D1598513

THE
BELOVED
VISION

THE
BELOVED
VISION

A HISTORY OF
NINETEENTH CENTURY MUSIC

STEPHEN WALSH

PEGASUS BOOKS

NEW YORK LONDON

THE BELOVED VISION

Pegasus Books, Ltd.
148 West 37th Street, 13th Floor
New York, NY 10018

First Pegasus Books cloth edition October 2022

ISBN: 978-1-63936-236-3

10 9 8 7 6 5 4 3 2 1

Printed in the United States of America
Distributed by Simon & Schuster
www.pegasusbooks.com

For Mary:
Die geliebte Gestalt

Contents

Acknowledgements

Family and friends have helped the book along in various ways. David Wyn Jones fed me information on Beethoven and the Vienna of his day; Robin Holloway, one of the most stimulating musical conversationalists I know, kept my ideas under firm scrutiny in long phone conversations; the late Bryan Magee talked to me about early-nineteenth-century philosophers and, of course, Wagner, and I have also been helped in the matter of Wagner by Barry Millington and Lionel Friend. Clare Hammond alerted me to the existence and significance of Hélène de Montgeroult. My wife, Mary, kept a firm check on my more wayward theorising, rightly insisting that good questions are more important than facile answers. My Faber editor, Belinda Matthews, has as ever provided massive support and encouragement, backed up by Anne Owen's wonderful team of copy editors and proof-readers, Sam Matthews and Kate Hopkins, fact-checker extraordinaire. Chuck Elliott and Leo Walsh kindly read the manuscript and constantly reassured me that the book was worth writing. But in the end everything herein is my own fault.

Welsh Newton,
June 2022

A Difficult and Dangerous Undertaking

On the wall of the music-room of my children's prep school in deepest Herefordshire in the 1990s was one of those time-line charts that simulate the flow of history in the form of a polyphony of overlapping lines. Music history began sparsely with Pérotin, Machaut, Dufay, then broadened out into the Renaissance – Josquin, Palestrina, Victoria, Tallis, Byrd, etc.: a well-populated era, it seemed. The seventeenth and eighteenth centuries, likewise, were busy times for music. But as the eighteenth century faded into the nineteenth there was a curious lull. In 1800, it turned out, there were only two composers worth mentioning: Haydn, still clinging on, and otherwise only Beethoven, thirty years old and monarch of all he surveyed. A few years into the new century things picked up again, but for a few short years it looked as if music history had practically died out, preserved only in the musical Noah's Ark by a single pair of composers.

Beethoven's superiority was certainly no myth. It was recognised in his own day by composers, performers, patrons and musical institutions all over Europe and even, from quite early on, America. In 1803, the Paris piano manufacturer Sébastien Érard sent him a piano as a gift that was also, of course, a promotional exercise. By 1808 Beethoven's reputation outside Austria was so great that Napoleon's brother Jérôme Bonaparte, the so-called king of Westphalia, invited him to take up the post of Kapellmeister in Kassel at a tempting salary of six hundred ducats (some sixty thousand pounds in today's money), while in Vienna his standing was such that a trio of aristocratic patrons put up an equivalent annuity to stop him leaving.

Above all, Beethoven's fame tended to act as a magnet for sweeping historical classifications, both in his lifetime and in the years that followed. Most notorious was E. T. A. Hoffmann's description of him, in a contemporary review of the Fifth Symphony, as 'a purely Romantic, and therefore truly musical, composer' (because, for Hoffmann, music was 'the most Romantic of all arts – one might almost say the only one that is *purely* Romantic'). Admittedly, Hoffmann also considered Haydn and Mozart to be Romantic, though his verbal portraits of their music suggest that their romanticism was largely in the mind of the writer. Haydn's symphonies, for example, 'lead us through endless, green forest-glades, through a motley throng of happy people. Youths and girls sweep past dancing the round . . . a world of love, of bliss, of eternal youth, as though before the Fall; no suffering, no pain; only sweet melancholy longing for the beloved vision floating far off in the red glow of evening.' Mozart, on the other hand, 'leads us deep into the realm of spirits. Dread lies all about us, but withholds its torments and becomes more an intimation of infinity.'[1] Hoffmann, as well as being one of the great novella and short-story writers of his day, was himself a composer and a knowledgeable music critic. His best-known opera, *Undine* (1816), though disappointing for anyone looking for the sources of Romantic music in the literary world of the early 1800s, is important as the first in a line of operas, songs and (eventually) instrumental works about water sprites who marry mortals against the best fairy advice and suffer the bitter consequences. There will be more to say about fairies; but it seems reasonably safe to assert, at this stage, that they are not a significant component of Beethoven's music.

So does it make sense, at the start of a book about Romantic music, to think of Beethoven and his immediate predecessors as in this or any other sense Romantic? The answer is clearly yes, but only because the idea of romanticism is something altogether broader and richer than might be deduced from Hoffmann's superbly imaginative definitions. To get at some kind of satisfactory image of what this much abused expression might signify in its particular application to music, we have somehow to get away from the habit of imposing on music our own emotional predilections and try to understand the nature and historical context of the phenomenon itself. After all, Hoffmann's description could just as well apply to Monteverdi, Handel or Bach, or even Josquin des Prez or Palestrina, as to composers like Schumann or Berlioz or Wagner, of whom he naturally knew nothing but whom we think of as Romantic. His idea of music as the most purely Romantic art plainly comes from the fact that instrumental music, at least, lacks overt subject matter and therefore lends itself to having subject matter thrust upon it in the privacy of the listener's mind. We can swoon to Brahms or Tchaikovsky, but we can also swoon, perhaps less dramatically, to Handel or Vivaldi. But if all 'Romantic' means is having the capacity to set us all swooning, we might as well pass on to some more interesting topic. Luckily, there is a little more to it than that.

It has seemed to me that the best way of exploring this complicated question would be through the entirely enjoyable process of writing a narrative history of what most of us think of as the Romantic epoch, very broadly defined; enjoyable, of course, because a lot of the research involved would be simply listening to an immense amount of music, including a good deal that, quite frankly, I had not heard before, and some that I barely knew existed. The nineteenth century was crucially a time of stylistic diversity, a time when a composer asserted his or her existential being through a recognisable, even idiosyncratic musical language, after several centuries during which composers were generally less concerned with self than with craftsmanship, and individuality emerged almost by accident, in small turns of phrase rather than wholesale linguistic contrasts. This is much truer for music than for literature, because music is less restricted by semantics; truer perhaps than for the visual arts, which, in the nineteenth century, were still largely tied to representation, or for the architectural design of buildings, which, after all, had to be lived in and to stay up.

Even within its seemingly rather strict grammatical rules, music turned out to be the most naturally deviant art form; the textbook rules proved less limiting than had been thought and could be broken without much damage as long as a coherent framework were preserved and could be perceived. I don't want to characterise Romantic composers as a procession of irresponsible tearaways. All the composers in this book were conscientious artists who knew what they were doing and who took the risks they took with a clear intention and an understanding of the always precarious balance between expression and technique. But risk-taking – the braving of the unknown – was certainly an important part of what they wanted to do, and that is as true of Chopin and Verdi as it is of Berlioz and Wagner. Perhaps one can say that the riskiest thing of all for an artist, the baring of the soul in language that might collapse under the weight of its own emotion, is an essential part of Romantic music, independent of categories and ostensible subject matter. But it is certainly not the only part. The new, the original, the unexpected, the beautiful, the sublime, but also the intimate and domestic, what Germans call the *gemütlich*, the supremely brilliant and the supremely simple: there is a range to Romantic music that is absent from the music of earlier centuries, with all its perfection. These things bring with them imperfections, disasters as well as triumphs. Writing music, when you leave the safety and comfort of the well-trodden, well-mapped path, is a difficult and dangerous undertaking, and what could be more Romantic than that?

In what follows I have tried not to be dogmatic about terminology. The academic fraternity, of which I was once a fortunate member, would be careful to limit what was meant by romanticism. We would hear about various categories: the Individual, Nature, the Outcast, Magic, the Antique, Dreams, Nightmares, Insanity, Folk Tales and Poetry, Myth, the Exotic, the Artist as God, etc., categories into which it would be hard or in one or two cases impossible to fit several of the greatest composers in what Eric Hobsbawm called the long nineteenth century. Verbal categories can be met by verbal, less well by instrumental, music. Programme music can help bridge the gap, but only if we take its assurances on trust, since they can hardly be demonstrated beyond question. If, on the other hand, we start with Hoffmann's idea and project it exclusively on to the music of his own time and the following hundred years or so, we may conclude that the issue is less about subject matter as such, more about freedom and individuality of style, allied to an increasing consciousness of self. More perhaps than in the other arts, the Romantic composer is the real subject of his own work, while any ostensible subject matter is merely its vehicle.

Most of this book has been written at a time when, for reasons that are all too well known, libraries have been closed, and research has mostly been limited to one's own bookshelves, the vast but by no means unlimited resources of the internet, and the remarkable amenity of overnight book deliveries – expensive but occasionally life-saving. I have availed myself of all these aids; and perhaps it has even been a mercy, with a topic of this kind, to have been denied the kinds of research facility that would have resulted in a still more tiresomely detailed, perhaps more erudite, probably longer and certainly later text than the present one. This is, in other words, an armchair book which, I optimistically hope, will also be an armchair read, at least for those who love this music and would like a conspectus of how it all came about, why it took the form it did, and indeed what it actually amounts to.

I

Longing for Chaos

The literary origins of romanticism are well, if a shade too precisely, documented. The standard source, cited in every book on the subject, is Goethe's early epistolary novel *The Sorrows of Young Werther* (1774), whose hero shoots himself at the end of a long correspondence with a friend about his unhappy love for the daughter of the high steward of a local prince; she is engaged to another man and, in the course of the novel, marries him. *Werther* rapidly became a cult novel; it was said that young men of a sensitive disposition would dress like Werther, go around with copies of the book under their arms, and even – in one or two not very well attested cases – carry pistols and shoot themselves. But Goethe's novel was only one of a number of books and plays of the 1770s and 1780s that portrayed the fate of the rejected poetic soul in a rational age. Werther is one kind of outcast, self-indulgent no doubt, but outcast none the less. Goethe's own play of a year earlier, *Götz von Berlichingen*, is based on the memoirs of a real-life sixteenth-century soldier-poet, portrayed by Goethe as a mercenary of the soul who stands out against the authoritarian Holy Roman Empire and dies in prison predicting evil times and crying, 'Freedom! Freedom!'

But Götz and Werther were only the latest manifestations of a growing reaction against the certainties of the Enlightenment, certainties so crisply summed up by Pope in his *Essay on Man*:

> And, spite of Pride, in erring Reason's spite,
> One truth is clear, whatever is, is right.

One could even characterise romanticism, in the most general sense, as a search for ways out of a world in which everything is properly ordered and nothing may be questioned. This point was well made by the poet and critic August Wilhelm Schlegel in a series of lectures in the early 1800s, where he used the term for what seems to be the first time as an aesthetic category opposed to the neoclassicism of the eighteenth century. Thinking of the Greeks, he observes that

> Ancient poetry and art is rhythmical *nomos*, a harmonious promulgation of the eternal legislation of a beautifully ordered world mirroring the eternal Ideas of things. Romantic poetry, on the other hand, is the expression of a secret longing for the chaos which is perpetually striving for new and marvellous births, which lies hidden in the very womb of orderly creation.[1]

This is, admittedly, a somewhat Romantic definition of romanticism. The earlier Romantics were interested not so much in disorder as in different kinds of order that took power away from the social and political status quo and handed it over to the imagination of the artist or the philosopher. One could, for instance, take refuge in a historical time other than one's own. Thomas Percy's *Reliques of Ancient English Poetry* (1765) was a highly edited, amplified and partly rewritten compilation of old ballads that Percy rescued from a friend's housemaid who was using the folio sheets to light the fire. More famously, James Macpherson's Ossian prose-poems, *Fingal* (1762) and *Temora* (1763), were presented as genuine translations from the Gaelic of the third-century bard Ossian, allegedly taken down by Macpherson from oral sources. They made a huge impact and were widely translated, and admired by poets as notable as Wordsworth and Goethe, if not for their poetic virtues – which are sometimes hard to detect behind the sub-Homeric prose – at least for their stirring evocation of ancient times when heroes were heroes and maidens were maidens, and blood flowed across the fields of battles fought for no discernible reason by indistinguishable warriors, as the wind howled through mighty oak woods and the moon cast its pallid light on the swirling waters of the western sea.

The past was preferable to the present, not always because it was more dramatic, but sometimes because it was simpler, purer, more authentic. The world, as the eighteenth century proceeded on its enlightened way, was an increasingly complex, confused, challenging and eventually dangerous place. The Industrial Revolution transformed urban life, by no means always for the better, gradually depopulated the countryside, and created a new, wealthy middle class ready for adventure, political, technological and artistic; it also created poverty and misery on a hitherto unknown scale. Yet when Rousseau opened his *Social Contract* in 1762 with the explosive 'Man was born free, and everywhere he is in chains,' he was by no means expressing a proto-Marxist response to the condition of the urban proletariat, which had scarcely emerged at that stage. On the contrary he was pursuing an argument – partly inspired by the republic of his native Geneva – about the relations between the individual and society that went back at least to Hobbes and Locke in the previous century, which did not prevent his ideas being taken up and distorted by the French Revolutionaries.

The past was also the repository of a great many things that the Enlightenment had either rejected or ignored. Neoclassicism was a kind of historical revival, true, but somewhat rigid and impersonal, like the society it represented. Writers and eventually musicians and painters were beginning to look for something more differentiated and less like the world they saw around them. Hence Ossian; but hence also the rediscovery of the Middle Ages, not necessarily as the source of Schlegel's Romantic chaos, but as a place of mystery and magic, of religious belief and divine intervention. The Middle Ages, broadly defined, were also the origin of a force that was to prove of overwhelming importance to Romantic artists, musicians especially, as well as to philosophers and, alas, in due course politicians: the force of national culture and identity. So far as this was already a political issue in the eighteenth century, its most lucid advocate was Edmund Burke, who (in his *Reflections on the Revolution in France*, 1790) saw nationhood as an aspect of the community spirit held together by centuries of tradition, descending in England's case from Magna Carta. But the broader originator of such thinking was the German historian and philosopher, Johann Gottfried Herder, who as early as 1773 read Ossian in German translation and found in it an authenticity, a truthful expression of the wild nature of the ancient northern tribes that he missed in 'the artificial Horatian style we Germans have fallen into at times'.[2]

Of all the great forerunners of romanticism, Herder was the liveliest and in many ways the most likeable. He was, it's true, a prime advocate of German national self-determinism; he argued for the German language, German art, German culture. He was in effect a proponent of German unification. But this was only one element of his general argument that every nation ought to identify and study its own particular character. Herder took up the concept of *Das Volk*, an untranslatable term that embraces not just the 'folk' in the rustic English sense of the word 'folksy', but the whole nation in its ethnic soul. To understand the importance of this concept for Germans in the 1770s and onwards one has to remember that until 1870 there was no such political entity as 'Germany', only a large agglomeration of highly disparate kingdoms, princedoms, dukedoms, and statelets of one kind or another. But Herder argued the same for other, non-Germanic peoples, particularly the European populations to the east: the Slavs and the Magyars, who were still under the rule of alien empires, and those farther north, the Scandinavians and Finns and the inhabitants of the Baltic region. These peoples, he maintained, should study their own history, their own myths, folk legends and music, speak their own languages, and above all not kow-tow to supposedly superior western cultures, especially the French, which had so dominated the Enlightenment. Folk song and folk poetry, which Herder himself collected, could tell us more about the inner character of the people concerned than the most elaborate verbal description; he called folk music 'the true voice of its organs of feeling'.

Of course, the vast majority of the people Herder was thinking of were never going to read his books. Nationalism, when it came, would, like so much else in the art and politics of the time, be a movement of middle-class intellectuals. But Herder was responding, with the sharp antennae of the original thinker, to changes that were in the air. Rousseau had already argued for a return to Nature as a corrective to the rigid, over-civilised world of mid-eighteenth-century France; and he had defended the simple, uncomplicated melodic style of Italian opera against what he regarded as the over-elaborate harmonies of the French, and had even composed operas (most famously *Le Devin du village*) illustrating the point. His distaste for society in the French sense had led inexorably to an elevation of the individual over the collective. 'I aspire to the moment', his pseudonymous Savoyard Vicar tells us in *Émile, ou de l'éducation*, 'when, released from the fetters of the body, I shall be *me* without contradiction, without sharing, and shall need only myself in order to be happy.'[3] Whatever Rousseau may have seen as the outcome of this individualism, it was plainly a direct challenge to the universalism of 'enlightened' France. It leads on to the subjectivism of Fichte and the relentless selfhood of early Romantic writers like Byron, Chateaubriand and Novalis.

Werther is often seen as a founding example of the so-called *Sturm und Drang* movement in 1770s Germany, the movement that first got romanticism into its stride. But 'storm and stress' (the usual English translation) had a number of manifestations in the literature and philosophy of the 1760s and 1770s. In *Werther* it favours excessive emotion and self-absorption to the point where suicide seems the only conceivable recourse. But in *Götz von Berlichingen* and Schiller's *Die Räuber* (1781), in Jakob Lenz's *Der Hofmeister* (1774) and *Die Soldaten* (1776), and in the Friedrich Klinger play by which the movement is known (*Sturm und Drang*, 1777), complex and often confused dramaturgy is marked by violence of various kinds, including sexual (the eponymous hero of *Der Hofmeister* castrates himself; the heroine of *Die Soldaten* is raped), and the classical unities are thrown to the four winds. All these works, and a number of others, represent a drastic rejection of the ideals of the Enlightenment. 'The Tree of Knowledge', Johann Georg Hamann wrote, 'has robbed us of the Tree of Life.'[4] A more precise encapsulation of the Counter-Enlightenment would be hard to find.

Where, then, does music fit into this turbulent narrative? For music, the Enlightenment version of classicism emerged late from the baroque initially in the form of what was known as the *style galant*, a light, gracious, agreeable instrumental manner partly derived from the simple melody-and-bass of Italian operatic arias. Essentially the *galant* style was a courtly reaction against the elaborate, learned counterpoint of the baroque, after which what we call the classical style evolved, most notably in the early works of Haydn, as a kind of Germanic intellectualisation of the (essentially French) *style galant*, rather than in any sense a revival of some notional pre-existing classicism, which simply didn't exist. But while Haydn and a handful of followers were working away at their symphonies and string quartets in Vienna, Prague and the north, opera in Italy and France pursued its untroubled course towards a very different *fin de siècle*. And meanwhile the supposed classical values of order, formal balance and cool emotional restraint were being disturbed, discreetly at first, in the extraordinary music of J. S. Bach's most talented son, Carl Philipp Emanuel.

The search for beginnings is always slippery, but it seems plausible to locate the first serious tremors of romanticism in the so-called *empfindsamer Stil* – literally the 'sensitive style' – which, in music, is associated with C. P. E. Bach. Like *Sturm und Drang*, *Empfindsamkeit* is more easily understood as first and foremost a literary tendency. Its master in Germany was the poet Friedrich Klopstock, best known today for his 'Resurrection' ode, which Mahler set in the finale of his Second Symphony, but famous in his own day for an epic poem, *Der Messias*, of which the playwright Gotthold Ephraim Lessing wrote that it was 'so full of feeling that one often feels nothing in it at all'.[5] Whether Lessing felt the same about the music of C. P. E. Bach, who was a friend of his in Berlin, where Bach was employed for almost thirty years at the court of Frederick the Great, is not as far as I know recorded. But Bach's version of *Empfindsamkeit* was not quite parallel with Klopstock's in any case. Whereas in *Der Messias* the hypersensitivity was part of the thought and its expression, in Bach it is a subversive element, an intervention in the smooth passage of a basically conventional musical language. Charles Rosen, a qualified admirer, called Bach's music 'violent, expressive, brilliant, continuously surprising, and often incoherent'.[6] The keyboard sonatas especially are frequently disrupted by unexpected silences, abrupt contrasts of dynamics, remote changes of key, and strange chromatic harmonies. One often feels, playing or listening to this music, that Bach is reacting as he goes along; the unpredictability is not always supported by weight of architecture, as it is in Beethoven. And yet his music is rich in possibilities that would be taken up later. Whereas a typical sonata or suite movement by his father would be based on a single thematic figure with a particular unifying *Affekt* or emotion, C. P. E. Bach will often have contrasting themes in contrasting keys, and will develop this material in the middle of the movement before bringing the themes back in a recapitulation. Thus what came to be known as sonata form begins to emerge from the simple binary forms of baroque music; with it comes the idea of conflict and dramatic tension so essential to Haydn and Mozart, and eventually the lifeblood of Romantic music.

Bach's music suggests a kind of opening out, a directness and variety unlike the concentrated seriousness of the high baroque. His *Essay on the True Art of Playing Keyboard Instruments* (1753, 1762), was both a thorough method, admired by Haydn and Beethoven, and a comprehensive style guide. It talks a lot about technique, about ways of playing. But it also constantly touches on questions of feeling, taste and communication. 'A musician', it insists, 'cannot move others unless he too is moved . . . In languishing, sad passages, the performer must languish and grow sad . . . Similarly, in lively, joyous passages, the executant must again put himself into the appropriate mood. And so, constantly varying the passions, he will barely quiet one before he arouses another.'[7] This is still perfectly good advice for the perfor-mance of his father's, and most baroque, music. But the explanation is post-baroque, more feeling-conscious, more *empfindsam*, and applies particularly to a music of volatile expression, like C. P. E's own.

It may nevertheless not sound all that much like romanticism. It is too stereotyped, and still bears a certain taint of classical rhetoric and the objective truths of the Enlightenment. The music itself, on the other hand, has a more genuine, even arbitrary, freedom, and it was this freedom – of expression, design and discourse – that in the 1760s and 1770s merged imperceptibly, both with Bach and with a younger gen-eration dominated by Joseph Haydn, into a kind of musical equivalent of the literary *Sturm und Drang*. Curiously, the musical storm blew up slightly earlier than the literary one, though the point can be overstated. The demonic finale of Gluck's ballet *Don Juan* (1761), often cited as an early example of *Sturm und Drang*, is after all no more than a vivid description of a frightful event, like the rending of the Temple veil in the *St Matthew Passion*. More to the point are a number of Haydn symphonies and string quartets from the late sixties and early seventies, many in minor keys, of which there are hardly any previous examples in his work in these genres. Suddenly we have Symphony No. 39 in G minor (1766 or 1767), the so-called 'Lamentation' Symphony, No. 26 in D minor (1768), No. 49 ('La Passione') in F minor (1768), No. 44 (the 'Trauer' or 'Mourning' Symphony) in E minor (1770 or 1771), and most famously No. 45 (the 'Farewell' Symphony) in F sharp minor (1772). Of the string quartets of these years, four are in minor keys, but there is an increasing emotional and intellectual intensity also in some of the major-key works. Haydn also composed major-key symphonies, some of which reflect the emotional unease of the time while some do not. It looks, in general, as if storm and stress was an aesthetic choice for particular works, rather than a consuming force that swallowed up everything in its path.

Whatever the origins of this extraordinary burst of passionate energy in music, they can hardly have been literary. True, Burke had theorised about the Sublime – the aesthetics of awe, fear and the epic, as opposed to the calm contemplation of beauty – as early as 1757. But it would be hard to imagine Haydn immersing himself in English writing (though he did set English poetry), and Ossian was not published in German until 1769. He certainly knew the music of C. P. E. Bach, some of which belongs to the late sixties and seventies, but some of which – including examples of the *empfindsamer Stil* – goes back to the 1740s and 1750s. It's difficult to resist the feeling, then, that these musical tendencies were a direct response to the ordered character of the late baroque and the elegant trivialities of the *style galant*, at first fragmentary and inchoate, then, in the hands of a master, reasserting the authority of formal design and discipline. In these minor-key symphonies and quartets Haydn does some strange, unorthodox things, but he hardly ever relinquishes control and sometimes asserts it through traditional methods applied in new ways. For instance, the brilliant fugal finale of the F minor String Quartet, op. 20, no. 5 (1772), retains the fizzing urgency of the G minor and F minor Symphonies, braced, however, by a strict baroque procedure. The 'Lamentation' Symphony reverts to the even older contrapuntal device of *cantus firmus*, in which a plainsong theme runs through a texture of free parts, imposing on it an oddly antique-feeling design. One is conscious of a certain tension between the flight of the passions and the discipline of the brain. The music is constantly disrupted by restless syncopations, unexpected silences, uneven phrase lengths. Loud unison themes, agitated string tremolos and other bold orchestral effects abound, and sometimes the music seems so anxious to hurry on that it can scarcely be bothered with more than one or two accompanying lines and the most basic harmonies.

Haydn was obviously the major figure in this brief musical midlife crisis. But he was by no means the only one, nor even the first. A G minor Symphony of 1762 by the French-based German composer Franz Beck already breathes, somewhat gaspingly, the air of *Sturm und Drang*, and there are fine symphonies by the Bohemian Johann Baptist

Vanhal, of which Haydn's biographer H. C. Robbins Landon counted thirteen in minor keys from the years around 1770.[8] In fact, so many composers of the time dipped into the *Sturm und Drang* as to make it seem like a fashionable resort, to be visited for a time in summer then abandoned in the autumn. Only two composers of any importance preserved the sheer energy and ferocity of the movement, and absorbed them into personal idioms of an emotional range that was to have significant consequences for the music of the next century. These composers were Christoph Willibald von Gluck and Wolfgang Amadeus Mozart.

The turmoil of Gluck's *Don Juan* finale was so specific to the action it was portraying that it hardly seems to qualify as a starting point for anything else. But his later, Paris operas are another matter. *Iphigénie en Tauride* (1779), for example, not only starts with an actual storm, it also has psychological storms and stresses, thrust from within (one possible meaning of *Drang*), and creates emotional ambiguities out of these feelings. When Orestes, pursued by the Furies for the murder of his mother and captured by the bloodthirsty Taureans, sings 'Le calme rentre dans mon cœur' he is, as Gluck himself famously remarked, lying, a fact made unforgettably clear by the orchestra, with its extremely uncalm, pulsating viola syncopations. But while his music had important admirers, his ideas about opera were if anything even more influential. In the preface to his opera *Alceste* (1767) he had already called for a less convention-bound approach to music drama: less indulgence of singers' vanity, less vocal display for its own sake, more fidelity to the particular needs of the drama. He argued for more musical continuity, for orchestral music more relevant to the action, and against the anti-dramatic convention of the da capo aria, and he sought 'a beautiful simplicity' and to avoid 'parading difficulties at the expense of clarity'. His target in all this, of course, was the long tradition of *opera seria*, the rigid operatic formula of the late baroque represented most notably by Handel, in seemingly endless successions of brilliant, very difficult da capo arias, separated by long stretches of dry recitative, and recounting convoluted, far-fetched plots about magnanimous Roman emperors, amorous crusaders, male lovers played, unpromisingly, by castrati, and other nonsensical but musically irresistible elements. Gluck had himself in earlier times made plentiful offerings on the altar of *opera seria*, and even has a lovelorn crusader in *Armide* (1777), one of his late reform operas. It is also true that his ideas were to some extent a distillation of changes that were afoot in existing operas, particularly in France, with its hybrid stage tradition represented most recently by the *tragédies lyriques* of Rameau, and in a variety of innovative works by Italian composers such as Tommaso Traetta and Niccolò Jommelli. But Gluck was the first to put forward thoroughgoing ideas of this kind while actually composing operas that demonstrate them coherently and on a grand scale.

Gluck's ideas for operatic reform may seem remote from the purely musical considerations of *Sturm und Drang*, and even more remote from the literary movement of Goethe, Lenz, Schiller and the rest. But behind all these various tendencies was one central preoccupation: emotional truth. The Enlightenment had sacrificed individual truth to universal truths. All was for the best, in Voltaire's satirical phrase, in the best of all possible worlds. One might indulge one's feelings in private, but in public society knew what was best and would, in due course with the aid of science and philosophy, cure whatever minor ills managed to survive the Age of Reason. *Sturm und Drang*, in its different guises, was at bottom a *cri de cœur* against this denial of human misery and passion and the variety of individual experience. Instrumental music could at first explode in a kind of fury, but as yet lacked the technical resources to express the range of emotion available to literature while maintaining the coherence that music required. In Mozart, this is no longer the case.

Mozart was almost two generations younger than Gluck, but as a reformer Gluck came late while Mozart started early. His G minor Symphony, K. 183, composed probably late in 1773 when he was seventeen, is *Sturm und Drang* in the same sense as Haydn's own G minor

Symphony (No. 39) of five or six years earlier, which Landon supposes Mozart will have heard in Vienna in the late summer of 1773. But whereas with Haydn *Sturm und Drang* was a phase, with Mozart it opened a door that he never closed. Mature masterpieces like the D minor and C minor Piano Concertos of the mid-1780s and the late G minor Symphony of 1788 obviously draw on the dark strains of the early seventies while absorbing them into an altogether richer emotional and technical experience. But most of Mozart's late instrumental music bears traces of this experience, even when the tone is not dark.

This must be why he responded so quickly to Gluck's late works, particularly *Iphigénie en Tauride* and the revised *Alceste*, both of which he heard in Vienna in 1781. At the time he was working on *Die Entführung aus dem Serail* (*The Abduction from the Seraglio*), a singspiel with dialogue that largely avoids the issues of reform. But *Idomeneo*, premiered in Munich the previous January, is a masterpiece that both does and does not show an active awareness of the issues involved. In a sense it argues the limitations of a work of art beholden to a theory. All right, it seems to say, let's have an overture that prepares the drama; let's get rid of empty vocal display and the stupid conventions that decree, for instance, that at the end of an aria the singer must leave the stage; let's have genuine continuities, music carrying the drama forward, not stopping all the time for applause and encores, and let's give the orchestra a dramatic role. But none of this will take us far in itself. What matters is that it should be the music, not the text, that dictates the shape of the drama.

Idomeneo, accordingly, was a reform opera that reformed through musical genius rather than doctrine. Many of its arias have formal reprises, rather than strict da capo repeats, and some even culminate – like any baroque aria – on half-cadences that invite expressive improvised roulades from the singer. But these devices are handled not just with discretion, but creatively. The reprise forms are often so highly developed that they resemble symphonic movements, with rich, often chromatic, harmony and middle sections that either develop the main ideas or at least serve as organic links to their recapitulation, without the more or less static formal divisions of the baroque. And this process is greatly enhanced by the variety of Mozart's writing for orchestra, strikingly so, for instance, in Ilia's 'Se il padre perdei', with its obbligato wind quartet. The characters speak for themselves, but the orchestra also speaks for them, so that they emerge fully rounded psychologically, realistic figures, not merely particular types in particular situations. Gluck had achieved something of the kind, but with less complex musical forms and generally less varied psychology. There is nothing in Gluck to compare with the quartet in the final act of *Idomeneo*, where the King is urging his reluctant son Idamante to leave the country in order to avoid being sacrificed, while Idamante's beloved Ilia laments the tragedy of their love, and the unloved Electra laments her jealousy of Ilia. Eric Smith once wrote that in *Idomeneo* 'traditional elements of *opera seria* struggle with innovations based on Gluck and the *tragédie lyrique*'.[9] But it is the fusion of these elements that generates the work's power and leads on to the even greater operas of Mozart's last years.

Le nozze di Figaro (*The Marriage of Figaro*, 1786) calls itself an *opera buffa*, which locates it at the end of a long tradition of comic opera that had begun in Naples in the early eighteenth century, spread to the rest of Italy, then beyond, and reached its peak with this masterpiece, first performed in Vienna (but with an Italian text, by Lorenzo da Ponte) in May 1786. Its two Italian-language successors are both labelled *dramma giocoso*, an even older designation that might seem to imply something weightier, arguable in the case of *Don Giovanni* (1787), less so, perhaps, with *Così fan tutte* (1790). In essence the categories are the same. *Opera buffa* had early on specialised in picaresque characters talking in dialect, but had later begun to include upper-class lovers and to address some of the social problems they encountered. Above all, these characters were presented as real personages with real mentalities, unlike the cardboard stereotypes of *opera seria*. Sometimes a sentimental component would obtrude, as in the French *comédie larmoyante*, where sad, potentially tragic events were eventually resolved in happy endings. In *The Marriage of Figaro* Mozart combines all these elements, but raises them to a musical and dramatic plane far above any conceivable model.

For a start his comic characters are not merely picaresque. On the contrary, they are intellectually and emotionally at least as complicated as their aristocratic master and mistress; they are as clever, and as thoughtful. Figaro loses his inflammatory political speech in the last act of Beaumarchais's play. But throughout the opera his behaviour, and above all his music, is inflammatory. He delivers his first-act cavatina, 'Se vuol' ballare, signor contino' – 'If you want to dance, Mr Countlet, I shall be playing the guitarlet' – to an empty room, but in the second act he sings a verse of it openly in front of the Countess. The music is an ironic minuet, a specifically aristocratic dance. On the other hand the Count is throughout made to seem ridiculous in his sexual advances on his female servants, and is eventually humiliated in front of his whole staff. Meanwhile the Countess (not herself from an aristocratic background, but originally – in *The Barber of Seville* – a ward of the middle-class Dr Bartolo) is subjected to the *larmoyant* element, in what are surely the two greatest of all arias of this type: 'Porgi amor' and 'Dove sono'. Mozart and Da Ponte have turned what was previously a more or less farcical genre into a profoundly serious character study, clinched by its music, addressing not only socio-political issues that were about to explode in violent reality in Paris but also issues of individual psychology that would soon be of lasting importance in the fields of art and philosophy.

With all these enrichments, *The Marriage of Figaro* remains an essentially eighteenth-century opera. Though it is free with convention, it is eighteenth-century convention it is free with. The same is broadly true of its immediate successor, *Don Giovanni*, and of *Così fan tutte*. But there are additional factors which, in the former, were to have an actual impact on early-nineteenth-century romanticism and, in the latter, were prophetic but exerted little or no influence.

Così fan tutte was not liked in the nineteenth century, presumably because its attitude to the Romantics' favourite topic, love, and the bourgeois institution of marriage was seen as unduly cynical, even depraved. *Don Giovanni* is another matter. While this, too, in its forms and conventions, is still essentially an eighteenth-century opera, there are factors at work that transport it into a very different arena. For a start, the happy ending common to all *opera buffa* and *dramma giocoso* is called into question, and Don Giovanni, a ruthless seducer, gets his deserts and is dragged down to hell, to the undisguised relief of the other characters. Violent death is not a normal concomitant of comic opera; and *Don Giovanni* not only ends with one, it also starts with one. Moreover, the force of the ending is that an exceptional human being has been obliterated while ordinary, commonplace human-ity looks on and applauds. That's what happens, it crows, to naughty boys. The other deviant factor is the supernatural element, the *deus ex machina* which, instead of rescuing the hero and/or heroine from a tragic fate – its usual role in *opera seria* (including *Idomeneo*) – here acts as the hand of vengeance against the anti-hero.

These could be comic devices, but are elevated into something approaching genuine tragedy by the character and power of Mozart's music. The overture begins in a grand, monitory D minor, music that will later accompany the arrival of the statue of the Commendatore, at which point it leads to a scene of positively infernal menace as the statue over and again demands Don Giovanni's repentance and he over and again refuses, until he finally, amid fire and earthquake, is swallowed up into the ground. These are not episodes that belong in comic opera as normally understood; and there are several other moments where the enormity of the events is echoed: the murder of the Commendatore; Donna Anna's recognition of Don Giovanni as her father's murderer; her great following aria, 'Or sai chi l'onore'; and the attempted rape of Zerlina.

The Romantics, of course, interpreted the opera in the light of their own preoccupations. For Hoffmann, in his short story 'Don Juan' (1813), Mozart's Giovanni is a superhuman figure, endowed by Nature 'with every quality that can exalt humanity, in its closest approach to the divine, above the vulgar rabble', but all this 'to no other end but that of dominating and defeating him'. From his hotel room, Hoffmann is able to go by way of a secret passage into a private box of the adjoining theatre, where Mozart's opera is about to begin. Instantly he is drawn into a world of nightmarish fantasy:

> In the andante, I was gripped by the terror of the frightful infernal *regno al pianto*; fearful premonitions of its horrors pervaded my soul . . . from out of the deep night I saw fiery demons stretching out their glowing claws upwards towards the life of joyful mankind, dancing happily on the thin crust of the bottomless abyss.[10]

For Søren Kierkegaard, on the other hand, Mozart's anti-hero is something still grander than a mere exceptional human being. He is the very spirit of sensuality, which, in the context of Kierkegaard's *Either/Or* (1843), a study of the relation between the aesthetic and ethical views of human behaviour, turns him into something like a foreshadowing of the Freudian id, or even Nietzsche's concept of the spirit of music, since in Kierkegaard's opinion music is the only art form that, because of its abstract nature, can adequately express something so physically immediate to human consciousness.

These interpretations take us a long way from the space between *The Marriage of Figaro* and *Così fan tutte* in which *Don Giovanni* was actually conceived and written, and perhaps they tell us more about the Romantic sensibility than about Mozart and Da Ponte's intentions in the year 1787. But taking account of Figaro's subversiveness and the confrontation in *Così* between social norms and individual passions, it hardly seems far-fetched to see Don Giovanni as a revolutionary figure intent on casting off the shackles of a well-ordered society in which all was for the best in the best of all possible worlds.

2

A Young Rhinelander

The events of 1789 in Paris, the fall of the Bastille and the revolution that followed, had an effect that still reverberates today. But they hardly came out of the blue. Leaving aside the social and political causes of the revolution in eighteenth-century France, there were plenty of warnings of impending change in the world at large. The striking thing is how seemingly diverse and unconnected these warnings were. Rousseau challenged the ideas of his time in almost everything he wrote. In *The Social Contract* (1762) he argued for political freedom and equality in a natural context devoid of the trappings of an over-sophisticated culture; in *Émile* (1762) for a liberal education freed from the impositions of a too prescriptive society; in the *Rêveries du promeneur solitaire* (1782) for an emotional absorption in nature itself and for solitary contemplation away from the distractions of urban life. Herder had undermined the whole concept of universal truth with his ideas of the autonomy of individual cultures and languages. *Sturm und Drang* had wiped the self-satisfied smile off the face of the Enlightenment. Above all the Industrial Revolution was creating a new, wealthy managerial class, a bourgeoisie with time and money to spare and in search of ways of spending them that, on the whole, the rigid eighteenth-century infrastructures did not provide. In the thirty years before the Bastille fell there had been a world war, the Seven Years War (1756–63), which robbed France of many of her colonies and left her with crippling debts; a revolution and war of independence in America against the British (1775–83); and serious anti-Catholic riots in London (1780). If there was a common cause in all this, it was the breaking of moulds, the overflowing of dammed-up waters, and it naturally sought an expressive outlet in the arts and philosophy.

In itself the French Revolution was a destructive outbreak of lawless violence on the streets of Paris (in particular) and of ruthless, doctrinaire idealism in the minds and behaviour of those – intellectuals, demagogues, rabble-rousers – who seized or assumed the mostly very temporary political power that it released. But it was at first greeted with enthusiasm by artists and intellectuals both inside and outside France. It was seen as a practical assertion of the ideas of liberty, equality and self-determination that Rousseau had argued for. The German philosopher Hegel, at the time a student in Tübingen, is said to have toasted the fall of the Bastille every 14 July thereafter, and the poet Wordsworth recalled his feelings at the time in lines that have entered the English language:

> Bliss was it in that dawn to be alive,
> But to be young was very heaven![1]

Most of these optimistic thinkers and feelers withdrew their enthusiasm after the Reign of Terror of 1793. But they still, like Wordsworth, preserved in their hearts the spirit of 1789, something they could manage because that spirit, for them, was an essence untainted by the day-to-day politics, the hatreds and bloodlettings, which were simply a false direction, a terrible mistake arising out of a misunderstanding of the true significance of this millennial transformation of history.

The Revolution promoted liberty, equality, fraternity. Good. But on the political and social front these were terribly mundane values, implying, for instance, that any Paris street urchin was as admirable and useful, not to say loveable, as the most brilliant philosopher or craftsman, or the most beautiful and virtuous woman. No doubt that was the theoretical intention. But the effect, in the mind of the artist at least, was subtly different. To the musician liberty meant release from servitude to aristocratic or ecclesiastical patrons and their bullying demands for weekly symphonies or string quartets or cantatas. It meant the freedom to follow one's own inspiration, to explore one's own inner emotional life and to respond to one's own experience. It's true that eighteenth-century composers had already in a few cases achieved this freedom. Mozart had discharged himself from the Archbishop of Salzburg's establishment in 1781 and spent the last ten years of his life freelance in Vienna. Haydn, too, effectively went freelance in 1790 by turning down a post in Pressburg (Bratislava) in favour of his first London visit. But Haydn, approaching sixty, was an ageing master resting on his laurels, while Mozart, far from entertaining grand ideas about the quasi-divinity of genius, was simply fed up with being treated as a skivvy so soon after his success with *Idomeneo* in Munich.

For one young Rhinelander who arrived in Vienna in November 1792 it would be a very different matter. Ludwig van Beethoven was the twenty-one-year-old grandson of a former Kapellmeister at the Electoral Court in Bonn. His father, more modestly, was a tenor in the electoral choir, but young Ludwig had shown exceptional talent from an early age as a keyboard player, with a special gift for improvisation, and solid competence as a composer in the received styles of the day. Bonn, though provincial by Viennese or Parisian standards, had, like many of the numerous princely courts of pre-unification Germany, a vigorous musical and thespian culture. There was a theatre which put on a wide repertoire of French, Italian and German opera, and in whose orchestra Beethoven had for a time played harpsichord continuo, then later viola; there was a court chapel where he acted as assistant to his teacher, the official organist Christian Gottlob Neefe; and of course there were secular concerts in which he will often have performed. In Bonn he had at some point met Haydn, who had thought well of a cantata Beethoven showed him, had accepted him as a pupil, and the young composer was now arriving in Vienna to take up Haydn's offer of lessons.

Like Mozart a decade earlier, Beethoven presented himself in Vienna initially as a pianist. But he also brought compositions, specifically chamber works with piano: a set of three quartets for piano and strings, and possibly also sketches for a set of piano trios which he must then have written up during his first year in Vienna, since they were played at Prince Karl Lichnowsky's house early in 1794 and published the following year as Opus 1 – almost, but not quite, his first publication.

These trios are naturally not yet full-blown Beethoven, but they already bear traces of the young lion who would soon be striding, somewhat rough-shod, through the salons of aristocratic Vienna. Their style is still essentially that of Haydn and Mozart, but the music could hardly be mistaken for theirs. It has a kind of laconic brusqueness, a love of the dismissive gesture, a take-that muscularity that goes with the different sort of person he evidently was, different in his Rhineland speech, and different in appearance – wigless in portraits of the time, unlike the always bewigged Haydn and Mozart: new independent versus old retainer. This is particularly striking with the third of the trios, in C minor, already a key that prompts some of Beethoven's most pugnacious writing. The short first theme, four quick bars for the three instruments in unison, is immediately extended by a repeat of its last two bars a semitone higher. This seemingly innocuous device, which might suggest uncertainty as to how to proceed, turns out to be a structural marker for the whole movement and its main thematic component. The instant change of pitch at once creates a fluid harmony that Beethoven is able to exploit in a variety of ways, even though the basic tonal framework of the movement is conventional. It's a risk; it risks destabilising the movement, but it repays the risk by greatly enriching the discourse, as long as the composer is equal to the technical challenge of controlling his ideas along unmarked roads. Beethoven will have learnt about risk from Haydn especially, from Mozart and C. P. E. Bach perhaps slightly less, hardly from any of the other in many ways excellent composers whose music was or may have been on the roster of chamber and orchestral music in Bonn, composers such as Ignaz Pleyel, Carl Ditters von Dittersdorf or Paul Wranitzky. In a sense their music, and that of countless lesser figures, marked out the safe, official route, much travelled, clearly signposted. But risk-taking, on an increasingly large scale, was to become one of the defining characteristics of Beethoven's music; and whatever the danger, his technique invariably rose to the challenge.

This quality can be traced through the twenty or so piano sonatas he composed during his first decade in Vienna. Essentially these are classical sonatas, varied in form but by no means spectacularly unorthodox, at least until the first of the two Sonatas 'quasi una fantasia', op. 27, no. 1, in E flat (1801), in which the four-movement template is diffused into a series of linked sections: A-B-A-C-D-C-E-F-E-F. All Beethoven's earlier piano sonatas (apart from the sonatina-like pieces in op. 49) have either three or four movements, nearly always with a sonata-form first movement (op. 26 has a set of variations), followed by a slow movement and/or a scherzo-cum-minuet, and a rondo finale. What is a lot less classical is the astonishing freedom and range of gesture, and the steep expressive gradient, the drastic contrasts between loud and soft, quick and slow, and the preference for short, punchy motifs, offset by silence or repetition. One recalls that Beethoven was a gifted improviser. In improvising at the piano the crucial issue is the almost physical contact with the sound, the sense of being in charge of a powerful machine that can do violence but can also create a deep tapestry of coloured sonority and can resonate for significant lengths of time while the player is doing hardly anything at all. Beethoven's piano of the 1790s was less powerful and secure than the instruments we play on today, and it had a smaller range. But it was improving rapidly, and like the early drivers of motor cars its players must have been chiefly conscious of its novelty in relation to what preceded it: the loud and soft expressed in its name. In Beethoven's early sonatas one can almost touch the exhilaration prompted by these new and expanding possibilities.

It's a mistake, though, to suppose that, because Beethoven was an improviser, his published piano music somehow embodies the looseness of design that those who argue this way imagine to be an inevitable concomitant of performing extempore. Beethoven seldom if ever published a slackly constructed work. On the contrary his genius, already in these early works and of course later, lay in his ability to manage apparently unruly or fragmentary material, and build it into a coherent narrative. He had, as his sketches show, an extraordinary architectural vision. He would foresee a pattern or structure, and work his way towards it by a process of artisan craftsmanship, like Michelangelo seeing his David in a block of marble and slowly chipping it out through sheer technical mastery. How else are we to understand the amazing variety of Beethoven's discourse: the bits and pieces of the first movement of the D minor 'Tempest' Sonata (op. 31, no. 2, 1802), on the one hand, and on the other the long, slowly unfolding line of the Largo Appassionato of the A major Sonata, op. 2, no. 2 (probably 1794), whose nearly motionless and perilously simple melody seems to defy the percussive nature of the instrument?

There is a distinct element of theatre in all this, and in retracing Beethoven's background one notes that, although by 1800 he had composed very little music for the theatre, he had spent a large part of his young manhood playing in other people's operas and ballets. It's hard to argue that he will have taken much of a specifically musical character from the *opéras comiques* of Grétry, Dalayrac and Gossec or even Salieri's so-called *dramma tragicomico*, *Axur, re d'Ormus*, a mixed-genre opera that was probably the last work Beethoven played in before his departure for Vienna. These were still essentially eighteenth-century works. But they may well have prompted a more stagey approach to the hitherto rather stereotyped forms of classical instrumental music. In any case it was an influence that was to be reinforced during the 1790s and early 1800s, when the more spectacular examples of French rescue opera began to appear, in print or in the flesh, in Vienna.

Beethoven was at first broadly sympathetic to the Revolution, if without the express commitment of writers like Wordsworth or Schiller, or philosophers like Fichte. And, unlike them, he was not openly disillusioned by the violence of the Terror. It seems that his republicanism, though strongly and sincerely felt, was contingent on more general ideals, such as freedom, honour, the brotherhood of man, which, as Enlightenment virtues, did not inevitably call for revolution, though they did not preclude it. He was happy with the concept of the enlightened ruler and slow to notice the practical failings or sheer hypocrisy that usually went with the outward image of political reform. He had no personal quarrel with aristocracy, on which in any case he depended for his survival in Vienna. His *liberté* and *fraternité* were emphatically not wedded to *égalité*. 'Power', he once wrote, only half joking, 'is the moral principle of those who excel others, and it is also mine.'[2] In modern jargon, he was an unashamed elitist, and the Revolution interested him as a distant assertion of republican values while its unpleasantness largely passed him by.

Its immediate impact on him, at least until the French occupation of Vienna in 1805, was mainly musical, and in particular operatic. Even before the Revolution, or after it but before the latest Paris operas hit Vienna, French opera was a major force on the Imperial stage. Beethoven just missed the Viennese premieres of Méhul's *Euphrosine* in 1790 and Grétry's *Guillaume Tell* in 1791, but he may have picked up subsequent performances of the latter work, with its villainous governor figure, Guesler, shot dead with bow and arrow in the final act by the populist liberator, William Tell. Grétry's music, which veers between folk operetta and *comédie larmoyante*, is unlikely to have made a huge impression on Beethoven. He may have been more struck by the printed copies of French revolutionary hymns, military marches and the like, brought to Vienna by no less a personage than General Bernadotte, who was French ambassador for a brief spell from February to April 1798: short, massive pieces like Gossec's 'Hymn to the Supreme Being', impressive, unsubtle music to be sung by a choir of thousands on the Champs de Mars in Paris. accompanied by hundreds of wind instruments and percussion. Perhaps the music included Gossec's 'Funeral Song on the Death of Féraud', a solemn, dignified tribute to a young deputy who had confronted and been killed by a mob of *sans-culottes* when they invaded the Chamber demanding bread on 1 Prairial Year III (20 May 1795). Beethoven might have inspected a score of this kind and thought, 'I can do that, and better.' Within two or three years he had done so, in the great A flat minor funeral march 'on the death of a Hero', the third movement of his A flat Piano Sonata, op. 26.

In the end, though, it was a slightly later series of encounters with French opera that seems to have had the most profound and lasting effect on his own work. In particular three recent operas by the Paris-based Italian composer Luigi Cherubini reached the Viennese stage early in the new century: *Lodoïska* and *Médée* in 1802, and *Les Deux Journées* in 1804. In between, Jean-François Le Sueur's *La Caverne* had its Vienna premiere in 1803, and at about the same time there were operas by Méhul, Dalayrac and Berton. These works were invariably what the French call *opéra comique*, but they were, on the whole, anything but comic: the designation meant only that they included spoken dialogue, unlike the *tragédie lyrique*, which was entirely sung. Several of them were 'rescue' operas, in which someone unjustly imprisoned is eventually released amid general rejoicing and the perpetrator punished or humiliated. Rescue opera was a symptom of revolutionary times: the triumph of the popular will over evil authority. But at least one notable example, Grétry's *Richard Cœur de Lion*, pre-dated the French Revolution, and involved, of course, the rescue of a king. Nor were all rescue operas political. In *Lodoïska* a Polish count rescues his beloved, a princess, from the castle of a bad baron with the help of a posse of right-minded Tartar guerrillas. In *La Caverne*, a noblewoman is captured by robbers but rescued by her husband who arrives disguised as a blind beggar. But when right triumphs, politics is never far away. The second most famous of all rescue operas, *Les Deux Journées* (sometimes known in English as *The Water-Carrier*), tells of a humble water-carrier at the time of the Paris civil war known as the *Fronde* (1648–53), who saves a member of the French *Parlement* from arrest by the royal army by hiding him in his water cart.

Beethoven seems to have been attracted to works of this kind partly because of their anti-authoritarian tendency. The girl in the castle, the woman in the cave, the member of parliament in the water cart, were all victims of tyranny, whatever their social class (all three, as it happens, were aristocrats). But there was a more direct reason for his interest in these operas, and that had to do with the character and quality of their music. His own instrumental works of the 1790s had already shown a tendency to dramatise the balanced classical forms, to disrupt them in various ways, or sometimes to enrich them with narrative or picturesque elements, as in op. 26 (where the march title was his own), or op. 27, no. 2 (the 'Moonlight' sobriquet came later), whose first movement does have an intensely poetic, inward quality, but whose finale is one of his most turbulent, unforgiving pieces, minor-mode throughout, an image of heroism against overwhelming odds. This is music (composed in 1801) that verges on theatre, and music that will have found an answering call in, for example, Cherubini's *Médée*, with its powerful, driven opening, the following year. In return, Beethoven was so impressed with the dramatic power of Cherubini's music that he quickly signed a contract with the Theater an der Wien for an opera of his own, which, after a false start or two, would bring about the most famous rescue opera of all, *Fidelio*.

Beethoven was a huge admirer of Cherubini, whom he considered the most important operatic composer of the day, and when he came to write his own rescue opera, *Leonore* – the first version of *Fidelio* – in 1805 it was natural for him to take as a model a work such as *Les Deux Journées*, of which he owned a score and from which he copied out passages. So *Fidelio* (to refer now to the familiar version) begins in a simple, song-like style, somewhat laboriously portraying the mundane normality of the gaoler Rocco's establishment, his very ordinary, not very bright, daughter, and her rather hopeless, rejected boyfriend, before the entry of the disguised Leonora immediately raises the dramatic tone and pushes these characters into the shade. Here the music becomes darker, richer and more complex, and the dialogue element

31

recedes. In the grave-digging scene of the second act Beethoven adopts a device Cherubini had used to powerful effect, that of *mélodrame* – accompanied speech. In the climactic scene of *Médée* (in its authentic, dialogue version),[3] Jason and Dirce's wedding is celebrated musically in the background while Medea speaks (shouts) her impotent fury in the foreground. In *Les Deux Journées*, Armand hides in a tree and speaks his concern for his wife over a soft accompaniment of four horns. The offstage trumpet that announces the arrival of the Minister in *Fidelio* – one of the most overwhelming moments in all opera – was also probably pinched from a French opera, Méhul's *Héléna* (1803), where offstage trumpets similarly announce the successful outcome of a prison rescue by a disguised wife.

Influences of this kind are transparent, and in Beethoven's case carry limited weight, since he never composed another opera. What he did, instead, was transport the influence into his instrumental music, which entered a new phase at precisely the time that he started contemplating an opera of his own. In the same year that he signed his contract with the Theater an der Wien, he composed his *Eroica* Symphony, No. 3 in E flat major, and began the *Waldstein* Sonata in C major, op. 53. And within the next four or five years he wrote the great works of his middle period, the Fourth, Fifth and Sixth Symphonies, the Violin Concerto and Fourth Piano Concerto, the 'Razumovsky' String Quartets, op. 59, the 'Appassionata' Sonata, as well as the first version of *Fidelio*, the three *Leonora* overtures, the *Coriolan* overture, and a good deal else.

These works are all arguably classical in general type. With the exception of the 'Pastoral' Symphony and of course the overtures, they have the usual three or four movements, are broadly regular in tonal design, have sonata-form first movements, rondo or sonata-form finales, and so forth. Yet they inhabit a completely new world. The best way of hearing how radically different these Beethoven works are from what might be deemed a normal path is to listen to the often excellent music composed by his Viennese and German contemporaries:

the symphonies of Gyrowetz, Wranitzky and Eberl (whose E flat Symphony was played a week after Beethoven's, and seems to have been preferred);[4] the piano music of Dussek and Tomášek, the string quartets of Anton Reicha – a close friend of Beethoven's from the Bonn years. These composers were not writing like Mozart or Haydn, but the scale and character of their work is recognisably in a straight line extended from them. By comparison, it is the sheer scale and daring of Beethoven's music of these middle years that strikes one first, once one has got out of the habit of regarding it as 'normal'.

The *Eroica* Symphony, to take the most obvious example, lasts in an average performance almost fifty-five minutes. Haydn's last symphony, No. 104, lasts under thirty, Mozart's last, the 'Jupiter' (No. 41), about thirty-five. The Eberl symphony plays for under half an hour (which may explain why it was better liked). Beethoven's orchestra is no bigger on paper than Haydn's, except for a third horn, needed not for extra noise but for solo entries in 'wrong' keys.[5] But the character of the writing is in every way bigger, with consistently full and active writing all the way down the orchestra, prolonged passage-work for the strings in all sections, and a greatly increased role for the wind, who not only play for more of the time, but have to blow harder for longer. This 'windy' quality in Beethoven's orchestration was much remarked in Vienna, where he came to be thought of as practically a wind-band composer. It suggests the influence of the revolutionary pieces shown him by Bernadotte, but also that of the French operas he had been hearing, written for pit orchestras with much more versatile wind sections than were usual in the stuffy salons of the German and Viennese aristocracy.

Beethoven's dynamic range was as notorious as his instrumentation. Even in his early piano sonatas the commonest dynamic marks are *sf* (*sforzando*: strongly accented), *ff* (*fortissimo*: very loud) and *p* (*piano*: quiet); but the most striking dynamics are the combinations: the *fortissimo* or *sforzando* followed rapidly by a *piano* or *pianissimo*. It's tempting to explain these sequences as the antics of an impetuous young pianist with a new and powerful instrument under his hands. But he was soon transferring the device to other kinds of music. In his string quartets, op. 18 (1798–1800), the *sforzando* is so common as to become almost a mannerism, often placed on weak beats, tending to contradict or undermine the natural metre.

Gesture had often been an important factor in the classical symphony. Better to start off with a strong, pithy idea that would lend itself to development later on, than with no matter how beautiful a melody that would simply have the audience longing for its return. Sometimes these ideas can seem like nothing more than a way of getting going. The slow opening of Haydn's Symphony No. 104 or the loud *vivace* triplets of Mozart's 'Jupiter' Symphony would be unprepossessing if it were not for something compelling in the gestures. With Beethoven such gestures become imperious. What, after all, is the significance of the two thumping E flat chords that start the *Eroica* if not to command the audience to stop chattering and listen? Even the theme that follows is nothing but a childish set of arpeggios with a swinging rhythm and a surprising finish, the descent to an alien C sharp, which is, so to speak, the question the rest of the movement has to answer. The famous four-note opening of the Fifth Symphony is so aggressive and absolute as to have become the butt of jokes about classical music. But having grabbed the audience's astonished attention, Beethoven then proceeds to build the whole first movement and parts of the rest of the symphony out of this four-note motif, so that gesture turns into substance in an essentially new way.

There are other examples, not only in orchestral music: the start of the E minor 'Razumovsky' String Quartet (two loud chords, arpeggios and a cadence); the 'Appassionata' Sonata (arpeggios and an ornamented cadence); later, the 'Hammerklavier' Sonata (a punch on the nose in B flat). These gestures have a certain 'look-at-me', lapel-clutching character that the classical precedents lack. And what is one to make of movements like the repetitious Allegro ma non troppo of the 'Pastoral' Symphony or the heavenly lengths of the 'Choral' Symphony, where monotony and the slowing down of time amount to new ways of compelling our reluctant attention, like Coleridge's Ancient Mariner holding the unwilling wedding guest with his glittering eye?

In such ways, Beethoven ceases to be the culmination of the classical era, and becomes instead the outsize individual, the great Romantic 'I am that I am'. Now each new work proclaims some aspect of this individuality. One thinks of the joke about Vivaldi, that he wrote, not six hundred concertos, but one concerto six hundred times. The same joke evolves somewhat through Haydn's hundred and four symphonies, because anyone can hear that these works are quite varied, and yet there are a hundred and four of them. Beethoven managed only nine, not just because he lived less long, or because he was unproductive or plain lazy, but because a work had become a statement. Haydn's eighty-something string quartets similarly compare with Beethoven's sixteen, his forty-odd piano trios with Beethoven's half-dozen or so. Only with the solo piano sonata is there even remote parity: fifty-two against thirty-two; but of these thirty-two, twenty were composed by 1802, at what might be termed a classical rate, only twelve in the remaining twenty-five years of Beethoven's life, a four times slower rate.

Often, as with the *Eroica*, Beethoven's scores of this period are simply on a grander scale, though this is hardly enough to account for the numerical difference. Nor is it always the case. The F minor String Quartet, op. 95, is no longer than any late Haydn quartet and a good deal shorter than Mozart's so-called 'Haydn' quartets. Its compactness, however, is an aspect of its scale. The ferocity of its opening bars depends on their abruptness. By contrast the opening of the 'Pastoral' Symphony is so matter-of-fact that Beethoven is able to chew it over to the point of boredom, like a Cumbrian shepherd tallying his flock, without actually boring anyone who has the wit to share the concentration of thought.

But while the gestural aspect of Beethoven's music may be superficially its most striking feature, it's the way he develops these ideas that really sets his music apart from that of his predecessors and creates a

35

completely new conception of form. The original idea of a development section in the classical symphony or sonata came, as we saw with C. P. E. Bach, out of the specific form of the baroque suite movement. Haydn, especially, played on the border between baroque and classical form in a particularly inventive way, but only from about the 1780s did he and Mozart, under each other's influence, begin to explore properly the idea of conflict resolved through musical argument that became the point of sonata form. Nevertheless the classical requirements of balanced form to some extent limited the argumentative element. Even in their last symphonies the development section was less than a quarter of the whole movement. In Beethoven's first two symphonies the proportions are almost exactly the same. But then suddenly in the *Eroica* the whole form explodes. In the first movement, itself almost as long as a complete Haydn symphony and with not two but four distinct themes or motifs in the exposition, the development section alone constitutes well over a third of the total and includes an important fifth theme in the remote key of E minor. What's more, the other parts of the movement also have a more fluid, developmental character than was normal even in late Haydn. In fact it's sometimes hard to say what is theme and what development.

Beethoven never wholly abandoned classical forms. They remain fundamental to his middle-period instrumental works, and still survive in many of the late works, albeit treated in an increasingly idiosyncratic way. Gone for ever is the balanced, well-behaved four-walls architecture of the classical sonata and symphony. Instead Beethoven seems to be acting out some deep internal intellectual drama, a sort of opera of the mind, whose *dramatis personae* are the old materials and concepts reconfigured so as to astonish them into new kinds of confrontation and ever more profound reflection. In the last three sonatas and all the late string quartets except the last, the discourse is fragmented and reassembled in a whole repertoire of ways. The Vivace first movement of the E major Sonata, op. 109, is twice interrupted by a florid Adagio espressivo, quickly yields to a scherzo-like Prestissimo, then settles into a long and increasingly intricate slow-quick-slow variation finale. The final sonata, in C minor, op. 111, is two movements only, a big sonata movement with slow introduction, and another long, long set of variations on an almost childishly simple C major melody, enriched, as it proceeds, by more and more elaborate figuration. After finishing this sonata, Beethoven took up another set of variations he had already begun on an even pottier C major theme, ending this time with a grand double fugue and, tongue more than slightly in cheek, a pompous minuet. This unpromising description masks one of his greatest piano works, the 33 Variations on a waltz by Diabelli, op. 120.

The sheer range of contradictions in this late music of Beethoven is what contemporary performers and audiences found so disconcerting, and why, unable to grasp the logic of its continuities and discontinuities, they increasingly tended to dismiss him as more than slightly crazy. The instrumental music of Reicha, Tomášek, Hummel and the others pursued a reasonably predictable course. The operas of Cherubini, Le Sueur and Méhul were, after all, operas (and French into the bargain). But what could you make of a chamber work like Beethoven's C sharp minor Quartet, op. 131, which started with a long slow fugue, then proceeded through a further six movements that, if tempo change were anything to go by, might be as many as ten or a dozen, with constant interruptions from one to the next; or the A minor, with its twenty-minute slow movement; or even the comparatively normal-seeming F major, op. 135, the master's very last 'significant' work, which kept asking itself a silly quasi-philosophical question ('Must it be? It must be.') before vanishing in a puff of pizzicato smoke?

Beethoven, profoundly deaf in his last years, was evidently exploring a private universe that had little contact with the Biedermeier world of 1820s Vienna. It was not, all the same, as private or detached as one might suppose. Abrupt contrasts and curtailments had been a feature of middle-period works like the Fifth Symphony and the E minor and F minor Quartets. It is easy enough to characterise these works as revolutionary. They continually challenge the settled, sociable spirit of the classical tradition from which they emerged. They shed its blood. They certainly defy its conventions, reinterpret its rules, break out of its limits. What they seem to express, perhaps unconsciously, is an idea that had become central to German philosophy since Kant, the idea of the freedom of the will. I've no idea whether Beethoven read philosophy, but great artists are themselves, in a sense, philosophers who create, as much as they respond to, the *Zeitgeist*. For Kant, the will was a necessary precondition for moral choice. For Johann Fichte it was a more energetic, existential force, which defined itself in relation to the resistance it encountered in the outside world. This concept of the will as a kind of embattled self-consciousness defining the world in its own image was a revelation for the Romantic artist, seeking a way out of the oppressive, anti-individualist eighteenth century, either by embracing the French Revolution or by abandoning the civilised world altogether. Beethoven embraced the Revolution for as long as it suited him, but when in his opinion it failed in its proper aims he simply went his own way, imposing his own will on received traditions and materials. Whether or not he knew that Fichte had said, 'I am not determined by my end. My end is determined by me,'[6] he might easily have said it himself.

3

Pleasing the Crowd and Escaping It

When Hoffmann wrote, in 1810, about music as 'the most Romantic of all arts', he was thinking above all of instrumental music. This seems natural enough in view of the particular strengths of the Germanic composers whose music prompted the remark. But at the time the idea would have seemed eccentric at best. Surely romanticism was an aspect of subject matter, whether narrative or at any rate verbal? Kant, who disliked music in general, had regarded instrumental music as trivial because it conveyed no definable thought. But for Hoffmann this was precisely its strength. 'Music', he insisted, 'reveals to man an unknown realm, a world quite separate from the outer sensual world surrounding him, a world in which he leaves behind all feelings circumscribed by intellect in order to embrace the inexpressible.'[1] An important aspect of this freedom from mundane concerns was the ability of music to create forms and new expressive vocabularies, new grammars, that emerged from the nature of the actual material without the limitations imposed by words or stories.

Hoffmann wrote with great eloquence, and his arguments are persuasive, even when he took refuge in private fantasy to give flesh to the thought. Nevertheless one searches in vain in the instrumental works of Beethoven's immediate contemporaries for any corresponding emotional or spiritual reach that might have inspired the same response if he had never existed. Hoffmann, who died in 1822, would have seen and heard his ideas fulfilled in Beethoven's late sonatas and string quartets had he lived. But in his lifetime the landscape was altogether less spectacular. Composers there were of real expertise, but they seldom broke, in instrumental music at any rate, with what one might describe as an early-nineteenth-century extension of eighteenth-century formulae.

More specifically they continued as providers to a changing market. The combination of the Industrial Revolution, the French Revolution and the Napoleonic Wars severely undermined the old settled world of court and Church musical establishments which had supported generations of composers in Germany and the Habsburg Empire. In France and Italy, where the theatre dominated musical life, the situation was different. But for the instrumental composers required by the small German courts, the world was turning upside down. Mozart, ground down by the philistine establishment of Archbishop Colloredo, had settled in Vienna in 1781 as a freelance musician, but failed to obtain a significant court appointment there. Beethoven lived on aristocratic support in Vienna, but never held a post of any kind after he left Bonn in 1792. A handful of leading composers succeeded in holding down long-term musical directorships: Gyrowetz at the Hoftheater in Vienna, Danzi at Stuttgart and Karlsruhe, Spohr at the Electoral Court in Kassel, Hummel eventually in Weimar. But for the majority of composers professional life became more and more a matter of trading their skills on the open market.

The old aristocracy could no longer afford large-scale musical establishments, but there was a new and growing public, moneyed and increasingly well-educated, that could and did. There was nothing particularly new about public concerts as such; music societies had existed at least since the early eighteenth century, presenting concerts for which tickets would be sold to the public, and concert organisations had emerged in cities, mainly to put on performances on those Holy Days – mostly in Lent – when theatre performances were prohibited. But well before the end of the century the audience for such events had begun to grow exponentially, and this growth can be charted through every aspect of music and musical life: larger, purpose-built concert halls and opera houses, larger orchestras, more powerful, more versatile musical instruments, music of a more public, less intimate character.

At the same time the market for printed music, to be played or sung in the home, expanded to the point where new methods had to be invented of printing at reasonable cost the complicated symbolic texts from which western musicians perform. When Haydn, in the 1770s and 1780s, had tossed off quartet after quartet, sonata after sonata, it had essentially been to meet the purely local needs of his employment. But when Beethoven's old Bonn colleague Anton Reicha composed some two dozen string quartets in Vienna in the early 1800s and two dozen wind quintets in Paris a decade or so later, it must have been with a view to selling the printed music to a domestic, amateur market. And that required the ability to print and distribute multiple copies on a scale hardly known before.

The explosion in music publishing just before 1800 was only one of the radical changes that came out of the revolutionary years, but it was one of massive importance. In meeting the increased social demand for domestic music, it created a commercial vehicle on to which composers hastened to climb, and the result was a corresponding explosion of instrumental music, chamber and solo, written generally with an eye to bourgeois, that is, conservative but not vulgar, taste. Paul Wranitzky, for example, a Czech composer working in Vienna, published more than fifty string quartets, among much else, between 1788 and 1805. Some fifty piano trios and forty-odd string quartets are listed for Adalbert Gyrowetz, another Czech, over roughly the same period. Franz Krommer, yet another Vienna-based Czech, published upwards of sixty string quartets and at least twenty string quintets up to about 1809. On the whole this music is conservative in idiom. One can still listen with pleasure to the Wranitzkys and Krommers, the Reichas and Ferdinand Rieses. Their best music is excellent and by no means deserving of the oblivion to which it is now largely consigned. But its individuality is mostly swallowed up in a certain general competence and predictability, or occasionally, as with Ries, involves seemingly unexplained oddities in a flattish landscape. Perhaps this is what prompted Beethoven to say of Ries, whom he taught for a time, that 'he imitates me too much'.

The piano was the one instrument that bred in musical terms the kind of individuality we think of as a main product of revolutionary thinking. It had been invented in about 1700 by an Italian called Bartolomeo Cristofori, a harpsichord maker from Padua; but its musical development had been slow, presumably because the essentially violent character of the instrument, whose strings are struck by hammers rather than, as with a harpsichord, plucked by quills, called for a much stronger design and construction. The point of the pianoforte was that it could play loud or soft according to the weight of touch on the keyboard and it could to some extent sustain the sound, and these properties gave it an expressive power not available on the harpsichord or its relatives. By the early 1800s it had settled into an instrument that could withstand the fierce dynamic contrasts required by Beethoven's early sonatas, even though the wooden frame still limited the weight and tension of the strings, and therefore the power and depth of the tone. Not till the 1820s were the first pianos made with cast-iron frames that could support the massive weight of thick metal strings at high tension over a full seven octaves. At the same time increasing refinements in the mechanism (the piano action) produced a highly sophisticated piece of machinery that could perform musical tasks of a previously unheard-of virtuosity and intricacy.

In its day the harpsichord had had its virtuosos; Bach himself had once challenged the French harpsichordist Louis Marchand to a contest, but Marchand had lost his nerve and left Dresden on the appointed day by an early coach. At the time (1717) both Bach and Marchand were in service. By contrast the emergence of the piano as a fully fledged concert instrument coincided with the disappearance of most such posts. When Mozart and Muzio Clementi competed at the Habsburg court in 1781, Mozart was unemployed, Clementi a virtuoso keyboard player on tour. Beethoven survived in Vienna on what amounted to charitable sponsorship. But many composers had already been forced out on to the open market. Some took up the newly expanding trade of music publishing, some took on pupils, some, like Hoffmann, became music critics. But a considerable number, like Clementi, cultivated their skills on the spectacular 'new' keyboard instrument and presented themselves to an eager and growing public as star performers, mostly playing music they had composed for their own use.

An important fact about these early virtuoso piano composers is that, although their music, apart from Beethoven's, is largely unknown to modern audiences and even most pianists, it was familiar to the next generation of piano composers, who are sometimes credited today with innovations in style and technique that they actually derived from their predecessors. This is not to claim that Cramer is remotely the equal of Chopin as a composer, or Dussek as good as Schumann. But Chopin certainly knew Cramer's two sets of studies (1804 and 1810) and was influenced by them in his own two sets, and perhaps also in his playing. Dussek, one of several talented expatriate Czech composers working around 1800, composed a huge quantity of music for or with piano, music uneven in quality but with flashes of individuality, especially of harmony, that often hint at the work of later composers such as Schubert and Schumann.

Jan Ladislav Dussek's life was as erratic as his music. In the best Rousseau tradition, he left his native Bohemia in 1779 aged nineteen, in the company of an Austrian captain of artillery, travelled with him to the Low Countries, gave concerts in Amsterdam and The Hague, for some reason proceeded in 1782 via Hamburg to St Petersburg, where he was patronised by Catherine the Great but was then implicated in a plot to assassinate her and had to flee to Lithuania, like Pushkin's False Dmitry, pursued by the Tsarist police. In Lithuania, for a year or so, he was music director to Prince Antoni Radziwiłł, but alas probably something more intimate to the prince's wife, so once again had to depart in haste. In Paris, two years later, he was, as *Grove's Dictionary* discreetly records, 'noticed by Marie Antoinette'. This time he seems to have left voluntarily, in the late spring of 1789, possibly on political grounds, or conceivably once again to escape a husband's wrath. With him travelled to England a certain Anne-Marie Krumpholtz, the young wife of the composer and harpist Jean-Baptiste Krumpholtz. A few months later poor Krumpholtz threw himself into the Seine and drowned.

Dussek's music is an important link between the classical eighteenth century and the generation of Mendelssohn, Schumann and Liszt. In a sense, it is a link that bypasses Beethoven, whose music created as many problems as it solved for his successors. Dussek's forty or so piano sonatas evolve gradually from the fluent, rather weightless pieces of the 1790s, with their decorative melodies and schematic (Alberti) basses, towards larger, more imaginative works like the so-called 'Farewell' Sonata (in E flat, op. 44), or the F minor 'Invocation' Sonata, op. 77, composed in 1812, the year he died. In these later works the textures are enriched by counterpoint and often quite complex chromatic harmony, with abrupt key changes; but the concentration and drastic gestures of Beethoven are absent, and the forms are conventional, four movements complete with minuet and rondo finale.

A different kind of link is provided by Dussek's younger compatriots, Václav Tomášek and his pupil Jan Václav Voříšek. By Dussek's standards, Tomášek lived a dull life, never anywhere but Bohemia and mostly in Prague. But his best music is interesting, to say the least, and often novel. His basic style in larger works (church music, three symphonies and a couple of sprightly piano concertos) is palpably Haydnesque/Mozartian, but there is a new and individual tone to some of his shorter piano pieces, especially a series of what he called *Eclogues*, miniatures in ternary (ABA) form modelled on the idea of the classical pastoral. Stylistically these pieces, composed in sets of six between 1807 and 1819, are straightforward to the point of plainness. They are largely devoid of counterpoint. But they are inventive, playful, highly pianistic and to some extent prophetic of the impromptus and *Moments musicaux* of Schubert. Perhaps Tomášek already knew Beethoven's bagatelles, op. 33, published in Vienna in 1803, but like Dussek's sonatas they are innocent of the disruptive element that Beethoven could not resist even in simple miniatures.

Voříšek is best known today for his one and only symphony (in D major, 1823), a superb piece that sounds a little like early Schubert. But Voříšek, a brilliant pianist in his own right, shone especially in music for his own instrument. Like his teacher's *Eclogues*, his *Twelve Rhapsodies* (1813–18) and *Six Impromptus* (1820) are uncomplicated ternary-form pieces, somewhat longer and richer-textured than Tomášek's, but with the same sense of classical style advancing towards the Biedermeier charm of 1820s Vienna, where Voříšek lived from 1813, and where he died of tuberculosis in 1825 aged thirty-four. Voříšek's pieces are especially fascinating because, unlike anything in Dussek or Tomášek, they bear faint traces of the ethnic Czech, nothing more than a harmonic twist here and there, certainly nothing folksy.

The outstanding case of a pianist-composer whose music bridges the gap between eighteenth-century classicism and the early Romantics is Johann Nepomuk Hummel. Hummel was born in Pressburg, today the Slovak capital, Bratislava, but at that time an Austro-Hungarian city – a mere fifty miles from Vienna, whither his family moved when he was eight. By that time young Johann was a child prodigy. Mozart heard him play, took him on as a pupil, then recommended a European tour like the one he himself had been subjected to at an even earlier age. Johann's father duly hauled him from city to city for five long years. Naturally he created a sensation everywhere, but he seems not to have come out well financially, since we next find him in Vienna, composing, teaching, by no means well off, performing comparatively seldom. Only much later, after returning to serious performing in 1814 at the time of the Congress of Vienna, did he become a proper celebrity, paid accordingly, and his best and subsequently most influential music was largely written after that.

Up to then he had composed prolifically in almost every medium except symphony. But these works are essentially eighteenth century in style. After about 1814 he concentrated on the piano, and at this point a significant change comes over his work. Already in the D minor Septet (1816), the A minor and B minor Piano Concertos (1816 and

1819), and the F sharp minor Sonata (1819) there is a warmer, more colourful approach to the sheer matter of sound, and a richer, more flexible harmony. The piano writing has a coruscating brilliance that seems to belong to a new, showy age of instrumental bravura, but there is also a strain of lyrical poetry prompted, no doubt, by the improved touch and sustaining pedal mechanism of the instrument itself. Above all, the relationship between the piano and the other instruments assumes a new kind of eloquence. The essential contrast between the melody instruments and the percussive piano is dramatised, and the formal processes take on an almost narrative character, as if we were being told a story with so many different characters interacting with one another. Probably Hummel was influenced in these respects by the recent concertos and chamber music of Beethoven, with whom he had cultivated a somewhat up and down friendship in Vienna. But as with Dussek and Tomášek, the fundamental violence of Beethoven is missing.

Hummel remains a transitional figure. Schubert, Schumann, Mendelssohn, Chopin all learnt from his example in one way or another. Schubert seems to have modelled his 'Trout' Quintet on Hummel's E flat Quintet, op. 87, for the same combination with double bass, and he certainly shared Hummel's taste for mediant relationships (keys or chords a third apart). The texture of Schumann and Chopin's piano concertos is to some extent Hummelesque. Something of Hummel's decorative piano writing also found its way into Chopin's solo piano music. But the greatest influence on Chopin in this respect was a quite different composer from a very different background, the Irishman John Field.

Field was born in Dublin in 1782 but came to London when he was ten and already a pianist of some note. In London he was apprenticed to Muzio Clementi, which seems to have meant being taught by him but also being employed to demonstrate the pianos built by the firm of Longman and Broderip, in which Clementi was a major partner. In due course this also entailed travelling with Clementi, first to Paris, then to Vienna, then in the winter of 1802–3 to Russia, which the twenty-year-old Field liked so much that he stayed there for most of the rest of his life, mainly in St Petersburg, partly in Moscow, where he died in 1837. Field had been a child prodigy, but to judge from his music he was a somewhat unorthodox kind of virtuoso. He cultivated a hyper-refined, rhapsodic manner in which a sustained lyrical flow was at least as important as the sheer bravura of Dussek and Hummel. His seven piano concertos are episodic in form and incorporate curious vagrant elements, traces of popular song, hints of Irish folk music, a Polacca finale to the third concerto, a storm in the middle of the first movement of the fifth concerto. But his most notable contribution to Romantic piano music was his invention of the nocturne. He wrote some twenty of them, typically four- or five-minute pieces in an almost entirely singing style of expressive right-hand melody accompanied by simple left-hand figuration, only rarely breaking into more vigorous motion. Chopin drew heavily on Field's nocturnes for his own, sometimes to an almost embarrassing degree of closeness, though he also dramatised the concept beyond anything in the model. There is nothing in Field that remotely approaches the grandeur of Chopin's C minor Nocturne. Yet Chopin's keyboard style in general would be hard to imagine without the precedent of Field, whatever its other sources.

Taken as a whole, these pianist composers of the Beethoven years are easy to see collectively as a product of the revolutionary upheavals of the 1790s. With their newfound expressive resources, their pyrotechnic brilliance, and their godlike uniqueness as they strode on to the concert platform (Dussek seems to have been the first keyboard soloist to perform sideways on, rather than with his back to the audience), they are icons of the emancipated individual, beholden to no one, like Adam in Haydn's *Creation*, 'erect before Heaven . . . a man and King of Nature'. But in their music, with the obvious exception of Beethoven himself, they measure up to this image rather seldom. Their music is more advanced because thirty years have passed, not because anything particular has happened in those years. If romanticism means overthrowing the past and seeing the world in a new light, then for its musical representatives we need to look elsewhere.

The revolutions of the late eighteenth century had a variety of origins and a variety of outcomes, but on the face of it they were all to do with practical living. The Industrial Revolution was made possible by the development of coke-fired blast furnaces and the invention of steam power. Its most significant consequences, beyond the obvious technological outcomes (mass production, faster and more efficient transportation, enhanced trade, improved sanitation and lighting, etc.), were social: the vast expansion of the mercantile and professional middle class, the creation of a large urban underclass, and the depopulation of the countryside. The French Revolution had other causes, but its effects compounded those of the Industrial Revolution. By shaking the foundations of the ruling aristocracy (and not only in France), it placed growing power in the hands of the new middle class. It made them richer and it gradually brought them political and economic freedoms. Above all it brought them leisure, and with it the demand for spare-time entertainment, edification and education of one kind and another.

Some of the consequences have already been mentioned. In music, public concerts and opera in larger concert halls and theatres were required and supplied. There was an explosion of domestic music-making provided, not by hired musicians, but by family and friends round the newly acquired grand or upright piano. Meanwhile in 1795 the first public music conservatoire had opened in Paris, for the first time offering advanced secular musical education, at least theoretically, to anyone with the talent to benefit from it. All this in turn led to a huge expansion of music publishing, not only of new music but of arrangements of existing music for every kind of instrument or instrumental group that might conceivably be found in somebody's home. It led to the composition of songs and piano music and chamber music with or without piano, on a previously unknown scale, or at least on a scale never before associated with the market-place. Meanwhile bigger concert halls demanded more powerful instruments. The piano could meet this demand as well. But other instruments had perforce to follow suit. It was during these years that most string instruments in general use were strengthened by raising the bridge, extending and angling the neck, and reinforcing the bass bar. Woodwind instruments acquired new keys. Brass instruments sprouted valves that enabled them to play full chromatic scales and evened out their tone. All these changes were facilitated by new industrial technology, which also rendered them economically worth making.

One might suppose that artists would like these developments, and of course some did. Gauging the market aright, you could sell your work, either directly or via a publisher, and become, if not rich, at least comfortable, and quite possibly famous. But for some artists this ready availability and, by extension, comprehensibility of their work was not necessarily a good thing. Many of the tenets of early romanticism, explicit or implicit, are in one way or another alienating; they contain some element of reaction against normality, against what the average person might be expected to feel or think, or against everyday life, especially modern life, with its factories and commerce, its machines and urban squalor, its matter-of-fact sanity, and its elevation of the common man with his common tastes, to say nothing of its violence and repression, whether in Paris at the time of the revolution, or practically everywhere else afterwards. As with Beethoven, the defining terms for the Romantics were difference, the unique, the individual imagination. But Beethoven had his aristocratic sponsors. For the true Romantic, saleability was the mark of Cain.

Romanticism of this kind has probably always existed, or has come and gone according to the temper of the age. In its early-nineteenth-century manifestation it can be traced to a whole swathe of writers, painters and philosophers in various countries in the 1790s: in England, Coleridge's Ancient Mariner alone on the Southern Ocean,

Wordsworth inspired by the wild woods and cliffs of the lower Wye to 'thoughts of more deep seclusion',[2] Blake in *America* and *The Song of Los* apostrophising revolution in Ossianic – even Messianic – language. But for all their genius, these writers exerted little influence on continental literature and none at all on its music. More important in these, if no other, respects were the French novelists François-René de Chateaubriand and Étienne Pivert de Senancour, both of whom, just after the turn of the century, published novels about young men alienated from society, abandoning their homes and wandering the world in despair, seeking quietus or oblivion. The eponymous hero of Chateaubriand's *René* (1805) is a young Breton aristocrat, like his creator-namesake, deprived of parental love and property, unhealthily attached to his sister, who to escape the overcharged atmosphere of his home travels aimlessly round Europe, eventually returns to Paris, finds that his sister has left and is apparently avoiding him, contemplates suicide but is rescued by his sister's return. Inexplicably she suddenly disappears into a convent, and when he follows her, she reveals her passionate love for him, a sin for which she is now atoning. All this René relates in Louisiana, whither he has fled, to an Indian chief and a Jesuit missionary. After a time he hears of his sister's death, and is soon afterwards himself killed in a fight between the Indian tribe and French troops.

Senancour's novel *Obermann* (1804) was preceded by a volume of beautiful descriptive nature writing called *Rêveries sur la nature primitive de l'homme*, which purported to be a Rousseauesque reflection on the troubles of this sublunary world caused by man's inability to free himself from the cares of daily life. 'I had found', Senancour writes, 'that everything was vanity, even glory and sensual pleasure, and I felt my life was of no use to me . . . Even unhappiness was questionable, and I realised that it made no difference whether one lived or died.'[3] Born in Paris, Senancour himself had been a sickly young man whose father supposedly wanted him to study for the priesthood. To avoid this fate, he ran away to Switzerland, married a Swiss girl, and settled in Fribourg, subsequently to-ing and fro-ing between Switzerland and Paris. Much of this is implied, rather than stated, in *Obermann*, an epistolary novel full of vivid, if somewhat morose, descriptions of wanderings in the Alps and the Jura and in the forest of Fontainebleau, interspersed with lengthy disquisitions on his own states of mind. Obermann, like René, is a prototype of what the French call *ennui* and the Russians later called the 'superfluous man', left high and dry by social and technological changes that left the upper classes with neither wealth nor function, incapable of reconciling themselves to the drab existence of the new bourgeoisie and the modern world in general. Their recourse to nature, preferably in its wildest, loneliest forms, is a search for annihilation and atonement, a washing clean of their humanity.

This French brand of self-absorption was a symptom of a much wider rejection of the universal truths and commonly held values that had informed much of eighteenth-century consciousness. In Germany it took a more systematic form, embodied in a series of short-lived artistic circles, of which the most important was the first, at Jena, from about 1798. The presiding genius of the Jena group was the playwright and novelist Ludwig Tieck, but its most significant products were the poetry and prose of Novalis (Friedrich von Hardenberg) and Friedrich Hölderlin, the philosophy of Fichte, and an even shorter-lived journal called *Athenaeum*, edited by August and Friedrich Schlegel. Tieck's plays and short stories are notable for their apparently random cultivation of the counter-rational, for instance in 'Der blonde Eckbert', where, after a long, fairly conventional fairy story with magical ingredients, it turns out that various central characters – the old woman who has cared for the heroine, the murdered (male) friend, and another (male) friend – are one and the same person, and Eckbert and his dead wife were incestuous half-siblings. Novalis, a trained lawyer and mineralogist as well as writer, explores this relation between the rational and irrational in his *Hymns to the Night* and the unfinished novel *Heinrich von Ofterdingen* which opens with a complicated dream and a vision of the blue flower that seems to draw Heinrich into a transcendental world beyond the terrestrial, towards night and perhaps death. The blue flower is a typical Romantic symbol, uniting the everyday world with a world of the spirit. One might see it as a doorway to Kant's unattainable other world of the noumenon, a doorway that Fichte had forced open by redefining the noumenon as a process originating with the inner self, the mind. 'All reality', Fichte insisted, 'is produced purely by the imagination . . . The imagination does not deceive, but presents the truth, the only possible truth.'[4] This was a philosophy that imprinted itself very readily on the Romantic consciousness.

One of the characteristic products of this privileging of the imagination was the literary fragment, invented as an aesthetic concept by Friedrich Schlegel in the pages of *Athenaeum*. Clearly Schlegel did not actually invent the fragment. The aphorism or maxim had been cultivated by many an author before, most famously by La Rochefoucauld in the seventeenth century. But the maxim was a complete thought expressed in concise form, pleasing above all for its aphoristic wholeness. Schlegel's idea of the fragment was something incomplete, a thought with crumbling edges. 'Many works of the ancients', he wrote, 'have become fragments. Many works of the moderns are like that from the start.'[5] This remark might have been meant as a fragment, though in fact it seems quite complete as a thought. If one looks through the hundred or more fragments (*Blütenstaub*, or *Pollen*) by Novalis in the first (1798) issue of *Athenaeum*, one is struck by their diversity of scale and form. Some are genuine aphorisms: 'We seek everywhere the absolute [*das Unbedingte*], and always find only things [*Dinge*].' Others are aphorisms whose meaning is deliberately arcane: 'Life is the beginning of death. Life exists for the sake of death. Death is at once ending and beginning, at once separation and closer self-fusion. In death is the reduction complete.'[6] Some are miniature essays. All, strictly speaking, make sense of a kind, if often without the razor-sharp precision of the old French maxims. The edges rarely crumble, and there is little of Schlegel's 'secret longing for chaos'. Yet the idea of the stray thought, left hanging, what musicians call the imperfect cadence, would survive as a Romantic fantasy, even within an art form like music, which scarcely works at all without closure.

While the French Revolution summoned up visions of freedom and political equality, the Industrial Revolution brought equality for some, squalor and poverty for others, and it created a world increasingly dominated by machinery and technology. From such things the Romantic artist flew in terror. René and Obermann had taken to the hills. But for the German Romantics escape was into something more like internal exile, into the privacy of the mind, into dreams and fantasy, the supernatural, the magical and the strange, or a longing for the past, especially the Middle Ages, when superstition reigned over the rationality that Hamann had so detested. Hence the multiple levels, medieval settings and fantastical narratives of Tieck's fairy tales; hence also the magical idealism of Novalis's hymns. 'Must morning always return?' Novalis pleads in the second of the six hymns. 'Will earthly power never end? Accursed busy-ness consumes the heavenly approach of night.'⁷

A striking aspect of these German works is their abundant use of musical imagery: Novalis's hymns, the melody of morning in Hölderlin, the magical bird in 'Der blonde Eckbert' who sings different songs that always begin and end with the same word, 'Waldeinsamkeit'. A special case is Wilhelm Heinrich Wackenroder's *Outpourings of an Art-Loving Friar*, a slim volume that, after an enthusiastic discussion of the beauties of Italian and German painting, concludes with a biography of an imaginary composer, Joseph Berglinger. Wackenroder was the son of a Prussian bureaucrat who wanted him to follow in his footsteps and was inflexibly opposed to his artistic leanings. Eventually the young man was forced into the civil service; but meanwhile he had befriended Tieck, an exact contemporary, and would certainly have fallen in with the Jena circle had he not died of typhoid fever early in 1798. Berglinger, like his creator, is a passionate music-lover whose doctor father refuses to countenance an artistic career, and who despairs of the way audiences in general treat music as just another amenity, to be enjoyed between one meal and the next. But when, after running away from home, he studies music and eventually becomes Kapellmeister at the nearby cathedral, he falls into fresh despair at the reduction of his adored music to sets of rules and routines. At last, after visiting his father on his deathbed, he is inspired to compose a masterpiece, a setting of the Passion, but is so drained by the effort that he dies soon afterwards.

Berglinger is the archetype of the Romantic composer who imagines that art is nothing but inspiration, akin to religion in its power to elevate the soul but to be corrupted by the mean-spirited bourgeoisie. Some fifteen years later, E. T. A. Hoffmann invented a comparable but more complex figure in the person of Kapellmeister Kreisler, similarly an *alter ego* who is represented as the author of various critical writings that are in reality the work of Hoffmann himself, including his essay on 'Beethoven's Instrumental Music'. Kreisler, like Berglinger, despairs of bourgeois music. He describes a tea-party at Councillor Röderlein's at which he is required to accompany the councillor's two daughters in a duet from one of Ferdinando Paër's operas. 'Actually,' he reports,

> the talent of the Miss Röderleins is not insignificant. I have now been here for five years, and a teacher in the Röderlein household for four and a half. During this short time Miss Nanette has progressed to the point where, after hearing a melody only ten times in the theatre and then playing it through on the piano another ten times at the most, she can sing it so well that one immediately recognises what it is supposed to be. Miss Marie grasps it after only eight times, and if her pitch is frequently a quarter-tone below that of the piano, then her dainty little face and most agreeable rosebud-lips make it on the whole easy to bear.[8]

Not altogether surprisingly, Kreisler soon vanishes without trace, leaving behind a number of sheets of music paper, on which 'brief essays, largely humorous in content, had been hastily scribbled in pencil during odd moments'.[9] Hoffmann's *Kreisleriana*, as he called these in fact substantial and by no means exclusively humorous essays (first published in 1814), was the start of the brief storytelling career – he died in 1822 – that has brought him fame even among those who never read music criticism or listen to classical music. Many of his stories involve music in one way or another, but more broadly they represent an important strand of Romantic sensibility somewhat rare in the writings of the Jena circle: that of satire and self-parody. The remarkable-looking man Hoffmann meets in a Berlin café in the year 1809 and enters into conversation with about the music of Gluck turns out to be the long dead Gluck himself; the bizarre eccentricities and diabolical musicianship of Councillor Krespel and his daughter Antonia play out in a world where everything else is commonplace. Hoffmann's brilliance, unlike Novalis's, lies in his gift for relating mad or appalling tales in a faintly ironic tone of straightforward rapportage. His stories are gripping, funny and frightening, but seldom if ever spiritually elevated.

There were precedents for this kind of writing, if nothing quite in the Hoffmann vein. An isolated case is Part One of Goethe's *Faust*, first published complete in 1808. In its original form, the so-called *Urfaust*, it belonged to Goethe's *Sturm und Drang* phase, but the finished play emerged from his time in Weimar, when, together with Schiller, he adopted a more classical, objective stance in literary matters and engaged in long discussions on social, philosophical and scientific questions with Herder, and Alexander and Wilhelm von Humboldt. The hero of his novel *Wilhelm Meisters Lehrjahre* (1795–6) is a would-be Romantic figure who abandons a business career to join a travelling theatre company, with for a time unfortunate but eventually fulfilling results – the whole point of what the Germans call a *Bildungsroman*, a novel of personal development. However, the narrative treatment is detached and gently ironic. Wilhelm is an idealist with a sententious streak, whose genuine search for spiritual freedom is constantly obstructed by the hard-nosed realities of life and the pragmatic nature of his fellow creatures. Faust, by contrast, is a rebel on the grandest scale who, with diabolic assistance, brushes aside the inhibitions of this world on condition of eternal damnation in the next: a sort of Don Giovanni of the soul. Of all the literary creations of the years around 1800, the Faust of Goethe's Part One is the most authentically Romantic, the one who reaches highest and falls farthest. *Wilhelm Meisters Lehrjahre* will attract composers exclusively for the poems the author puts into the mouths of his two least flesh-and-blood characters, the child Mignon, who adopts Wilhelm as surrogate father but dies partly because of his neglect, and the mysterious harper, the old man who turns out to be Mignon's actual father. *Faust*, on the other hand, will attract as a whole, as the ultimate topic for musical treatment, the summit of human and artistic aspiration (bearing in mind that in Part Two, completed only in 1831, Faust is redeemed). Yet Goethe's play, written almost entirely in rhyming verse, is devoid of pomposity or self-importance as a work of art, but treats its tragic subject with a degree of wit and verbal bravura that belie the terrors of the plot as surely as Mozart's grace and transparency belie those of *Don Giovanni*.

One other writer who adopted a partly ironic stance towards romanticism was the now largely forgotten Johann Paul Richter. Jean Paul (as he called himself) is important to musicians today chiefly as an influence on Schumann, who imitated his prose style and borrowed imagery from his novels in some early piano works. For Schumann the key works were the novels *Siebenkäs* (1796–7) and *Flegeljahre* (1804–5), in both of which Jean Paul explores the idea of the *Doppelgänger*, or double, but in the metaphysical sense, as he describes it in *Siebenkäs*, of 'Leute, die sich selber sehen'– people who see themselves. In *Flegeljahre* these are the twins Walt and Vult, separated at birth, whose personalities, when they meet, turn out to complement one another: Walt is thoughtful, reflective, and steady; Vult is mercurial, volatile, intuitive, quick-witted. (Schumann matched them with his own personal doppelgangers, Eusebius and Florestan, of whom more later.) For Jean Paul the idea fed into the rapid mood changes and elaborately metaphorical language that he cultivated.

Jean Paul lived for a few years around the turn of the century in Weimar, but did not consort with the Goethe circle. Schiller is supposed to have regarded his work with contempt, disliking its satirical tone; and certainly there is little in common beyond the German language between the two writers' work. Schiller, though he wrote poetry, philosophy and history, is most important as a playwright, whose plays often emerge from his historical research. For instance his *Don Carlos* (1787), with its subsidiary theme of freedom for the Dutch, was preceded by a history of the Dutch revolt, and his Wallenstein trilogy by a history of the Thirty Years War. His later plays are mostly about great figures at turning-points of history: Wallenstein murdered by agents of the Emperor, Mary Stuart executed as a rival claimant to the English throne, William Tell fomenting the fourteenth-century Swiss revolt against the brutal Austrian occupation. And it was surely the grandeur and psychological complexity of these portraits, including of the Marquis of Posa and Philip II in *Don Carlos*, and Joan of Arc in *Die Jungfrau von Orleans* (1801), that attracted so many opera composers in the years after Schiller's death.

Schiller himself was a Romantic on the grandest intellectual scale. He had been an enthusiastic supporter of the French Revolution, until it fell victim to the brutality of the Terror and the fanaticism of its ruling spirits; but his liberalism was allied to a strong feeling for the revitalisation of German culture, specifically through the theatre. His nationalism was essentially political in character; it was about liberty, fraternity, equality (perhaps) and unity. But German romanticism harboured another sort of nationalism that was more specifically ethnic, more to do with language, local history and folk culture, exactly as articulated by Herder. It came in two specific forms: as a collection of folk poetry published in three volumes (1805 and 1808) under the title *Des Knaben Wunderhorn* (*The Youth's Magic Horn*) edited by Achim von Arnim and Clemens Brentano, and as a single volume of fairy tales (first published in 1812) called *Kinder- und Hausmärchen*, edited by the brothers Jacob and Wilhelm Grimm.

The collecting of folk tales and folk songs was a symptom of the dawning consciousness of a specifically national spirit, something that defined who one was in contradistinction to those who lived far away, spoke other languages, ate different food, wore strange clothes. Herder himself had published a collection of folk songs, *Stimmen der Völker in Liedern* (1778–9), and strictly speaking the issue for him had been less the nation state, as understood later on, than the nation as a self-defining local group, often barely conscious of where it might be on the map of Europe. But the German situation was peculiar because Germany actually had no existence as a totality, and instead comprised a large conglomeration of independent states and statelets, all speaking German of one kind or another, and with a growing consciousness of their common political and cultural identity. Thus a tendency that, for most parts of Europe, was fissile, in the German lands spoke for unification, and even for a certain latent hostility to non-Germans.

The poems of *Des Knaben Wunderhorn* reflect many aspects of a damaged rural society. The title comes from the first song, about an elephant's horn (tusk), decorated with four golden bands, pearls and rubies and a hundred little bells, which a handsome boy on a swift steed places in the Empress's hand. At the slightest pressure from her finger, he tells her, the bells will ring, as no harp ever sounded, and no bird or mermaid ever sang. But the happy tone is not maintained. Many of the songs reflect the horrors of war, recalling, perhaps, that barely a century and a half earlier the German lands had been ravaged by the Thirty Years War. There are love songs, of course, love lost and gained, but also comic songs, children's songs, ballad (story) songs, and songs of hope in the next world, such as 'Urlicht' ('Primeval Light'), made famous by Mahler's setting in his Second Symphony. The question of authenticity, however, is real, because Arnim and Brentano were both poets in their own right, members of the Heidelberg group

founded in 1806 in the shadow of the Jena group, and the poems generally have a degree of sophistication that argues at least the editorial
if not the composing hand. Not that this in any way diminishes – if
anything it increases – the significance of the collection as a monument to the growing sense of German nationhood. In sorrow and
joy, these are poems about German people, German countryside and
places, German society, a land of forests and rivers and ancient magic,
far from the courtly elegance of France and the civic splendour of Italy.

Grimms' fairy tales were the product of a similar intention and were
perhaps even prompted by Arnim, who was in Kassel with the Grimm
brothers in about 1808. In certain ways the fairy tales cover similar
territory to the poems. We are mostly in or close to the German forest, far from the city, among the poor, the deprived and those whose
sole hope is in the next world. But there are crucial differences. War is
largely absent from the tales, and love is usually satisfied with a certain
amount of guile and a great deal of magic. In these pocket kingdoms
where talking to the king and marrying his son or daughter might be
a simple matter, magic both good and bad is a universal force, often
acting as a kind of wish fulfilment. 'In olden times when wishes still
helped . . .' are the opening words of the very first tale, 'The Frog King
or Iron Henry', and in many of the tales the capacity of wishing to
bring about the most improbable result is the chief mechanism of the
plot. But wit and courage are also required. Hansel and Gretel outwit the witch without the help of magic, and the Brave Little Tailor
achieves astonishing feats with a mixture of trickery, luck and sheer
derring-do and accordingly ends up with half the kingdom and a princess wife.

Many of these stories are older than the versions the Grimm brothers collected from German sources. Their informants were frequently
educated bourgeois with knowledge, for instance, of the French tales of
Perrault; the peasants were often unwittingly relaying oral traditions of
great, sometimes non-European antiquity. But for the Grimms, these
were German stories with a purely German resonance. Jacob Grimm

was also a philologist, a student of the German language and its parentage. Like the *Wunderhorn* poems, the stories told of a life rooted in Germanic soil, a soil many times before, and now once again, trampled by the boots of foreign soldiers and foreign officials, a life that might, as Herder had argued, be revitalised by tapping down into the native earth or exploring the memories and knowledge of the oldest and least sophisticated members of the rural community.

4

Operas Grand and Grotesque

'The enemy was at the gates,' the narrator, Theodor, announces at the start of Hoffmann's dialogue *The Poet and the Composer*:

> But Ludwig sat in his little back room, completely absorbed and lost in the wonderful, brightly coloured world of fantasy that unfolded before him at the piano. He had just completed a symphony, in which he had striven to capture in written notation all the resonances of his innermost soul; . . . to speak in heavenly language of the glorious wonders of that far, Romantic realm in which we swoon away in inexpressible yearning . . .'[1]

Hoffmann's Beethoven of the Napoleonic years is perhaps not altogether ours, and it is striking how this poet-composer, writing in 1813, identifies so precisely a Romantic music that hardly existed as yet. But this is also the music of Jean Paul's Victor in his novel *Hesperus* (1795), who enquires of it ecstatically: 'Art thou the evening breeze from this life or the morning air of the life to come?'[2] The fact that the music that inspired these transports was Friedrich Beneken's pathetic little hymn 'Wie sie so sanft ruhen' played on a jew's harp, merely underlines their unfocused, essentially literary character, unconnected with any particular music.

Through all these years, the Hoffmann/Jean Paul romanticism was struggling to find its musical equivalent. There is actually little trace of it in Beethoven, and hardly any in the instrumental music of his contemporaries. It begins to emerge spasmodically in French opera of the 1790s and 1800s, but even here the emphasis is on classical or occasionally Gothic tragedy, heroic in tone, with a persistent 'rescue' element that proclaims its origin in the public world of revolution rather than the private world of dreams. A quality we do, perhaps vulgarly, think of as Romantic rather than classical begins, however, to invade the style, and with it the technique, of several of these works. This is the psychological factor that drives Cherubini's *Médée* (1797) or, even earlier, Méhul's *Euphrosine* (1790) and *Mélidore et Phrosine* (1794). Behind these works lies the influence of Gluck, especially his Iphigenia operas and *Armide*. But there is a ferocity in the portrayal of emotion that goes beyond the model, and a new kind of technical richness that begins to evolve with it. *Mélidore et Phrosine* became notorious for its adventurous (at times eccentric) harmony and unusually colourful orchestration, which went with a plot about fratricide and incest – topics of surpassing interest to the Romantic mind. In one other crucial respect these French operas created a precedent that was to have powerful implications for nineteenth-century music. The reminiscence motif – the brief but recognisable theme used to remind the audience of some previous incident or element in the drama – had only a modest history before Méhul transformed it, in *Euphrosine*, into an organic psychological resource. Méhul uses a simple two-note figure – the minor third, D-F – as a recurrent image of the jealousy that the Countess of Arles maliciously arouses in the anti-hero Coradin and his consequent attempt to poison Euphrosine. This is not quite the leitmotif of Wagner, but it has a similar intention in rudimentary form. The idea of binding a dramatic work by a device that integrated it musically as well as psychologically was to find an instinctive response in the Romantic obsession with the inner self and the operation of fate. The effect is still limited in Méhul by the *opéra comique* format, with spoken dialogue constantly interrupting the musical flow, but a new formula was in the making that would do away with this disadvantage, in favour, however, not so much of greater integration as of sheer spectacle of sight and sound.

Not for the first time in French opera, the new impulse came from an Italian. Gaspare Spontini had been born in Maiolati in the Papal States in 1774, had studied in Naples, and composed a dozen or so *opere buffe* which were performed with moderate success in Italy before, in 1802, he moved to Paris and switched to composing operas in French. Here he somehow acquired the patronage of the Empress Joséphine, and it was with her support that his first *tragédie lyrique*, *La Vestale*, reached the stage of the Opéra in 1807.

After various vicissitudes under the Revolution, the Opéra had reopened in 1804 under Napoleon's patronage with a new name, Académie Impériale, and with a new grand opera, *Ossian, ou les bardes*, by Le Sueur. It would be hard to imagine a subject that caught more precisely the spirit of romanticism, and Le Sueur had treated it on the grandest scale in five acts, with massive choruses of Caledonian and Scandinavian bards, a series of ballets, an elaborate dream sequence for Ossian himself, and a setting that combined the misty forests and lakes of Scotland with the ghastly impedimenta of Odin worship and human sacrifice. After a successful first run, *Ossian* made little headway, but it set the tone for what was to become not just a major operatic genre in Paris of the First Empire and the Restoration, but a lasting influence on the development of music drama thereafter. Le Sueur himself followed *Ossian* up with a work on a still grander scale called *La Mort d'Adam* (*The Death of Adam*, 1809), with a cast described by Winton Dean as 'the entire human race . . . and the total complement of heaven and hell'.[3] But the work proved too big for its boots and soon vanished from the stage. It was left to Spontini to lead the way towards a more viable, if no less spectacular, version of grand opera.

La Vestale (*The Vestal Virgin*) returns to the classical Roman world so beloved of *opera seria*, but in a completely transformed musical and dramatic context. Gone for good are the da capo arias and dry recitative, the castrato heroes, and the interminable confusion of characters in love, assassination plots and magnanimous emperors. Spontini's models are again the Gluck of *Iphigénie en Tauride* and, to a lesser extent, the Mozart of *Idomeneo*. His music flows from beginning to end, arias leaking into accompanied recitative, choruses fading into arias, and with the orchestra a potent force, as in Mozart, but much freer use of the woodwind and brass that had become so strong and numerous in Parisian pit orchestras after the Revolution. Spontini's orchestral writing was thought noisy, and his writing for voice is certainly strenuous. But dramatically the work is compact, and there is nothing in the story (about the reluctant Vestal Virgin in love with a victorious Roman general) to compete with the scenic diffuseness of *La Mort d'Adam*. The main weakness of *La Vestale*, an influential piece in its day, is its *deus ex machina* ending in which the hidden deity releases Julia from her vows and the assembled virgins and priests rejoice. When Bellini treated the same subject in *Norma* some twenty-five years later he avoided this mistake.

The Gluck legacy comes out in one other way, the essential realism of psychology and action, within an admittedly highly artificial context. But soon Spontini was turning to actual history and to stage effects on the grandest scale, with psychology pushed into the background. His *Fernand Cortez*, as first staged in 1809, was the original cast-of-thousands grand opera, complete with horses, battles, the firing of the Spanish fleet, a siege, stage bands and the suicide of the heroine. Spontini's musical idiom is by no means advanced for its day, though its clothing is topical. He knew how to dramatise through abrupt shifts of tonality and by sheer volume. But he never achieved, either in *Fernand Cortez* or in his one subsequent French grand opera, *Olimpie* (1819), the emotional truth that in its modest way shines through *La Vestale*. In 1820 he left Paris to take up a post as Generalmusikdirektor at the court of the Prussian king Friedrich Wilhelm III in Berlin, and thereafter composed operas in German, of which the most notable, the grand historical *Agnes von Hohenstaufen* (1829), was supposedly admired by Wagner but left no particular mark otherwise.

Meanwhile these new trends in Parisian opera began to exert an influence abroad, but the leakage was slow and for a long time unspectacular. Italian opera continued with a productivity like a factory line, still largely preserving the old distinction between *opera seria* and *opera buffa*. An interesting partial exception is Simon Mayr, a Bavarian who moved to Italy in his mid-twenties and spent the rest of his long life there, writing almost seventy operas and a great deal of sacred music, like any well-brought-up Italian composer. Mayr seems gradually to have incorporated into the standard Italian genres various attributes of the German music of his youth: harmony of a less stereotyped kind, a certain flexibility of form, more versatile ensemble and chorus writing, and a richer orchestral palette. These tendencies come to a head in his *Medea in Corinto* (*Medea in Corinth*), a work unashamedly influenced by Cherubini's *Médée* and Spontini's *La Vestale*.

Nine months before the Naples premiere of *Medea in Corinto* in November 1813, a new *opera seria* had gone on the stage of the Fenice in Venice that announced the arrival of an Italian-born genius whose work would transform both the serious and comic forms of Italian opera. *Tancredi* was the twenty-year-old Gioachino Rossini's tenth opera, but the first to set the echoes ringing beyond the narrow operatic world of northern Italy. Rossini had been born in Pesaro on leap year day 1792, had studied at the Bologna Conservatorio, and had worked regularly as continuo player at the Teatro del Corso in that city. His parents were both musicians, and Gioachino had himself sung on the operatic stage at the age of thirteen in Paër's *Camilla*. The theatre was entirely in his blood, including the factory-line rate of production. In 1813, as well as *Tancredi*, no fewer than three other operas of his had their premieres, one of them the sparkling *L'italiana in Algeri* (*The Italian Girl in Algiers*). Within a year of the premiere of *Il barbiere di Siviglia* (*The Barber of Seville*) in February 1816, three further operas reached the stage, including *Otello* and *La Cenerentola* (*Cinderella*), two masterpieces that pale only beside the incomparable brilliance of the *Barber*.

Rossini's speed of production was helped by various conventions. In *opera buffa* he was mostly working within established norms, occasionally using existing libretti, sometimes adapting other composers' ideas, often transplanting pieces of his own from one opera to another. All the same, his handling of these conventions reflected the new tendencies in French opera. His comedies still alternated set-piece arias or ensembles with *secco* recitative with harpsichord. But these set pieces were often of considerable complexity, involving several characters and frequent changes of pace and texture. This was particularly true of the Act 1 finales, where the comic confusion would boil up in an accelerating crescendo of repetition as in the first finale of the *Barber* in Bartolo's house, with Count Almaviva disguised as a drunken army officer but avoiding arrest by flashing a credential of some kind at the police captain.

The fact is that, while Rossini's early *buffo* operas are understandably his most popular, his work evolved along much more individual lines in the serious operas that predominate after 1816. Already in *Otello*, his second opera for Naples, where he took up the post of musical director in 1815, he moves away from the rigid *seria* conventions towards a more organically conceived *dramma per musica*. The individual numbers are still separate; they end with perfect cadences, the musical equivalent of the full stop. But increasingly they contain plot developments, dramatic gestures, sudden changes of mood. The single mood aria, linked to the next by more or less dry recitative, begins to give way to a mobile dramatic concept in which the music maps itself fluidly on to the text. There is even in *Otello* a sense of the music controlling the drama, generating atmosphere, creating the sound space within which the action unfolds.

Of Rossini's later Neapolitan operas (he left Naples in 1822), the most interesting are *Mosè in Egitto* (*Moses in Egypt*), *La donna del lago* (*The Lady of the Lake*), and *Maometto II*. They all take further the musico-dramatic enrichments of *Otello*. *Mosè in Egitto* was composed for performance in Lent (1818), when secular subjects were banned from the stage, and it bears the somewhat devious label *azione tragico-sacra*. In some ways it is more like an oratorio than an opera, at least an Italian opera. It has big choruses and grand, statuesque scenes as well as a mysterious non-scene, the very opening in total darkness (one of the plagues of Egypt), and it is a tragedy only for the poor Egyptians, who get swallowed up by the Red Sea. By contrast, *La donna del lago* (1819) is a strikingly picturesque, landscaped score, apparently the first opera (of many) based on Sir Walter Scott, whose long narrative poem had come out in 1810. Rossini responds to the Highland setting and the clan warfare of sixteenth-century Scotland in true Romantic style. At curtain-up, shepherds are watching their flocks, and Elena (Ellen Douglas) appears on the lake singing an exquisite barcarolle. Soon hunting horns are heard – six of them on the stage – and at the end of the first act a bardic chorus with harp and pizzicato strings. As with Le Sueur, it was no doubt the wild scenery and the kilted warriors with their attendant music that attracted Rossini to the subject. But the treatment remains purely Italian, with plenty of bel canto *fioritura* which tends to leave the disguised King James V (alias Uberto) sounding not very different from Count Almaviva in the *Barber*.

Maometto II (1820) is the climax of this development in Rossini's Italian operas, notwithstanding its rickety plot involving another disguised (in this case Turkish) ruler calling himself Uberto, and unsuccessfully in love, like James V, with his enemy's daughter. The music is now continuous, often in lengthy, more or less unbroken sections in which choruses, ensembles and solos flow into one another, linked by orchestrally accompanied recitative that is itself musically substantial, tending towards arioso. It's clear that Rossini was influenced here by French opera, especially Spontini, whose *Fernand Cortez* he had just been conducting at the Teatro di San Carlo. Six years later he adapted *Maometto II* in French for the Paris Opéra, transferring the action from Negroponte to Corinth, and retitling it *Le Siège de Corinthe* (*The Siege of Corinth*). He reduced the solo *fioritura*, added dances and choruses and a new overture: in short he gallicised the work. A year later he performed a similar service for *Mosè in Egitto*, changing rather more, secularising it somewhat, and putting it on at the Opéra in 1827 as *Moïse et Pharaon, ou Le Passage de la Mer Rouge* (*Moses and Pharaoh, or the Passage of the Red Sea*).

A recurrent element in Rossini's Naples operas that helped him carry them over on to the Paris stage was their candid political content; theirs was the romanticism of liberty, fraternity and equality. Two years before *The Siege of Corinth* opened at the Opéra, Lord Byron had died of septicaemia at Missolonghi while helping the Greeks defend their town against the Turks. Liberation was in the air: Moses freeing the Israelites, the resistance at Negroponte or Corinth, even the clan rebellion against James V. These were subjects close to the Parisian, if not the Bourbon, heart. Rossini himself wrote a short cantata in Byron's memory, and then, finally, what would turn out to be his last stage work, a grand opera about the famous, though perhaps mythical, fourteenth-century Swiss liberator, William Tell, based on the play by Schiller and premiered at the Opéra in August 1829. This was Rossini's only original opera in French (apart from *Le Comte Ory*, much of whose music originated in the Italian opera *Il viaggio a Reims*), and it is the closest he came to opera on the scale that Giacomo Meyerbeer would shortly make his own.

The key to grand opera at its best is the conflict between the public and the private, between the great, sometimes violent, sometimes ceremonial, events that make newspaper headlines, and the lives and loves of individuals. In *Guillaume Tell* (*William Tell*), Arnold Melchthal, the son of the village headman, is in love with the Austrian princess Mathilde and serves in the Austrian garrison. When his father is taken hostage and murdered by the Austrians, Arnold has to decide between his love and his fellow countrymen. The choice is obvious but cruel. 'No longer any hope for our love,' Mathilde sings despairingly in a wonderful, frenzied third-act aria. Meanwhile, the world goes on its way. The Swiss peasants dance their dances, Jemmy Tell wins the archery competition, there are hunting horns and a *ranz des vaches*, and a big ensemble scene in the town square where the occupying Austrian soldiers force the townspeople to dance and sing, and to bow to the governor Gesler's hat on a pole. When William Tell refuses to bow, Gesler condemns him to shoot the apple off Jemmy's head (a bigger challenge, perhaps, for the stage director than for the archer himself). Finally Tell is rowed across Lake Lucerne in order to be torn apart by the crocodiles of Küssnacht Castle, but a storm arises, Tell is released to steer the boat, and the rebellion is signalled.

This proto-cinematic range of historical events, human emotion and local colour is entirely characteristic of grand opera, and it had a powerful influence on the two greatest opera composers of the nineteenth century, Verdi and Wagner. It required the ability to write on both the grandest and the most intimate scale and above all to switch convincingly from the one to the other. It called for expertise in writing for voice and, particularly, for the orchestra, which had now to paint the landscape as well as the emotions, and respond to a steep dramatic gradient at every point. To this extent, grand opera was the natural climax of a period in which the orchestra was expanding to meet the demands of a growing middle-class public and ever larger theatres, and voices were being trained to compete with them from behind the footlights. It was the age of Malibran, Pasta and Nourrit, singers of a power and expressive range that could project over a large orchestra pit for the four hours of *William Tell* or Meyerbeer's *Robert le diable*. It was also a time of new or newly available orchestral instruments, the serpent, the ophicleide, and a whole battery of trombones, released from their traditional association with sacred music and the operatic *deus ex machina*. In Parisian theatre orchestras by the late 1820s horns, trumpets and cornets with the newly invented valves had become standard, enabling those instruments to play for more of the time in more kinds of music. Parisian grand opera was well known for sheer noise, some of it from the stage, some from the pit. *William Tell* is not the loudest work of its kind, but it is certainly among the most colourful orchestrally, with a richness and refinement of sound that Rossini could barely have dreamt of when writing his early comedies.

For a long time before and after 1800, German opera was inhibited by the example of Mozart's singspiels, especially *Die Zauberflöte* (*The Magic Flute*) with its blend of exotic lands, magic, good and evil and low comedy, all of which might have led to something new and fertile if the composers had been good enough. One or two isolated works hint at a way forward. Louis Spohr's *Alruna, die Eulenkönigin* (*Alruna, the Owl Queen*, 1808) plunges deep into the German forest and stays there for three whole acts in which the Owl Queen attempts unsuccessfully to seduce the hero, Hermann, away from his Pamina-like beloved, finally hunting him through the woods, only to be defeated by a magic shield supplied by the ghost of one of Hermann's ancestors. Some strong, individual music is weakened by a heavy dependence on *The Magic Flute* at crucial moments, not least the overture, a partial but unmistakable crib. More interesting is an opera called *Silvana* completed in a Stuttgart debtor's prison in 1810 by the king of Württemberg's brother's outgoing private secretary, Carl Maria von Weber. Silvana, who, unpromisingly for an operatic heroine, is dumb, has been living wild in a cave in the forest, but is found by Count Rudolf and taken back to his family castle, where, in due course, it turns out she is the long-since abducted sister of Rudolf's unloved fiancée, Mechthilde. After more forest adventures and the inevitable storm, all ends happily and Silvana recovers her voice in time for the celebrations. Weber had been encouraged in this work by an older Stuttgart colleague, Franz Danzi, who was himself the author of successful singspiels and would soon produce another, *Der Berggeist* (*The Mountain Spirit*, 1813), on a subject that Weber had himself contemplated a few years earlier. The Silesian folk tale concerns an evil gnome called Rübezahl (literally 'turnip number'), who abducts a beautiful princess to his magic garden but unintentionally lets her go when she sends him out into the garden to count turnips while she is whisked off home by a griffon. Danzi's music for this nonsense is mostly charming and folksy in the old singspiel way, but it has some sinister features, including ghostly music and voice-overs (melodrama), a dramatic scene in gnome-land and, of course, a storm. The search in these works for a musical equivalent of Grimms' fairy tales is almost palpable. Always we are in a dark forest or a magic garden, or on a wild mountain, inhabited by strange creatures and where the laws of nature are mysteriously suspended. The magical, otherworldly element conveys a sense of difference, something specifically German and not French or Italian. The landscapes are those of the German painter Caspar David Friedrich, the gnarled trees and stormy skies and mist-clad mountains and lakes, the dark strangers, always with their backs turned, a dream world where cathedrals rise up in the forest and calvaries grow on mountain-tops. In short, reason is in retreat. Factories and steam power and gaslight, the discoveries of science and the home comforts of the bourgeoisie may be all very well, but for the artist, the exceptional, liberated soul, such things are worse than irrelevant – they block the view to the higher beauty; they inhibit experience; they breed materialism. For painters, the imagery of this rejection of civilised life is easy to imagine, if harder to execute: Turner's *Shipwreck* (1805), Géricault's *Raft of the Medusa* (1819), combine technical brilliance and innovation with a powerful sense of the beyond, the uncontrollable, the open sea. To establish exactly how such ideas could be rendered in music, and above all to learn how to do it, would take longer, because music is not imagery in any literal sense; it can only become imagery on its own terms and by means of a symbolic exchange.

Two operas premiered in 1816, both singspiels, begin to show what might be possible in these ways, without fully achieving it themselves. Spohr's *Faust*, composed in 1813 but not staged until September 1816 when Weber conducted it in Prague, is a Romantic opera in the sense that it deals with man's bid for moral and spiritual freedom and his confrontation with supernatural forces at the limits of civilised life.[4] It has nothing to do with forests or gnomes or magic spells (and not much, incidentally, to do with Goethe: Joseph Carl Bernard's libretto draws mainly on older sources). Faust's pact with Mephistopheles is already in place before curtain-up, but he now wants to break it and only do good. Alas for his intentions, Mephistopheles traps him into a series of unfortunate love affairs, at the climax of which he seduces Kunigunde at her wedding, kills her fiancé in the ensuing duel, and is dragged off to hell as his other lover, the pure Röschen, commits suicide. Spohr is not quite equal to the more diabolical aspects of this tale. When, for instance, Mephistopheles invokes the witch Sycorax to give Faust a potion that will make him irresistible to women, Spohr writes an undeniably delightful chorus for her retinue that Winton Dean reasonably suggests 'would serve equally for shepherdesses or mermaids'.[5] His virtues are those of a symphonist; he composed ten symphonies, as well as fifteen concertos for the violin, an instrument on which he was a virtuoso performer. He tends to develop his material without regard to the drama, and his handling of reminiscence motifs is in the same way somewhat neutral. The score's real strength lies in the simple quality of its best music and the highly accomplished writing for voice and orchestra.

Hoffmann, brilliant writer, storyteller and music critic, was certainly no match for Spohr in compositional technique. On the whole his music lacks the flair and technical range of his fictional composer, Johannes Kreisler. Nevertheless his 'magic opera' *Undine*, first staged in Berlin a month before the *Faust* premiere, is a key work in musical romanticism, if only for its subject matter, which became archetypal for composers of opera and programme music. Friedrich de la Motte Fouqué's tale of a water sprite who comes ashore, loves and marries a mortal against the advice of the elder water spirit Kühleborn, but is duly betrayed by her lover with disastrous results for them both, is a classic allegory of man's search for a balance between his material and spiritual nature. It reappears many times in various forms, in an early opera by Wagner, in Heinrich Marschner's *Hans Heiling* and Dvořák's *Rusalka*, in piano works by Debussy and Ravel, and elsewhere.

Hoffmann's version is a patchwork. The fairy atmosphere is intense, and is established from the outset as the curtain rises on Huldbrand (the knight loved by Undine) and Undine's adoptive father, the Fisherman, standing by the Fisherman's house door lamenting her disappearance into the night-time forest, 'where ghosts and bestial creatures live'. Although Hoffmann did not write the libretto (it was by Fouqué himself), the dramatic span is comparable to that of his greatest stories, *Das Fräulein von Scuderi* or 'Rat Krespel'. It plunges *in medias res* and maintains focus to the end. But the score lacks the ironic humour of the tales. It veers between a simple song-like style, mapped squarely on to the verse of the text, and something approaching through-composition in the final scene, where Undine reappears at Huldbrand's wedding to the mortal Berthalda and kisses him, as she says, to death. Here Hoffmann rises at last to the situation, described prophetically, and oddly enough approvingly, by the priest Heilmann as 'a pure love-death [Liebestod]'. But elsewhere the music, though it has lyrical charm and skilful orchestration, is short-winded and short-sectioned, the tone relentlessly earnest. It's a chastening thought that within four years of the first performance of *Undine* Hoffmann created his novel *Lebensansichten des Kater Murr* and the *Serapionsbrüder* compilation, prose works of a wit and fantasy entirely absent from *Undine*.

Yet *Undine* exerted an influence beyond its own quality. It was admired by Weber, who reviewed it favourably in the *Allgemeine musikalische Zeitung* and took from it certain elements for his own opera, *Der Freischütz*. *Undine* was performed only in Berlin, where it ran for twenty-three performances, soon after the last of which – ironically for an opera that ends in the water – the Schauspielhaus burnt to the ground, and the costumes and scenery were incinerated. There was a Prague production in 1821, then nothing for a hundred years and no published score until 1906. So John Warrack must be right that Wagner cannot have known it.[6] Wagner did, on the other hand, know Hoffmann's prose writings, both his stories and his quasi-theoretical essays, such as *Kreisleriana* and *The Poet and the Composer*. Hoffmann echoed Gluck in his advocacy of an integrated music drama (he labelled it *Tongedicht* – tone poem) in which every element sprang from a close reading of the libretto: 'true musical drama', he called it in a review of Gluck's *Iphigénie en Aulide*, 'in which the action moves forward without stopping from one moment to the next'.[7] This kind of unified music drama – Wagner's *Gesamtkunstwerk* (total work of art) – was a typical early Romantic concept, which went with the idea of the artwork as a complete, indivisible expression of the artist's soul.

Several other aspects of this particular slice of music history are symptomatic of artistic life in the early stages of romanticism. For the first time, leading composers are theorising about the aesthetics, not just the technicalities, of music; and for the first time a major literary figure is writing *about* music, as well as writing music and getting it performed on a major national platform. All of a sudden music is being regarded as a vehicle for ideas, not merely in the sense of intelligible words being set to music, but in the sense of music as itself capable of intelligible exegesis. In the past, composers had been musicians first and last. It isn't necessary to regard Bach or Mozart or Haydn as idiot automatons in order to suggest that for them music was a completely self-contained language in no need of verbal explanation. They were born musicians; music was what they did, and there was no need to discuss it.

Weber came from a somewhat different background. His father, Franz Anton Weber, was Stadtmusicus at Eutin, on the north German Baltic coast, when Carl Maria was born there in 1786. But the following year he resigned his post, upped sticks, and started a travelling theatre company, consisting mainly of his family, and performing straight plays and operas on a more or less perpetual tour that over the next seven years took in cities as far apart as Hamburg, Meiningen, Augsburg, Nuremberg and Vienna. What their performances were like can only be imagined, but we can form a general picture of their lives from Goethe's *Wilhelm Meisters Lehrjahre*, whose eponymous hero similarly abandons his father's business and joins a company of none too expert travelling actors. One might even speculate that Goethe picked up ideas for that part of his novel from the Weber company, since Franz Anton's wife Genovefa had for a short time in 1794 been a member of Goethe's Weimar theatre company. In any case, Carl Maria trailed along, having no choice, limping from a congenital hip deformity, and suffering what must have been fairly perfunctory music lessons from his father and half-brother on the way. By some miracle, he emerged a good enough musician for his father to entertain visions of his son as a new Mozart. So the travels continued, now focusing on the young prodigy: Salzburg, where Carl Maria had lessons from Michael Haydn (and Genovefa died of tuberculosis), Munich and Freiberg (Saxony), and from 1802 a tour of north German cities ending in Hamburg, then back to Vienna, where father and son at last separated, Carl Maria entered on adult studies with the Abbé Vogler, and met Joseph Haydn, Hummel and Salieri (but not, it seems, Beethoven).

This footloose, homeless childhood must have had an adverse effect on Weber's musical development, which in adulthood never settled into a clear, unmistakable pattern. He became a brilliant pianist, as is evident from his own writing for the instrument. The effect is generally showy rather than weighty in the Beethoven or Schubert sense, and the same goes for his writing for other solo instruments, most notably the clarinet, for which he composed two fine concertos, a quintet with strings, and a Grand Duo with piano that generations of students have staggered through to some or no avail. But it was in the theatre that he made the biggest impact and experienced the biggest disappointments. By his fourteenth birthday he had composed two operas, including one, *Das Waldmädchen*, that was performed in Freiberg. Both are lost. He wouldn't have minded. 'Puppies and first operas', he said later, 'should be drowned.'[8]

A third opera, *Peter Schmoll und seine Nachbarn* (*Peter Schmoll and His Neighbours*), a singspiel of somewhat Mozartian cut, followed in 1803. Then in 1804, still only seventeen, he got his own first post, as conductor of the theatre orchestra in Breslau. Here another aspect of his theatre 'training' sprang into action. Inured as he was from childhood to an ad hoc, pragmatic approach to theatrical not to mention living arrangements, he at once began making changes with a view to raising the standard of the orchestra's playing. He altered the seating plan, introduced sectional rehearsals, hired additional players and fired those past their prime. He also interfered with the stage production and design, and generally made himself an idealistic nuisance to musical jobsworths who not unnaturally resented being pushed around, however amiably, by a mere slip of a teenager, especially one with a probably spurious aristocratic 'von' to his name. Perhaps not surprisingly, he composed rather little during his two years at Breslau. He tinkered at another fairy opera, the aforementioned *Rübezahl*, but managed only three or four numbers, including an overture which he later reworked as a separate concert piece called *Der Beherrscher der Geister* (*The Ruler of the Spirits*). Then one evening in 1806 he took a swig from a wine bottle that had been refilled with engraving acid, collapsed on the floor and had to be resuscitated. During his two-month convalescence the theatre management reversed his reforms, and when he returned to work he had no choice but to resign.

From Breslau, the peripatetic young composer proceeded via Karlsruhe to the Württemberg capital, Stuttgart, where, as we saw, he became private secretary to the king's younger brother, Duke Ludwig Friedrich Alexander. Here he composed *Silvana* and started another singspiel, *Abu Hassan*, a one-act piece about a heavily indebted cupbearer to the Caliph who fakes his wife's death, while she fakes his, in order to claim double funeral money from the Caliph. To call this plot autobiographical might seem absurd. But in fact Weber had, precisely, been engaging in the fraudulent conversion of ducal funds while raising loans against the promise of court favours that he was unable to deliver. In the opera Abu Hassan escapes prison thanks to the Caliph's well-developed sense of humour. The Stuttgart court was less easily amused. Weber was imprisoned for a week, then kicked out of Württemberg.[9]

By this time he had, in his messy fashion, touched on a whole range of ideas and colourings and ways of life that would belong exclusively to the new century. Not all of it was Romantic fantasy. His Breslau reforms were those of a practical-minded new man unimpressed by the hallowed conventions of an old provincial theatre, and his repertoire, then and later in Dresden, where he was Kapellmeister for the last nine years of his life, was notably short on concessions to Biedermeier taste. He was also one of the first composers of the front rank to write about music as well as composing it. Hoffmann had doubled these roles too, but rather as a writer who composed than a composer who wrote. Weber's journalistic writing was by no means all hack-work, though he undertook it partly to keep the wolf from the door. He used it to promote ideas that were slowly and painfully emerging also in his music. Like Hoffmann he argued for the integrity of the musical work. In opera, as we saw, this meant the coherence of all the ingredients in what was by its nature a hybrid art form; in instrumental music it meant the organic connection of the melodic and harmonic elements within a lucid overall design. Music was the outward sign of the inner consciousness. But he tended to distance himself from the intensely conflicted character of Beethoven's symphonic music (the 'chaotic arrangement of his ideas', he called it in a letter of 1810[10]). His own instrumental music is distinguished by its clarity of line and texture, and its general avoidance of harmonic terrors. Above all, it has a real freshness and originality of tone colour. Sometimes this seems to be the lack of inhibition of the free spirit, schooled on the open road. But there is seldom anything random about the effect. In *Peter Schmoll* the writing for recorders, piccolos and, in Minette's romance, divided violas might look like the perversities of a fifteen-year-old; but the effect in each case is enchanting. The wind scoring in both *Silvana* and *Abu Hassan* is arresting and vivid. As for his piano writing, that was to prove in some ways more influential than Beethoven's, precisely perhaps because of its lack of such a heavy musical cargo.

The question of German nationalism in Weber's music, or in his criticism, hardly comes up before he is thirty. His operas have German texts, of course, but that was normal in the singspiel tradition out of which 'Romantic' works like *Silvana* emerged. However in 1817 he took up an appointment as Director of Music to the Roman Catholic court of the king of Saxony in Dresden, specifically in charge of a new German opera company, as against the established Italian Opera run by the court Kapellmeister, the composer Francesco Morlacchi. The relationship between the two companies says a great deal about the state of opera at the time. For everyday opera-lovers, opera was Italian. Not only was the repertoire dominated by Italian operas, but it was also normal to perform non-Italian opera in Italian. The idea that Germans might compose serious operas in any other language, or at all, was still quite hard for the layman to grasp. French opera had begun to assert itself, but even the works of Cherubini (an Italian, after all) and Méhul were sung in Italian outside France. The fact that Weber's new job involved performing opera in German automatically put him at a disadvantage. He had to make do with whatever singers were available and could sing in German; he was not allowed to duplicate Morlacchi's repertoire; and as before his attempts to modernise seating arrangements and other practical details of performance ran into difficulties.

It was nevertheless under these unpromising conditions that his most famously German opera began to take shape soon after his arrival in Dresden. A leading member of a local poetry-reading circle (*Liederkreis*) was a poet by the name of Friedrich Kind, and he and Weber were soon in discussions over an opera libretto based on a ghost story by Johann August Apel about a hunter, Max, whose skill has deserted him just when he needs to win a shooting competition in order to marry the head forester's daughter, Agathe. A fellow hunter, Caspar, who has a pact with the devil, Samiel, hauls Max off to the sinister Wolf's Glen at midnight, where they cast the magic bullets that will win Max his bride and damn his soul; but Samiel has destined the crucial final bullet for Agathe, and she is saved only by the timely intervention of a hermit, who redirects the bullet instead at Caspar. The opera, *Der Freischütz* (*The Free-Shooter*), had its first performance at the opening of the newly built Schauspielhaus in Berlin on 14 May 1821. Almost at once it took on a kind of symbolism as the first German national opera, partly because its production had been seen as a blow struck against the unpopular Franco-Italian Spontini, now in post at the Hofoper. Everything about *Der Freischütz* was different from Spontini's grand operas. Far from the classical or historical grandeur of his settings, Weber's work played out in the German (or at any rate Bohemian) forest with a cast of seventeenth-century villagers and not an aristocrat in sight. In place of the sumptuous splendour of *Fernand Cortez*, Weber supplied rustic gatherings, drinking songs, and a general atmosphere of muddy boots, lederhosen and beer tankards. The intimacy and sense of place in *Der Freischütz* struck a chord with audiences across Germany who yearned, like children, for stories set in their own landscape. The one thing it shared with Spontini, the *deus ex machina* ending, was as much an expression of the difference: a Christian redemption replacing a bit of pagan jiggery-pokery.

Der Freischütz is still a singspiel with dialogue, and it draws on that tradition in its use of a kind of folk lyricism, choruses obviously of folk type (like the Act 1 chorus where the villagers make fun of Max), and songs and ensembles of a certain innocent beauty, however heartfelt. The characters are types: the earnest, up-against-it hunter and the evil hunter, the pure beloved, offset by a soubrette of a cousin who takes life lightly, and so forth. But the intervention of evil inspires a situation and music unlike any ever heard before, on or off the opera stage. The centrepiece is the twenty-minute scene in the Wolf's Glen with the casting of the magic bullets. Here Weber uses every resource from French rescue opera to Romantic fairy opera, but with an uninhibited power unmatched in any existing work. The effect is of a kind of aural cinema, in violent contrast with the touching but essentially flat scene between Max and Agathe just before. First we hear the chorus making diabolical incantations against dark mutterings on the strings and (in some productions) ad lib crashes of thunder. Then Caspar negotiates with Samiel over the substitution of Max's soul for his. Here Samiel speaks against Caspar's singing, an astonishing melodramatic effect borrowed, with heavy interest, from Danzi. 'At the gates of Hell!' Samiel yells, 'Tomorrow, him or you!' When Max arrives, the casting begins. His dead mother's ghost appears, warning him away, also a vision of Agathe, her hair in disarray, about to throw herself into the waterfall. Each bullet is accompanied by successive forms of orchestral panic and various increasingly supernatural apparitions: birds flutter round the fire, a black boar crashes out of the undergrowth, a sudden storm smashes the treetops, there is the cracking of whips, the drumming of hooves, flaming wheels roll across the stage, a mysterious hunt dashes by. With the sixth bullet the heavens darken, lightning flashes, the earth flames; and on the seventh (Samiel's bullet), the black hunter appears and takes Max's hand, at which point Max makes the sign of the cross and faints.

Weber's handling of this barrage of audio-visual effects is unforgettably exciting. His orchestration, never less than imaginative and individual, is here of devastating vividness and precision, especially in the treatment of woodwind and brass. His timing, too, is superb. Everything moves swiftly, but not too fast, and the gradual increase in terror to the final climax is paced magnificently. Berlioz and Wagner learnt more from this one scene than from the whole repertoire of French opera. Where, one might ask, did Weber suddenly discover this genius for the theatre? The answer, of course, is *in* the theatre, where he had lived and worked for literally most of his life. We know from his reforms that he understood everything about the stage, about stage movement and design, and about how music and stage action worked together. The trouble was he had not had the opportunity to immerse himself in theatrical composition. He had struggled early on with poor dramatic material, then been distracted by the battle with recalcitrant employers and musicians. Now, though, he had arrived. *Der Freischütz* blew through the German theatre like a gale; it was staged everywhere in no time, in Germany and abroad, often, it's true, in corrupt versions and under different titles. It set the agenda for romanticism in music, as well as for the idea of rustic opera about people from one's own countryside singing the sort of music that might be sung there: nationalism, not in any political sense, but in Herder's sense of local communities finding their own particular voice. This would prove a huge discovery, and there is a case for arguing that it was Weber who made it.

While *Der Freischütz* was still unfinished, he had toyed with a comic opera called *Die drei Pintos*. But then with the Berlin success came a commission for a new opera for the Kärntnertortheater in Vienna, and though Vienna, as usual in such cases, wanted another *Freischütz*, Weber had different ideas. He had made up his mind to compose a grand opera, and to find a subject and a librettist he went back to the *Liederkreis*, and this time settled on Helmina von Chézy, a journalist and poet who had worked in Paris and who, among other topics, suggested the medieval French romance of Gérard de Nevers and his beloved, 'the very virtuous, very chaste princess Euriant de Savoye'. Chézy's version of this chivalric tale, *Euryanthe*, has good claims to be regarded as the most impossible libretto ever set by a great composer. The outline of the plot is simple enough. Adolar (the Gérard of the romance) is betrothed to the absent Euryanthe, but Lysiart is also in love with her and wagers with Adolar to prove her unfaithfulness. Meanwhile Eglantine, herself in love with Adolar, befriends Euryanthe while secretly hating her, and extracts from her a secret connected with Adolar's sister, who poisoned herself after the death in battle of her lover. When Lysiart, in league with Eglantine, reveals this secret, Adolar at once accepts the betrayal as proving Euryanthe's infidelity, drags her off to a mountain gorge and is about to kill her when they are attacked by a huge snake; she tries to protect Adolar, who is touched by her gesture and, after killing the snake, decides merely to abandon her. Euryanthe is found by the king's hunt and convinces him of her innocence. Lysiart stabs Eglantine and is himself led away. All ends happily.

On the face of it, this is run-of-the-mill operatic nonsense. But the nonsense is aggravated by a monumental shortage of motivation. Even allowing for the chivalric mentality, Adolar's acceptance of the wager, which will cost him all his property if he loses and is in any case in the worst possible taste, makes no sense. Lysiart produces no evidence but is merely theorising about women – a Don Alfonso without the wit. The secret, presumably the sister's suicide, hardly justifies Adolar's abrupt switch from adoring swain to vengeful murderer, but once he has decided to kill Euryanthe his change of mind is hardly less bizarre. Needless to say nobody, not even her fiancé, bothers to investigate the charge against her, and she in turn doesn't bother to defend herself. Alas, great drama cannot hang on so fine a thread.

The tragedy of *Euryanthe* is that Weber's music is some of his very finest, and the whole design of the drama, from a musical point of view, suggests a masterpiece. Donald Tovey considered it superior to Wagner's *Lohengrin*, which was indeed strongly influenced by it. 'The whole work', Tovey wrote, 'is of such a quality that a single glance at an unknown fragment of it would convince you that here is the style of a great man; and there is no form of dramatic music . . . which is not here handled with freedom and power.'[11] Comedy, it may be objected, is missing. But as grand opera, a genre not famous for its humour, it ticks every box. Weber's aspiration to truthful, all-embracing music drama required a through-composed score, with recitative in place of dialogue, and a flexible arioso linking the set pieces to one another without strong breaks in the musical flow. All this Weber manages superbly. True, there *are* set pieces, but so there are in *Lohengrin*, only not marked as such in the score, and the musical quality of the ariosi is on a par with that of the arias and choruses. These are not time-marking linkages, but a crucial part of the musical discourse, added to which Weber employs what will one day be called leitmotifs, that is, reminiscence motifs that feed into the fabric of the orchestral score, helping to integrate it both as music and as music drama. What *Euryanthe* lacks, as well as narrative sense, is psychological truth. There is hate music but no love music: Euryanthe and Adolar are never together onstage until the scene in which he denounces her. Without exception the characters are absurd, like the cardboard figures in a toy theatre, moving around on the ends of rods, shapeless, fleshless and often irritating to behold. Not surprisingly, despite its brilliant music, it has seldom reached the stage since its first Viennese production in October 1823, which explains why one of the major connections between French revolutionary opera and Wagner has been represented by a gaping hole.

Another plug in that hole might be Spohr's *Jessonda*, which was premiered in Kassel three months before *Euryanthe*, and is likewise a work of much greater quality than its almost total neglect might suggest. *Jessonda* is also a grand opera with recitative and arioso, but closer than the Weber piece to the origins of that genre in the work of Spontini. Set in early-sixteenth-century Goa, it brings exotic spectacle, politics, war and human emotion into conflict. It has human sacrifice, invading Portuguese, Brahmin priests, a procession of bayadères, hair flying, with torches and drums, and a violent thunderstorm which knocks over a huge statue of Brahma. Jessonda herself, threatened with suttee (ritual immolation on the death of her husband, the rajah), is in love with the Portuguese general. Yet curiously, Spohr's music responds to hardly any of this. Just as in *Faust* the diabolical element is missing, so here there is barely a trace of Asian colouring, little distinction between the European and Indian characters or their respective cultures. Even the storm, though picturesque (with flickers of flute lightning), would hardly knock over a candlestick, though it terrifies the chorus. The music itself is on a high level, finely honed, richly scored, if sometimes too locked into the regular metres of Eduard Gehe's libretto. For some reason, much of it is in triple time, with polaccas and waltzes, and a more or less redundant ballet early in the second act.

These two important, flawed operas were to some extent off the main track of German Romantic opera, which, in *Der Freischütz* and Danzi's *Der Berggeist*, among a bevy of lesser works, retained its links with the specifically Germanic tradition of singspiel. But the dialogue aspect of that tradition was starting to fade. Spohr's own version of the

Berggeist story, first performed in Kassel in 1825, is through-composed like *Jessonda*, but entirely forest and fairy magic, as the subject requires. On the other hand two later works by Heinrich Marschner, briefly an associate of Weber's in Dresden, and his stand-in while he was away in London in 1826 supervising his final stage work, *Oberon*, develop further the idea of singspiel as a series of complex scenes made up of set-piece arias, choruses and ensembles interwoven with arioso and recitative, and separated by relatively few stretches of dialogue.

Marschner's *Der Vampyr* (1828) is a strange piece in one sense, in another sense not strange enough. Like *Der Freischütz* it belongs to the world of Gothic horror (what Germans call *Schauerromantik*) of which the most famous example in literature is perhaps Mary Shelley's *Frankenstein*. The vampire of the title is a Scottish earl called Ruthven, who has been told by his vampire-master that he must sacrifice three virgin brides and suck their blood before one o'clock the next morning or else he will himself die. The first two he manages, as he himself boasts, with ease, though on each occasion he is killed by the bride-groom, only to be revived – as vampires, it seems, can be – by direct moonlight (not perhaps a dependable phenomenon in Scotland). The third bride is his own intended, a liaison forced on her by her father; but at the last minute her true, non-vampire lover, who knows Ruthven's secret but had vowed not to reveal it, denounces him. The inevitable thunderstorm blows up and, as the clock strikes one, lightning strikes Ruthven and he tumbles down into Hell.

Marschner, unlike Spohr, is fully equal to the demonic aspects of this bloodthirsty tale; at its best the music is thrillingly sinister, fast-moving, and colourfully orchestrated. The weakness dramatically is that, although we hear a lot about the flesh and blood of the female characters, they never become actual flesh and blood. Like Ruthven, Marschner treats them as disposable, in a faintly pornographic sense, though the opera contains no sex as such. The music for the first two victims tells us nothing much about them except that they are on the menu. No. 3, Malwina, has more, but it rather lacks profile; she is, so to speak, a vulnerable soprano, but she lacks psychology. Ruthven, after all, is not much more than a pantomime devil masquerading as a human being, and Marschner never quite explains, through the music, why anyone would be taken in by him. He fails, in short, to link the two worlds, the supernatural and the everyday. This, however, will be precisely the subject of his finest opera, *Hans Heiling* (1833).

Like *Der Vampyr*, *Hans Heiling* starts in the nether regions, in this case the under-earth realm of the Queen of the Earth Spirits, who is Heiling's mother. In a long, elaborately composed prologue he informs her, against her protests and those of the assembled earth spirits, of his intention to return to the world of mortals to be with his beloved Anna. Alas, when he gets there things do not go well. Anna, an ordinary village girl, really much prefers her former boyfriend, the gamekeeper Konrad, to this mysterious and sometimes ill-tempered otherworldly presence with his disconcerting gifts of jewellery, and in the end Heiling accepts the inevitable and returns to his mother's subterranean arms. A number of episodes in Marschner's score are evidence of growing powers of music-dramatic discourse. The prologue and overture together add up to almost half an hour of highly theatrical music with only the one break between them, and several later scenes deal in a musically effective way with strong dramatic situations: Anna dancing with Konrad at the farmers' dance while Heiling tries vainly to intervene; Anna lost in the forest suddenly confronted by the earth spirits and the Queen herself; Anna's mother Gertrude in her hut brooding on her daughter's failure to return from the forest as a storm gathers outside. Here Marschner uses melodrama skilfully to create an intense atmosphere of fear and anxiety. But his continued use of dialogue between these sections unfailingly deflates the drama, while perhaps suggesting that he lacks the last degree of confidence in his ability to sustain it through musical means alone.

All the same, *Hans Heiling* is an impressive achievement, a nearly complete evolution of Romantic opera out of the fusion of singspiel and turn-of-the-century French opera. If Marschner had been a stronger melodist to go with his developing command of chromatic harmony and the organic use of motifs, and if he had had the courage to pursue his approach to its logical conclusion, he might conceivably have preceded Wagner in the creation of true music drama. Wagner himself thought *Hans Heiling* stylistically obsolete.[12] But obsolescence is always the lurking fate of music not quite of the front rank, and it has been the not always deserved fate of all but one of the many operas by German composers between 1814 and 1843.

Hoffmann
(überaus ähnlich)

ROSSINI, par GILL

(*top left*) Beethoven, by J. W. Mähler (1814–15).
(*top right*) E. T. A. Hoffmann, self-caricature.
(*bottom*) Rossini, caricature by André Gill.

(*top*) Weber, *Der Freischütz*, the
Wolf's Glen scene (Weimar, 1822).
(*above*) Schubert, about 1820.
(*right*) Liszt, by Richard Lanchert,
1856.

(*top*) Chopin, original daguerrotype by Louis-Auguste Bisson, Paris, 1847.
(*bottom*) Berlioz conducting at the Cirque Olympique des Champs-Élysées, 1845

(*top*) Revolution in Berlin, March 1848.
(*above*) Verdi in 1860.
(*right*) Wagner in 1870.

(*top*) The Balakirev Circle, caricature by Konstantin Makovsky, 1871. Left to right: Cui, Balakirev, Stasov, Borodin (to the rear), Rimsky-Korsakov (with the Purgold sisters, one of whom he married the next year), Musorgsky, and their imagined enemy, the composer Alexander Serov, as Jupiter hurling thunderbolts.
(*bottom left*) Mahler in Toblach, 1907. (*bottom right*) Hugo Wolf, *c.*1895.

(*top*) Sibelius at his desk, 1915.
(*bottom*) Debussy after the premiere of Pelléas et Mélisande, 1902.

5

Landscapes of the Heart and the Mind

In 1813 a book came out in London, in French, about Germany, by the exiled daughter of the former director of Louis XVI's finances, Jacques Necker. Madame Germaine de Staël had fallen foul of Napoleon over her openly expressed opposition to his expansionist policies and her – as he considered – anti-French writings, and had been sent into exile in 1803, forbidden to approach within forty leagues of Paris for the next ten years. She had gone first to Germany, and spent six months there, including more than two months at Weimar, where she met Goethe, Schiller and the elderly poet Christoph Martin Wieland, and six weeks in Berlin with August Schlegel. Her book *De l'Allemagne* was the result of these and other encounters. It contained detailed observations about the society in the various cities where she stayed (including Vienna, which she disliked), together with extended critiques of the leading German writers.

Among much else, it developed a crucial theory about the differences between French and German culture in general and literature in particular. German literature, she claimed, was virtually unknown in France. And this was partly due to a radical difference in attitude. In France the essential models were classical, for the English and the Germans they were medieval, chivalric and above all Christian. Classical art (she calls it the 'art of the ancients') was the expression of a fundamentally unitary mental world in which everything knew its place. 'Man, reflecting little, always directed the activity of his soul outwards; consciousness itself was represented by external objects, and the torches of the Furies brought down remorse on the heads of the guilty.' But the modern mentality was something very different and could not readily be represented by classical models.

Writers who imitate the ancients are subjecting themselves to the most severe rules of taste; for, being unable to consult either their own nature or their own memories, they are having to conform to laws according to which the masterpieces of the ancients can be adapted to our taste, even though all the political and religious circumstances which gave birth to these masterpieces have changed.

She finds it significant that, of all European poetry, French poetry is alone in being generally unknown to ordinary people. With pardonable exaggeration she maintains that Tasso is sung by Venetian gondoliers, settings of Goethe are to be heard up and down the Rhine, and every Englishman knows his Shakespeare (perhaps this was the case in 1813). Neo-antique poetry, by contrast, 'no matter how perfect, is rarely popular, because nowadays it has nothing to do with the people'.

The modern mentality is moulded by Christianity, individually self-aware, preoccupied by suffering, atonement and the Cross. 'Honour and love, bravery and pity, are the sentiments that symbolise chivalric Christianity; and these dispositions of the soul can only reveal themselves through dangers, exploits, loves, misfortunes, finally Romantic interest, which continuously varies the picture.' The Romantic, for Germaine de Staël, as for Schlegel, is the whole disordered pattern of the emotional and moral existence of the individual.

Classical poetry has to pass through memories of paganism to arrive with us: the poetry of the Germans is the Christian Era of the fine arts: it avails itself of our personal impressions in order to move us: the genius that inspires it addresses itself directly to our heart, and seems to evoke our very life like the most powerful and terrible phantom of all.[1]

A year after the London publication of *De l'Allemagne*, a seventeen-year-old schoolteacher sat down in a Viennese suburb, and in a single day made a setting of a lengthy poem from Goethe's *Faust* that would revolutionise the art of the German lied. Franz Schubert had been writing songs at least since he was fourteen, and while there is nothing earlier to compare with this Goethe song, 'Gretchen am Spinnrade', the songs that survive are not juvenilia but serious contributions to an existing repertoire. Nevertheless the change was dramatic, and it was to have dramatic consequences.

Before 1800 the history of the lied had been confused and without clear direction. It had evolved as a minor spin-off of whatever was the dominant form of the day. In the sixteenth century it was a simple polyphonic part-song to a secular text; in the baroque period it was a solo song with continuo accompaniment in which only the bass line was given, with the harmonies represented by a system of figures; in the mid-eighteenth century it declined into not much more than an instrumental piece with added text. Of course, throughout this time people sang, and if there was an instrument to accompany them, so much the jollier. But the results were inherently limited. Either the accompaniment was no more than a support, chords and a few twiddles, or the vocal line was a mere peg on which a poet, with or without a subservient composer, hung his verses. Equal partnership between voice and instrument was scarcely to be seen. And since the prevailing verse forms in the eighteenth century were clear, regular, balanced, in short classical, the music tended to mimic those qualities and sit squarely and respectfully on the text like children in a school reading competition.

Why this started slowly to change in the 1780s and 1790s is a question I have already tried to answer in relation to other kinds of music. *Empfindsamkeit* and *Sturm und Drang* placed a strain on the stable forms and idioms of the classical style. Then Mozart came along, and with him everything to do with vocal music began to shift. Compared with his Italian operas and concert arias, his German songs (including the ones in his singspiels) remained mostly simple. The majority are strophic, the same music to each verse, as in the classical lied. In a few cases the strophic form is modified, and in two or three the text is set straight through without formal divisions, most famously in 'Das Veilchen' ('The Violet'), which tells a sad tongue-in-cheek story about a violet that longs to be pinned to a pretty shepherdess's breast but is trodden on by her instead, and still dies happy that it was *her* foot; and in 'Abendempfindung' ('Evening Feeling'), which muses sentimentally on sunset as an image of death.

The majority of Beethoven's early songs are likewise in strophic form. A few are on a larger scale, more in the nature of concert songs, a slow section followed by an Allegro, like a German version of the Italian aria-plus-cabaletta. Of his mature songs the most lied-like are a beautiful strophic setting of 'Kennst du das Land' (1809) from Goethe's *Wilhelm Meisters Lehrjahre*, and a brief but intense Goethe song called 'Wonne der Wehmut' (1810). But work of this quality and sophistication is somewhat scattered in Beethoven's songwriting. It never feels like the thing he most needs to do or does best.

For all Schubert's reverence for Beethoven, his lieder emerge from another tradition altogether. For one thing, he was a singer as well as a competent pianist and violinist. He entered the Stadtkonvikt (Imperial seminary) in Vienna as a choral scholar in 1808 when he was eleven, and sang in the Imperial Court Chapel under Salieri, the court Kapellmeister. Unlike Beethoven's, his background was purely Viennese, and suburban at that. His father was a schoolmaster in the Himmelpfortgrund, a mile or so outside the city Ring, and while his children were well taught, musically and otherwise, their intellectual and social horizons were bourgeois. At the Stadtkonvikt Franz made friends with bookish as well as musical boys; and one can picture his later circle of friends and admirers, poets, playwrights, painters, as well as musicians of varying degrees of expertise, growing from these beginnings. One can also see why, while Beethoven turned naturally to piano chamber music and sonatas, Schubert was drawn early on to the setting of poetry.

His models in this were two prolific song composers from the German lands, Johann Rudolf Zumsteeg and Johann Friedrich Reichardt. The Swabian Zumsteeg composed many short songs in a simple strophic form, but his speciality was the ballad, a narrative form generally in a number of short sections, like a dramatic recitation set to music. Schubert must have known Zumsteeg's ballads because not only did he compose several of his own, but his earliest surviving song, 'Hagars Klage', is a setting of a ballad text that Zumsteeg also set, and Schubert's version has so many passing similarities to his, including mostly the same sectional divisions, as to rule out coincidence. The ballad form seems laborious to us now, but it gave Schubert useful practice in the matching of music to situation and atmosphere; and perhaps it gradually taught him to reject storytelling in favour of the single, concentrated psychological image.

Reichardt, a Prussian from Königsberg, also wrote ballads, as well as shorter songs in a ballad-like, recitative style that respected the text perhaps too earnestly. Goethe, whom he knew in Weimar, wrote that Reichardt was 'the first to make my lyrical works known through music, in a serious and steady manner',[2] a compliment which – bearing in mind that Goethe never really came to terms with Schubert – looks like a bad sign. Nevertheless Schubert certainly knew and respected Reichardt's songs, and he set many of the same poems. The comparison is instructive. Reichardt's settings of lyrical texts are mostly extremely simple, strophic, harmonically limited. For instance, his 1809 version of Goethe's 'Der Musensohn' is entirely strophic; it stops at the end of each verse, then sets off again. Schubert knew this song, and to some extent copied it. He has the same bouncing six-eight metre and even some melodic shapes that have been listening to Reichardt. But Schubert's wanderer never stops; he rides from verse to verse aboard the piano accompaniment, which also twice flips him into different music in a different key.[3] So where Reichardt has five identical verses and four restarts, Schubert's five verses alternate in an A-B-A-B-A sequence and never stop at all. A nice, unpretentious ditty has become a sharp image of the restless, self-centred Romantic genius, filling the world with his radiance, and barely so much as remembering his sweetheart back home. Reichardt also set 'Erlkönig' (1795), Goethe's ballad of the child assailed and killed by the demon Erlking as he and his father ride home through the stormy night. Here too Reichardt's setting is rigidly strophic, eight verses to identical music, with the sole exception that the Erlking always sings on a monotone against the strophe music on the piano. Schubert's 1815 setting, by contrast, is not strophic at all, but charges ahead, like the father and child on their horse, sharing their desperation and catching at every moment the menace of the terrifying phantom the child can see and the father cannot. Another setting of Goethe's poem made at about the same time as Schubert's, by the North German Carl Loewe, follows the ballad incident more closely from verse to verse, in the manner of incidental music, with a result that is more varied but less gripping. Loewe, like Schubert, was a singer as well as a composer, and he made something of a speciality of the long narrative ballad, which in his hands often has a genuine storytelling power that Schubert's ballads, 'Erlkönig' notwithstanding, sometimes lack. But he also wrote many shorter lieder that hardly deserve the almost total neglect they have suffered, including a charming setting of Adelbert von Chamisso's *Frauenliebe* poems (1836) that Schumann may have known when he composed his own, much richer, cycle four years later.

In Schubert's hands the ballad ceases to be a recitation with music, and the lied is no longer a poem, a tune and a dutiful accompaniment. From now on words and music, piano and voice, combine to create an image, man and woman in a landscape of the outer world and the inner consciousness. Gretchen's spinning song in *Faust* is a beautiful poem in the play, but the spinning is not much more than a prop, reflected in the words only by the monotony of the rhyming dimeters and the twice repeated refrain, 'Meine ruh' ist hin' ('My peace is gone'). In Schubert's song, however, the piano is the spinning wheel, and what it spins is Gretchen's emotional torment, echoing her thoughts, following her through the changing keys of her fluctuating moods, and only pausing when, at the memory of Faust's kiss, she takes her foot off the treadle, at which the piano is so put out that it takes four bars to pick up the thread again. The integration of the scene, the girl spinning, and her mental turmoil, is so complete and so exact, the music so arrestingly beautiful, that one has constantly to remind oneself that the song was composed by a boy of seventeen.

In the next fourteen years before his tragically early death at the age of thirty-one, Schubert composed more than six hundred songs, and while opera during these years embodied the Romantic dream, Schubert's lieder did so too, in a more lifelike, human way, and to a degree of perfection hardly ever encountered in the shreds and patches of the opera house. Song, after all, was a domestic medium. In 1810 there was no such thing as a professional song recital; singing took place in the home, either as a group activity, or simply for the pleasure of one or two singers with a keyboard accompanist, probably, by 1810, a pianist.

The piano is the real key to Schubert's professionalisation of the lied. We saw how improvements to the instrument's structure and mechanism were reflected in the music composed for it; and this was no less true in its role as accompanist. With Schubert, suddenly, the piano is a participant. In a sense it creates the song. In 'Gretchen am Spinnrade' it is both the treadle and her troubled feelings; in 'Erlkönig' it is both the desperate ride and the panicky child. Many of his accompaniments depend on the piano's resonance being much stronger than the harpsichord's. The soft rolled chords of 'Meeres Stille' (another Goethe song of 1815) or of 'Lied eines Schiffers an die Dioskuren' (Mayrhofer, 1816) would be lifeless on the harpsichord, and the gradual crescendo in the chords that introduce 'Nähe des Geliebten' (Goethe, 1815) would be impossible. In general, the piano's ability to mimic the expressive refinements of poetry is a major factor in the complex relationship it enjoys with the voice in Schubert's greatest songs.

The world of his songs is the open air. His heroes are walkers, wanderers, riders, stargazers, or simple idlers by the brook or on the seashore. In musical terms he is a landscape painter, in an age of great landscape painters – Constable, Turner, Caspar David Friedrich – and great landscape writers – Wordsworth, Byron, Goethe. Landscape had been a problem for eighteenth-century critics because, lacking the human element, it seemed not to relate to the emotions in any specific way. Schiller had tried to solve this problem by requiring landscape painting and poetry to create an analogy with the abstract workings of the heart and mind, to operate, in effect, like music. Schiller was thinking of instrumental music, and would probably have argued that insofar as word-setting might suggest a landscape of the emotions it was only because the poet had done so already.[4] For instance, in Goethe's 'An den Mond' the poet finds in the veiled moonlight over the woods and fields a release from the sorrow of a lost love, something precious and unique that (like the moon) 'wanders at night through the labyrinth of the heart'. But the poem's imagery is vagrant and unstable; the moonlight brings solace but the stream reminds the poet of his loss, the fun, the kisses, the trust. Any song that tried to follow all these meanders would risk falling apart, but Schubert (having already, in the same year, 1815, composed a simple strophic setting that barely touches the poem's changing moods) at the second attempt produced a song in modified strophic form that embraces its ambiguities in the piano prelude and interludes, but sets the words in an agonisingly calm tone, until thoughts of the stream carrying everything away prompt a moment of agitation, before the deathly calm of the ending.

Schubert made a speciality of such landscapes of the mind, and eventually they became a central element of his style. In 'Des Mädchens Klage' (1815) a girl sits on the seashore at night in a storm, grieving for lost love. The wind howls in the oak-wood, the clouds fly past, the sea heaves, and the girl weeps uselessly, while Nature, in the piano left hand, grinds away remorselessly. Often, though, mankind's feelings are in tune with Nature, and sometimes the waters are benign. In the 'Lied eines Schiffers an die Dioskuren' the sailor hymns the twin stars of Gemini, thanking them for comforting his soul as he plies the ocean waves. In the later 'Auf dem Wasser zu singen' (1823), the boat glides on the water, the boatman's soul glides on the waves of time, and gradually we lose all sense of space and time in the incessant rocking of Schubert's barcarolle semiquavers. His technique, leaving aside the question of meaning, is the conventional one of unifying the song by means of a persistent accompaniment figure appropriate to the general image of the poem. Only, he takes the method to its limits, risks monotony in the interests of intensity, and trusts the quality of his inspiration to justify the risk.

The risk works also in the opposite direction. 'Meeres Stille' must be one of the most uneventful songs ever written, but it conveys a depth of meaning out of all proportion to its surface content. Now the wind has died completely and, like Coleridge's Ancient Mariner, the sailor looks about him in despair at the flat, deathly calm. Goethe's eight lines, their scansion as flat as the sea they portray, hardly invite musical setting, but Schubert accepted the challenge and set the poem with an accompaniment of nearly motionless rolled semibreve chords and the marking 'very slow, troubled [ängstlich]'. His most famous song of this type is another Goethe setting, 'Wanderers Nachtlied' (II, c.1823). Here we are among trees, but again there is scarcely a breath of wind. The birds are silent, and soon, the poet warns, 'you too will be at rest'. The setting is more active than 'Meeres Stille', and to get the right scale Schubert repeats the words schweigen ('are silent') and warte ('wait'), as well as the whole final couplet with its music, thereby intensifying the warning: silence equals death. He also slides through the carefully patterned rhymes, so that Ruh and du, Hauch and auch no longer, in effect, rhyme. The poem is transformed into music, and Goethe would surely have hated it.

One could spend years discussing nuances of this kind across the whole range of Schubert's songs. What was previously a limited, stereotyped genre becomes with Schubert a complete repertoire of expressive and descriptive possibilities within the capacity of a solo voice with piano. He certainly never abandoned the simple strophic song. From 'Heidenröslein' (1815) to 'Jägers Liebeslied' (1827) he stayed loyal to that form that everyone enjoys, the form which ensures that, by the time it's over, even the dullest singer (even Kreisler's Misses Röderlein) will know the tune. Sometimes, of course, there is an irony behind the repetitions. In 'Heidenröslein', the pocket tragedy of the rose picked by the naughty boy is brushed aside by the final refrain, not a minor chord in sight. More often, Schubert will make music of the irony. In one of his very last strophic songs, a setting of Rellstab's 'Frühlingssehnsucht' published posthumously in the *Schwanengesang*, spring sets off the usual longings, but the poet, it seems, has nobody particular in mind. Each verse ends with a question. The breeze blows, but where to? The stream entices, but why? The bright sun brings tears: why? Each time, Schubert stops spring in its tracks with a musical question mark, a momentary darkening of the melody and harmony. Then in the final verse, the longing gets the better of him, and he sets off in B minor instead of major, and the minor key leads the harmony off, briefly, in a new direction. But the question at the end remains: who will cure this trouble? 'Nur du' – only you, the poet insists, but the music assures us that the identity of that 'du' is still unknown.

Schubert's great virtue as a composer of strophic song was, of course, his wonderful melodic gift. One has only to think of songs like 'An Sylvia', 'Frühlingsglaube' or 'An die Musik', to marvel not only at the simple beauty of the tunes, but also at the way they redefine the words. But the piano also makes a melodic contribution. In 'Frühlingsglaube' it has a completely separate tune of its own, by way of prelude, interlude and postlude; in 'An Sylvia' (Shakespeare's 'Who is Sylvia?') the dotted figure in the piano left hand is almost as much a defining feature as the main vocal theme; and the melody of 'An die Musik' is the sighing piano postlude as much as what the voice sings – a melody that never strays, in either part, from the seven diatonic notes of the key of D major. Moreover he could manage this same trick of the piano setting its own seal on the melodic character in those uniquely

Schubertian songs that skim along with a kind of unstoppable impulse from start to finish. In 'Auf der Bruck', for instance, the rider is trotting home after three days separation from his beloved, but if the piano is the horse, the trot is an extended one, to put it mildly, and the singer-rider had better hold on tight.

Such brilliance in accompaniment is unknown in lieder before Schubert. But for him it was a resource that could release a degree of dramatic power well beyond the normal lyrical reach of the lied. His 1820 setting of Friedrich Schlegel's 'Im Walde' has its origins in a masterly but straightforward storm-in-Nature, storm-in-the-heart song such as 'Rastlose Liebe'. But whereas Goethe's lyric is concise and focused, Schlegel's is wild, overwrought, rich in discursive imagery. We are in the forest at night, but every manifestation of nature has its correlative in the philosophical mind. The trees rustle, the spirit soars; dawn breaks and the light on the fields is pregnant with death; the babbling streams conjure flowers from grief. It is a manifesto of the Romantic soul in five stanzas. In Schubert it inspires something akin to a voice-and-piano tone poem, for which as it happens the poem itself is insufficient and much repetition is needed. The images throw up a succession of themes in a succession of keys, and then the whole thing is tied together by a kind of sonata recapitulation prompted by Schlegel's ending with a varied reprise of his own first verse. Above all, Schubert's writing for voice has an almost operatic power and emotional range: short, rhetorical snatches in dialogue with, rather than merely accompanied by, the piano, and with little or no trace of conventional, melodious lyricism.

A song of this type has nothing to do with Zumsteeg, and not much to do with opera as such, a medium that Schubert had already, by 1820, attempted on several occasions without showing much grasp of the stage. Yet in the humble medium of song he could generate a positively operatic voltage. This comes out in two contrasted settings of Goethe from around 1820: on the one hand 'Prometheus', about the Titan who stole the creative fire of the gods, and on the other hand 'Grenzen der

Menschheit', about the limits of humanity and the need for humility towards the gods. 'Prometheus' is a dramatic monologue for bass voice in a series of short sections, recitative and arioso alternating, harmonically free (it starts in B flat and ends in C, and goes through some chromatic contortions on the way), superbly characterised. 'Grenzen der Menschheit', by contrast, is a musical homily, cast in a single, slow tempo and impressively long-breathed, a kind of cross between the Commendatore and Wagner's Erda, and even bolder harmonically than 'Prometheus'. Both these songs look forward to the intense Heine settings in the *Schwanengesang* at the end of Schubert's life. But his growing powers of dramatic narrative are perhaps best shown by an extraordinary ballad-type song of late 1822 or 1823, a setting of a poem by Matthäus von Collin called 'Der Zwerg' ('The Dwarf').

The dwarf of the title is a court jester on a ship with a young queen, accompanying her, perhaps (nothing much is clear about the story) to fulfil her new role as wife of the king of somewhere or other. We are in time to witness the dwarf strangling her with a silken cord. She offers no resistance, but dies, she says, willingly, having it seems loved the dwarf but accepted the king. Both are in tears; but this is no suicide pact, no *Liebestod*. The dwarf kills, weeps, tips the body overboard, then sails away for ever. Fortunately Schubert made no attempt to penetrate the bizarre psychology of this tale, and instead composed a gripping background score, thick with atmosphere, but retaining certain bardic elements, recurrent melodic figures, and touches of antique harmony, like the minor cadence on 'mit ihrem Zwerge', which recurs in various forms, apparently as a marking device, with no obvious narrative meaning. The overall effect is curiously detached, as if the music had a separate history from the poem, as in a way it does, since the most prominent motif is a presumably conscious reference to the main theme of Beethoven's Fifth Symphony, and – more directly – is lifted, together with the right hand's semiquaver figure, from the first movement of Schubert's own B minor Symphony, which he had just composed, but which, for unknown reasons, he was destined to leave unfinished.

One might suggest that 'Der Zwerg' was written in response to a reviving interest in narrative. But the song cycle that Schubert composed soon afterwards is too different in form and character to sustain so facile a parallel. *Die schöne Müllerin* (*The Lovely Mill-Girl*) was composed in the autumn of 1823 a mere two years after the publication in Berlin of Part I of Wilhelm Müller's *Poems from the Posthumous Papers of a Travelling Horn-player*, the cyclic form itself comes from Müller and so do the story and the telling. The simple tale of the young miller wandering in the countryside who follows a brook downstream, comes to a mill, is taken on to work, falls in love with the miller's daughter but is thrown over by her for a passing hunter, and in despair drowns himself in the brook, is told in a sequence of twenty-five short poems, mostly in simple rhyming forms that are like salon versions of *Des Knaben Wunderhorn*. Schubert omitted five of the poems, set the rest in Müller's sequence, and reverted to a musical idiom that fitted the not-quite Biedermeier style of the verse. Nine of the twenty songs are strophic, and even the more free-wheeling numbers belong mostly to genres that he was already cultivating in his teens. For instance 'Eifersucht und Stolz', where the miller tells the brook to go and tick the girl off for her wanton behaviour towards the huntsman, clearly harks back to 'Rastlose Liebe' of 1815. The songs in *Die schöne Müllerin* are lovely, but the cycle is a masterpiece as a whole, rather than containing anything startling in this or that song.

As a concept the work has few precedents. There was nothing new in the idea of a song collection, or *Liederkreis* (literally a song circle), based on the work of either one or a number of poets, but the idea of a story, implied or stated, told exclusively in song was comparatively new. One might regard it as a specifically Romantic notion: the hero as a wanderer or outcast, confiding his thoughts and feelings to the natural world, carving his name on the tree of the world forest, finding then losing his heart's desire, and ending his life in the embrace of nature. The obvious precedent was Beethoven's *An die ferne Geliebte* (*To the Distant Beloved*, 1816), a short cycle of six songs sung by a young man sitting on a hillside and longing to be with his beloved far down in the valley. There is no story as such and no particular outcome; the songs are messages in bottles, carried by the stream or the birds or the breeze, but they are linked, one to the next, by key sequence and musical continuity, and bundled up at the end by a varied reprise of the first song. *Die schöne Müllerin* is musically less coherent; the songs are not connected, there is no obvious key sequence and no thematic links. Its coherence is narrative, sometimes verbal (as in the shared colour green of 'Die liebe Farbe' and 'Die böse Farbe'), and stylistic, and as if to clinch its unity the individual songs are mostly so contrived as to be hard to extract, hard to programme separately. And this is even more the case with the still greater cycle that Schubert based on poems by Müller four years later, in the year before his death.

Schubert first came across Müller's *Winterreise* (*Winter Journey*) poems early in 1827, in a journal that contained only twelve of them. He quickly composed these twelve, then later that spring he read all twenty-four in the second part of the horn-player's papers, and by the late autumn he had completed the cycle. It had been a miserable year for him. He was suffering more and more from the syphilis that would kill him a year later. In March he had been a pall-bearer at Beethoven's funeral, and his lifelong friend Josef von Spaun recalled that

> Schubert had been in a gloomy mood for some time and seemed unwell . . . One day he said to me: 'Come to Schober's today. I shall sing you a cycle of frightening songs. I am curious to see what you will all say to them. They have taken more out of me than was ever the case with other songs.'[5]

It almost looks as if he is telling Spaun that the cycle is autobiographical: not literally, no doubt, but psychologically. But his mood was by no means impenetrable. Between composing the two halves, in June 1827, he wrote 'Das Lied im Grünen', one of his happiest inspirations, and when he had finished the cycle, in November, he at once started the E flat Piano Trio, music of an entirely positive, energetic turn of mind.

Whatever it may tell us about Schubert's own mood, *Winterreise* itself is almost unremittingly tragic. The story packs a heavier punch than *Die schöne Müllerin* because all we know about the situation is what the increasingly desperate hero tells us, whereas in the earlier cycle we witness the beginning and end of the affair and may feel, when the miller drowns himself, that he is making a bit of a mountain out of a molehill. In *Winterreise* something more disturbing has evidently taken place. There has been a love affair, marriage was mentioned, then everything disintegrated, a rich suitor appeared and our hero was shown the door. All this we know by the end of the second song, 'Die Wetterfahne' ('The Weather Vane', alias the unfaithful girl). For the rest of the cycle, he staggers through the winter landscape, the snow and ice an unchanging image of his despair and the frigidity in the girl's heart. He hurries past the lime tree, which seems to be calling him (it has good, strong branches for a rope). Other living creatures are few. The distant posthorn reminds him of the town from which he will not receive any letters; a crow flies round his head, dogs bark in the village. Eventually he comes to a cemetery, which he thinks of as an inn where he might lay his head. But the inn is fully booked. Finally he meets the hurdy-gurdy man, the only other human being in the landscape, another traveller, his plate for ever empty. Denied death and burial, the hero has to settle for insanity.

On the face of it, *Winterreise* looks like a cycle very similar to *Die schöne Müllerin*, but in detail it is different, both more individual and in some ways more inventive. For a start it has only two overtly strophic songs: 'Gute Nacht' and 'Wasserflut', and even 'Gute Nacht' is in modified form, with a varied third verse, a fourth verse in the major (the song is in D minor), but shifting abruptly back to the minor for the piano postlude. Several others have the same music for each verse, but written out in full. This may be because of minor changes of detail. But Schubert probably thought of the songs as continuous expressions, to be felt through from start to finish, not simply hung on the single tune. They are mostly short, and continuity is crucial. For instance, 'Die Wetterfahne' fades on to a weak half-beat, as if calling for the next song. Sometimes there are thematic connections; the triplet figure in 'Wasserflut' is derived from the previous song, 'Der Lindenbaum'. Later on the sequence accelerates, and, though none of the songs particularly invite performance outside the cycle, the last six or seven more or less forbid it, so swiftly do they advance towards the conclusion. The final song, 'Der Leiermann', is strophic apart from a brief coda, but has to be felt as a single, almost expressionless thread.

Winterreise is the culmination of Schubert's lifelong exploration of lied form. Phrase after phrase, section after section, recalls the simple, innocent world of 'Heidenröslein' and 'Der Fischer'; in fact, the tragedy of the cycle works precisely against that background. 'Der Lindenbaum' would be meaningless without it; the hymnic character of 'Das Wirtshaus' ('The Inn', but actually the graveyard) and 'Die Nebensonnen' go back to the 'Dioskuren' and 'An die Musik' but turn them into images of death. 'Frühlingstraum' conjures up a pair of folk tunes and sours them both. Such undercurrents were always latent in the folk poetry of the *Knaben Wunderhorn*, but to make music of them needed a genius who had lived so completely with song that to dramatise it was second nature.

How did he manage it musically? Schubert's melodic gift practically never let him down. But his command of the harmonic language he inherited from Bach, Mozart and Haydn was hardly less complete. *Winterreise* is seldom harmonically complex, is chromatic only here and there and within tight limits. Instead it manipulates tonality, the sense of key, to interrogate the words and situations. No fewer than seventeen of the twenty-four songs are in minor keys, but within the songs there is a constant shift between minor and major, as memory of the past is clouded by the present, or casts an ironic light on it. In 'Gute Nacht' the D major of verse four is sarcastic ('I won't trouble your dreams; that would be such a shame'), but turns on the singer at the end in an abrupt flip back to D minor. In 'Rückblick', as the protagonist stumbles along in G minor, tripping on stones and showered with snow from the roofs, he remembers (in G major) his kindlier arrival in the town, thinks resentfully (in G minor) how he would like to stand in front of her house once again, until the resentment turns back to nostalgia in G major. In 'Auf dem Flusse' he arrives at a stream, once a torrent, now frozen and silent. The E minor drops a semitone to D sharp minor for the silence, marked *leise* (gentle), then uses that semitone to take us back through B major to E major, as he jauntily scratches the girl's name and relevant dates on the ice. This miniature drama of keys then serves, in the second part of the song, to remind our hero that carving names on ice changes nothing. At the far end of all this tonal subtlety, the whole point of 'Der Leiermann' is that it never moves away from A minor. Mind and memory are dead, feeling is numbed. To make a great song such as this out of total inertia is perhaps the surest mark of supreme genius.

If Schubert had died after finishing *Winterreise*, he would certainly be remembered as one of the greatest composers of song, but not perhaps as a profound innovator cut off before his most significant achievements. The final year of his life, November 1827 to November 1828, changed all that. In those twelve months he produced, as well as a number of incomparable songs and the Mass in E flat, a barely credible sequence of instrumental masterpieces: one, or possibly two piano trios, the C major String Quintet, three big piano sonatas, several impromptus for solo piano and the F minor Fantasy for piano duet, all of this while suffering unknown torments from his illness. He had previously, of course, written a great deal of instrumental music, not to mention a vast quantity of choral music and many part-songs, with or without piano. But much of this work pales beside his best songs. Of the eight symphonies performable today, only the B minor ('Unfinished', 1823) and the 'Great' C major (probably 1825) rank with the last works, and of the large body of chamber and solo piano music, only perhaps the last three string quartets, the 'Trout' Quintet and the Octet.

In later years, Schumann referred to the 'heavenly lengths' of the 'Great' C major Symphony, the score of which he acquired from Schubert's brother in Vienna in 1838 and whose premiere Mendelssohn conducted in Leipzig the following year. But this sublime monotony originated in the songs; it might be traced to Schubert's treatment of strophic form. At the end of *Die schöne Müllerin*, the poor miller is rocked by the stream in five long, slow, unchanging verses harmonised like the tolling of funeral bells. Even quick songs like 'Auf der Bruck' and 'Fischerweise' depend for their effect on a kind of repetitiousness that curiously never becomes boring. But Schubert was already writing on similar lines when he was seventeen; 'Gretchen am Spinnrade' is precisely a study in monotony by obsessive repetition. And at the very end of his life, in the Adagio of the String Quintet, Schubert composed music that placed an unprecedented strain on his performers' technical control (not to mention his listeners' concentration), so motionless yet intense is the writing. He may well have been encouraged by the example of Beethoven's late quartets. But Beethoven's discourse is nearly always, even at its slowest, argumentative. Schubert's is serene, contemplative, hypnotic. And this is not an isolated example. The slow movements of the B flat and A major Piano Sonatas, the middle section of the F minor Impromptu, and in its very different way the finale of the C major Symphony, all treat extension as a substitute for development, and – against the odds – it works. The curious thing is that, while Schubert was indulging the heavenly lengths of such pieces, his songs were shrinking, in a few cases, to a concentrated nucleus that threatened to deny their origins in lyric forms altogether.

Admittedly this was largely in response to a single poet, Heinrich Heine. Heine, an exact contemporary of Schubert's, specialised in brief love poems with a sting in the tail, or an emotional contradiction at the core. Schubert was plainly intrigued, and quickly set half a dozen poems from Heine's just-published *Buch der Lieder* (1827), mostly in a completely new, elliptical manner prompted by the terse ironies of the verse. Probably he intended these songs to form part of a cycle. But after his death, when the publisher Tobias Haslinger wanted to bring out a volume of his last, unpublished songs, he put the Heine songs in with a series of very different settings of poems by Ludwig Rellstab, and one, 'Die Taubenpost', by a certain Johann Gabriel Seidl, and titled them, *Schwanengesang*, as if this particular swan, like his dying feathered friends, had never sung before.

The seven Rellstab songs are on a high level, but they hardly break new ground. They include one of his most famous songs, the subtle, languid 'Ständchen', perhaps the classic example of Schubert's fluid switching from minor to major and back. But, with one exception, the Heine settings inhabit a completely new world. Heine's imagery is mostly conventional enough, his cast of characters Schubertian: Atlas, another Prometheus, chained to his fate; the beloved's face ever present to the abandoned lover; the distant town of the unfaithful love; the sea an image of flowing tears. But he has no interest in facile metaphor for its own sake. His images are the images of disappointment, of disillusion expressed with a dismissive wave of the hand. Or they may be images of deception. In 'Das Fischermädchen' the poet tries to seduce the fisher-girl by comparing himself to the sea, which, he points out, she trusts despite its unpredictable nature. This is the one case where Schubert, enticed by the picture of the girl and the sea, misses the sinister point and composes a conventional, charming barcarole in A-B-A form, ignoring the treachery of the last verse. In 'Am Meer', by contrast, the only slightly modified strophic form works because the poisoned tears that he drinks from her hand in verse two already cast their shadow over the start of the song, with its tense, somewhat repressed lyricism and its broken phrases and uneasy harmony as the fog rises, the sea heaves, and the gulls fly back and forth, music to which, in the second verse, his soul dies in his wasting body.

But the great Heine songs are those that, as it were, resist their imagery, that share the poet's bitterness and draw from it new musical resources. The sheer brutality of 'Der Atlas', the violence of its melodic gestures and harmonic shifts, is like a foretaste of Wagner's giants in *Das Rheingold*, while its superb abruptness is a flat denial of any kind of Romantic self-indulgence. The song is electrified by the fear that Atlas might, after all, drop the world and march off in disgust. 'Ihr Bild' ('Her Portrait') is perfunctory in a different way. The poet remembers falling in love with the girl from her picture, in which (typical Heine) she was smiling and weeping tears of sorrow. The poet was weeping too. And now, he can't believe he has lost her. The subtlety of Heine's language, in this brief lyric, is fascinating; he talks throughout about 'her' portrait, 'her' smile, etc., but suddenly in the final line it is 'you' he has lost. This time Schubert picks up all these nuances, in a song so economical and 'thin' he captures exactly the conflict of then and now, her and you.

'Die Stadt', which follows after 'Das Fischermädchen', is possibly the most musically uncompromising song in the whole history of the lied. We are on the water somewhere in a rowing boat, and the town appears in the twilight mist, lit by a last ray of sunlight. But what town *is* this? It is the town (Heine again waits for the final line to inform us) 'where I lost my best beloved'. But for Schubert this is a sinister place from the outset. The whole scene is described in misty, mysterious arpeggios of diminished seventh chords over a 'drum-roll' pedal C; and, astonishingly, Schubert leaves this dissonant harmony hanging, unresolved at the end. This is very dark, but 'Der Doppelgänger', the final Heine song, is darker. The poet stands outside the house where his lover, long departed, once lived; and he sees, already there, a man staring up at the house, wringing his hands in grief. In a shaft of moonlight, he realises the man is his double, a shadow of his own lovesickness, and of the many nights he stood mournfully outside this very house. This is Jean Paul's fantasy idea of 'the people who see themselves' translated into a nightmare image of revisitation. Schubert sets the poem as a slow passacaglia in B minor over a series of eight chords repeated three times, then varied, then part-repeated as a coda, a series of musical doppelgangers. The piano plays almost nothing but chords, low down (always in the bass clef), with much doubling of the hands; and the vocal line is not much more than an embroidered version of the note F sharp. The impact of these two pieces is as if the greatest composer of lieder had decided to abandon everything he had ever put into a song and compose only the experience that had accumulated in the process.

Schubert's death in November 1828 deprived him and us of possible successors to these extraordinary last works: the enigmatic, laconic songs on the one hand, the expansive instrumental works on the other. In barely fifteen years, he had transformed the whole concept of the solo song, and with it many aspects of musical language, from a simple essence at the bottom end of the creative and intellectual scale to a rich and complex form capable of expressing an almost unlimited range of feeling and imagery. More even than Beethoven, he had extended the harmonic vocabulary of tonal music, mainly from inside the supposed rule-book. This included restricting it, slowing it down, at times almost to a standstill, both on a large scale, and in quite short songs. At the same time he hugely expanded the role of the piano, turning it into an equal partner, no longer a mere accompanist. A lot has been written about the shadow cast by Beethoven over nineteenth-century music, the sense of inadequacy he induced in his successors, the misguided need to emulate. Schubert, by contrast, created only possibilities, all or most of which were taken up by composers who might not always have admitted their debt. The tragedy is that Schubert did not survive to take them up himself.

6

Geniuses, Young and not so Young

When Beethoven and Schubert died, less than two years apart, Vienna
ceased to be the centre of the musical universe. It became, instead, its
playground.

It's true that its musical infrastructure remained intact, even
expanded, in the years following the Congress that marked the end
of the Napoleonic Wars in 1815. The old, largely defunct aristocratic
patronage had been replaced by a vigorous civic culture of music publishing and marketing, instrument (especially piano) manufacture,
musical journalism and domestic music-making typified by the so-
called Schubertiads – drawing-room gatherings which, in the last decade or so of his life, were the main outlet for performance of Schubert's
songs and piano music. The Gesellschaft der Musikfreunde (the city's
music society) had started up in 1814, established the Conservatoire in
1817, and in 1831 opened Vienna's first ever public concert hall, at last
filling an astonishing gap in the resources of a city that had somehow
provided a platform for Mozart's late piano concertos and Beethoven's
nine symphonies and seven concertos, and a great deal else besides.

Yet behind all this activity, behind all the marketing and study
and amateur enthusiasm, behind the grand façade of what was now
the capital of a new (since 1806) pan-European empire, there was a
curious void. Hardly any music of lasting substance was composed or
premiered in Vienna for thirty-four years after Schubert's death, until
Brahms played in the first performance of his A major Piano Quartet
there in November 1862. After the Congress, Austria had effectively
become a police state under its powerful chancellor Metternich and
his sinister chief of police, Graf Sedlnitzky, with a harsh censorship

regime that certainly was not encouraging to new works of art, and the situation was aggravated by the assassination in 1819 of the conservative playwright August von Kotzebue, at his home in Mannheim, by a student member of the nationalist *Burschenschaft*, which led to the Carlsbad Decrees against free universities and a free press, and a further tightening of censorship on the arts and ideas.

The theatre naturally suffered worst. In Vienna Metternich's thought police kept a close eye on the written word, whether in print or on the stage, and the natural outcome of their attentions was a retreat into frivolity, vacuousness or the revival of existing work that posed no threat. You could go to the theatre or the opera, but it would always be Rossini or Paisiello or the latest singspiel or pantomime by Wenzel Müller or Joseph Weigl. Standards of performance followed the quality of the product down the hill. Only in one kind of music did the quest for oblivion yield something new that could both elevate the spirits and stand the test of time.

The Congress of Vienna, the prince de Ligne had famously remarked, 'ne marche pas, il danse'.[1] And soon Vienna itself was discovering its soul on the dance floor. The waltz craze that emerged in the twenties had its origins in the music of the tavern bands that had been touring the city since before the Congress, and its two most famous early exponents, Joseph Lanner and Johann Strauss, were both self-taught violinists who played in such bands and then broke away to form their own. In 1816 Lanner started a trio that by 1823 had expanded into a small orchestra with Strauss as a viola player, then in 1827 Strauss started his own orchestra, and within two years had established it as the resident band at the Zum Sperlbauer dance hall in the Viennese suburb of Leopoldstadt. Strauss's son Johann, together with his younger brothers, Josef and Eduard, would in due course fix the Viennese waltz and polka in the imperishable form of pieces like the 'Blue Danube' Waltz (1886) and the 'Thunder-and-Lightning' Polka (1868), not to mention *Die Fledermaus* (*The Bat*, 1874), the younger Johann's most successful operetta, which elevates these dances into irresistible vocal-dramatic forms. But it was their father who more or less invented the international image of the dancing Viennese, composed the music for them to dance to, and made it famous and lucrative by touring Europe with his orchestra, playing for balls and banquets, and giving concerts that included symphonic pieces as well as dance music. The nineteen-year-old Richard Wagner heard Strauss play and conduct in Vienna in 1832 and was transfixed.

> This demon of the Viennese musical folk spirit trembled at the start
> of each new waltz like a Pythia on the tripod, and veritable whinnies
> of delight from the auditorium, befuddled to tell the truth more
> by his music than by the drink, whipped up the enthusiasm of this
> violin-magician to a, for me, almost alarming height.[2]

Wagner would come to detest Vienna in later years. But in the twenties and early thirties the sheen had not completely rubbed off. For young musicians from eastern Europe, Vienna was the natural landfall. For Czech musicians like Hummel it had been a mere step from Pressburg or Prague. But for one family from the Burgenland it was even nearer, and since it housed some of the most brilliant piano teachers anywhere, it was the obvious first stop for Adam Liszt, a clerk at the Esterházy estates near Eisenstadt, his wife, Anna, and their ten-year-old pianist son Franz, who had already, more than a year earlier, given concerts in Oedenburg (Sopron) and Pressburg to huge acclaim, and was now receiving an annual stipend from a group of Hungarian aristocrats towards his future studies.

Young Franz was taken on as a pupil by Carl Czerny, himself a piano pupil of Beethoven, and the author already of a whole repertoire of keyboard exercises and studies which, to this day, form the bedrock of any serious teaching of piano technique. He later gave a vivid account of his first meeting with the young prodigy. Adam had initially brought Franz to see him when the boy was eight.

He was a pale, delicate-looking child and while playing swayed on the chair as if drunk, so that I often thought he would fall to the floor. Moreover, his playing was also completely irregular, careless, and confused, and he had so little knowledge of correct fingering that he threw his fingers over the keyboard in an altogether arbitrary fashion. Nevertheless, I was amazed by the talent with which Nature had equipped him.[3]

In just over a year, Czerny succeeded in channelling the wildness into a comprehensive, 'infallible' technique, without it seems suppressing the boy's musical sensibility (and, incidentally, without charging Adam a single thaler). At the end of that time, Adam announced his intention of taking his son to Paris. Czerny was not pleased; he disapproved of what he saw as a Mozartian attempt to cash in on the child's precocity, just when he needed more time to cement his piano technique and work harder on his composing. Nevertheless off they set in September 1823, and after three months' travel and a spectacular series of concerts in Munich, Augsburg, Stuttgart and Strasbourg, they arrived in the French capital on 11 December. On the morning of the 12th they appeared at the Conservatoire and were ushered into the presence of the Italian director, Luigi Cherubini. Might this young boy, a favourite pupil of the great Carl Czerny and already an acclaimed performer across half of central Europe, be admitted to this august institution?

Alas, Cherubini regretted, it was not permitted to enrol a foreigner on the Conservatoire's piano course. 'There are so many foreign pianists. Your son is doubtless gifted; but there are so many . . .'

There are fathers who will undermine their own lives in order to promote their children's musical careers, and there are fathers who will undermine their children's lives rather than allow anything of the sort.

While Adam Liszt was abandoning job, income and home for the sake of his brilliant son, a local doctor in the Dauphiné, one Louis Berlioz, was doing his best to bully his son out of his insistence on pursuing a career in music instead of medicine. Hector Berlioz was seventeen when he arrived in Paris at the start of November 1821 and enrolled at the École de Médecine. To say he was a reluctant medical student would be a grotesque understatement. He loathed the whole prospect. But on the face of it his musical prospects were hardly more encouraging. Far from being a child prodigy, he couldn't play the piano at all and was no more than moderately competent on the guitar and flute. He had composed, but nothing survives beyond two melodies he later re-used, in the overture to *Les Francs-Juges* and the introduction to the *Symphonie fantastique*. In Paris he continued to write, while dutifully pursuing his medical studies, until two crucial things happened that changed his life: first, late in 1822, the École de Médecine closed its doors as a result of political disturbances involving medical students; then, at about the same time, Berlioz managed with the help of a music student friend to gain entrée into the Conservatoire composition class of Le Sueur, who – perhaps surprisingly – looked at the music Berlioz brought with him, declared him raw, untutored but clearly talented, and admitted him as a non-enrolled member of his class.

The contrast with Liszt, a few months later, was stark. Here was this jumped-up nineteen-year-old with big ambitions but little or no technique, and not even the beginnings of competence on a keyboard instrument, usually regarded as a *sine qua non* for a serious composer, being accepted as an admittedly unofficial student in the world's greatest advanced music school, while eleven-year-old Franz, patently a genius on the piano and already a halfway competent composer, was about to be refused admittance. Yet Le Sueur's intuition was not without foundation. The cantata Berlioz showed him that first time has not survived, but one or two large-scale works he composed just afterwards have, in whole or part, and they show that, however rough his technique, his musical personality was already strong enough to shine through. In particular a *Messe solennelle*, composed in 1824, would be instantly recognisable as a work by Berlioz, if only because it contains several ideas that he plundered for later works. Something similar happened to his opera *Les Francs-Juges* (1826), though at least the Mass was performed, the opera not.

His problem was that his invention ran far ahead of his technical skill. Le Sueur himself looked at the Mass and is supposed to have remarked: 'That young man has the devil of an imagination. His Mass is astonishing; there are so many ideas in it that with his score I could write ten of my own.'[4] This remained Berlioz's problem, even after entering the Conservatoire as an official student in 1826. In 1828, after reading Gérard de Nerval's newly published translation of Goethe's *Faust*, he promptly set eight unrelated sections of it to music – music of such richness and individuality that when he came to write *La Damnation de Faust* seventeen years later he was able to incorporate nearly all of it, some of it not much altered, in what is beyond question one of his greatest works. And after trying three times unsuccessfully for the Prix de Rome, the grand climax of the Conservatoire composer's student career, he at last accepted that his only way of winning was to moderate his idiosyncrasies and write a conventional cantata (*La Mort de Sardanapale*, 1830) that would not disturb the examiners' intellectual slumbers. Yet even here there was enough of his own self to be of use in later works, including a pair of fragmentary themes that reappear in *Roméo et Juliette*; and there may have been more; most of the score is lost.

How was it possible for so musically untaught a young man to pour forth ideas on such a scale and with such creative energy, when anyone who has ever had anything to do with teaching young composers knows that their usual problem is continuity, extending their ideas beyond the first few thrilling bars? Admittedly, Berlioz was spending a lot of time with big things. In 1827 he was reading Walter Scott and turning *Waverley* into a concert overture, and it was in September of that year that he saw Shakespeare on the stage for the first time and was overwhelmed by Charles Kemble's Hamlet and Romeo, and especially by the Irish actress Harriet Smithson's Ophelia and Juliet, performances that left him desperately in love with her. *Faust* came soon afterwards. But long before that he had been obsessed with classical literature, in particular Virgil's *Aeneid*, which he read as a child with his father, in Latin. As for music, Paris was the best city in the world for an ignorant twenty-something to fill the gaps left by a provincial childhood. Parisian concert life was sketchy, but the Opéra was another matter. From the start, Berlioz was an opera regular. He heard Salieri and Méhul, Cherubini, Spontini, Le Sueur, and, above all, Gluck. He had read as a teenager about Gluck's genius but knew hardly a note of his music until hearing *Iphigénie en Tauride* at the Opéra soon after his arrival in the capital and being so moved, he tells us in his memoirs, that he at once firmly made up his mind to become a composer himself.

Finally there was Beethoven. Berlioz was not up on the Viennese classics or on German music in general. He had been excited by a heavily adapted version of *Der Freischütz* at the Odéon at the end of 1824. Mozart he was for a long time inclined to despise because, he admits, Mozart meant *The Marriage of Figaro* and *Don Giovanni*, Italian operas that drew the anathema automatically directed by the young Conservatoire bloods at Rossini, Paisiello and co. And of Beethoven he knew hardly anything until, in March 1828, François-Antoine Habeneck, the chief conductor at the Opéra, conducted what was probably the first fully professional performance of the *Eroica* Symphony in Paris, and followed it a few weeks later with the Fifth Symphony, a work not previously heard at all in France. For Berlioz it was another of those lightning strikes to which he was so susceptible. 'The shock was almost as great as that of Shakespeare had been. Beethoven opened before me a new world of music, as Shakespeare had revealed a new universe of poetry.'[5]

Putting all these enthusiasms together, we can form a picture of Berlioz's mentality that coincides with the character of his early music.

He was excited by grandeur and grand passion, by pulsating colours and heart-on-sleeve emotion, by the sheer linguistic sweep of Shakespeare (though he knew hardly any English), of de Nerval's Goethe, of the *Aeneid* and the *Iliad,* and by public ceremony of all kinds, but also by dramatisations of the inner life, by the poetry of the soul. Above all he believed in the authenticity and authority of the great artist, whether in quest of the beautiful or the sublime (in Burke's sense), the grotesque, even the ugly. 'Away with the unities,' Victor Hugo wrote in the book-length preface to his play *Cromwell* (1827). 'Art supplies wings, not crutches. Let us take the hammer to theories and poetic systems . . . The beautiful has but one type, the ugly has a thousand.'[6] And when his *Hernani* created a riot at its first performance in February 1830, the immediate cause was not the political tensions that would erupt in the July Days later that year, but a battle of ideas between the defenders of the classical tradition of French drama and the supporters of the new Romantic theatre, with its deliberate abandonment of the rigid conventions of Racine and Corneille, the unities of action, time and place, the purity of diction and lofty avoidance of the specifics of daily life. Berlioz was in the audience for *Hernani* along with a noisy group of Hugo's supporters. Then the following December he conducted the first performance of his own *Symphonie fantastique* in the Conservatoire's concert hall, a work that in its way was no less of a challenge to the classical proprieties than Hugo's play, though the manifesto that accompanied it had nothing to do with such matters but instead was a kind of novelette about the composer's love life under the subtitle 'Episode in the life of an artist'.

French composers of Berlioz's day did not make a habit of writing symphonies, and though his own was at least partly inspired by the encounter with Beethoven, that hardly shows in the form, style or detail of the result. The symphony's hero is a kind of René figure, wandering helplessly through the alpine terrain of life (the original programme, later modified, specifically referred to Chateaubriand). In Berlioz's case, the trouble is Harriet Smithson, for whom his love has begun to turn rancid. He broods on his 'malaise of the soul' before he met her and his volcanic passion when he did; he glimpses her at a ball, then one evening in the countryside; he takes opium and dreams he has killed her, is condemned to death and guillotined; finally he is at a witches' sabbath, and she is there too, grotesquely altered, 'participating in the diabolical orgy'. The five movements are linked by a single theme, the *idée fixe*, which stands for his fixation and pops up unbidden at various points, sometimes worked symphonically – Berlioz lifted it from one of his Prix de Rome failures, a cantata called *Herminie*. Other rebrandings include the fourth movement, 'March to the scaffold', which had begun life in *Les Francs-Juges*, and the main theme of the 'Scène aux champs' ('Scene in the Fields'), from the *Messe solennelle*. But for all these borrowed and hallucinatory elements, the work itself is tightly constructed, a masterpiece *sui generis*. The influence of French opera is clear, not least in the orchestra, which includes instruments not usually found in Viennese symphonies: harps (four of them), timpanists (also four), cors anglais, cornets, and two ophicleides, the poor, doomed keyed bass bugle soon to be displaced by the tuba. The pictorial vividness also suggests the theatre: the beloved suddenly appearing on the dance floor, the distant thunder in the fields, the guillotined head dropping into the *tricoteuse*'s basket. At the climax of the finale, the witches perform a round dance to a strict fugue.

It would be tempting to see the *Symphonie fantastique* and for that matter *Hernani* as symptoms of the three July Days that finally unseated the Bourbon kings, even though neither work was political in motivation. Hugo may have been a revolutionary in artistic matters, but politically he was, at this time, royalist. Berlioz was more sympathetic to the rioters, but was locked in for the first two days completing his Prix de Rome score, and only able to join in on the third day, roaming the streets with a pair of unloaded pistols and later providing an unrivalled description of the 'blessed rabble . . . the frantic bravery of the guttersnipes, the enthusiasm of the men, the wild excitement of the whores, the grim resignation of the Swiss and Royal Guards, the strange pride of the working class in being, as they said, masters of Paris and taking nothing.'[7] It was perhaps as a result of this experience that he began to take an interest in the utopian social theories of the Comte de Saint-Simon, who had died in 1825 but whose idea of a scientifically and industrially based programme of social reform was in the air in the late summer of 1830, when Berlioz first contacted Saint-Simon's collaborator Father Barthélemy Enfantin, and perhaps attended group meetings.[8] But he was probably too sceptical and wayward temperamentally to involve himself for very long in such single-minded group-think.

Liszt also dabbled. Since his father's death in 1827 he had become disillusioned with the interminable concert tours, the empty praise of the Paris salons, and the futility of teaching their owners' pretty but untalented daughters. Liszt, unlike Berlioz, had retained a strong religious streak from his Catholic upbringing, was a keen reader of devotional literature, and for a time dreamt of taking holy orders. He, too, was drawn for a while to Saint-Simon's social theories, attended meetings, and even played the piano for the assembled Saint-Simonians, until in 1832 what had become not much more than a cult was closed down by the police, and Liszt judiciously lost interest.

Liszt had first met Berlioz at the performance of the *Symphonie fantastique* in December 1830. Just over a year later, on 26 February 1832, he was at another concert by a fellow composer whose music would transform the image of the piano at least as much as his. Fryderyk Chopin was a twenty-one-year-old Pole from Warsaw who had arrived in Paris the previous September partly by accident, after being detained in Vienna in November 1830 by news of the uprising in Warsaw against the occupying Russians. Chopin had felt unable to return home and had instead drifted to Paris, where he at once formed part of a large Polish diaspora of artists, writers and political exiles.

Though only a year and a half older than Liszt, Chopin was already a more mature composer and also to some extent a more individual pianist. In Warsaw he had written music in the 'brilliant', bravura manner of Hummel, but he also brought with him to Paris a number of pieces that explored a more intimate, less ostentatiously gymnastic style. Good examples are the two piano concertos, in F minor and E minor, which contain a lot of bravura writing, but lack the towering virtuosity favoured by the school of travelling keyboard trapeze-artists of whom Liszt was in danger of becoming the best known. Also in Chopin's baggage were several études that would eventually appear as his op. 10 in 1833, together with two sets of mazurkas, opp. 6 and 7, and some of the nocturnes that would form opp. 9 and 15. This is a defining body of work. The études are technical studies in the conventional sense that each piece develops mastery of a particular technical or musical problem; but they are also genre pieces calling for the ability to make musical sense of the purely mechanical challenges. For instance, the steepling arpeggios of the first, C major, study are underpinned by a slow bass line that is actually the main theme of the piece. The famous third study, in E major, is a deceptively difficult nocturne requiring a sustained legato and steady hand positions for the sequences of variously shaped parallel chords that alternate with the tune. The sixth study, in E flat minor, demands the ability to play a disguised four-part texture with an even legato throughout.

Most of the nocturnes are technically straightforward, apart from the sometimes tricky embroidery Chopin applies to his melodies on second and third playing. The initial inspiration for this kind of piece was, as we saw, Field, though Chopin's melodic extensions and harmony are already beyond Field's scope. In op. 15, however, he introduces an additional element not found in his predecessor's nocturnes: the contrasting middle section. These B sections tend to be un-nocturne-like. The stormy F minor interlude in the F major Nocturne, and the *doppio movimento* (double speed) in the F sharp major, question the lyrical tone only briefly, but the effect on the form is electrifying. It's as if Chopin were already thinking in terms of a bigger architecture erected on lyrical foundations. This involved some experimentation. In the G minor Nocturne, op. 15, no. 3, what feels like a middle section, *religioso*, in fact displaces the G minor music, which never comes back. On the other hand the Scherzo in B minor, op. 20, probably drafted in Vienna at the start of 1831, has a nocturne-like middle section, based on a Polish Christmas carol, which tempers the ferocity of the scherzo music (provoked, Alan Walker believes, by anti-Polish remarks overheard in a Viennese restaurant⁹). The first climax of this tendency is the Ballade in G minor, op. 23, also probably sketched in Vienna but not fully composed until 1835. Here the lyrical nocturne is transformed into something on the scale of a Beethoven sonata movement, but in a highly original form that uses the sonata idea of themes in contrasting keys to trigger a ten-minute movement in which the real contrast is between the lyrical themes themselves and the bravura episodes that explode out of them, the whole process controlled by a rigorously thought-through harmonic scheme.

All this music is the work of a seriously well-taught, intellectually engaged artist. The old idea of Chopin as the creator of delicate musical flowers suitable for nice young ladies to play more or less badly in suburban drawing rooms, or to be fenced off in special Chopin recitals by pianists who seldom played anything else, can hardly survive careful listening even to these relatively early pieces. Chopin had played and studied Bach's 48 Preludes and Fugues in Warsaw, and though his music is seldom contrapuntal in that sense, it everywhere shows an expertise in voice-leading, the relating of the individual lines to the whole texture. At times it also shows at least an awareness of Beethoven, a composer for whom Chopin is supposed to have had no more than grudging respect. Beethoven stands audibly behind the so-called 'Revolutionary' Study in C minor, op. 10, no. 12, whose main theme is partly lifted from Beethoven's C minor *Pathétique* Sonata, op. 13, and which also quotes from the first movement of his last C minor Sonata, op. 111, at the exactly parallel moment, the final eight bars.

One influence Chopin would not have denied comes out in the other group of pieces he brought with him, the two sets of mazurkas, opp. 6

and 7. The mazurka was a Polish dance from Mazovia, the region of Poland that includes Warsaw, as well as Chopin's birthplace thirty-odd miles to the west, and Chopin, though he was brought up in urban Warsaw itself, plainly knew about it before arriving in Paris, where it was already a fashionable dance. In any case, he used the mazurka as an excuse for a variety of irregular harmonic and instrumental devices derived from the folk music that would presumably have accompanied the dance on its home ground. Drone basses, originally played on the bagpipe (*duda*), figure in several of the early mazurkas, most notably in the central episode of the well-known op. 7, no. 1 in B flat, where the drone, on a dissonant G flat–D flat chord, seems to be making fun of the average out-of-tune rustic bagpipe. Features of nearly all Chopin's fifty-odd mazurkas are the curiously inflected melodies and harmonies that are like memories of the modal scales of east European folk music. Our familiarity with the very first, F sharp minor, mazurka of op. 6, or the A minor, op. 7, no. 2, may deafen us to the strangeness of the extremely fluid chromatics in these pieces. And behind this shift in style there seems to lie a kind of virtual Polishness, an idiom never heard in rural Poland or anywhere else, but one created in the mind of a musical genius dreaming of his unhappy, abandoned native land. Perhaps not surprisingly, therefore, some of the most striking examples of the mazurka style are pieces composed soon after his arrival in Paris, such as the A minor, op. 17, no. 4 (1832 or 1833), with its curiously evasive opening (repeated, even more curiously, at the end), and its studious avoidance of the home key until bar 20; or the B flat minor, op. 24, no. 4, with its descending sequences of oscillating chromatic sixths and sevenths, and its brief vision halfway of unclouded folk melody, like a sudden news flash from Poland.

By comparison, Chopin's waltzes, more showy pianistically, are harmonically and rhythmically more conventional, either with an accented downbeat (unlike the mazurka's accent on the second or third beat), or with cross rhythms created by deviant groupings, as in the F major, op. 34, no. 3, whose four-quaver groups cut across the six-quaver metre.

The mature polonaises, on the other hand, starting with the two of op. 26 (C sharp minor and E flat minor, 1834–5), are harmonically colourful and rhythmically powerful but lack the experimental flavour of the mazurkas. Their Poland is the Poland of the court and the army, a world of stately processions and military parades, with the peasants and their fiddles and dudas nowhere to be seen. At their finest, in the F sharp minor, op. 44, and the A flat, op. 53, there is a thunderous ferocity not found elsewhere in Chopin, including octave passages that demand muscular coordination on a positively Olympian scale.

Chopin was no political activist. All his life he remained a very private person; he detested rhetoric or ostentation of any kind, disliked and rarely gave public concerts, and always preferred to display his musical wares in the private households and salons of the Parisian upper classes. It was typical of him that he should confine his expressions of patriotism and homesickness to a discreet, superficially innocuous dance form like the mazurka. Yet he stayed in touch with the more active wing of the Polish diaspora and with his family in Poland, though he never went back there.

Poland, for neither the first nor the last time, was something of a special case in the early rise of nationalism. The self-determinism argued for by Herder often emerged in more scholarly forms, in collections of folk tales and poetry, in the myth-making of James Macpherson and Elias Lönnrot, the author/compiler of the Finnish *Kalevala*, in histories like Nikolay Karamzin's twelve-volume *History of the Russian State* and the historical novels of Walter Scott, or the work of lexicographers like the Czechs Josef Dobrovský and Josef Jungmann or the German Jacob Grimm. In their different ways, these were all by-products of romanticism. They were part of the deification of the particular or the individual; they sought out the antique or the mythic, and when these things failed to provide the necessary assurances, the authors provided them instead. In a sense nationalism at this stage was simply a branch of Romantic fantasy, which could share its obsession with place and time, with the wild and the remote and the grotesque. The only difference was the sense of (legitimate) belonging; and this could easily be supplied, like a false passport.

Berlioz, emerging in 1831 from the trauma that had inspired the *Symphonie fantastique* and another trauma, that of being jilted by his fiancée, a pianist called Camille Moke, cobbled together a so-called 'Return to Life' (later rechristened *Lélio*) consisting of longish stretches of self-regarding monologue interspersed with musical fragments rescued from his student years. He then turned once again to Scott and composed an overture to *Rob Roy*, complete with 'Scots, wha hae' as a main theme and plenty of Scotch snaps, before withdrawing this piece and transferring two of its other themes to his next work, a four-movement symphony with concertante viola, entitled *Harold en Italie* after Byron's long poetic travelogue, *Childe Harold's Pilgrimage*. Commissioned by the great Italian violinist, Niccolò Paganini, *Harold en Italie* may nevertheless also have begun life as a Scottish piece about 'The Last Days of Mary Stuart' before acquiring the Byronic tag and migrating south of the Alps. But it never had much to do with Byron, whose oddly named Childe Harold never wanders in the Abruzzi, never witnesses pilgrims singing their evening prayer, and certainly never attends an orgy of brigands, whatever that might be. Byron was himself hardly the melancholy viola hero of Berlioz's symphony. Childe Harold, it's true, is in flight from an empty world and a wasted youth, like René and Obermann; but his travels prompt not gloomy introspection but a learned diatribe on ancient and modern history and its topography in five hundred dazzling, galloping stanzas. Berlioz's Harold is more of an Obermann, witness to scenes of sorrow, piety, love and revelry but unable to participate in any of them, as the viola wraps its theme round each in turn, then in the finale reminisces about them one by one before falling silent in the face of the world's unseemly exuberance.

Paganini took one look at Berlioz's first movement, with its modest bravura and many bars rest for the soloist, and lost interest. He never played the work, but when he eventually heard it in 1838, four years after the premiere, he evidently had a fit of remorse and promptly sent the indigent composer a cheque for twenty thousand francs. Berlioz, for his part, was destined never to hear Paganini play; but Liszt heard him, in Paris in April 1832, and the experience changed his life yet again.

Paganini was already forty-eight years old when he first appeared in Paris in March 1831, playing his First Violin Concerto and some variation sets on the stage of the Opéra; but his reputation had long preceded him, together with various lurid tales purporting to explain what he had been up to in the missing years. One particularly juicy theory had him serving a long prison sentence in Italy for murdering his mistress and manufacturing a violin E-string from her intestine. In prison, with only a violin for company, he had forced from it its most diabolical secrets, and now appeared as the Devil incarnate, thin and cadaverous, lank black hair to his shoulders, black coat and waistcoat, 'probably such as are prescribed by infernal etiquette at the court of Proserpine'.[10]

Liszt was not at the 1831 concert, and only heard Paganini for the first time a year later, in April 1832. Perhaps he was influenced by the violinist's appearance, but it was his playing that overwhelmed him. 'For the past fortnight my mind and fingers have been working away like two lost spirits,' he wrote to a pupil. 'Ah! provided I don't go mad you will find an artist in me! . . . What a man, what a violin, what an artist! Heavens, what suffering, what misery, what torments in those four strings.'[11] Having lost his sense of direction as a common or garden virtuoso, he heard in Paganini's playing previously undreamt-of possibilities of the relationship between instrumental mastery and musical depth. Nevertheless the first fruits of this study were chiefly attempts at finding a keyboard equivalent of Paganini's technical wizardry. The fantasy on *La Clochette* (*La campanella*), the finale theme of Paganini's B minor Violin Concerto, is the formidable start of a series that would culminate five or six years later in the twelve *Grandes études* and the six Paganini studies, themselves staging posts on the way to the *Études d'exécution transcendante* and the *Grandes études de Paganini*, published in 1851. Even amid the atrocious technical difficulties of these studies, Liszt never completely lost sight of the ideal of musical beauty. But the most striking thing about them, beyond the high-wire aspect, is the sense of exploring the potential of the instrument itself, which had continued to grow in power and responsiveness since Sébastien Érard's introduction of the iron frame and the double escapement action in the 1820s. Liszt was a strong, physical pianist who wrote for and played on instruments that could withstand the considerable weight of young arms on necessarily thin wire strings, as compared to Chopin, who played mostly in drawing rooms on less virile pianos. Their music tends to reflect this difference. Liszt did, in fact, often break strings. Chopin, it was said, was often barely audible at the far end of the room.

All the same, a poetic streak also begins increasingly to colour Liszt's music after his encounter with Paganini. It starts with his own reading. Romanticism, after all, first emerged in literature, and as it gradually transferred to music in the 1820s and 1830s it did so especially in the work of composers who read books. In Liszt's case it seems to have been dissatisfaction with the empty life of the adolescent virtuoso that triggered other parts of the mind. By the time he was eighteen he was reading Hugo and Lamartine, Voltaire, Rousseau, Chateaubriand, anything, it seems, that he could lay his hands on. There was no pattern. On one occasion he rushed up to a lawyer friend and cried, 'Tell me everything about French literature!'[12] Social questions and religion fed the confusion. Saint-Simon was succeeded by Lamennais, whose *Paroles d'un croyant* Liszt read as soon as it came out early in 1834. Lamennais's idiosyncratic mixture of political libertarianism and Christian piety appealed to the young musician's unformed mentality, and he promptly wrote to Lamennais, who invited him to stay at his estate in Brittany.

At La Chênaie Liszt imbibed Lamennais's views on the sanctity of the artist's role in society, and he composed: a three-movement suite called *Apparitions*, inspired by a poem of Lamartine about a moonlight visit to his lover's grave, and a single piece called 'Harmonies poétiques et religieuses', the title of a recent collection of Lamartine's verse. Liszt seems, in this music, to be feeling his way towards a new and individual style, only partly glimpsed. He sits at the piano and allows his feelings to lead him where they will, through strange, incomplete harmonies, uncertain rhythms and metres, punctuated by apparently random bravura flourishes, as if his pianism were impatient of his reflective hesitations. The *Apparitions*, especially the first two, stand alone as beautiful and individual if curiously improvisatory pieces; the 'Harmonies', however, will be revealed some years later as a mere outline for the more elaborate 'Pensée des morts' in a cycle with the same collective title, *Harmonies poétiques et religieuses*. This process of reacting to impressions then allowing them to mature and change, sometimes over long years, was to prove fundamental to Liszt's spontaneous, rule-free way of composing.

Some time late in 1832 he had met a certain Countess Marie d'Agoult, the estranged wife of a much older French cavalry officer, and very soon they were conducting a clandestine affair under cover of her marriage. Liszt's summer at La Chênaie was perhaps a planned separation; but it came to an end because of the sudden death that December of Marie's six-year-old daughter, which precipitated a crisis at the climax of which she returned to Liszt and their affair resumed. By March 1835 she was pregnant; very soon the affair was public knowledge, and to avoid the likely scandal the couple decamped to Geneva. It was the start of what Liszt would refer to as his 'années de pèlerinage', his pilgrim years. They were in Switzerland for two years, then, after a brief return to France, they proceeded to Italy: Bellagio, then Venice, Rome and Lucca. Their sight-seeing in Switzerland was recorded by Liszt in a series of piano pieces in a three-volume collection called *Album d'un voyageur*, some named after particular places, others embodying generic types, *ranz des vaches*, peasant dances and so forth. Seven of these pieces later reappeared, in some cases heavily revised, in the first volume of *Années de pèlerinage*. Italy, by contrast, was remembered in the second volume through works of art: Raphael's *Marriage of the Virgin* (*Sposalizio*), Michelangelo's *Il penseroso*, three Petrarch sonnets, etc.

Liszt's response to these visual and verbal stimuli produced what amounts to a radically new kind of music, not necessarily revolutionary in style but groundbreaking in concept and form. The larger pieces – *Chapelle de Guillaume Tell, Vallée d'Obermann, Sposalizio, Après une lecture de Dante* (the so-called 'Dante' Sonata) – are tone poems in which, however, the form derives, not from any specific descriptive impulse, but from the composer's thoughts as he contemplates the scene or painting or poem and allows his imagination to roam through the subject. In one or two cases these thoughts are backed up by epigraphs. *Vallée d'Obermann* is prefaced by poetic quotations from Senancour and Byron, *Eglogue* by a disquisition from *Obermann* on the *ranz des vaches* – the Alpine herdsman's horn-call – and the Romantic sounds of the mountains.

This is very different from anything in Chopin, who never gave titles or epigraphs to his piano works. His generic titles may imply the idea of a back story. A ballade, after all, is a narrative poem, and it's conceivable that Chopin used this title for four of his greatest works in order to suggest the narrative mode. Yet their form is essentially abstract. If one compares the Ballade No. 4, in F minor (1842), with Liszt's *Vallée d'Obermann* in its definitive version (early 1850s), the difference is unmistakable. From the start the Ballade has the structured feeling of an unorthodox sonata form, rather free in tonality but with balanced periods linked, as in the G minor, by passages of bravura that are themselves, in general, thematic. Development, with Chopin, tends to be a matter of decorative variation rather than the tight working of motifs, but there is never any loosening of control, no padding, no vagueness in the design. The wonderful effect, for instance, of the re-emergence of the introduction theme in the remote key of A major is brilliantly calculated so as to lead back to the actual recapitulation in F minor.

With Liszt the feeling is quite different. Whether or not there is any such place as 'Obermann's Valley' is beside the point. The opening of Liszt's piece reveals it as a territory of the mind. The marking 'quasi cello' on the left-hand melody may suggest a particularly legato technique; but 'molto legato' would have done for that. The cello is an instrument of the soul, just as the 'oboe' (at bar 9) is the voice of rural despair. What follows is an extended rhapsody on these two brief ideas, growing in intensity, once or twice exploding into a kind of passionate protest represented by bravura of a typically Lisztian violence. But at the end nothing much has changed, and the poet quits the scene unappeased.

One other point is worth making in this comparison. With Chopin, a superb melodist, harmony is generally classical in the sense that it both serves and controls the discourse. Strange things happen now and then in the mazurkas, but these are rustic, modal colourings within mainly orthodox procedures, however imaginatively deployed. In Liszt, a less spontaneous melodist, the rhapsodic approach often leads the music into remote territory where normal harmonic behaviour no longer applies. Sometimes this is because of his love of irrational melodies like the opening theme of *Vallée d'Obermann*, which by twists and turns visits almost every note of the chromatic scale; or he may investigate chords for their particular sound, rather than for their correctness in terms of voice-leading. These are partly the habits of the improviser; but not many improvisers possess the ear or indeed the hands of the great Liszt, or know how to handle harmony that has somehow wandered off the beaten track.

Of all the assorted virtuoso pianists who lived in or converged on Paris in the 1820s and 1830s, only one seems to have matched Liszt in this exploratory relationship between the mechanics and technical demands of the instrument on the one hand and its musical possibilities on the other. This was Charles-Valentin Alkan, a Parisian of such precocious talent that he had already enrolled at the Conservatoire when he was six, and won a *premier prix* for piano at the age of ten. At the end of his life Liszt claimed that 'Alkan had the finest technique of any pianist he knew'.[13] But Alkan also possessed a complex, introverted personality which turned him eventually into a recluse who for the last forty years of his life hid away in his Paris flat, seeing few people except a handful of students and emerging only to give an occasional concert. His own music he seldom played at all in public, with the apparent result that few pianists took it up subsequently; though much of it was published, it was simply not known about. Even today, the one thing people know about Alkan, who was Jewish, is that he was crushed to death by a bookcase which fell on him while he was reaching for a copy of the Talmud. And this one 'fact' may be apocryphal.

Alkan's music remains neglected today, but this is clearly not just because it is extremely difficult; not all of it is, and in any case transcendental works by Liszt, Chopin, Balakirev, Rachmaninov and others are in the standard repertoire and regularly performed by the nimble-fingered. One problem is that it doesn't fit into categories, or even programme timings. His *Grande sonate* (1848), subtitled *Les quatre âges*, lasts forty minutes and has four disparate movements that, like man and woman as they age, go from very fast to very slow. His *Douze études*, in all the minor keys, op. 39 (1857), play for two hours and include a four-movement symphony, a three-movement concerto, an overture and a set of variations, all for solo piano. On the other hand, the *Vingt-cinq Préludes* (1847) are comparable to Chopin's set, which Alkan, who was on good terms with Chopin, certainly knew well. He has a more complicated key sequence (beginning and ending with pieces in C major), and his preludes are slightly longer and more diverse in content. But they add up to an excellent study of Alkan's individual way with mid-century keyboard idioms, his slightly quirky approach to harmony and to piano texture and sonority, and, to be candid, his relatively modest melodic gift.

7
Opera as Politics, Politics as Opera

The real focus of music for Parisians in the 1820s and 1830s remained the opera. Liszt was a keen opera-goer, and a significant proportion of his own music during this period consisted of fantasies or 'reminiscences' based on themes from the popular operas of the day. He was by no means alone in cultivating the operatic fantasy. Pretty well every virtuoso pianist of the day would routinely programme such pieces, usually of his or her own composition, sometimes no doubt more or less improvised, sometimes elaborate, written-out works of some substance. When Liszt came back to Paris from Switzerland in 1837 to take part in a keyboard duel with Sigismond Thalberg, both pianists played pieces of this kind: Thalberg his fantasy on Rossini's *Mosè in Egitto*, Liszt his fantasy on Pacini's *Niobe*. Most of these works were more or less showy variations on or heavily embroidered medleys of themes from the operas in question. But occasionally there would be an attempt to make something more substantial, even complex, out of the basic material. Liszt's *Réminiscences de Norma* (1841) has a grandeur of its own derived from, even going beyond, the opera itself. His *Réminiscences de Lucrezia Borgia* (1840–8) openly treats the operatic material as a pretext for a display of outrageous keyboard bravura.

Chopin was also a regular opera-goer from his Warsaw years. But he never seems to have contemplated writing an opera, and he wrote no operatic fantasies for piano apart from the early variations with orchestra on Mozart's 'Là ci darem la mano' and a set of variations on an aria from Hérold's *Ludovic* (1833). As a composer his most productive debt to opera lay in the general character of his melody, which was consciously influenced by the ornamental vocal melody of Italian opera. The piano, being a percussion instrument, is not able to play a true vocal legato, but it can fake one with the help of the sustaining pedal and through touch and timing by the fingers, hands and wrists, and it can successfully mimic vocal coloratura. Chopin's arrival in Paris in early October 1831 coincided with the first performance there of any opera by Vincenzo Bellini: *La sonnambula*, which opened on the 28th. Whether or not he attended that performance, he certainly heard *La sonnambula*, as well as Bellini's *Il pirata*, the following year. His melodic style was already well set by that time, partly under the influence of Rossini, whose operas he had seen in Warsaw. But he came to love Bellini as well, and there is plenty of evidence in his subsequent music of Bellini's famous long melodic line working on his own extended, much-decorated melodies.

By the early thirties, Rossini had abandoned opera, and although occasional works by Pacini and Luigi Ricci leaked out of Italy and turned up in London or Paris or one or other of the German cities, and post-Rossinian operas by Saverio Mercadante were heard in Paris before the composer appeared there in person in 1836, Bellini and his slightly older contemporary Gaetano Donizetti were by far the most widely performed abroad of any Italian composers apart from Rossini.

Donizetti was born in Bergamo to poor, working-class parents, and was fortunate that the *maestro di cappella* at the local cathedral was Simon Mayr, a selfless and hard-working teacher as well as a successful opera composer. Mayr took the boy under his wing, oversaw his studies, and eventually fixed his first opera commission. But this helping hand merely pitched him into what Verdi later called the galley years, and he had composed no fewer than thirty operas for Italian theatres (mainly Naples and Rome) before the thirty-first, *Anna Bolena*, attracted attention abroad and was taken up by London and Paris in 1831, the year after its Milan premiere.

Italian composers had been able to write so many operas because the conventions of the genre were like bottles of a given shape that had simply to be filled with a similar liquid over and over again.

Any attempt to alter the bottle tended to be frowned on (Donizetti's teacher at the Bologna Liceo, Stanislao Mattei, who had also taught Rossini, thought his innovations 'had brought dishonour upon his school'[1]). Donizetti himself seems to have worked fairly happily for most of the time within these limitations, while discreetly stretching them in certain ways, especially in terms of characterisation and dramatic situation. Above all, his sudden preoccupation in the late 1820s with English and Scottish history prompted a distinct broadening of approach. *Anna Bolena* had been preceded in 1829 by *Elisabetta al castello di Kenilworth*, after Scott's *Kenilworth*; and soon afterwards came *Maria Stuarda* (1834, after the play by Schiller), and *Roberto Devereux* (1837, about Elizabeth and Essex), with in between, among eighteen or so other operas, his most successful of all, *Lucia di Lammermoor* (1835, on Scott's novel *The Bride of Lammermoor*). Needless to say, Donizetti was not much interested in the actual history or specific plots, only in the, mostly invented, dramatic confrontations. Admittedly, the superbly unhistorical meeting between Elizabeth and Mary in *Maria Stuarda* was a fabrication of Schiller's; but *Anna Bolena* is a brilliant compendium of unlikely interviews variously between Anne Boleyn, Jane Seymour, Henry VIII and Anne's brother and assorted lovers or would-be lovers, culminating near the end of Act I in a stirring sextet for the entire crew. As for *Lucia*, the librettist Salvatore Cammarano rewrote Scott mainly to provide a big baritone role for Lucia's brother Enrico, in the process killing off their mother, the main destructive agent in the novel.

Amid all this historical and literary mayhem Donizetti was able to adapt the fixed forms of Italian tragic opera strongly enough to create powerful human drama without completely abandoning the forms themselves. Insofar as bel canto opera is absurd, Donizetti is absurd. When in full vocal flow the characters remain, on one level, coloratura sopranos and tenors. Villains are usually baritones, nurses mezzo-sopranos (not to upstage their soprano employers). The orchestra's main task is to support, to cheer on, but not to interfere. Performances of even the best of these operas to this day are governed almost as much by audience response as by what happens onstage: the routine hollering at the end of showpiece arias, however well or mediocrely sung, and the response of the singers, who, in true nineteenth-century fashion, still rewrite their music here and there to suit their vocal strengths.

Donizetti never tried to evade these issues, but he learnt to use them in the service of the drama. His vocal writing, well peppered with cadenzas and general *fioriture*, is always beautifully tailored to the voice and subtly, sometimes deeply, expressive. At the same time he took from Mayr and Rossini the constant flow, rather than simple alternation, between aria and recitative. By this means he could control the pace of the drama, in the manner of speech coloured by bursts of feeling, points of reflection, humour or irony, with arias or set-piece ensembles when one or more characters take centre-stage. The mad scene in *Lucia* and the meeting of the queens in *Maria Stuarda* are only the best-known examples of this technique. The penultimate scene of *Maria Stuarda*, in which Cecil delivers Maria's death warrant and she makes her confession to Talbot, is a non-stop montage of *secco* and accompanied recitative, aria fragments and duet in quasi-dialogue form. And perhaps it was comparable episodes in *Anna Bolena* that appealed to Paris audiences; after all, they had come, by a roundabout route, from French opera. They also helped the pacing of Donizetti's two best comedies, *L'elisir d'amore* (*The Love Potion*, 1832), a master-piece of controlled sentiment and witty, cartoon-like portraiture, about a fake elixir which nevertheless helps Nemorino win the love of the proud, mocking Adina, and *Don Pasquale* (1843), on the well-worn topic of the rich old *buffo* bass wanting to marry the beautiful young soprano who is actually in love with the handsome young tenor, and getting his comeuppance with the help of various forms of legal skulduggery.

That autumn of 1831 Parisians had their first opportunity to com-pare Donizetti and Bellini, his main Italian rival. *La sonnambula* (*The*

Girl Who Sleep-Walks) is dramatically a quite different kind of work from *Anna Bolena*. Where Donizetti's opera taps into the Romantic fascination with history, Bellini's is a love story set in a Swiss village, combining a pastoral setting with strange goings-on in the heroine's mind. Nevertheless their stylistic background was much the same. Bellini was Sicilian, born in Catania in 1801, then trained at the Conservatorio in Naples under Niccolò Zingarelli, an elderly composer who, like Mattei in Bologna, seems to have regarded Rossini (at that time himself based in Naples) as first cousin to the Antichrist. He encouraged Bellini to avoid Rossini's sinful complexities, and in a sense Bellini took his advice and developed a manner that still seems exceptionally pure, a wonderful demonstration of the power of song as a vehicle for drama of a direct, natural kind. He achieved something of this perfection early on, with a pair of full-length operas composed and performed in Naples when he was barely out of college, and he was then twice commissioned by La Scala, for *Il pirata* (1827) and *La straniera* (1829). But Bellini was never a rapid producer like Donizetti, and in his admittedly short life (he died in 1835 aged thirty-three) he composed only ten operas and, after graduating, little else but a few songs.

La sonnambula is perhaps the most refined, least stereotyped of his four or five fully mature works. It is a genre piece about well-rounded individuals, neither particularly good nor particularly bad. Amina is engaged to Elvino, but seems to have arranged an assignation with the local squire, Rodolfo, when she is spotted one evening climbing through the window of the inn where he is staying by the innkeeper, Lisa, who is herself in love with Elvino. In the end it turns out that Amina was sleepwalking, and it is the flirtatious but essentially honourable Rodolfo who reveals this to the villagers. Bellini catches the atmosphere and tensions of village life largely through the exquisite refinement of his melodic writing, his gentle handling of his characters, and the skilful use of the chorus. In his subsequent operas he moved more towards a grand manner: in his portrayal in

Norma (1831) of the druid priestess in love, like Spontini's Julia, with a powerful Roman, and in *I puritani* (1835), a typical grand opera subject of the love of a Puritan girl for a Cavalier aristocrat against the background of the English Civil War. *Norma* is the Bellini opera most people know best, and perhaps the one that best exploits his skill at characterisation through vocal style: in the tragic expression, for instance, of the long monologue 'Dormono entrambi', in which Norma draws back from murdering her children by her lost Roman lover (a piece that had a palpable influence on Chopin), and in the prayerful but authoritative tones of 'Casta diva', in which the more elaborate *fioritura* masks her true motive for refusing permission to make war on the occupying Romans.

One looks in vain, in these late bel canto operas, for any actual political engagement. Italy was still a divided territory, ruled in the north by the Austrian Habsburgs, in the south by the Spanish Bourbons, with the Papal States in between. But there were already stirrings of the Risorgimento, the move towards unification. By its nature, this was a nationalist movement; unification meant kicking out the occupying foreigners. But it was a different kind of nationalism from Herder's cultural particularism. It wasn't merely a question of finding and cultivating the roots of your own tribe, it was a question of literally doing battle with those whose roots grew elsewhere but had spread to threaten yours. Giuseppe Mazzini and Giuseppe Garibaldi, the leading members of the revolutionary Young Italy movement in the early 1830s, promoted violent insurrection against the Austrians, Spaniards and even the Papacy. Alessandro Manzoni's great novel of 1827, *I promessi sposi (The Betrothed)*, is not only an allegory of the alienation of the common people from the centres of power, but a covert argument for a common Italian language, based like Dante's *Divine Comedy* on Tuscan dialect. But it would be hard to see *Norma* or *Lucia di Lammermoor*, or Donizetti's Tudor operas, as political in any such sense. The druids in *Norma* are agitating against the Romans, but the opera is actually about the inconvenience for a druidess of having had two children by a Roman proconsul. Donizetti's interest in the Tudors and Stuarts had much more to do with their personal relationships than their power politics.

The truth about opera in the 1830s is that it liked to seize on the political issues of the day and dramatise the human predicaments they created. But politics had a way of fighting back and treating the theatre as a suitable arena for its own battles. The most famous example was Daniel Auber's opera *La Muette de Portici* (1828), a tragic tale of a dumb girl (played by a dancer) seduced by the son of the Spanish viceroy in Naples, against the backcloth of the 1647 revolt against Spanish rule. The libretto was by Eugène Scribe, the most important and prolific author of operatic texts in Paris between the 1820s and his death in 1861. Though it makes spectacular capital out of the actual revolt, led by the silent heroine's brother Masaniello, *La Muette de Portici* is not really a political work. The seducer, Alfonso, suffers remorse and is treated rather sympathetically; Masaniello, on the other hand, refuses to take advantage of Alfonso when he comes seeking shelter from the insurrection. Revolution here is little more than an excuse for rousing choruses and a final battle accompanied by an eruption of Vesuvius, while the heroine throws herself off a high terrace into the lava flow – 'a remarkable feat', Winton Dean suggests, 'even for a French ballerina'.[2] The Paris premiere went off quietly, and the work was staged in Brussels a year later without incident. But a revival there in August 1830 seems to have coincided with a planned revolt against Dutch rule, and when Masaniello and his fellow rebel Pietro launched into their second act duet, 'Better die than go on being miserable', with its climactic 'Sacred love of the fatherland', the audience drowned out the singers with their shouting, and before the fifth act was even properly underway they poured out into the street and enthusiastically joined in the demonstrations that led, within a few months, to the creation of an independent Belgium.

In music history, as against the history of revolutions, *La Muette de Portici* is chiefly important as the start of a new wave of grand opera.

French revolutionary opera had been rich in works on a broad historical or epic canvas, with large choruses, spectacular scenery and ending in natural or quasi-natural disasters like the blazing temple at the end of Cherubini's *Médée*. But these, apart from two or three by Spontini, were with dialogue; grand operas were fully composed. And it so happened that the decade following Auber's piece brought forth half a dozen such works on the largest scale and destined to exert an influence well beyond their individual artistic merit. Auber himself rarely tackled the genre again. His *Gustave III* (1833) is the only full-scale exception in a string of comic operas that indicated Auber's true *métier*. He specialised in lively, uncomplicated melodies, simply harmonised, brightly scored: his best-known comic opera, *Fra Diavolo* (1830), illustrates these qualities to perfection. They belong to an essentially Gallic tradition stretching from Boieldieu's *La Dame blanche* (1825) to the operettas of Offenbach, and on to the songs and operas of Poulenc. It's a style that lives by making elegant fun of its own vacuousness, like a wit whose silly conversation conceals subtle parodies of the social world it inhabits. It takes us as far as possible from the world of grand opera, a world in which almost anything is possible except wit.

The immediate successor of *La Muette de Portici* was Rossini's *William Tell*, which went onstage at the Opéra eighteen months later, in August 1829. But the biggest event in the evolution of grand opera came two years after that, in November 1831, with the premiere on the same stage of Meyerbeer's *Robert le diable*. Meyerbeer was the descendant of rich Jewish entrepreneurs and bankers in Berlin, well connected through his mother's salon there, and from childhood a brilliant pianist, a pupil first of Zelter, then of the Abbé Vogler in Darmstadt, the teacher also of Weber, who became a close friend. In Darmstadt, perhaps under Weber's influence, he had turned to writing operas, but it was only when he moved to Italy in 1816 that opera became the main focus of his work. He was in Italy for nine years and in that time composed half a dozen operas, all of them staged more or less successfully in Italian theatres. Broadly these works are Italian in style; they make serious vocal demands (the last of them, *Il crociato in Egitto*, even has a major role for a castrato). They are the work of Giacomo, rather than Jakob – a name change he adopted at about this time.

The Italian success soon spread abroad, eventually to Paris, where *Il crociato in Egitto* (*The Crusader in Egypt*) was staged in 1825, *Margherita d'Anjou* in 1826, both with success. The commission for *Robert le diable* was the direct outcome. Originally it was ordered by the Opéra-Comique as a three-act piece with dialogue; but when the commission fell through it was picked up by the Opéra and became the five-act grand opera that most opera-goers in the twenty-first century do not know, for the strange reason that a work which created a sensation in its day, and remained one of the two or three most performed operas in the nineteenth century, withered away in the twentieth into a mere history-book name, regarded with routine contempt largely because of the immense prestige of its detractors.

By the time *Robert le diable* took the stage, Meyerbeer was forty and an experienced, highly intelligent theatre composer and an accomplished musician with an eclectic range of traditions behind him. Like Rossini, a friend and admirer, he had no interest in simply importing more Italian opera for the Parisians to hum along to. On the contrary, he and his librettist (Scribe again) saw the opportunity offered by the exceptional resources of the Opéra, its huge stage, its large, high-quality orchestra, its recently installed gas lighting, and, not least, its relatively new and still expanding middle-class audience, well-educated up to a point, but with the usual complement of businessmen, bankers and lawyers of a type more interested in spectacle and a good night out than anything that might be classed as great art. This didn't necessarily preclude great art, of course. It only meant it had to be presented in a vivid, highly coloured, if you like disguised form, not effects without causes, as Wagner later complained, but causes with plenty of effects. It was a prescription that *Robert le diable* fulfilled to the letter.

The title is in fact a misnomer. Robert, an invented thirteenth-century duke of Normandy, is not himself the devil in question, but his son. He has come to Sicily having been hounded out of Normandy for 'sowing grief in families . . . beating husbands, abducting wives and daughters'. But he is pursued by his (unrecognised) father, Bertram, who is actually a devil, and whose infernal task it is to capture Robert's soul by midnight on a certain day. His campaign consists mainly of obstructing his son's attempts to marry the fair Princess Isabelle by impugning his honour, tricking him into gambling away all his possessions, enticing him away from a tournament for Isabelle's hand, and finally conjuring up a ballet of deviant nuns who seduce him into stealing a sacred cypress branch. But Robert has also been followed to Sicily by his virtuous half-sister Alice, who performs a kind of filibuster on Bertram so that midnight chimes before Robert can sign the diabolical contract. All ends happily as Isabelle appears miraculously in her bridal dress, and Bertram vanishes in a cloud of dust.

It is easy enough to pick holes in this scheme. The plot is poorly motivated and not a single relationship is properly explained: how Robert and Isabelle come to be in love, why Alice should trek from Normandy to Sicily, postponing her wedding, to save her feckless halfbrother, why Bertram is in thrall to Satan, etc. A lot of the incidental detail is plainly inserted for its shock value. Robert himself has been described as 'a veracious portrait of the moral uncertainties of that epoch, that vacillated so restlessly and so painfully between virtue and vice'.[3] But not much about Robert is veracious, and his final wavering between a father who is plainly leading him to perdition and his beloved waiting at the altar is not much more than what another writer has called 'a suspense effect'.[4]

Yet *Robert le diable* was not merely a success; it was a phenomenon. One measure of this is the curious way its music has of sounding vaguely familiar even on first hearing, which is only partly because Meyerbeer learnt from the music of other composers. More important, it is because his own music exerted such a strong influence on a whole array of later composers whose music we know very well. Verdi is the most obvious case, but there are also pre-echoes of Gounod and his pupil Georges Bizet, of Berlioz, of Wagner, and even of Offenbach (in *The Tales of Hoffmann*).[5] Time after time Meyerbeer comes up with imaginative motifs, rhythmic figures, or orchestral effects that collude with the dramatic situation, intensify it or lend it colour; structure and dramatic pacing are handled with great expertise. Done complete, *Robert le diable* runs for some four hours, but it seldom drags or loses its way. It's true that Paris opera-goers in the 1830s would not necessarily feel obliged to stick it out for a whole evening; they would arrive late, come and go, talk, drink and eat in their boxes. And Meyerbeer's eclectic, eventful style played to audiences of this kind.

It was chiefly this aspect of Meyerbeer, his acute sense of his audience, that provoked the scorn of serious-minded Romantics like Schumann, for whom art was akin to religion, and for whom any kind of flaunting of sexuality or drunkenness onstage, or any sensationalising of Christianity or the Church, was anathema. 'To astonish or tickle is Meyerbeer's highest maxim,' he wrote in a review of *Les Huguenots*, 'and he succeeds, too, with the rabble'.[6] But there was prejudice involved in this kind of judgement as well. Schumann was no anti-Semite, but he was, at least in adulthood, a strait-laced German, and clearly suspicious of Meyerbeer's melting-pot approach to composition, which combined Italian melodic and vocal style with Germanic richness of texture and polyphony, and a French love of orchestral colour. This fusion, however, was precisely Meyerbeer's strength. It gave his music depth, and helped its continuities; the brilliant orchestration went with the riveting visual spectacle, the fast-flowing action, the crowded stage, the choruses of drunken knights, courtiers, devils and nuns, the ballets, not just for titillation (though that was certainly not precluded), but built into the action, and the dazzling stage picture. Perhaps melody was not Meyerbeer's strongest suit, though there is sustained vocal writing of real beauty, notably in the third-act confrontation between Bertram and Alice, and in the Act 5 trio, which Verdi seems to have had in his head when he composed Rigoletto's encounter with Sparafucile. Meyerbeer makes heavy demands on his solo singers, who must display bel canto athleticism over an exceptional vocal range while riding orchestral accompaniments of much greater variety and power than were normal in Italian opera. Problems of casting may be another, more practical reason why performances of his operas remain a rarity.

Meyerbeer extended his mastery of the genre with two operas, like Auber's *Muette*, on specific historical subjects, personalising them with invented characters who become inextricably caught up in the more or less historical narrative. *Les Huguenots* (1836) is framed by the events leading up to the St Bartholomew's Day massacre of Protestants in Paris in August 1572, culminating in the massacre itself, mainly, though not entirely, enacted offstage. The real-life context of the massacre was the attempted reconciliation of Catholics and Protestants through the marriage of the king's sister Marguerite to the Protestant Henri III of Navarre, and Meyerbeer fleshes this out in the person of the Protestant Raoul de Nangis, whom Marguerite wants to marry off to the Catholic Valentine de Saint-Bris. Unlike in *Robert le diable*, the motivations are finely drawn; this is a genuine drama of character. Raoul himself is willing to befriend the generous, easy-going Catholic Comte de Nevers, but he rejects Valentine because he believes her to be Nevers's mistress, while Raoul's servant Marcel, a stern, incorruptible Calvinist, will have nothing at all to do with Catholics, and accepts Valentine, after Raoul has realised his mistake, only when she converts.

Les Huguenots lacks the splendid diabolism of *Robert*, but in its place it has a kind of cinematic vividness and realism of narrative and historical detail. Schumann objected – rather absurdly – to Meyerbeer's prominent use of the Lutheran chorale 'Ein feste Burg'. But this is only one aspect of the musical canvas, which is a kind of polyptych of the warring factions and social and ethnic types, the religious processions and chanting, the gypsy dancers, the night watch, and the ladies of Marguerite's court, who before our eyes perform a bathing ballet in gauze wraps. Meyerbeer's skill lies in the fusion of all these colourful elements with the love story that lends them a certain grim, ironic significance. It was easy to ridicule the sheer inclusiveness of this sort of thing, its determination to throw every imaginable chemical of city and courtly life into a cauldron that will finally explode in a big bang of passion, piety and out-and-out violence. But there was scarcely any serious operatic composer after Meyerbeer who failed to learn some lesson or other from these two works, or from his third Paris opera, *Le Prophète* (1849, about the Anabaptist takeover of Münster in 1534).

No doubt, in the end something was lacking. For the poet and critic Théophile Gautier, Meyerbeer's 'grandest effects, those which stir the heart most vividly, seem the result of long meditation rather than to spring spontaneously from the composer's feelings'.[7] Berlioz admired *Les Huguenots* but came to have doubts about *Le Prophète*. Meyerbeer's supreme competence and the overwhelming brilliance of the stage spectacle, the constant appeal to both the ear and the eye, could wear thin over time, and perhaps this is the true explanation of why the influence survived but the works, in the main, have not.

The influence could work both ways, especially when most of the libretti were by the same Eugène Scribe. Auber's one post-*Muette* grand opera, *Gustave III*, about the assassination of the Swedish king at a masked ball in 1792 (a Scribe libretto later adapted by Antonio Somma for Verdi's *Un ballo in maschera*), ended with a ball scene of such splendour that even *Les Huguenots*, three years later, had nothing to match it. There were three hundred on the stage, spectacularly, many of them grotesquely, costumed, participating in an extended ballet including, for good measure, a duple-time as well as triple-time minuet, a triple-time as well as quadruple-time march, and a wild galop, all more or less in Auber's *opéra comique* vein, before the tragic dénouement. Fromental Halévy's *La Juive* (1835) lacked a ball scene and instead ended with its heroine and her adoptive father being thrown into a cauldron of boiling water by the pious Christian citizens of fifteenth-century Constance. Halévy's title is ironic: Rachel, the Jewess of the title, is not Jewish at all, but a gentile adopted by a Jewish goldsmith, a fact unfortunately not revealed until too late to prevent her execution for daring to be seduced by a Christian. *La Juive* was also staged on a massive scale, but in some ways its best music is intimate, especially Rachel's beautiful Act 2 romance and the goldsmith Eléazar's 'Rachel, quand du Seigneur', with obbligato accompaniment for two cors anglais.

La Juive had distinguished admirers, including Wagner, but not Berlioz, who had been forced by sheer indigence to take up music criticism in 1833, but had declined (in 1835) to write a review of *I puritani* or of 'that wretched *Juive*; I had too many bad things to say about them – it would have been put down to jealousy'.[8] For, of course, he was writing an opera of his own, and was all too keenly aware of the crucial role played by personal influence and string-pulling in the turbid world of Parisian theatre. His idea for an opera with dialogue about the sixteenth-century Florentine sculptor, goldsmith, poet and soldier Benvenuto Cellini had already been turned down by the Opéra-Comique, and was now being worked up with recitative for possible performance at the Opéra. But it was worryingly unlike the grand operas that had been pulling in the crowds there. It had one spectacular scene, the casting of Cellini's *Perseus*, and one fast-moving carnival scene, but was otherwise more like an eighteenth-century *opera buffa* with a lot of rapid comings and goings, a father trying to marry his daughter off to an unloved but influential suitor (Fieramosca), while she and her actual love, Cellini, decide to elope. It had two acts instead of five; and perhaps trickiest of all, a couple of appearances by the Pope, Clement VII, who had commissioned the *Perseus* and was demanding its completion in return for a free pardon for Cellini, who had killed a man in a carnival brawl.

Paris has never taken kindly to artistic or linguistic innovation, and Berlioz was exactly the kind of flagrant original who could expect to hear the slamming of doors in the old city. But by the mid-1830s he also had his supporters. Liszt adored his music and backed him in various ways, most publicly by arranging and publishing his previously unpublished *Symphonie fantastique* for piano, thereby enabling its circulation, in France and elsewhere. Above all Meyerbeer, always a generous supporter of younger colleagues, was on his side. According to Berlioz's biographer David Cairns, it was largely through Meyerbeer's influence that *Benvenuto Cellini* was finally accepted for performance at the Opéra in September 1838 (with the Pope demoted to Cardinal for the occasion).[9] But it was not a success, partly because of problems with the libretto, which was deemed vulgar, partly because of disturbances prompted by personal animosity towards Berlioz the critic and towards his music in general, partly simply because the music itself was annoyingly brilliant, but too unconventional to be acceptable to the all-knowing connoisseurs of the greatest opera house in the world. There were four complete performances followed by three of the first act in a double bill with a ballet. Then *Benvenuto Cellini* vanished from the French stage until the 1970s.

Its most striking quality is its buzzing, nervous energy, but this isn't simply a matter of speed. It has as much to do with something mercurial in the pacing of the music, and this in turn is part and parcel of Berlioz's response to the subject and its principal characters. Cellini himself is resourceful, quick-witted, impulsive, rough and ready, and a genius who stakes everything on the final throw of the dice. On the spur of the moment he persuades Teresa to elope with him, on an impulse he kills Fieramosca's friend Pompeo, and at the last minute he orders all his metal sculptures to be melted down to make up the quantity for the *Perseus*. His whole life (as in his *Memoirs*, Berlioz's source) is a tapestry of escapades, violent encounters and last-minute redemptions, which is no doubt why Teresa, though in love with him, reacts nervously when he turns up at her father's door.

Berlioz catches precisely this conflict in a young girl's heart in the edgy cabaletta to her first aria, 'Quand j'aurai vôtre age' ('When I'm your age, my dear parents, it will be time to be more sensible'), cast as a rondo, which helps the feeling that she is talking herself into an indiscretion. But it is also worth examining Berlioz's setting of the French language here and elsewhere. A native speaker and thinker, he makes skilful use of the virtually accentless property of French, which frees the music from the usual routines of the upbeat and downbeat and the four-bar phrase. Time and again one is conscious of a rhythmic and metric fluidity quite unlike anything in Berlioz's rivals in the setting of French, Gluck (a German), Spontini and Cherubini (both Italian), Meyerbeer (another German). The effect is conversational, quick and interactive, strikingly so in the trio where Cellini is instructing Teresa in the elopement plan, overheard by Fieramosca, and in the confusion of the carnival and the final scene in Cellini's foundry. This informality infects the melody as well, and even the harmony. We know from Berlioz's pre-Conservatoire music that he had never had particular respect for the textbook rules that were supposed to govern those matters. At that time he hardly knew them in any case, and since he played no keyboard instrument, he was shielded from the pianist's left-hand, right-hand instincts, the feeling that the two hands have to combine, work together, and end properly on the right chord. Berlioz's melody is curiously liquid, like his word-setting, and one often feels that the harmony is simply following in its wake, mostly behaving itself, occasionally sticking out its tongue at normality. At this stage, Berlioz knows the rules perfectly well, but has not been brainwashed into obeying them by habit, and the result is a highly individual, sometimes startling freedom of language that his contemporaries found hard to accept but was to prove an inspiration to later instinctive lawbreakers.

While the Opéra was agonising over *Benvenuto Cellini*, another, very different project came Berlioz's way, nothing less than a government commission to write a grand work in memory of the victims of an attempt on King Louis Philippe's life in 1835, to be performed in the church of Les Invalides in July 1837. Berlioz licked his lips at the thought of a requiem with 'five or six hundred performers at my command . . . What a Dies Irae!!'[10] And when he completed the work, and it was eventually performed that December, he was still counting; not only does the score specify just over two hundred voices, and just under two hundred instruments, but a note on the first page allows these numbers to be doubled or even tripled.

It was this *Grande Messe des morts*, together with the Te Deum (1849), with its choir of eight hundred including six hundred children, that gained Berlioz his long-standing reputation as 'a mere noise-maker, who could only ever appear in the company of so many dozen trombones'.[11] It's true that there is a lot of noise in the Requiem, notably in the Tuba Mirum, with its thunderous timpani and its four brass bands placed at the four corners of the main body of the choir and orchestra. Berlioz was clearly excited by the spatial possibilities of music in a very large building; it brought to mind the spectacular outdoor musical ceremonies of the Revolution, with their huge choruses and wind and percussion orchestras. And the fact that he, a non-believer, presumably did not fear the Last Judgement was evidently no reason not to dramatise the terror that even atheists and revolutionaries are perhaps able to conjure up in those rare moments when it occurs to them that they might be wrong.

All the same, the Requiem is actually a predominantly restrained work, much of it quiet and slow, sometimes intensely polyphonic, as at the start of the Dies Irae or the Quaerens Me, and for long stretches reflective and uninsistent in tone. Admittedly this is not the silence of the grave, but the dramatic, frightened calm of what has been happily called God's waiting-room. Several movements begin with solo lines, and while the model here is Palestrina, the image is modern: the lonely soul in the vast hall of eternity. Berlioz was in the depths of his creative being a dramatist, and all his musical resources were ultimately at the service of theatre. So in a live performance of the Requiem the huge forces spread out in front of one enhance the power of the stillnesses by virtue of the massive restraint they imply. And one becomes aware of Berlioz's delicacy, his refined and varied orchestral colouring, at least as much as the uninhibited racket that might at any moment break out.

Not long after the Requiem performance, he received a second government commission, this time for a work to accompany an actual open-air ceremony, the symbolic reburial of the dead from 1830 on the tenth anniversary of the July Days. One can only imagine the effect of the *Grande symphonie funèbre et triomphale* performed by two hundred wind and percussion players marching along Paris streets swarming with an excited, noisy crowd on a sweltering summer's day: music of an outdoor character but sophisticated in form, with quieter episodes that will have been totally inaudible even, probably, to the players themselves. But fortunately for Berlioz, Paganini's amazing generosity had given him the freedom to compose music out of his own head, music he and nobody else demanded, and the result was a completely different kind of symphony, what he called a Dramatic Symphony, based on Shakespeare's *Romeo and Juliet*. He had briefly thought of it as an opera, but seems in the end to have positively preferred what, in a later age, might have emerged as a radio opera, a drama performed partly in the theatre of the mind, sometimes with text, sometimes not, a profoundly Romantic concept that, as it were, invites the listener to enter the composer's head and share directly the products of his fantasy.

The result, though it contains some of Berlioz's most beautiful and brilliantly imagined music, is curiously hybrid as a whole. It starts (after a brief orchestral introduction) and finishes with mainly vocal music, while its main substance – those parts that deal with the core of Shakespeare's drama, plus one piece that takes advantage of Mercutio's Queen Mab speech as pretext for a symphonic scherzo – is orchestral, which Berlioz justifies in the preface to the score as being 'a language richer, more varied, less fixed, and, by its very imprecision, incomparably more powerful in such a case'. There is more than a hint of special pleading here. When he came, a few years later, to compose *La Damnation de Faust* – a similarly hybrid work, neither quite opera nor quite oratorio – he took the opposite view and included no purely orchestral music except for a dramatically irrelevant march and a pair of dances. And he was plainly uneasy about *Roméo et Juliette* in this respect, going to the trouble of explaining the procedure in his preface, then, before the orchestral section that describes the play's tragic ending, making the extraordinary suggestion that the general public lacks imagination; accordingly, pieces which appeal solely to the imagination have no public. The following instrumental (orchestral) scene is an instance hereof, and I am of opinion that it should always be omitted, unless played to a select audience familiar in every respect with the fifth act of Shakespeare's tragedy as conceived and represented by Garrick, and endowed with a highly poetic mind.[12]

David Garrick, whose version of the play Berlioz had seen in Paris in 1827, had changed the ending to allow for a passionate scene between Juliet and the dying Romeo, and Berlioz's orchestral sequence follows the same plan, before reverting to Shakespeare's ending, with the reconciliation of the warring families, which Garrick had omitted. Perhaps nothing shows more clearly that, in planning his *Roméo et Juliette*, Berlioz was still locked into his passions of the Harriet Smithson time, and perhaps this explains the slightly undercooked quality of the vocal sections, especially the contralto soloist's scene-setting prologue and the over-long setting for solo baritone of Friar Laurence's final speech.

The fact remains that the orchestral sections contain some of the finest and most original music Berlioz ever wrote. The Queen Mab scherzo may be irrelevant to the drama, but it is such an exquisite piece of orchestral colouring – the opposite in every respect of the 'so many dozen trombones' – that relevance itself is silenced. It is preceded, on the other hand, by two long orchestral movements that go some way to justifying Berlioz's claim that the very imprecision of instrumental music can open psychological doors which the precision of words can sometimes leave closed. It's true that 'Roméo seul – Tristesse', refers in the play to his unrequited love for another Capulet relation, Rosaline. But for Berlioz he is mourning his impossible love for Juliet, which then bursts forth in the passionate avowals of the love scene that follows. This great movement may count as the apotheosis of early Romantic love music, gorgeously orchestrated, and touching depths of emotion

147

that words might well find hard to reach without sententiousness. The secret seems to lie, oddly enough, not in the individual gesture, the wonderful tune, the expressive temperature, the varied instrumental colour, important though they are. The movement makes its impact in the same way as a classical work, through formal balance and control of timing, a lesson that, in all music but Romantic music especially, separates the mature master from the untutored genius.

By the time he wrote *La Damnation de Faust* (1845–6), incorporating his *Huit scènes* from the twenties, Berlioz had the hybridity itself under control. Perhaps nothing in his adaptation of Gérard de Nerval (with Faust irretrievably damned) rises to the emotional level of *Roméo et Juliette* at its best. But for sheer variety of imagery, aural spectacle and consistent quality of invention, he surely never composed anything better. Many composers wrote their Fausts, but Berlioz is the only one to grasp the full range of Goethe's diabolical wit and mercurial energy. *Faust* is, among much else, a very funny play (Part One at least), and Berlioz gets this quality: in Brander's song about the rat (and the Amen fugue based on it: 'bestiality in all its candour,' Mephistopheles sneers), Mephistopheles's own song of the flea and, especially, his irresistible serenade with the will-o'-the-wisps, evil delicacy in a choir of flutes and oboes. Berlioz is also better than any of his predecessors except Weber at the actual diabolism, culminating in the Ride to the Abyss and the Pandaemonium, music of genuine terror at the far end of the spectrum of the Sublime, conveyed not only in the panic-stricken string ostinatos and the weird satanic patois of the demons, but also, hauntingly, in the chromatic meanderings of the solo oboe, which visits all twelve notes of the chromatic octave in its travels. Yet the score also contains two of the most exquisite early Romantic songs, Marguerite's ballad of the king of Thule with solo viola, and the Romance, 'D'amour l'ardente flamme' with cor anglais. The astonishing thing about these songs, as also about Brander's and Mephistopheles's tavern songs and the latter's serenade, is that all of them were among the *Huit scènes* of 1828–9 (the Serenade for tenor with guitar, but otherwise all with only quite minor changes). Berlioz's individuality, as we saw earlier, preceded his technical mastery, which simply evolved to accommodate it.

Like *Roméo et Juliette*, *La Damnation de Faust* is not a theatre piece, but a masterpiece of virtual theatre. Its design is more recognisably narrative, and it has often been staged. But it seldom succeeds in that form, perhaps because it tells too much of its story through what one might call 'insets', set pieces that belong to the plot but don't advance it (plus one or two, like the Hungarian March, that do neither). It's one of the ironies of this great composer that his best dramatic works were not written for the theatre, while his three operas, for all their fine musical qualities, have often proved problematic on the stage.

Berlioz conducted three performances of *Roméo et Juliette* in the Conservatoire in November and December 1839, each time to a capacity audience, eager to hear what this noted lunatic would do to one of Shakespeare's most popular plays. There will have been many musicians, many writers, many artists in the audience, among the usual social and political grandees, and one insignificant figure, recently arrived in Paris, and almost certainly in one of the very cheapest seats: a young composer by the name of Richard Wagner.

At twenty-six, Wagner was still quite unknown outside the German-speaking lands, and not much better known inside them, though he had completed two operas, had one of them staged, and had conducted a large number by other composers in a variety of provincial German theatres, from Magdeburg to Riga. Born in Leipzig in 1813, he was probably the son of a police actuary, Carl Friedrich Wagner, who died when he was six months old, and he was accordingly brought up in the family of his stepfather (or possibly father), an actor called Ludwig Geyer. Carl Friedrich had himself been a passionate theatre-goer; several of his children became actors, and young Richard was generally surrounded by theatricals of one kind or another until, in 1833, his brother Albert wangled him a job as chorus master at the theatre in Würzburg. Between then and July 1839, when he and his actress wife Minna fled Riga and his creditors under cover of darkness and with a large dog in tow, he had learnt theatre and opera the hard way, by browbeating modestly talented singers and instrumentalists into acceptable performances of mostly contemporary operas that were often, we can be fairly sure, strictly beyond their powers. From somewhere he had acquired an acute musical ear and score-reading ability; he had studied music in desultory fashion for a few months at Leipzig University and harmony and counterpoint privately. But his real secret seems to have been an extraordinary ability to learn by a kind of disguised imitation: by doing, while altering, what somebody else had done before him, and usually doing it better.

His first completed opera, *Die Feen* (*The Fairies*), draws variously on Hoffmann (especially his dialogue *The Poet and the Composer*),[13] Weber, especially *Euryanthe*, Marschner's *Hans Heiling*, which was premiered in Berlin in May 1833 then staged in Würzburg in September, and Beethoven, in the hero's last-act mad scene, which has Florestan's aria in *Fidelio* somewhere behind it. Wagner was still only twenty when he finished the score at New Year 1834. Yet at many points it outstrips its models. Particularly in the use of the orchestra and chorus to carry the drama forward, there are hints at a new kind of power, a certain weight of expression in the writing for strings, a magisterial quality in the brass. There are incipient Wagnerisms: melodic turns, processional music that looks forward to *Lohengrin*, one or two themes later adapted for *Tannhäuser*, and plot devices, notably the ban on asking the name (as in *Lohengrin*). *Die Feen* was never performed in Wagner's lifetime. Yet the score is strong for a first opera preceded by so little: a symphony, some operatic fragments, one or two overtures. Its successor, though, was a disappointment. Wagner adapted *Das Liebesverbot* (*The Ban on Love*) from Shakespeare's *Measure for Measure*, but jettisoned the play's disturbing critique of hypocrisy in high places in Vienna in favour of a farcical study of authority caught, literally, with its trousers down in

Palermo. The music is a kind of Germanised Rossini, garrulous and noisy, with occasional stretches of a more northern lyricism, a fine monologue for the heroine, Isabella, and a big aria (with cabaletta) for the governor Friedrich, Shakespeare's Angelo. But it all led nowhere. Wagner managed a single, shambolic performance in Magdeburg, where he was music director, in March 1836, but a planned second performance was cancelled because of a punch-up between the prima donna's husband and her onstage brother, Claudio, with whom she was having an affair, and the work was never again performed in the composer's lifetime.

After escaping from Riga, he and Minna (and the dog) took ship from Königsberg to London, and from there, after about a week, to Boulogne, where, by one of those mysterious chances that peppered Wagner's life, Meyerbeer was temporarily in residence. By another such chance, Wagner had met on the boat friends of Meyerbeer's who had supplied an introduction, so he accordingly presented himself to the famous composer and read him the libretto of an opera he had been working on about the fourteenth-century Roman demagogue, Cola di Rienzo, based on Edward Bulwer-Lytton's novel *Rienzi, the Last of the Roman Tribunes*. Meyerbeer seems to have listened patiently, and even agreed to look through the music of the first two acts which Wagner had already composed. The whole episode tells us a lot about Wagner's character, his relentless habit of talking about himself, and his impenetrable self-confidence. The aftermath would tell us more. Meyerbeer seems to have been impressed by what he saw of *Rienzi* and to have made genuine moves to help its composer while he was in Paris. It was almost certainly with the help of a recommendation from him that *Rienzi* was accepted for performance in Dresden in 1842. Wagner, though, seldom acknowledged and never forgave help of this kind, and when (for other reasons) he came to write his notorious essay *The Jewish in Music* in 1850, Meyerbeer, though not named, was his unmistakable image of everything that was wrong with music by Jews.

Hans von Bülow called *Rienzi* 'Meyerbeer's best opera'; Charles Rosen called it 'Meyerbeer's worst opera', and John Deathridge, one of the world's leading Wagner scholars, retorted that the work owes more to Auber, Spontini and the Rossini of *William Tell* than to the composer of *Les Huguenots*.[14] It was certainly designed as grand opera from the outset. Its five acts and the sheer scale of the action, with huge crowd scenes setting off a drama of public versus private loyalties culminating in the destruction of the Capitol with Rienzi inside it, make it a classic of the genre. Its historical subject clearly aligns it with *La Muette de Portici* and *Les Huguenots*. Even its length – almost five hours, as compared with the three of *Die Feen* and *Das Liebesverbot* – helps define it. But these crude statistics tell us nothing about the quality of the work. At its core is the first of Wagner's great conflicted heroes: later there will be Tannhäuser, torn between carnal and spiritual love; Walther, forced to temper inspiration with technique; Parsifal, stripping away the body to reveal the soul. Rienzi is the pure-minded popular leader, trusted by the people to restore the grandeur of Rome, brought down by arrogance, intransigence and divided emotion, through his sister's love for the son of his chief patrician enemy, Stefano Colonna. The portrait is vivid and touching, convincing to an extent not found in Meyerbeer, whose Robert, Raoul and Jean de Leyde are strong but not engaging figures.

As with Wagner's two previous operas, there are times in *Rienzi* when things happen in the music that simply do not happen in Spontini, Auber or Meyerbeer. One feels in the presence of a larger musical spirit, one who, even in small gestures or for brief moments, can draw from a situation a radiance or a dark power whose absence is not felt in the work of those other composers because its possibility was unsuspected by them or their audience. This is Schopenhauer's distinction in action: talent hits targets others can't hit; genius hits targets others can't see. Yet *Rienzi* is not like that all the time. It sprawls and drags itself out, it repeats itself, strains the patience and sometimes credulity. The germs of the great Wagner are here, but there is a lot, too, that he needed to discard in the search for a new synthesis that would learn the lessons of these three very different early operas and avoid repeating their mistakes.

8

The Mendelssohn Set

One Sunday morning in October 1825, in the summerhouse of a large mansion on the outskirts of the city of Berlin, eight string players sat down to play a new octet by one of the viola-players. It was an unusual enough work, nothing like an eighteenth-century string divertimento, but a genuine double string quartet lasting fully half an hour and worked out in the manner of a middle-period Beethoven quartet. But the most unusual thing about it was that the composer, the son of the house, was a mere sixteen years old, yet already, it seemed, a complete master of these complicated forms and techniques and able to invest them with musical ideas of great brilliance and sophistication. The composer Felix Mendelssohn's father was a well-to-do Jewish banker by the name of Abraham Mendelssohn who had recently bought and refurbished a semi-palatial but dilapidated house in ten acres just off the Leipzigerplatz and had converted its outsize summerhouse into a concert room with seating for a hundred.

It's hard for us today to think of old Berlin as an emancipated city, but the fact is that, as early as the 1780s, it had been possible for young Jewish women of an intellectual tendency to hold salons attended by leading figures in the city's literary, artistic and political life. At the salon of Henriette Herz, for instance, you might meet the Humboldt brothers, Schiller, Jean Paul, and various members of the Jena group, including Friedrich von Schlegel and the theologian Friedrich Schleiermacher. Another lively salon was that of Dorothea Veit, Abraham Mendelssohn's elder sister, an unconventional, independent-minded woman who in due course left her banker husband and lived openly with Friedrich Schlegel, to the dismay of her family and the horror of the strait-laced Berliners. At her salon in the early days you might, if you were lucky, have coincided with her father, the philosopher Moses Mendelssohn, friend of Lessing and Lavater, who had made money in textiles, was intellectually and socially comfortable in the easy-going bourgeois salons, but steadfastly refused to ease his life further by converting to Christianity.

Dorothea, by contrast, did convert (in 1804, in order to marry the Lutheran Schlegel), and so, somewhat later, did Abraham, his wife Leah, and their four children, Fanny, Felix, Rebecca and Paul. Abraham seems to have had mixed feelings about this step, no doubt conscious of his father's refusal. But conversion would open every door, especially for his children. The atmosphere around his father, Jewishness tolerated for its intellectual brilliance and spiritual force, would be replaced by the bright openness of a garden salon in the most desirable part of the city, where his dazzlingly talented older children could perform to an audience of the most distinguished artists, thinkers and doers in post-Napoleonic Berlin, without any but the most racially bigoted raising an eyebrow or turning on their heel. And it worked. As Abraham himself put it wistfully: 'Once upon a time I was known as the son of my father, now I am known as the father of my son.'

He might just as well, in other times, have been known as the father of his daughter. Fanny, four years older than Felix, was hardly less of a phenomenon. Both as a pianist and as a musician of the mind, she was probably his equal, and there is evidence in the music she composed that she might, given the opportunity, have matched him as a creative genius. She was limited, of course, by 'contemporary social thought on women in the public sphere'.[1] Her own father told her, when she was fourteen, that while 'for [Felix] music will perhaps be a profession, for you it can and should always be only an adornment, never the ground-bass of your being and doing'. With one part of her doing, Fanny accepted this, with her being emphatically not. For much of her life, at least until Felix's marriage in 1837, she lived musically happily in his shadow, acted as sounding-board for his music, often performing it at the Sunday mornings, and above all deferring to his advice against publication of her own work – advice probably given with good intentions but clearly influenced precisely by the considerations that had prompted Abraham's little homily. There was a conventional streak in Felix's make-up that came out in judgements of music as well as of behaviour. Fanny's husband, the painter Wilhelm Hensel, whom she married in 1829, seems not to have shared this attitude; but he was not musical and could not apply pressure in that department.

Where Fanny could not accept her father's advice was in the act of composition itself, and throughout her life, until her sudden tragic death from a stroke at the age of forty-one, she composed prolifically, more than five hundred works, including a large number of songs and short piano pieces, but also a handful of larger works: piano sonatas, cantatas, a masterly string quartet and, at the end of her life, a piano trio that is hardly overshadowed by her brother's two great trios. The plethora of short pieces probably reflects nothing more than that, in the absence of publication or public performance (since the Sunday audiences were by invitation), composition was rather in the manner of a diary, a private activity that mostly precluded the grander gestures of the concert platform or the theatre. All the same these pieces, and especially the songs, are by no means facile homages to the domestic family style. Many of Fanny's songs have a beauty and individuality quite distinct from anything in her brother's vocal music and often its superior. In particular the best of her numerous settings of Goethe, whom she knew and revered, and of Heine, whom she knew and disliked, show an imaginative response to words, or at least verbal atmosphere, comparable to Schumann's, though her piano accompaniments are mostly more conventional – chords, arpeggios, marking the harmony. Her piano pieces, often of a brilliance that presumably reflects the quality of her own playing, are extremely varied in type, and by no means always salon music. A good conspectus is provided by her hour-long cycle *Das Jahr* (*The Year*), composed in 1841, one piece for each month plus a postlude. It includes character pieces like the 'Spring

Song' for May, the hunting song (not so-titled) for October, and a pair of serenades for June and July. But the overall tone is big, bravura, the work of a pianist in complete command of her instrument. The influence of Chopin, whom she had met in Paris in 1835, is apparent in several pieces, most obviously in 'December', whose oscillating thirds resemble those in Chopin's G sharp minor Study, op. 25, no. 6. But Bach is also not far away, in the Easter chorale prelude of 'March', and in the postlude, a setting of the chorale 'Das alte Jahr vergangen ist'. Finally her brother Felix is distinctly audible in 'February', a conscious memory, surely, of his *Rondo capriccioso*.

It seems extraordinary that music of such quality should have gone unnoticed simply because of its composer's gender. The prejudice was not absolute. In France, during these years, there was more acceptance of women in senior musical posts, if not much more enthusiasm for their creative efforts. Hélène de Montgeroult, a pupil of Clementi and Dussek, was herself a piano professor at the Conservatoire from its beginnings in 1795, and wrote an inventive series of *études* that seem to have pioneered the idea of the study as a Romantic character piece, were highly regarded for many years by her Conservatoire successors, but soon vanished with barely a trace from the public sphere. A half-century later, Louise Farrenc was likewise appointed professor of piano at the Conservatoire and composed several accomplished if not highly original chamber works (including a fine pair of piano quintets with double bass, as in Schubert's 'Trout'), which were widely performed in 1850s Paris, but then sank into the oblivion of twentieth-century prejudice until revived in the 1990s by one or two groups in search of fresh repertoire. In Germany meanwhile, Clara Wieck could pursue a successful career as a virtuoso pianist, sometimes playing (and publishing) works of her own, which included a good deal of skilfully wrought, if sometimes rather ordinary, solo piano works, and an excellent piano trio that has at last in recent years begun to achieve the performances it deserves. But Clara rejoiced in – suffered from – an aggressive, pushy father and a broken home. By contrast the Mendelssohns, recent converts, rich, stable and class-conscious, were wary of social deviance, and this, in the Biedermeier age of domestic solidarity, was the more normal attitude.

For all its astonishing mastery, Felix's Octet hardly disrupts this image. On the contrary, its freshness and self-confidence reflect closely, if imaginatively, the optimistic certainties of the new, enlightened Berlin. It was very far from his first substantial work. He already had to his credit a baker's dozen of sinfonias for string orchestra, three piano quartets, four or five concertos, an overture for wind-band, and a full-blown orchestral symphony in C minor. Most of these works had been performed at the Sunday mornings, usually conducted by their composer; and he had also written a series of singspiels or dramatic entertainments, the latest of which, *Die Hochzeit des Camacho*, would shortly find its way on to the stage of the Berlin Schauspielhaus. He and Fanny had been studying music theory with Zelter and singing in his Singakademie choir, and in 1821 Zelter had taken the twelve-year-old Felix to Weimar and introduced him to the septuagenarian Goethe. At sixteen, he might well have burnt out, like many an over-fêted child prodigy. The Octet, on the contrary, showed that he could make an early transition to adulthood and write music that needed no grudging 'brilliant-for-a-teenager' label, and this was confirmed a year later by his Shakespeare overture, *A Midsummer Night's Dream*, an orchestral piece of startling originality and vividness, incorporating graphic effects – scurrying fairies, a braying donkey, rustling leaves, courtly ceremony – in an immaculate sonata design, orchestrated with complete assurance. By the time he was twenty he had added to this tally a pair of beautiful string quartets (in A minor and E flat), a string quintet, a piano sonata, an array of songs, piano pieces and short choral works, and another masterly concert overture, *Meeresstille und glück-liche Fahrt* (*Calm Sea and Prosperous Voyage*), inspired by two poems of Goethe.

The striking thing about this music, taken as a whole, is its freshness of invention, combined with an extraordinary fluency and expertise. It completely lacks the gaucheness of the six-years-older Berlioz at this time, though it perhaps also lacks his potential range. Mendelssohn's technique, along with many aspects of his style, is essentially classical, modelled, one might say, on Mozart rather than Beethoven, though the A minor String Quartet, op. 13, is in part a homage to Beethoven, composed soon after his death in 1827 and alluding to his late quartets. A more modern feature of op. 13 is its cyclic form: not in the sense of a Schubert song cycle, but in the sense that the same musical material comes up, more or less altered, in more than one movement. The basic idea comes from a short song called 'Frage' ('Question', op. 9, no. 1), which Mendelssohn had composed, to his own text, a few months before. 'Is it true?' he asks; he was in love with a local girl, but the musical idea, quoted in the first and last movements of the quartet and distantly alluded to in the other two, comes from Beethoven's F major Quartet, op. 135, with its mysterious last-movement enquiry, 'Muss es sein?' ('Must it be?'), and its answer: 'Es muss sein.'

This is a Romantic thought, but also a Romantic process. The growing use of reminiscence motifs in (especially) French opera of the last thirty years was not merely a way of keeping the audience abreast of the plot, it was an internalisation on the part of the composer. These events, it says, are all connected by my consciousness; through them I offer my experience to you whole. A couple of years after Mendelssohn's quartet, Berlioz would use his *idée fixe* to represent, not the girl, but his obsession with her (the terminology gives the game away). For Mendelssohn, a less self-dramatising character, the device was not so typical, and while he became fond of linking movements physically, for instance, in his Third and Fifth Symphonies and his E minor Violin Concerto, he seldom did so thematically after the Octet and E flat String Quartet, op. 12, whose finales repeat earlier music. For him, the Romantic took pictorial form and came out in a response to landscape or local atmosphere. It was the musical equivalent of the postcard or letter home, as well as in his case – since he was also a gifted artist – the sketch or watercolour: personal but distanced, passionate within decent limits. So, for example, his A minor Symphony (No. 3, the 'Scottish') and his *Hebrides* overture, both inspired by a trip to Scotland in 1829, are musical images of place and atmosphere: the ruined chapel at Holyrood, a bagpipe festival, the storm-tossed sea at Fingal's Cave. But they are model images, beautifully formed, classically conceived. The Grand Tour itself was like that, and it was rather in Mendelssohn's line. It took you by rough roads to wild places, beautiful and sublime, to historic cities and ruins, showed you rustic life and great art of other cultures and your own, but mainly at a safe distance, with a good meal and a comfortable bed at the end of the day. Felix's A major Symphony (No. 4, the 'Italian') is a kind of album of such a trip, made in 1831–2: the thrill of arriving in the southern Alpine valleys, the sudden warmth, the brilliant light, the sounds and smells; a religious procession in Naples (indebted, though, to the Armed Men in Mozart's *Magic Flute*); a graceful minuet in, perhaps, Florence; a breathless saltarello in Rome, ending the major-key symphony, unusually, in the minor. The 'Italian' Symphony is a masterpiece *sui generis*. Yet Mendelssohn seems to have been dissatisfied with it. He conducted it once in London in 1833, but never in Germany, not even in Leipzig, where he went as conductor of the Gewandhaus Orchestra in 1835. Nor was it published in his lifetime.

Mendelssohn may well have had Beethoven in mind, and specifically, one might guess, his Seventh Symphony, also in A major. The parallels are striking: an exuberant, extrovert first movement in six-eight time, a solemn, minor-key processional, a dance-till-you-drop finale. The crucial difference – apart from the third movements, which have nothing much in common – lies in Beethoven's grand, extended slow introduction, which lends a certain rhetorical weight to what follows. His symphony, one feels, is a powerful statement of the Dionysian spirit, where Mendelssohn's is an album of marvellous vignettes, like the exquisite watercolours that still adorn his house in Leipzig. He may have felt this himself, and it will have troubled him. For German composers of his generation Beethoven was both model and obstacle. Whatever they thought about the late works, the 'Choral' Symphony, the last piano sonatas and string quartets, which were still, in the 1830s, quite widely regarded as impossibly eccentric, they could hardly ignore the great works of the middle period, which had recalibrated the whole concept of symphonic music and of classical discourse in general, were successful with audiences, but were dangerous models for young composers who might find difficulty in extracting workable principles from music of such extravagant, transformative power. Brahms's famous remark to Hermann Levi in 1872 – 'I shall never compose a symphony! You don't have any idea how it feels if one always hears such a giant marching behind one.'[2] – spoke equally for the previous generation. Mendelssohn completed five symphonies. But of the five, Nos. 5 and 4 (actually second and third in composition order) were withheld by the composer and published posthumously, and No. 2 (actually fourth) is really a cantata with a three-movement sinfonia as overture; it was published quickly, as was No. 3, the 'Scottish', after its Leipzig premiere in 1842, though it had taken Mendelssohn thirteen years to complete. Only the First Symphony, in C minor, written at the carefree age of fifteen, takes Beethoven on in any serious sense, but perhaps more especially Mozart, in the shape of his late G minor Symphony.

All in all this is a patchy record for so gifted a composer who excelled in instrumental forms and was acutely aware of the tradition in which he was writing. His two piano trios, in D minor and C minor, are major works in the line of Beethoven's op. 70 and op. 97 trios, except that he fights shy of the scale and intensity of their slow movements. His six numbered string quartets, all of which were published in his lifetime except for the great F minor (composed in the shadow of Fanny's death and shortly before his own), are an authentic Romantic approach to an essentially cerebral genre, transferring to it a certain controlled sentimentality within a masterly handling of classical forms and processes. On the other hand, he perfected a new type of orchestral piece that had been slowly crystallising in the work of Beethoven, Weber and, recently, Berlioz: the single-movement, programmatic concert overture.

Beethoven and Weber's concert overtures were mostly connected with dramatic works from which, for various reasons, they became discon-nected. Berlioz's *Waverley* (1827) has notes on the title page of the auto-graph linking the music to Scott's novel, and his *Le Roi Lear* and *Rob Roy* overtures (both 1831) refer obviously to their literary sources. But these works are not the young Berlioz's best, whereas Mendelssohn's *Midsummer Night's Dream* overture is a near-perfect snapshot of the play, and *Calm Sea and Prosperous Voyage* (1828) is a highly effective rendering into music of the Goethe poems. Mendelssohn's technique is to take the various aspects of his source and absorb them into the more or less normal components of a classical orchestral movement. The *Hebrides* overture (1830), inspired initially by the sea at Oban before he and his friend Karl Klingemann embarked for Fingal's Cave, is a superb seascape that at the same time conveys the idea of a voyage, with themes that pass through different weathers before making landfall in a roughly orthodox recapitulation, somewhat compressed.

Mendelssohn had one other great project in the year of the Anglo-Scottish tour. On 11 March 1829 he sat down at the piano in the Berlin Singakademie and directed the first public performance any-where for more than eighty years of Bach's *St Matthew Passion*. Five years earlier he had been given a manuscript copy of Bach's score by his grandmother (who had had it from Zelter), and it is clear from two or three of his own works of the mid- to late twenties that he had studied Bach's music closely and sought to absorb its methods. There was, though, nothing particularly new about this enthusiasm. The Singakademie had been founded in 1791 partly with a view to the performance of Bach's choral music, and Zelter himself had held rehearsals of the B minor Mass and the *St Matthew Passion*, but had concluded that they were no longer performable. Mendelssohn's per-formance thus turned a specialist study into a newsworthy event. It was important that Bach was a German composer, and that choral singing was a collective activity in ways that instrumental music, previously regarded as Bach's true terrain, was not. It went with another musical institution that had emerged in Berlin out of the Singakademie, the smaller *Liedertafel,* or male-voice group, that Zelter organised for the singing of part-songs in regular informal gatherings around the supper table. The *Liedertafel* idea spread widely in Germany and rapidly became a symbol of German bourgeois identity, an urban equivalent of the forests and glens of *Der Freischütz.*

The explosion of amateur choral singing in the early nineteenth century catered for the aesthetic and leisure-time needs of the growing middle class as surely as the building of concert halls and the mass publication of music for the home. The Berlin Singakademie was only the oldest of a growing number of choral societies in Germany, Switzerland and Great Britain in the early decades of the nineteenth century; and while the basis of their repertoire tended to be the oratorios of Handel and Haydn, their existence had naturally spawned new work before the Bach revival of the late twenties. Not much of this work survived into the twentieth century. The most popular oratorio of the early 1820s in Germany, Friedrich Schneider's *Das Weltgericht* (*The Last Judgement*), first performed at Quedlinburg in 1820, was all too expressive of the inevitably limited taste of the average amateur singer or audience member in provincial Saxony. Spohr's treatment of the same subject (1826) at least survived long enough to figure as one of the Mikado's sadistic little punishments in Gilbert and Sullivan's operetta of 1885. These scores were part of the musical landscape in the 1830s when Mendelssohn, having absorbed Bach's greatest choral work, himself turned to writing for choir and orchestra. His immediate response was a beautiful cantata, *O Haupt voll Blut und Wunden* and a superb setting of Psalm 115, both candidly Bachian, richly polyphonic, far removed from Schneider's simple harmony and counterpoint. But he followed these sacred pieces with a crisp choral setting of Goethe's druidic poem *Die erste Walpurgisnacht,* more in the style of Weber, if without the satanic venom of the Wolf's Glen. Then in due course came the three oratorian masterpieces that would clinch his reputation alike in Lutheran Germany and Victorian England: *St Paul* (1836), the second symphony, *Lobgesang* (*Hymn of Praise*, 1840), and *Elijah*, this last actually composed for England, though to a German text, and premiered in Birmingham in 1846.

Modern opinion is ambivalent about these works. Obviously skilful in their creation of an updated version of the Handel oratorio and (in *St Paul*) Bach chorale styles, they nevertheless suffer badly in the comparison. In *St Paul* the tendency of the choruses to break into fugue at every opportunity becomes a mannerism. The formal pietism of Bach reappears now and then as the merely pious, the plain, often predictable harmonies as ever-so-slightly smug. Perhaps Mendelssohn, as a convert from Judaism, was a little too ready to appeal to the sturdy, untormented spirituality of the Protestant soul. Certainly these works made the best headway, and maintained their popularity longest, in the areas of popular hymnody, in Lutheran Germany, and nonconformist northern England and south Wales. But Queen Victoria liked them as well, and this has usually been seen as a bad sign by a later, harder-nosed age with a poor opinion of Victorian taste.

Mendelssohn finally left Berlin early in 1833 to take up a post in Düsseldorf, then in 1835 moved to Leipzig as conductor of the Gewandhaus Orchestra, a position he would hold, in one way or another, for the rest of his short life. The move brought him into contact with a much deeper strand of German music than anything Berlin could offer. Not only was Leipzig the city of Bach, but the Gewandhaus Orchestra was one of the oldest municipal orchestras in Europe and its concert hall one of the oldest halls. In Leipzig, furthermore, were published two of the most important musical journals of the day, the *Allgemeine musikalische Zeitung*, and the recently established *Neue Zeitschrift für Musik*, founded and edited by Robert Schumann. Schumann had had to abandon hopes of becoming a concert pianist because of an accident to his right hand. But as a music critic his right hand would serve music more effectively than any single pianist could ever have done; and as a composer he would carry forward the line of German musical romanticism begun by Weber.

Schumann was only a year or so younger than Mendelssohn, but his background was very different. His father was a book dealer and publisher in Zwickau, but also himself a writer of poetry and Gothic novels, a lexicographer of note, and above all the translator of Byron, Scott and Bulwer-Lytton. The atmosphere in the Schumann home was therefore bookish, and Robert's musical talent, though it appeared early and developed quickly, seems to have sprung from nowhere in particular. Until his late teens literature and music ran neck-and-neck in his affections. At school he helped organise a book club, out of which emerged especially a passion for the novels of Jean Paul. He wrote poetry of his own, translated Theocritus, sketched several plays, and started a diary that tells us a great deal about the inner life of the budding Romantic artist, its passions and obsessions, its profound sense of self, its weakness for sententious philosophising in bits, in the manner of Novalis's pollen. 'Flowers', he muses, 'cover the tears of people in the grave; tears fall on the grave-flowers from people's eyes; thus in life and death every flower is wrapped in tears.' More to the point, he reminds himself that 'everyone has had a time in his life that he would rather not think about'. He does, nevertheless, think about such times. In often painful detail, we read about his loves and losses, the girls who do and don't, and, in due course, the disease, which he never names, referring only to his 'wound', almost certainly the syphilis that would eventually destroy his mind.[3] Above all, the diary is a foretaste of many of the qualities that would make Schumann's music unique; it reveals a mind concentrated not on rules but on experience.

By August 1828 he had started lessons with a Leipzig piano teacher, Friedrich Wieck, and then, after an abortive year studying law in Heidelberg, he returned to Leipzig in 1830, moved in as Wieck's lodger, and began serious work as a pianist-composer. In music theory he was still almost completely untaught. With some reluctance he embarked on theoretical studies with a certain Heinrich Dorn, studies that Mendelssohn, and almost every professional musician before him, had absorbed practically with their mothers' milk. Schumann was perhaps, with Wagner, one of the first musicians in the new mould, in a sense an incomer, profoundly musical in his sensibility but innocent of the textbook.

His first mature works coincided with the start of his lessons with Dorn; they reflect the mental habits of the diarist braced by the disciplines of the piano teacher and the theorist. The verbose title of his op. 1, *Thème sur le nom Abegg varié pour le pianoforte* (1830), is that of a fantasist. The work's dedicatee, Mademoiselle Pauline Comtesse d'Abegg, didn't exist as such, but was at least partly invented by Schumann to explain his theme, which consists of the notes A-Bb-E-G-G, itself a fantasy idea, somewhat cryptic in musical flavour. But the work itself is tightly composed, compact (three variations and a finale), and densely thematic, as well as technically demanding.[4] Op. 2, *Papillons (Butterflies)*, completed in 1831, is a different kind of fantasy. Here a sequence of a dozen short pieces is presented in a montage of sharply defined images, with a few seemingly casual thematic links and a very fluid key sequence. The inspiration for this unusual piano suite was the penultimate chapter of Jean Paul's novel *Flegeljahre*, the account of a masked ball in which the twin brothers Walt and Vult compete for the love of a young Polish girl called Wina, who is actually in love with Walt. The issue is resolved by way of an exchange of costumes, and Vult, angry and disappointed, leaves the ball and the next day vanishes from Walt's life, playing the flute as he goes. *Papillons* is accordingly a dance suite, largely in triple time. In his copy of *Flegeljahre* Schumann marked the passages that related to his work. But with one or two exceptions (notably the ending, which, after the clock strikes six, fades out like Vult) they are not strongly profiled in the music. The real importance of the Jean Paul connection lies in the type of musical discourse, which would become a defining characteristic of Schumann's piano music for the next ten years.[5]

In *Papillons*, Schumann created a kind of music radically different from the essentially classical flow of a contemporary work like Mendelssohn's E flat string quartet. Here everything is momentary, like a thought that vanishes with the next thought, or like figures in the half-light. The pieces are fragments, in Schlegel's sense, 'half-torn pages of life', Schumann called them. After a six-bar introduction, the first *papillon* flies past in under a minute, the second in half a minute, even with repeats of every section. This almost promiscuous sequencing may well have been inspired by Jean Paul's scattergun approach to metaphor:

'Love,' interrupted Vult, 'to speak in your flute-language, is eternally a pain, either a sweet, or a bitter pain; always a night, in which no star arises, until another has gone down – friendship, on the contrary, is a day, where nothing goes down, but, at last, the sun itself – and then – and then, it is dark night, and the devil appears. But, to speak seriously, Love is, at the same time, a bird of Paradise, and a mockingbird – a phoenix of weak ashes, without the sun.'[6]

Music can do this without semantic absurdity, and it can to some extent create its own grammar and its own intuitive continuities. Schumann, as we know from his correspondence and diary, was a tireless improviser. One pictures him at the piano, allowing the ideas to flow under his hands unchecked by best musical behaviour. One idea suggests another which in turn perhaps recalls something familiar, like the antique 'Grossvatertanz' which he quotes twice at the start of the finale of *Papillons*. Nor is this the last time this melody will pop up in his music; or, for that matter, the last time we shall hear the first theme of *Papillons*.

For some years Schumann completed nothing but works for solo piano. At the piano he was in his element, but there was another possible reason for the preoccupation. Friedrich Wieck had a daughter, Clara, eight years old when Schumann first came for lessons, but already an accomplished enough pianist to be performing in public concerts, and destined to grow into one of the finest pianists of the day. Clara probably fell in love with Robert soon after he moved into the house, and no doubt had to grit her teeth as women came and went in his life, including a certain Christel (surname unknown), perhaps a servant of Wieck's, who is sometimes credited with infecting him with syphilis, and culminating in his engagement in 1834 to a fellow Wieck pupil, a certain Ernestine von Fricken. But it was while still engaged to Ernestine early in 1835 that his feelings for Clara crystallised; he soon broke off his engagement, made a secret commitment to the now sixteen-year-old girl, and was then confronted with her father's furious prohibition. Early in 1836, Wieck despatched his daughter to Dresden, where Robert visited her covertly (missing his mother's funeral). Their enforced separation lasted eighteen months, until just before her eighteenth birthday in September 1837, and was followed by a three-year legal battle for her father's consent to their marriage.

But their keyboard relationship pre-dated all this. There were duets, sight-reading, and in 1833 he composed a set of Impromptus (op. 5) on a theme that he attributes to Clara but was actually by him, subsequently borrowed by her. Evidently such intersections arose out of many hours playing together. And, as we have already seen, mystifications of one sort or another were an intrinsic part of his thinking about music. One day in June 1831 he noted in his diary: 'From today I shall give my friends nicer, more suitable names. So I baptise you as follows: Wieck becomes Meister Raro – Clara becomes Cilia – Christel Charitas' and so forth. On 1 July: 'Quite new personages appear in the journal from today – two of my best friends, but who I've never seen before – Florestan and Eusebius.'[7] It turns out that these are simply aspects of Schumann himself. Florestan is the extrovert, outspoken, rather noisy, emotionally unkempt Robert; Eusebius is his quiet, reflective, poetic, self-contained alter ego. Eusebius it is who, later that month, enters the room and places a score on the piano, with an ironic smile, and the remark: 'Hats off, gentlemen – a genius!' The work in question is Chopin's Variations on Mozart's 'Là ci darem', 'An Opus 2', as Schumann labelled his review-cum-short-story in the *Allgemeine musikalische Zeitung* later that year.[8] Thus began both the public career of his alter egos and his own distinguished career as a music critic: the literary and the musical inextricably entwined. Three years later the founding of the *Neue Zeitschrift für Musik* would give him a regular platform for his discussions of the past, present and future of music.

Meanwhile, Florestan and Eusebius popped up in his own music. In 1834, while engaged to Ernestine, he began a work that would embody all his charades and cryptograms. *Carnaval* is one of the great original masterpieces of nineteenth-century piano music, and it would be that even without the elaborate verbal scaffolding that Schumann erected round it. Like *Papillons*, it is a sequence of short movements, fragments almost, joined by subtle threads of similarity for which, however, there is now an encoded explanation. Ernestine's home town was Asch (now Aš), in the Sudetenland, and Schumann, remembering Abegg, is quick to notice that (in German nomenclature) ASCH are all musical letters: A-Eb-C-B. Or it can be read as Ab-C-B. And, being Schumann, he also noticed that the musical letters in his own surname were exactly the same: SCHA = Eb-C-B-A. All three patterns are set out in the score after the eighth movement, labelled 'Sphinxes', in musical notation though clearly not meant to be played. Movement 9, significantly, is called 'Papillons', and movement 10 is 'A.S.C.H.–S.C.H.A. (Lettres dansantes)'. But the letters dance in every piece, mainly Ernestine's four-letter code in the first half of the work, her three-letter code in the second half, Schumann's code everywhere by implication.

All twenty-one movements carry titles, and some of these are characters, real or invented, in Schumann's recently conceived *Davidsbund*, his imaginary League of David against the Philistines in art. Eusebius and Florestan are here, of course, alongside Chiarina (his new name for Clara), Estrella (Ernestine), and – no doubt to their surprise if they came across the Paris edition in 1837 – Chopin and Paganini. Various members of the *commedia dell'arte* put in an appearance: Pierrot, Harlequin, Pantalone and Colombine. The final movement is a 'March of the "Davidsbündler" against the Philistines'. But the real key to *Carnaval* lies in the way Schumann binds it all together. The work is not quite a set of variations, though all the movements except the first pay at least passing homage to the Sphinxes; nor is it a sequence of apparently unrelated improvisations like *Papillons*, though there is a distinct sense of the composer at the piano 'thinking' his three- or four-note motif into different shapes. Behind this flicker of musical ideas lies a serious attempt at a new kind of form, one that arises naturally out of the ideas themselves, and allows them to flow in a network of associations that sometimes goes back on itself while the music hurries on from piece to piece, linked by key sequence, by occasional random-seeming recapitulations, and by the curiously open-ended character of the individual movements, as if each thought can only be completed by the next.

This is the Romantic fragment moulded into high art. Novalis's pollen had spread on the intellectual wind, fertilising through the efforts of others. Music, which exists solely in performance, cannot function in this way. It is a rounded event, or it is nothing. When it stops it finishes, and bleeding ends go on bleeding. This at any rate is the message of *Carnaval*, a continuous, self-contained thirty-minute compilation of organically related incompletenesses forming a completeness. Throughout the 1830s Schumann was searching for large-scale forms to replace the classical forms that had apparently been superseded by the late works of Beethoven. After *Carnaval* he composed a companion piece, the *Davidsbündlertänze* (1837), riskier, because lacking the motivic bonding of its predecessor and somewhat freer in its tonal structure, but if anything still more compelling in its sheer imaginative bravura. This time Schumann initials each dance with an F for Florestan or an E for Eusebius, or both, and closes, not with a defiant march, but with a deprecatory little waltz, ending quietly in C major. Significantly, Clara completely failed to understand these two works. *Carnaval* she called 'my favourite among the smaller pieces you've written' and never played it complete in public until the year he died, while the *Davidsbündlertänze*, though it starts with a quotation from a mazurka of hers, she never played at all until 1860, four years after his death. The concept of a large design that was not a sonata- or variation-type was too novel.

More interestingly, it looks as if Schumann himself was unsure of these works on the classical scale of values. He also tended to refer to the dances as 'these pieces' rather than 'this work', and he certainly acquiesced in the selective performance of *Carnaval*, by Clara, Liszt and others. There was a part of his mind that still believed that great music could only inhabit great forms, and that these forms were, in general, the traditional ones: symphony, sonata, variations. Otherwise there were suites of pieces and books of pieces; the *Davidsbündlertänze* were published in two books. Mendelssohn's *Lieder ohne Worte* (*Songs Without Words*) came out in a series of books, but nobody would think of regarding an individual book as a 'work'; and Schumann himself composed several books of pieces in this sense: two sets of Paganini studies (1832 and 1833), the *Phantasiestücke* (1837), the *Novelletten* and *Kinderszenen* (1838). But there is always something about these works as entities. The last of the *Phantasiestücke* is 'Ende vom Lied', and the last of the *Kinderszenen* is 'Der Dichter spricht' ('The Poet Speaks'), a wise nod of the head at the childish antics of the earlier pieces. Neither end-piece would make much sense on its own. *Kreisleriana* (1838) consists of eight distinct pieces or movements, linked by key sequence, clearly intended to be played complete. Finally there are actual sonatas, in F sharp minor (1832–5) and G minor (1833–8), and the *Concert sans orchestre* in F minor (1835–6), a three-movement sonata in all but name (it was later republished as a four-movement *Grande Sonate*). But perhaps the finest of all the sonata-like works is the *Fantasie* in C major (1836–8), a three-movement piece that starts with an unorthodox sonata movement and ends still more unorthodoxly with a long slow movement, one of his most beautiful pieces of sustained lyrical writing. Schumann originally called the first movement 'Ruins', and with this in mind Charles Rosen described it as 'the triumph of the musical Fragment'.[9] What sets out as a sweeping, passionate Allegro gradually disintegrates, re-forms, digresses into a long, intensely worked intermezzo ('Im Legendenton'), recovers its early momentum, again disintegrates, then finally emerges in a quotation from the final song of Beethoven's *An die ferne Geliebte*: 'Accept them then, these songs, which I sang to you, my beloved.' The *Fantasie* was composed during the separation from Clara, and when he had finished it he wrote to her that it was 'the most passionate thing I have ever composed – a deep lament for you'.

Schumann's reputation as a composer was slow to develop. In his lifetime it probably never equalled Clara's as a pianist, and was certainly far below Mendelssohn's, a fact that he himself seems to have accepted as perfectly reasonable. In musical circles he became best known as a music critic and as editor of the *Neue Zeitschrift*, which he took over as sole editor in January 1835. He rapidly transformed the twice-weekly journal into a mouthpiece for his own strongly held views on the flow of music history. Much of the content he wrote himself: reviews, descriptive articles, think-pieces. His style was sometimes novelistic, with Florestan, Eusebius and Meister Raro prominent, sometimes straightforward, sensible, occasionally analytical, above all astonishingly broad-minded and well-informed by the standards of his time. His reviews, especially, are an invaluable and illuminating guide to the German musical scene from the mid-1830s to the mid-1840s, when he handed over the editorship to Franz Brendel. They are a great encouragement to explore music that, often for reasons other than its quality, has since fallen by the wayside.

Some of this is by composers already discussed in these pages. Schumann took it for granted that composers such as Spohr, Hummel and Field were of major importance in the recent history of music alongside the Liszts and Chopins and Berliozes, whom he recognised as towering figures. His enthusiasm for their work is infectious. Of Field's Piano Concerto No. 7 he assures us that 'the best review would be for the *Zeitschrift* to insert a thousand copies of the concerto for its readers'. But there was also a younger generation of composers 'whose destiny', he wrote, 'seems to be to unchain an epoch that still hangs by a thousand links on the old century'.[10] This was at the start of a long and guardedly appreciative review of a set of piano studies by Ferdinand Hiller (1811–85), a composer, pianist and conductor whose name runs like a thread through the biographies of other composers at this time, but whose own music has vanished from the repertory.

A not dissimilar case is that of the Englishman William Sterndale Bennett (1816–75). Bennett had been a child prodigy in England, a chorister at King's College, Cambridge, a Royal Academy student at the age of nine, and a good enough pianist to perform a Dussek concerto at an Academy concert at twelve. When he was seventeen Mendelssohn heard him playing his own first piano concerto, and promptly invited him to visit him in Germany. Bennett took up the invitation three years later, played and conducted at the Leipzig Gewandhaus at the start of 1837, and was properly befriended by Mendelssohn and by Schumann, who lionised him in the *Neue Zeitschrift* and subsequently reviewed a number of his works, always favourably. But one of Schumann's very first Bennett articles, a review of his *Three Musical Sketches* for piano, already sounds a complimentary note that rings like a death-knell. 'Anyone', he writes, 'will be instantly struck by the speaking family likeness to Mendelssohn.'[11] In fact Bennett's music up to this time, including four piano concertos, five symphonies and two or three attractive symphonic poems, is quite Mendelssohnian, but with poetic elements of its own that might have developed into something still more personal, if he hadn't returned home and allowed himself to be caught up in the stultifying life of the musical institutions of Victorian Britain. Perhaps he welcomed the avalanche of paperwork as an excuse for compositional inertia. Perhaps inspiration failed, though a handful of late works suggest not entirely. In any case, his reputation faded, and some excellent if not very individual music died with it.

Finally there was Norbert Burgmüller, whose death from an epileptic fit in 1836 at the age of twenty-six was certainly one of the great tragedies of early-nineteenth-century German music. Schumann compared it to the loss of Schubert, but had to admit that Schubert had at least composed a great deal of wonderful music in his brief life, whereas Burgmüller had barely started. He had composed a C minor Symphony and most of a second symphony in D, a piano concerto and a twenty-minute piano sonata in F minor, together with a pair of early string quartets and some other piano music. The music is generally somewhat raw, the orchestration in the symphonies rather thick. But there are the beginnings of a distinct individuality and a command of large-scale thinking that is impressive in a composer of such scant experience.

After taking over the *Neue Zeitschrift*, Schumann somehow managed to combine reviewing and editing with composition, occasionally lapsing into periods of depression lubricated by copious quantities of alcohol, until in August 1840 a Leipzig court gave judgement in his and Clara's favour against Wieck, and they were free to marry. And suddenly, at the start of 1840, he abandoned solo piano music and turned to a medium that seemed to make explicit what had previously been implicit: that of song. Over the next year he composed well over a hundred lieder, many of them of a highly original kind that owed comparatively little to the obvious models, Reichardt, Beethoven, Weber, Schubert and Mendelssohn.

Why this abrupt change of direction after a decade of piano music? The previous year he had been in Vienna, had visited Schubert's brother Ferdinand, and been shown a pile of unpublished manuscripts, including the C major Symphony and a number of songs. The symphony, obviously a major find, he had brought back to Leipzig, and Mendelssohn conducted its premiere at the Gewandhaus in March 1839. But perhaps the songs (we don't know which ones) got into his bloodstream and gave him ideas. Not that his own earliest songs are strikingly Schubertian. If Schubert's lieder were built on the expanding possibilities of the piano, Schumann's studiously avoid giving the instrument prominence, at least at first. From the start, in the *Liederkreis* (op. 24, poems by Heine) and *Myrthen* (op. 25, various poets), there is a strong sense of dialogue, of piano and voice springing from the same material. At the same time, the material itself has become simpler, with none of the intricacy of the piano writing in recent works such as *Kreisleriana* or the *Humoreske*. Schumann was clearly aware of the need to aim his songs at an amateur market, but he seems also to have wanted to focus on the words, to make sure that his settings were integrated and coherent extensions of poems that he chose, in his opinion, for their quality as verse, where Schubert had tended to respond to strong images in sometimes mediocre poetry.

These ideas had begun to emerge in Schumann's critical writings of the late 1830s. But they only became precise in the early 1840s, when he had himself begun composing songs. Not surprisingly, in view of his own literary obsessions, he insisted that the song should respond to every nuance of the poem, the voice having the job of capturing its atmosphere, while the piano painted in the detail. Schubert's unbroken accompaniment figures, like the treadle in 'Gretchen am Spinnrade' or the stream in 'Liebesbotschaft', struck him as too general, and a dangerous model, one he nevertheless occasionally adopted in his own songs, especially in the lush settings of Eichendorff in his second *Liederkreis* set, op. 39: the soughing treetops in 'Schöne Fremde', the trembling thrill of spring in 'Frühlingsnacht'. More often, though, there is a meticulous quality about the piano writing, as if the composer were listening intently for the poet's hidden nuances. A fine early example is 'Der Nussbaum' in the *Myrthen* set, where the piano weaves a pattern of melody round the words, like the 'fragrant, airy foliage' of the walnut tree. More profound is the setting of Eichendorff's 'Zwielicht', which expresses the fear and distrust of falling darkness as a sinister, creeping polyphony of piano lines in the manner of a Bach fugue.

Op. 39 is a *Kreis*, literally a circle, but not yet a cycle in the narrative sense, though it has recurrent topics: night, fear, alienation, the thrill of Nature or remote antiquity, all authentic Romantic themes. But in the spirit of his cycles for piano, it was natural for Schumann to take the extra step and compose a narrative or quasi-narrative cycle in which a story, if not actually told, is clearly implied, in the thoughts and memories of a central character: the singer. His first work of this type, *Frauenliebe und -leben* (*A Woman's Love and Life*), is a setting of eight poems by Adelbert von Chamisso, tracing the brief history of the heroine's love from its beginning, through marriage and motherhood to widowhood. Schumann then returned to Heine and composed *Dichterliebe* (*A Poet's Love*) out of a selection of twenty – eventually reduced to sixteen – poems from Heine's *Lyrisches Intermezzo*. *Frauenliebe und -leben* presents certain difficulties for modern taste because of the heroine's abject devotion to her apparently flawless husband, whose only fault is to die young, leaving her with nothing but retreat into her inner self. It is, nevertheless, a work of great beauty, formally balanced, subtle in word-setting, marvellously well written for, ideally, the mezzo-soprano voice. Whether or not Schumann saw his coming relationship with Clara in this light, he was surely thinking musically above all. The piano's return at the end of the final song to the music of the opening is a purely structural device, presumably not meant to contradict the poem by suggesting that the woman is now emotionally where she was at the start of the affair, as if nothing had happened in between.

Dichterliebe is both psychologically more convincing and a more intricate design. It similarly traces an affair of the heart from its radiant beginning to its bitter end, brought about, however, not by death, but by infidelity, as described in a burst of rage in the eleventh song, 'Ein Jüngling liebt ein Mädchen'. This time, Schumann links the songs as a series of brief or actually incomplete fragments, like consecutive diary entries that imply a sequence of events by detailing the feelings they aroused. Throughout, this incompleteness hints at an anxiety. The extraordinary first song, 'Im wunderschönen Monat Mai', is, as it were, a piano piece in F sharp minor with a song in A major on top of it; but the voice ends in the wrong key (the subdominant, D major), the piano ends without resolving its own harmony, and the tiny second song, eventually in A major, starts on a chord that might be in either of the first song's two keys. So the fair month of May is already shrouded in mist; and soon Heine's ironies begin to do their own damage. 'When you say "I love you," I can only weep bitter tears' (in No. 4); 'I shan't complain, even though you break my heart' (No. 7); 'I dreamt you were still faithful, and woke up with tears streaming down my face' (No. 13). Schumann picks up every detail. The uncomplaining 'Ich grolle nicht' complains superbly, violently, from start to finish, in a majestic C major. The piano's fiddle music in 'Das ist ein Flöten und Geigen' dances along untroubled by the poet's jealousy at the girl's dancing with another, but in a mocking minor key. Near the end he dreams of her; she greets him kindly but shakes her head sadly, gives him a cypress frond, then says something that, when he wakes up, he can't remember; and in a soft three-chord ending, the piano forgets it as well. This is the end of the affair. In the penultimate song it dissolves like foam, but then at the very end the poet orders a dozen giants to lay his songs and dreams, his love and his pain, in an enormous coffin and dump it in the sea. So much for the foam; but we know how he feels, and so does the piano. In a beautiful coda – more precise than the one in *Frauenliebe und -leben* – it reminds the poet of the wise advice of the birds at the end of an earlier song (No. 12): 'Don't be cross with our sister, you pale, unhappy man.'

Schumann's treatment of the voice/piano relationship here reaches a pitch of refinement that even Schubert seldom achieved. The technique is to simplify the vocal lines in the general direction of folk song, while the piano, like a sympathetic bystander, sometimes casts doubt, sometimes agrees, occasionally teases, comments all the time, especially in the postludes that have by this time become a Schumann trademark. It catches beautifully the shifting meanings so typical of Heine, and it does so with a masterly economy of means that Schumann had learnt composing his piano suites. *Dichterliebe* is about the same length as *Carnaval* or the *Davidsbündlertänze*, and similarly made up of fragmentary, quasi-incomplete units; but the music now speaks its mind, where previously the thoughts were locked up in a fascinating but secret code.

9

The Nation Takes the Stand

Wagner had left German soil furtively, by night, escaping creditors and evading border guards and the harbour watch at Königsberg. His return, in April 1842, was altogether more legitimate, if only marginally more comfortable: five days in the Paris–Dresden coach instead of three storm-tossed weeks on the Baltic and North Seas. He had a new opera, *Der fliegende Holländer* (*The Flying Dutchman*), up his sleeve that was in some ways a memory of that earlier trip and that he hoped to get performed in Berlin. Meanwhile Dresden, thanks in large part to Meyerbeer, was programming *Rienzi*, initially in the summer, then eventually in October. Approaching his thirtieth year, Wagner remained without even the slightest significant success as a composer and with little to show for his other musical activities. All that, however, was about to change.

The first performance of *Rienzi* was conducted by the Kapellmeister of the Dresden Court Opera, Karl Reissiger, and it lasted well over five hours. As the evening dragged on, Wagner became more and more convinced that the audience would give up on it and go home early. He seemed not to hear the tumultuous applause for each act, and was of course unaware, in his stage box, of the excited babble of foyer conversation in the intervals. The opera was a triumph, and its success transformed Wagner's entire situation. Suddenly, from being a mere nuisance, known only to the harassed theatre managers and music directors whom he had plagued with his persistent importunings, he became a figure of some public fame whose work was in demand. Munich had turned down *The Flying Dutchman*, Berlin had equivocated about it; but now Dresden was planning to stage the premiere in the new year and Wagner was in the relatively happy position of having to prise the score out of a reluctant Berlin directorate. In the event the *Dutchman*, an opera of an utterly different type from *Rienzi*, was received coolly in Dresden; but Wagner had by this time already been mooted as second Kapellmeister at the Court Opera, and he was duly appointed in February 1843, with a job description that gave him, in theory, the power to institute changes, initiate reforms, generally impose himself on what he now saw as the lax musical and operatic standards prevailing at the court of the Catholic king of Lutheran Saxony.

Wagner's tenure would last just over six years until May 1849. *The Flying Dutchman* would be followed, in 1845, by *Tannhäuser*, by the composition but not yet performance of *Lohengrin*, and by the first drafts of the scenario of the *Ring*. As if that were not enough mental activity for a busy Kapellmeister, he also drew up two major reports of a practical nature, one in 1846 proposing reforms to the orchestra, covering issues such as seating arrangements in the pit, the hiring and firing of players, their salaries, holidays and deputies, all matters that Weber, in his time at Dresden, had also tried to reform; the other in May 1848 in the form of a plan for a German National Theatre in Dresden, involving a complete restructuring of the directorate, the founding of a drama school, expanding the orchestra, and other such trivial reforms guaranteed to meet with the approval of officials whose jobs would effectively be abolished in the process. Discretion was a virtue unknown to Richard Wagner. Revolution was in the air, and both proposals were rejected. Yet they remind us that he was no wild visionary, but an experienced practical man of the theatre, with lofty artistic ideals, certainly, but also a clear sense of what was possible and desirable in the performance and production of complex operas.

The Flying Dutchman was the first work that Wagner regarded as authentically his. His first three operas had arguably been sacrifices on one or another altar; the *Dutchman* was his alone. Old-fashioned in some respects, no doubt; it still bore traces of the magical German romanticism of *Der Freischütz* and the various *Rübezahls*

and *Berggeists*. The Dutchman's search for a faithful woman to rescue him from his eternity of seafaring is not essentially different from
Undine's need, in Hoffmann's opera, to marry a mortal in order to gain
a soul. Only, Wagner's treatment endows the redemptive idea with a
spiritual weight that was beyond the reach of his predecessors. The
Dutchman's monologue when he first lands on the shore at Sandwike
has a psychological force that distantly foreshadows the angry Wotan
of *Die Walküre*. When Senta and the Dutchman soar up to heaven in
each other's arms, an ending that Wagner revised several times, we are
already moving towards *Tristan und Isolde*. It's true that a lot else is
four-square and singspielish. The spinning chorus, pretty and cleverly
scored as it is, would not be out of place in *Der Freischütz*; Daland's
'Mögst du, mein Kind' perhaps reflects a shade too flatly his mercenary soul as he introduces his daughter to the unexpected goldmine he
has just met on the beach; Erik, Senta's hunter-fiancé, is Weber's Max
gone north, a tormented, not a heroic, tenor. Even Senta's ballad, comparatively sophisticated though it is musically and though it contains a
number of the work's main musical ideas, stands out rather too sharply
as a 'set piece', a lied in modified strophic form. At times, *The Flying
Dutchman* can have the feeling of a number-opera in disguise.

Yet Wagner was certainly thinking in quasi-symphonic terms, in
the *Euryanthe* rather than *Freischütz* mould. The work is saturated
with motifs of the sea and the wind, providing a continuity of imagery
that to some extent overrides its sectional character: the Dutchman's
horn calls, the swirling, gusty string figures from the overture, various melodic and rhythmic ideas from the Steersman's song, the sailor's
choruses, and Senta's ballad. The whole score is coloured in that way,
turning reminiscence motifs into something approaching the leitmotifs
of the *Ring*. Wagner's real model in all this was Beethoven, and especially the 'Choral' Symphony, an obsession of his since he had made
a piano transcription of it as a schoolboy. The very start of the opera,
with its *tremolo* string fifths and open fifth horn calls, is a clear echo of
the symphony's first page, in the same D minor. In Beethoven's finale, a

bass soloist leaps to his feet, interrupts the orchestra, and demands 'not these sounds, my friends! but let us sing ones more pleasant, and more joyful'. It's as if the Beethoven problem were in the minds of instrumental composers. Its solution lay with the human voice, in opera.

One other aspect of Wagner's source-consciousness is hinted at in *The Flying Dutchman*. He was a voracious reader who would pick up an idea from some book or other, then allow it to brew in the company of other, superficially unrelated ideas from the next book. He always wrote his own librettos. He had a genius for lateral thinking, for the synthesis of concepts. His *Dutchman* was a reasonably compact example of this mental habit: a well-known legend, of the ship's captain who swore he would round the Cape of Good Hope if he had to sail till the Day of Judgement, passed through the filter of stories by Heine and others. But even while at work on this fairly straightforward project, he was turning over in his mind a more complex subject, which finally emerged in 1845 as *Tannhäuser und der Sängerkrieg auf Wartburg* (*Tannhäuser and the Song Contest on the Wartburg*).

Tannhäuser is another variation on those operatic tales about the conflict between the dull everyday world and the enticing but dangerous other world of magic and eternal delight. Tannhäuser is a thirteenth-century troubadour who, when the opera begins, has somehow strayed into the mountain of eternal sex known as the Venusberg. We find him in Venus's arms surrounded by nymphs, naiads and the rest, but already weary of the sensual life and anxious to escape. In due course he succeeds, meets his former fellow troubadours and is able to take part in their song contest to be judged by the pure Elisabeth. But when his turn comes to sing, instead of praising virtuous love in the accepted manner, he raves about the delights of the Venusberg and urges them all to follow him thither. Barely rescued by Elisabeth from the fury of the assembled knights, he is ordered to Rome to plead for forgiveness. But the Pope, on hearing the details of his sin, refuses him absolution 'until this staff of mine should sprout leaves'. So Tannhäuser comes back to Thuringia intending to return to the Venusberg, only to find that the dying Elisabeth has redeemed him by her prayers, just as the staff of some passing pilgrim duly bursts into leaf.

Tannhäuser is a grander opera than *The Flying Dutchman*, and more in the Parisian mould, with a big ceremonial central act, a ballet, a lot of chorus and group participation, and a more diffuse, less concentrated dramaturgy. Wagner revised it many times, for Paris in 1861, and again for Vienna in 1875. But it remains, in every version, an uneven work, mixing original invention with passages of a rather stolid conventionality. Even in the original Dresden score of 1845, the harmonic language (especially in the Venusberg music) sometimes looks forward to the modernisms of *Tristan*. But Wagner is making a point. The sensual existence is disorientating psychologically, hence harmonically. But when Tannhäuser emerges into a sunlit valley near the Wartburg, the music has to convey the honest normality of the knightly troubadours, and the holy simplicity of the pilgrims. Wagner clearly found this contrast hard to make convincing without overstating the vulgarity of Venus's subterranean brothel on the one hand and the purity of everything else on the other.

Tannhäuser brings together two unrelated medieval legends: the story of Heinrich von Ofterdingen, a troubadour who solicits the aid of black magic to help him win the song contest, and the tale of Tannhäuser, who while travelling the world fetches up in the Venusberg, wearies of its delights, goes to Rome to be shriven, but on receiving the Pope's refusal, returns to the Venusberg.[1] The melding of these legends suggests various levels of allegory. Most obviously, it argues the difficulty of balancing our spiritual and sensual passions, and by presenting this conflict in musical terms it raises the issue of new-versus-old, familiar-versus-unfamiliar, which will come up again in *Die Meistersinger von Nürnberg*. But there is a cruder argument going on here as well. We are in the thirteenth century, so the main participants (except presumably Venus) are Roman Catholics. But Wagner draws a distinction that strictly belongs to a post-Reformation time. The Germans on the Wartburg are sturdy, upright citizens who say their prayers and love the whole person, not just the body. They have read, one feels, Luther's *Ninety-five Theses*. The Pope, by contrast, an Italian, is a hypocrite who preaches one thing, but performs its opposite. There is even something *parisienne* about Venus and her scantily clad (albeit Wagnerian) courtesans. *Tannhäuser*, if not quite a nationalist tract, can easily be read as an invitation to divide nations into types.[2]

Throughout these years, Wagner read and read. He read history, especially German history; he read literature (not only German), and about literature; he certainly knew his Grimm, his Hoffmann and his Tieck; and he explored Teutonic and Nordic mythology. He was acquiring a Herderian sense of German culture, and at the same time he was evolving political views that would colour his work and complicate his life. Already in the early 1830s he had befriended a political activist called Heinrich Laube, a leading light in the Young Germany movement which stood out against the autocratic structure of German politics and the conservatism of German society, advocating democracy, individualism, free love and the emancipation of women. In particular, Laube and co. detested romanticism of the escapist kind, the forests and fairies, the medieval castles and magic bullets. Art, for them, had to be engaged, politically active, a bearer of ideas rather than mere images or moods. Not all of this was what we would now call socialism; it was utopian, anarchist, but at the same time proto-nationalist, at least in the German context, where the abolition of local autocracies naturally implied unification. Wagner swallowed all this, and its effects are to be seen in his music and in his increasingly voluminous prose writings of the 1840s. Admittedly his politics always contained an element of self-interest; the political changes he advocated were largely towards conditions that would favour the performance of his own somewhat complicated operas. He wanted less power in the hands of apparatchiks, more in the hands of artists.

Nationalism was associated with liberalism in other ways in the years before the revolutions of 1848. In the German states it meant unification, but in the non-German territories of the old Habsburg, now Austrian, Empire, it was particularist and separatist. The Czechs of Bohemia and Moravia, the Poles in Galicia, naturally resented the Germanising tendencies of their rulers; a Czech or Polish government would be more liberal, more attentive to the needs of non-German local people. Nationalism of this kind was, like most ideas, slow to emerge in music, not least because the dominant model, which happened to be German, was so overpowering. Wagner's nationalism had no need to find new modes of musical expression and could concern itself exclusively with subject matter. For non-Germans the issue was less straightforward. Chopin could incorporate Polish turns of phrase in mazurkas, but his larger pieces mostly lack that element. Liszt's music up to about 1839 has many individual qualities and much new thinking, but none of it is noticeably Hungarian. He never felt Hungarian (his mother tongue was German), until 1838, when he read about the catastrophic floods in and around Pest, the low-lying half of the not yet unified Hungarian capital. This seemed to trigger some latent patriotic feelings. He at once programmed a series of fundraising recitals in Vienna, and in 1839 travelled to Hungary for the first time since his childhood. His first musical tribute was an arrangement of the Rákóczy March. He visited a gypsy encampment, listened to gypsy music, and composed his *Magyar dallok*, the original versions of the *Hungarian Rhapsodies*, in the so-called *verbunkos* style that was subsequently regarded as gypsy, not Hungarian. The distinction hardly matters. Liszt believed himself to be writing in an ethnically Hungarian style, as he might have donned national costume for some welcoming ceremony in Budapest.[3]

In Budapest he will certainly have met a young composer called Ferenc Erkel, chief conductor at the recently founded Hungarian National Theatre. Erkel was at work on an opera, *Bátori Mária*, a fairly stock through-composed tragedy in an idiom essentially derived from Weber by way of Rossini, but with *verbunkos* touches that Erkel extended in his next opera, *Hunyadi László*, premiered in 1844. Here the subject is specifically Hungarian; the Hunyadis were an important fifteenth-century Hungarian family of soldiers and politicians, but the opera deals with the fate of one in particular (László), who had enemies, and the misfortune to be betrothed to a girl whom the king also loved. The opera, which ends with László's execution, is musically a striking piece of work with a superb soprano part for the hero's mother; but the Magyarisms are still fairly localised – a few rhythmic details, some cadential shapes, a csárdás dance in Act 3. Not till 1861 did Erkel produce a profoundly Hungarian work in *Bánk bán*, a setting of one of the best-known nineteenth-century Hungarian plays, saturated with *verbunkos* elements and simpler, earthier in style than *Hunyadi László*, which perhaps explains its continuing popularity in Hungary. But the earlier work has stronger claims on performance abroad, and is perhaps only held back by the difficulties of the Hungarian language, with its persistent first-syllable accent and complex word-formation, which make translation awkward.

These early proto-nationalist operas seldom concern themselves with the political issues of the day. They are still largely about the antics of the historically remote aristocracy, who are admittedly often shown in a bad light. It seems that the urban, and even the rural, poor were still regarded as unsuitable subjects for serious art. One partial exception is *Halka* by the Polish composer Stanisław Moniuszko, composed in 1846–7 and set in a Tatra mountain village of that time. Halka is a peasant girl who has been seduced and had a child by an impoverished aristocrat, who, to Halka's despair, is now marrying a rich girl of his own class. Moniuszko's villagers are poor and downtrodden but not noticeably rebellious, while the toffs are unblushing autocrats yet warm-hearted enough to show sympathy for poor Halka, who eventually drowns herself in the river. The image is of a perhaps regrettable but rigid social order that has its personal misfortunes, rather than of evil landowners trampling heartlessly on the peasantry, and the music observes the class distinctions but avoids moralising through satire or exaggeration. So the wedding guests are associated with the courtly polonaise, while the villagers dance the mazurka and the *goralski*, and

Halka sings in a kind of enriched folk-song idiom. The net result of all this is a degree of emotional realism, though the form is conventional, with arias, ensembles, choruses and dances.

In Italy, as we saw in connection with Bellini and Donizetti, nationalism had become less a purely cultural matter, more a question of politics. The Risorgimento was all about unification, and that meant ejecting foreign rulers. So central was this movement to Italian political consciousness in the 1830s and 1840s that it's surprising how few operas concerned themselves with it, even when, as was often the case, their subject matter was in a broad sense political. The two next most important opera composers in Italy in the thirties, Mercadante and Pacini, composed about a hundred and forty operas between them, but hardly any of them seem to deal noticeably with this burning issue. Mercadante was politically liberal, but in his various posts, in Lisbon, Madrid, and as director of the Naples Conservatory, it was more important for him to keep in with the ruling monarchies. The composer most closely associated with the Risorgimento is Giuseppe Verdi, the son of an innkeeper in the village of Roncole, a few miles south of Cremona, who had spent most of the first quarter-century of his life as a small-town organist, conductor and music teacher in nearby Busseto, but eventually, in 1839, contrived to have an opera of his, *Oberto*, staged at La Scala, in Milan. *Oberto*, a tale of rape and revenge in thirteenth-century Bassano, was successful enough for the manager of La Scala, Bartolomeo Merelli, to commission further work from the twenty-six-year-old composer, beginning with a comic opera, *Un giorno di regno* (*King for a Day*), which crashed disastrously at its first performance in 1840. Merelli, however, kept faith, and Verdi's third opera, *Nabucco*, staged at La Scala in March 1842, rewarded them both with a spectacular success that overnight turned Verdi into the most wanted composer in Italy.

Verdi considered *Nabucco* to be the real beginning of his career. Yet what it actually did was subject him to his 'galley years', during which the typically Italian demand for opera after opera resulted in works of uneven quality and for a time undermined his health. It also ensured that his work would remain broadly within the existing tradition of Italian opera. Here and there he would attempt to vary individual conventions. But there is little in early Verdi comparable to Wagner's move towards the symphonic style that culminated in his theoretical essays around 1850. Verdi had ideas and intentions, but he never theorised. It's worth comparing his early operas in this respect with the work of Italian contemporaries. At his best, Mercadante can sound as good as early Verdi, and even rather *like* Verdi. Pacini's *Saffo*, staged in Naples in 1840 and supposedly one of his best operas (of about eighty), sometimes suggests Verdi in his lighter moments, but without the emotional range or melodic brilliance that Verdi already commanded in *Nabucco*. At his worst in the galley years, Verdi was more energetic and athletic, noisier, sometimes cruder than these older composers. Works like *I due Foscari* (1844) and *I masnadieri* (*The Robbers*, after Schiller, 1847), are enjoyable to hear now and then, but the experience is a little like watching a good western; broadly one knows what to expect, and great subtlety is not on the agenda. *Nabucco* is a different matter. Temistocle Solera's libretto about the Babylonian captivity had previously been rejected by Otto Nicolai, the future composer of that comparative rarity, a genuinely witty and tuneful German comic opera, *Die lustigen Weiber von Windsor* (*The Merry Wives of Windsor*); and the story goes that, after the failure of *Un giorno di regno*, Verdi contemplated giving up opera altogether until Merelli handed him Solera's libretto and he was smitten by its combination of monumental choruses and intimate emotional drama. Whether it occurred to him to think of the captivity as in some sense an allegory of 'occupied' Italy, the audience at the premiere certainly saw it that way. The choral writing throughout has a kind of collective splendour that, in the context, inevitably puts one in mind of great popular movements, while the way Verdi projects these feelings downwards, so to speak, into the hearts of his individual characters whose lives are afflicted by events on the world stage reveals a genius for transition that Wagner, who once called opera 'the art of transition', should surely have admired. Here it is perfected in the unison chorus, 'Va pensiero', where personal longing and public protest come together in what amounts to a choral lament of the purest simplicity: 'Go, thought, on gilded wings; go, settle on the hills and slopes, where the gentle breezes of our native soil spread a cool, soft fragrance . . . Oh my country, so beautiful and lost!'

The success of *Nabucco* encouraged Verdi to give an important role to the chorus also in his next opera, *I Lombardi alla prima crociata* (*The Lombards at the First Crusade*), the fourth and for many years last of his Milan premieres (1843). And he repeated the unison idea in the one after that, *Ernani*, in which a Sullivanesque chorus of conspirators against the king draw their swords and vow to end their supposed servitude, to the splendid tones of 'Si ridesti il Leon di Castiglia'. But *Ernani* is a different kind of opera from its two predecessors. Though Hugo's play had started a riot fourteen years before, its subject matter is a typically arcane Spanish entanglement of love and honour, in which the hero Ernani, the elderly knight Silva, and the young king Carlos of Spain fight it out over Silva's niece, Elvira, whom the crusty old knight is himself planning to marry. For Verdi, this is a drama of character, with the three male leads distinguished by voice type: the tenor Ernani, the brash, Romantic outlaw robbed of his lands by Carlos's father; the baritone Carlos himself; and the ponderous old bass Silva. These are very far from pasteboard figures. They evolve both in themselves and in relation to each other, and the music reflects these changes, while poor Elvira looks on, helplessly defending her honour while being handed around like a bottle of wine, until Ernani, having finally won her, stabs himself, apparently for no better reason than some obscure promise to Silva. *Ernani* is a work of considerable melodic and harmonic presence, and rhythmically incisive, though not without the time-honoured Italian oompahs in the quicker cabalettas and choruses. The plot is of course absurd; but by creating musically believable characters, Verdi somehow persuades us to accept their bizarre behaviour.

The only other galley opera on anything like this level is *Macbeth*, composed in 1846–7 and premiered in Florence in March 1847. Verdi was a huge admirer of Shakespeare; all his life he intended, but never managed, a *King Lear*. But no doubt he was drawn to *Macbeth* especially for its powerful character portraits and the sombre Scottish atmosphere that surrounds and engulfs them. In particular the lengthy confrontations of Macbeth and his wife, and her sleepwalking scene, are the most complex things he had yet composed. Their scene together after the murder of Duncan is a genuine, self-contained dramatic *scena*, the music following the broken, tortured character of the conversation in a manner quite different from the normal recitative/aria pattern, with telling contributions from the orchestra. Lady Macbeth's sleepwalking scene is subtly different. Here Verdi writes what is essentially an aria, underpinned by a persistent rising figure in the strings, but with the lyricism of the voice part fragmented and reassembled as a musical soliloquy. The effect of looming insanity within a formal frame is both horrifying and curiously touching. The work has its crudities as well: its crowds of witches and murderers and castle personnel, its rattling cabalettas and rousing choruses. This is not yet the fully mature Verdi, though he seldom composed anything more fascinating than the mysterious scene of the apparition of the eight Scottish kings. Oddly enough, this was disliked by the hard-nosed Italian critics, who apparently regarded the *genere fantastico* as some kind of transalpine aberration.

Like Mercadante, Verdi was a friend of the Risorgimento. But this is only occasionally apparent from his operas. *Giovanna d'Arco* (*Joan of Arc*) is close in subject matter, but not strong enough to make the point musically. *Alzira* and *Attila* involve invasion or foreign occupation (Peru and ancient Italy respectively), but treated as exotic settings for personal rather than political conflict. *Macbeth* is about 'who rules?'; and so forth. The truth probably is that Verdi, like other Italian composers, was drawn to subjects where political circumstances created emotional divisions (*Don Carlos* and *Aida* are classic later examples), though it is also fair to point out that in the 1840s any open or implied advocacy of the Risorgimento would have brought the censors down on one's head. Verdi's one unequivocal liberation opera, *La battaglia di Legnano*, about the expulsion from Italy of the German emperor Frederick Barbarossa by the Lombard League in 1176, was composed in the year of revolutions, 1848, and performed in Rome in January 1849 during the brief Roman Republic under Mazzini and Garibaldi. When the Republic collapsed in July it vanished from the stage.

Nationalism and opera were natural bedfellows. As Herder had argued, every country had its stories, its legends and myths, not to mention its language and folk songs. But in music without narrative – instrumental music – it was at first a fragile growth. Writing about the Danish composer Niels Gade in 1843, Schumann observed that 'it looks as if the nations bordering on Germany have wanted to emancipate themselves from the dominance of German music; a Germanist might perhaps regret this, but to the deeper thinker and connoisseur of human nature it will seem only natural and gratifying'. However, he added the cautious hope 'that the artist doesn't somehow drown in his nationality . . . Every artist might be urged first to achieve originality then to reject it, shuffling off his old skin like a snake when it begins to crush him.'[4]

Gade, for one, took Schumann's advice. A native of Copenhagen, he had been for several years a violinist in the Royal Danish Orchestra and a moderately successful composer of songs and chamber music when in 1840 he won a competition with an orchestral piece called *Efterklange af Ossian* (*Echoes of Ossian*), and then soon afterwards sent his First Symphony to Mendelssohn, who duly conducted its first performance in March 1843. Presumably as a result of the success of this performance, the Danish government paid for Gade to go in person to Leipzig, and there he got on so well that within a short time he was appointed Mendelssohn's deputy. He stayed in Leipzig until 1848, by which time, Mendelssohn having died the previous year, Gade had become the orchestra's chief conductor. He left Leipzig only because of the outbreak of war in Schleswig-Holstein.

Echoes of Ossian and the First Symphony (of, eventually, eight) do have a distinctly Nordic flavour, though it's hard to put one's finger on exactly why. Something in the voicing of the string chords at the start of the Ossian piece suggests an ear attuned to the open spaces of the far north (though Copenhagen is hardly that), and both here and in the symphony folk music is somewhere in the background of the material, though the procedures are textbook. Perhaps the fact that the symphony is partly based on an earlier song of Gade's might suggest that the Danish language has had an influence on the music's tone. But as time went on, Gade regressed (or as Schumann might have argued, progressed) increasingly to the Leipzig image, gradually shedding his Scandinavian snakeskin, and turning into a lively product of the conservative German school.

Schumann's idea that originality, in the sense of unorthodoxy, might be limiting may seem strange, considering that, for the Romantic composer such as he had himself palpably been as a young man, originality was a first requirement. But Schumann was influenced in the end by his conviction that, to be a great composer, it was necessary to succeed in the great classical genres, which might well mean stifling the more wayward impulses. He probably never encountered the symphonies of the Swede Franz Berwald, which were played in Vienna, but not in Leipzig. Had he done so, he might have found them unusual but lacking in depth. Berwald's music is unorthodox in a number of respects; its forms are highly individual, and its harmonic vocabulary sometimes strange to the point of eccentricity. It is a thoughtful, independent-minded music, not ethnic but the work of a free-spirited northerner. There is little warmth in it, and hence a certain limitation of feeling. 'Art', he told himself, 'may be coupled only with a cheerful frame of mind. The weak-willed should have nothing to do with it. Even if

interesting for a moment, in the end every sighing artist will bore listeners to death. Therefore: liveliness and energy – feeling and reason.'⁵

The 1840s were a time when new kinds of composer were popping
up all over the place. Opera in particular had everywhere become the
bourgeois entertainment *par excellence*. Works like Michael Balfe's *The
Bohemian Girl* (1843), Vincent Wallace's *Maritana* (1845) or Friedrich
von Flotow's *Martha* (1847) were sentimental Romantic comedies of
an unashamedly commercial character consisting of series of instantly
hummable tunes, including, in *Martha*, an already popular ballad,
'The Last Rose of Summer'. In Paris, the more sophisticated tradition
of Boieldieu's *La Dame blanche* and Auber's *Fra Diavolo* was maintained by Adolphe Adam's *Le Postillon de Lonjumeau* (1837), not to
mention his ballet *Giselle* (1841), another tale of fairyland, and the
apotheosis of the decorative style that characterised French Romantic
ballet before Delibes. In Germany, Albert Lortzing composed a series
of witty, musically stylish comedies, including *Zar und Zimmermann*
(*Tsar and Carpenter*, 1837, about Peter the Great's time as a ship's carpenter in Holland) and *Der Wildschütz* (*The Poacher*, 1842), works that
skilfully and elegantly updated singspiel into the Biedermeier period.
Lortzing, incidentally, is a tragic illustration of the injustices of an age
before a proper royalty system and enforceable copyright law, a particular problem in Germany, with its plethora of independent mini-
states. Lortzing's best works were wildly successful but brought him
little income beyond the initial theatre payments, and he spent his last
years in poverty while his works continued to play in theatres all over
Germany.

Balfe and Wallace were both Irishmen, and their success inevitably
raises the much asked, seldom answered question why English music
of this period was so generally undistinguished. The curious English
assumption that composers had to be foreigners, or at least have foreign names, might serve as an explanation, though it is, of course, not
that at all, but a raising of the question in other terms. Opera had to
be in Italian; in the early 1900s, *Il seraglio* and *Il flauto magico* were still

to be heard at Covent Garden. English was the language of oratorio, but even here the field was dominated by foreigners: Handel, Haydn and Mendelssohn. There was certainly a social stigma against professionalism in the arts, while on the other hand the new professionals, in business and industry, had neither the time nor the taste for such frippery. The English welcomed great music and musicians from abroad. Haydn's London symphonies were premiered there, and Beethoven's Ninth, commissioned by the Philharmonic Society, would have been if it had been completed in time. Mendelssohn's *Elijah* had its first performance in Birmingham, and its composer was fêted by Queen Victoria and Prince Albert, who revealed to their guest that he, too, was a composer. But then, he was German as well.

The one area in which English composers excelled, if in a modest way, was church music. England may have lacked the many provincial opera houses of Italy and Germany, but it made up for it in the number and dignity of its cathedrals and collegial foundations. These, with few exceptions, had musical establishments: they had organists, precentors and choirs, and it was one of the tasks of a cathedral organist to supply music for the liturgy. Unfortunately most of these establishments were in a run-down state in the first half of the nineteenth century. Many cathedral choirs had barely enough singers to provide four-part harmony, and where the numbers were adequate, the quality usually was not. The music written for such choirs naturally reflected their limitations, but the exceptions suggest that the situation was improving, or at least that serious composers were looking for ways of exploiting such quality as existed. Samuel Sebastian Wesley's anthem *The Wilderness*, composed for Hereford in 1832, is a fifteen-minute miniature cantata calling for solo voices (SATB) and with a big final chorus in an updated Handelian manner. Wesley was the outstanding Anglican church composer of the years around 1850, himself the son of a composer, Samuel Wesley, and great nephew of John Wesley, a founder of the Methodist Church. He held a succession of cathedral and important parish church posts between 1832, when he was appointed to Hereford Cathedral, and 1876, when he died with his boots still on the pedals of Gloucester Cathedral organ, and during that time he produced a body of church music that set a standard for generations of organist composers whose names still resonate round the ancient walls of the buildings they served, and are more or less unknown outside them: names like John Goss, John Stainer, Thomas Attwood Walmisley, Charles Steggall, and, less obscurely, Hubert Parry and Charles Villiers Stanford. It's a colourful, pious repertoire, often unexpectedly aware of musical goings-on outside. *The Wilderness* itself was condescendingly described by one of the judges for the Gresham Prize as 'a clever thing, but not cathedral music', which one is tempted to understand as 'not old-fashioned enough', or perhaps simply 'not dull enough'. Wesley's music is still frequently sung in Anglican cathedrals and college chapels, but you are unlikely to hear a note of it anywhere else.

Lortzing, a Berliner, moved to Leipzig in 1833, and his four most successful operas, including *Die beiden Schützen* (*The Two Rifle-Men*, 1837) and *Hans Sachs* (composed in 1840 to mark the quatercentenary of Gutenberg's invention of printing) were all premiered there. It would be nice to think that Schumann or Mendelssohn went to see them, but in any case Schumann did not write about Lortzing, which suggests a somewhat lofty attitude on his part to the frivolities of *Spieloper*. As we saw, he had long aspired to compose an opera of his own, and it seems clear from the various subjects he contemplated that whatever else it might be, it would not be light-hearted. 'Do you know what I pray about morning and evening?' he wrote to the critic Carl Kossmaly in 1842. 'It's German opera. There's something to be done there.'[6] Had he known about *The Flying Dutchman*, shortly to be staged in Dresden, he would perhaps have recognised it as an example of what he meant, though he might not have liked it much. Then in 1844 he and Clara decided to move to Dresden, partly because Clara's father, with whom they were reconciled, was now living there, but also because Schumann saw the Saxon capital as a better prospect for the opera he wanted to write.

Soon after his marriage in September 1840, he had turned abruptly away from his obsession with song and back to large-scale instrumental forms. In 1841 he composed two whole symphonies (No. 1 in B flat, and the first version of what ended up as No. 4 in D minor), a part-symphony that he eventually left as an *Overture, Scherzo and Finale,* and a *Phantasie* for piano and orchestra that later became the first movement of his piano concerto. He then, in 1842, wrote three string quartets, a piano quartet and a piano quintet. No doubt this wholesale rediscovery of classical genres had something to do with his newfound domestic stability. It was certainly encouraged by Clara, who had told her diary in 1839 that 'my highest wish is that he should compose for orchestra – that is his field!'7 She was expressing a widely held view about the superiority of the old forms, a view Schumann himself shared.

In reverting to classical genres, Schumann had to suppress (or forget) the more capricious aspects of his youthful masterpieces. Yet the quality of invention remains amazingly high, and there are original features in almost every work. Of the symphonies, the most innovative is the D minor, No. 4. In the re-orchestrated 1851 version Schumann marked the four movements to be played without a break. But this was already clearly present as an idea in 1841, though not marked except in the transition to the finale. Musically the continuity is obvious, and confirmed by thematic links that run through the whole work. And these links tell us something else as well. This is not really a four-movement symphony at all, but a complex one-movement work with a truncated first part that is elaborated and completed in the finale, while in between are a slow episode and a quick episode that use the same music for their middle sections. This is a much more organic version of cyclic form than Berlioz's in the *Symphonie fantastique.* A closer model might have been Schubert's 'Wanderer' Fantasy of 1822, which joins its four movements and bases them on the same theme, but lacks the formal complexity of the Schumann symphony.

As we saw with Mendelssohn's A minor String Quartet, this fusing of the different elements of a large-scale work into a single unit was a typically Romantic idea. It proclaimed 'this is all about me'. Schumann, however, adopted the tactic rarely in his symphonic works and only once in chamber music, in the link to the brilliant finale of the D minor Piano Trio. His own string quartets are, by comparison, models of formal rectitude, their main oddity being that the first movement of the so-called A minor (op. 41, no. 1) is actually in F major after an A minor introduction, while the second quartet is also in F major, and the third in A major, almost as if Schumann, writing these three works in rapid succession, was thinking about them all at once. There remains a feeling that he is most at home when there is a piano involved. The opening pages of the piano quintet and piano quartet, both in E flat, have a sheer excitement that he seldom captured in his music without piano. An exception is the opening of the third symphony, the so-called 'Rhenish', also in E flat, which he composed after arriving in Düsseldorf in 1850 as the new municipal director of music, and which has an exuberance comparable to the opening of Mendelssohn's 'Italian'. The 'Rhenish' is also an exception in terms of its form. It has five movements, the extra movement being the solemn ceremonial fourth in E flat minor supposedly inspired by the installation of a new archbishop in Cologne Cathedral. Nothing in the score mentions this or any other programmatic detail, and in general Schumann was evasive about such matters and inclined to withdraw references like the original movement titles of the 'Spring' Symphony (No. 1 in B flat). Only in piano music, his personal diary, was he free with titles, allusions or veiled hints. The classical forms and genres he cultivated after 1840 were above such things.

All the same, much of his thinking in the ten years from 1843 was directed towards dramatic music of one kind or another. This was not a new idea for him; in the past he had considered a variety of possible subjects, including *Hamlet* and Hoffmann's *Doge und Dogaressa*. By 1841 it was Calderón, and – his eventual first choice – Thomas Moore's *Paradise and the Peri*, out of which, after thinking of it as a stage piece, he fashioned a secular oratorio about the peri (the fairy offspring of a mortal and a fallen angel) denied admission to Paradise until she can bring to its gate 'heaven's most cherished gift', which turns out to be a tear from the cheek of an elderly sinner who has repented at the sight of a child at prayer. *Das Paradies und die Peri* is in some respects a more complex work than either of Mendelssohn's oratorios; its form and texture are more fluid, less Handelian, though not without that influence. Unfortunately it is made difficult for modern audiences by its subject matter, with redemption attached to so mawkish a condition. Schumann's music is more robust and colourful than that implies. But engagement with the story remains tricky.

Less than three months after the *Paradies* premiere in December 1843, he was pondering an altogether grander redemptive concept, in the form of an opera on Goethe's *Faust*. *Faust* was in the air; only a year later Berlioz would be working up his own *Damnation* out of his original *Huit scènes*. But Schumann's plan was quite different. He started with the final scene of Goethe's Part 2, which had not yet been published when Berlioz wrote his scenes, and wouldn't in any case have fitted his subsequent intention to damn Faust. Then, by the end of 1844 Schumann had abandoned the idea of an opera on the subject, and set it aside in favour of other possible topics, eventually landing on a recent play, *Genoveva*, by Friedrich Hebbel. But *Faust* was still very much on the stocks, and while composing *Genoveva* in 1848 he continued to tinker with Goethe's final scene. It would be 1850 before he completed what he, too, ended by calling *Scenes from Goethe's Faust*, and another three years before he added the overture. Meanwhile *Genoveva* was completed and performed, and Schumann had in 1849 concocted yet another theatre work out of Byron's narrative poem *Manfred*, a hybrid piece involving the reciting of an abridged German version of the poem, sometimes with musical accompaniment in the form of melodrama, sometimes interspersed with musical settings.

The move to Dresden in December 1844 brought Schumann into

frequent contact with Kapellmeister Wagner, both in person and in the shape of his latest work. *Tannhäuser* opened in October 1845 and Schumann saw it the following month. Wagner had given him a copy of the score in advance of the performance and Schumann had studied it and made some disobliging remarks about it to Mendelssohn; but then after seeing it on the stage he had the humility to retract some of his criticisms. 'It makes quite a different effect on the stage,' he told Mendelssohn. 'Much of it impressed me deeply.' Schumann's problem was, evidently, a certain inability to prejudge the effect of an opera in performance. Wagner seems to have talked incessantly about his theories, with Schumann contributing the occasional monosyllable, while inwardly thinking Wagner a bad musician with a flair for the stage. But when he came to compose *Genoveva*, he had to endure Wagner's criticisms of the libretto, no doubt couched in terms of its suitability for musical treatment. Wagner will have spotted at once the poor motivation and lack of narrative shape in the story of the Brabantine Count Siegfried who embarks on a crusade leaving his wife in the care of his servant, Golo, who at once makes advances that Genoveva repels with disdain. Golo's response is to bring a false accusation of infidelity against her, as a result of which she is condemned to death, then rescued at the last minute when Siegfried learns of her innocence. As in *Euryanthe*, the whole issue of the pure wife's supposed adultery is dealt with in a cursory, psychologically inept fashion, with apparently neither her absent husband nor anybody in a castleful of people who must have known her and Golo well entertaining the slightest doubt about her guilt. Wagner perhaps talked about his *Lohengrin*, the opera on which he was then working, also set in medieval Brabant, and likewise hingeing on a false accusation. He will surely have urged Schumann to give time for his characters to evolve musically and for the situations to be properly elaborated. But he could have saved his breath. Schumann, at home in cyclic works that functioned like *tableaux vivants*, had no instinctive feeling for the pacing of music drama in the theatre, and *Genoveva*, a work full of lovely music in his best mature vein including a very fine overture, flopped when staged in Leipzig in 1850, and has rarely resurfaced since.

The *Scenes from Faust* were another matter. Here theatrical coherence had ceased to be an issue and Schumann simply composed the scenes that stirred his musical juices, assuming, of course, that his audience would know the story, who was who, and why it ended as it did. He was chiefly drawn to Goethe's Part 2, which deals with Faust's redemption in largely spiritual terms. He started with this in 1844, put it aside, worked on it again in 1847 and 1848 and only thereafter, in 1849, set three scenes from the original, more action-packed *Faust* of 1808, before completing the work with three earlier scenes from Part 2, including the scene where Ariel pleads for Faust's redemption, and the scenes of Faust's blinding and death. The result was a narrative hotchpotch. The garden scene from Part 1 introduces us to Gretchen and Faust and their initial lovemaking, Gretchen prays in her distress at the shrine of the Mater Dolorosa, then is assailed in the cathedral by an evil spirit accusing her of her mother's death. The rest – three quarters of the two-hour score – is Part 2, and especially the long final scene, the classic expression of the curious but strangely compelling Romantic concept of the *Ewigweibliche* – the eternal feminine, which 'draws us upwards'.

Muddled as this may be as narrative, it has real power musically. Freed from the need to achieve a grand discourse from start to finish, Schumann responded sharply to the imagery and atmosphere of each scene, and this drew him into a range of expression that he had seldom achieved in his symphonic works. He may have ignored Wagner's advice about *Genoveva*, but he heard his *Tannhäuser* and by his own admission was impressed by its effect as theatre. *Faust* gave him an avenue for achieving some equivalent power in a medium that suited his particular gifts. The style of course remains his own, that of the Second Symphony, the Cello Concerto and the best pages of *Genoveva*, but with bolder, sometimes more inventive chorus writing and orchestration, especially for brass. It's true that the demonic element, so vivid in Berlioz, is played down. Moments of pure theatre, like the explosion of the Dies Irae into the cathedral scene, are few. On the whole, the lyrical element predominates, and there are times, especially in the final scene, when the music is a little too subservient to the poetic metre. Clearly it was the radiance of Faust's redemption, more than his blood pact with the devil, that captured Schumann's imagination; it was where he started, after all.

The Schumanns were in Dresden in May 1849 when fighting broke out after the king dissolved the Saxon parliament and called in Prussian troops to help quell the resulting disturbances. Schumann himself, though sympathetic towards the revolutionaries, had no stomach for street-fighting and escaped with his family through the back garden to avoid being pressed into service by the rebels.[8] He was already on the look-out for a salaried post, and after failing to get the directorship at the Gewandhaus in July, he was offered and accepted the post of municipal music director in Düsseldorf, starting in September 1850.

The Rhineland city would be his penultimate home. At first everything went well; his concerts were successful, he conducted and rehearsed efficiently, and with Clara as a solo act there was a feeling that Düsseldorf had done well to attract them. But soon things started to go less smoothly. Schumann's lack of conducting experience began to create difficulties with the chorus, and – what was worse – his health showed worrying signs of deterioration. At first there were the familiar nervous attacks, depression and periods of inexplicable exhaustion; he became touchy, irritable and self-absorbed when his conducting required him to be outgoing and communicative. Then he was assailed by a severe tinnitus, began to ignore the practical needs of performance, and on one occasion went on waving his baton after the work he was conducting had come to an end. By November 1853 the situation had become intolerable to all parties, and his appointment was terminated. Three months later, after further aural hallucinations involving imaginary angelic music and the ululations of wild animals, he walked out of the house and threw himself into the Rhine. Some fishermen who had seen him jump hauled him out of the water, he was taken to a mental asylum at Endenich, in a park outside Bonn, and there, on 29 July 1856, he died.

The supreme irony of Schumann's mental and physical decline, aside from its sheer clinical ghastliness, is that these years, especially 1850–3, were among his most productive. Early on there were the marvellous Third Symphony, the Cello Concerto, the completion of the *Faust* scenes, concert overtures, and a large number of songs, the two violin sonatas and the third piano trio, among other chamber works. In 1852 he turned to choral music and composed a Mass and a Requiem, and in 1853 he wrote his solitary violin concerto as well as a substantial fantasy for violin and orchestra, a *Konzertstück* for piano and orchestra, the *Faust* overture, various smaller chamber works and a visionary piano suite called *Gesänge der Frühe* (*Songs of the Early Morning*).

The controversy that has simmered over Schumann's final illness and the music he wrote while suffering it is one of the more bizarre corners of modern musicology. The extensive medical literature is inevitably speculative, but one of its side effects has been to encourage the idea that the music is itself somehow sick and mentally defective. This view fails to take account of a handful of masterpieces and several other highly performable works alongside the undeniable disappointments. Schumann perhaps composed too much in these years, and sometimes in media that didn't suit him. The Mass and Requiem both contain fine things, but on the whole are too self-consciously churchy, too correct in technical matters (such as fugal chorus entries) that Schumann could do perfectly well but didn't fire his imagination. The songs of 1851 have been subjected to sometimes ferocious criticism,[9] and do include some dross, but also many imaginative and novel inventions. Schumann had always had a soft spot for pallid, sentimental verse of the pink-edged variety, and his settings of the Russian child poet Elisabeth Kulmann, who died in 1825 at the age of seventeen, reflect too readily the girlish pathos of the verse. Yet a few months later he composed the violin sonatas in A minor and D minor, music on a high technical and inspirational level for which no special pleading is necessary.

The most interesting aspect of this late period is the number of works that seem to be feeling their way towards a new manner. A certain obsessiveness enters into Schumann's music at about this time. The four *Märchenbilder* for viola and piano (1851), for instance, are studies in repeating figures that teeter on the edge of monotony but with intriguing consequences. The motif, instead of being a subject for development, becomes an object of contemplation: the decorative figure at bar 9 of the first piece, the dotted figures in No. 2, the semi-quaver triplets in No. 3. The intensely expressive fourth piece almost gets lost in its own *Innigkeit*, its inwardness. It is easy to disparage this kind of music, but it is effective in performance and a delight to play. Some of the songs share this quality, not in the Schubertian sense of a running accompaniment but in the sense of a recurring image: the prancing horse in Mörike's 'Der Gärtner', the vanishing evening drift in 'Abendlied'. These are not perfect songs, but they are fascinating. An extreme case is the set of five Mary Stuart songs, settings of poems supposedly by the tragic queen herself. Four of the songs, the last Schumann wrote (in December 1852), are in E minor, the other in A minor, five studies in single-minded lamentation. To suggest Schumann failed to notice the lack of variation would be absurd. He was still lucid. The concentration on one thing from different angles is plainly intentional, an aesthetic decision, whether or not completely successful. It suggests a desire to strip away the diversity and superfluity of romanticism in favour of a simplified, intensely concentrated, possibly more objectified, but agonised vision.

New Paths, Different Directions

More even than the French Revolution, the revolutions of 1848 changed the political and social complexion of Europe irrevocably. Whereas the 1789 revolution had been largely confined to France, had triggered a European war that dislodged ruling dynasties, but had been succeeded by restoration backed up by police states, the revolutions of 1848 were Europe-wide from the start and either brought immediate and permanent change, or created a turbulence that brought it about gradually. In France, King Louis Philippe abdicated and the monarchy collapsed. In Germany the attempt to create a National Assembly with a liberal constitution merely had the effect of cementing the authority of the Prussian king, Friedrich Wilhelm, and eventually helped bring about German unification under the Prussian crown. In the Austrian Empire, by contrast, the revolutions had the opposite effect, weakening the centre and in due course forcing the devolution of powers to the ethnic regions. 1848 was also a crucial year for the newly emerging Communist League. That February the *Communist Manifesto* was published in London, and while the revolutions erupted in city after city the manifesto followed them round. Marx himself was expelled from Belgium for supplying the workers with guns, then from Germany for subversive activities; from there he retired to London and the reading room of the British Museum. Meanwhile its most spectacular expression would be on the barricades of Dresden in May 1849, in the wild, larger-than-life person of Mikhail Bakunin.

But while Europe blazed, European music seemed to wilt. In November 1847 Felix Mendelssohn had died in Leipzig at the age of thirty-eight, brought down by a congenital vascular weakness in the brain aggravated by overwork and the shock of his beloved sister Fanny's death six months earlier. His last completed work, a furiously emotional string quartet in F minor, is perhaps the lasting expression of that shock, a masterpiece of unassuaged grief. When revolution broke out in Paris three months later, many who could afford to travel did so, abandoning the French capital and depriving Chopin and others of much of their teaching. Soon Chopin, too, left and took up an invitation from an aristocratic Scottish pupil, Jane Stirling, to visit Britain. But he was already a sick man, consumptive and wasted, and though he just about survived Scotland, the return to Paris in November 1848 was to be his final journey. Less than a year later he died in his apartment in the Place Vendôme, attended by his sister Ludwika, the doctor, two or three other friends, and with an anteroom crammed with souvenir hunters, sketchers, photographers and assorted princesses.

Chopin's second decade in Paris had been no less productive than his first, yet different in important ways. In 1838 he had started what had developed into a lasting affair with the novelist George Sand, an affair which began passionately but settled into a calm relationship that somehow accommodated their very different temperaments. Sand (real name Amantine Lucile Aurore Dupin) was not simply, like George Eliot, a female novelist who had adopted a masculine pen name in order to bypass prejudice. She was a genuine cross-dresser who wore male clothes, smoked cigars, and expressed herself like a man, with outspoken republican and agnostic views and a generally flamboyant, unladylike manner. Chopin, by contrast, was reserved, quietly spoken, fastidious, conventional in his social opinions, politically disengaged, apart from with his Polish friends, whom Sand mostly disliked. Yet for nine years they were, in modern jargon, an item, and there is not much doubt that the relationship benefited Chopin's work, and probably hers as well. The most famous image is of them together in a monastery on Majorca, where they spent their first winter together, the rain pouring down and dripping on the slate roof as Chopin composed his D flat major Prelude, with its 'dripping' A flats/G sharps. The scene was invented by Sand and denied by Chopin. But they certainly were in Majorca, it did rain excessively to the point of seriously damaging Chopin's already precarious health, and he did complete the preludes in the monastery, on a piano shipped by Pleyel from Marseilles and somehow hauled up the trackless thousand-foot mountain. Back in France, he was able to spend successive summers, peaceful and dry, at Sand's family home, the Château de Nohant, in the Berry region of central France, and here he composed several of his greatest works.

The Twenty-four Preludes are unusual for Chopin in being genuine miniatures, fragments almost, rather than merely short single-movement works. Nearly half of them are less than a minute long each, and it's clear that Chopin thought of them as a set, since they lead from one to the next by way of either common or adjacent pitches that are partly a consequence of the key sequence, which goes major-relative minor through the cycle of fifths (C–A minor–G–E minor, etc.). Presumably he was thinking of Bach's '48'. But Bach's arrangement is a catalogue: every key in alphabetical order (two sets). Chopin's is a design. The preludes took Schumann, at least, by surprise. 'I must admit', he wrote, 'that I expected something different, something executed like his studies in the grandest style. Almost the opposite: these are sketches, study beginnings, or if you like, ruins, individual eagle's pinions, all in a wild confusion of colours.'[1] Did Schumann perhaps think back to his own fragmentary sequences, or recall the original title of the first movement of his C major Fantasy: 'Ruins'? If so, he suppressed the memory. He was puzzled, too, by the prelude-like presto finale of Chopin's B flat minor Sonata a year or two later – 'more like a leg-pull than any kind of music . . . a sphinx with a mocking smile'.[2] But though Schumann made up his mind that Chopin had simply thrown together 'four of his maddest children' in the four movements of this sonata, the finale is a perfectly coherent response to the famous funeral march that precedes it, a bitter, dismissive gesture, in the spirit of Schumann's own hero, Kreisler. One has only to imagine what an 'appropriate' finale to a sonata on this scale might have been like to recognise the elusive perfection of Chopin's inappropriate version, a swirling minute-and-a-half of quaver triplet octaves which go by so quickly that the ear senses, rather than follows, the music's built-in harmonic logic.

Chopin composed two sonatas after this one, the great B minor for solo piano (1844) and a cello sonata in G minor (1845–6), his one and only mature piece of chamber music. But while the B minor Sonata, especially, shows that he was perfectly at home with classical forms, his best response to those forms shows up, as before, in single-movement late works like the F minor Fantasy, the F minor Ballade and the E major Scherzo, which evolve new formal concepts from classical principle rather than practice. Chopin never seems to have fretted over the superficial limitations of the old genres and dance idioms. Like Bach, he clearly enjoyed elaborating basic concepts, as in the Barcarolle, op. 60, or the Polonaise-Fantasy, op. 61, which takes a courtly dance and turns it into a big sonata-type movement with lyrical accessories. The 'fantasy' tag is the sole recognition that anything out of the way has happened to the dance type. Usually, though, the elaborations hide behind the generic title, into which Chopin smuggles all kinds of musical enrichments, like the tonal complexities and sheer formal variety of the C minor Mazurka, op. 56, no. 3, or the exuberant polyphony of the coda of the Barcarolle. As before, there is never any programme. His melodies sing and his dances dance, but they sing and dance nothing but themselves.

For Liszt, 1848 was a watershed in a quite different way. Ten years earlier, after his Vienna concerts in aid of the victims of the Pest floods, he had heard of the failure of an appeal to raise money for a monument to Beethoven in Bonn, the city of the Master's birth, and had promptly offered to raise the money himself. This naturally meant still more concerts, starting once again in Vienna at the end of 1839. And this time the concerts created a momentum that for almost a decade did not let up. Once more he became a touring virtuoso, with a schedule that would terrify the most energetic of modern jet-setting pianists. In nine years he gave more than a thousand concerts across the whole of Europe, from Portugal to Russia and from Ireland to Romania and modern Ukraine; and these were for the most part solo recitals, without the supporting artists that were then still normal. His repertoire was enormous, much of it played from memory – another novelty for the time. In most places his recitals (a term he invented) were like pop concerts, attended by large, noisy crowds, with swooning women desperate for souvenirs: a lock of hair, the dregs of a coffee cup, a cigarette end, a discarded glove. In St Petersburg in 1842 he performed on a platform specially erected, like a boxing ring, in the middle of the Assembly of the Nobles, with two pianos facing in opposite directions, so that he could play alternately to different sections of the audience.

Perhaps not surprisingly, composition sometimes took a back seat for Liszt during this so-called *Glanzzeit* (glitter-time). In Italy in 1838, after his Viennese concerts, he had composed the second (Italian) book of the *Années de pèlerinage*, and also in 1838 the first versions of the six Paganini Studies and the twelve Transcendental Studies. He had been working on what became the *Harmonies poétiques et religieuses*, though none of this music was published until the 1850s or later. After visiting Budapest and rediscovering his Hungarian roots he worked on the *Magyar dallok* (*Hungarian National Melodies*). But the overwhelming impression of these years is of a continuous work in progress, a constant search for better, more inventive, more transcendental ways of performing on this instrument that had itself not yet reached its final form. Liszt's constant revising of his piano works reflects this provisional character of virtuoso performance and composition. On tour, he never knew what kind of piano would greet him, or even what condition it would be in. At Bad Ems, in the presence of the Russian tsarina Alexandra Feodorovna, the old piano's strings snapped one by one until the tsarina had the wit to announce it was teatime. At Clonmel, in Tipperary, the piano was 'a small Tompkinson upright which rattled and shook as [Liszt] performed'.[3] Nevertheless it must have been on these forties tours that he perfected his keyboard technique, not in the sense of sheer mechanistic brilliance (that was already in place), but in the sense of what the instrument itself was capable of, its possibilities of colour and touch and the various resources provided by the pedals. Under Liszt's hands mastery of the keyboard evolved from pure display to the creation of a whole palette of sound colours that would be appropriated by later composers in a way that would eventually transform the actual style and grammar of the music they wrote.

In March 1846, Liszt embarked on his last and longest tour. It took him from Vienna up to Prague, then eastwards to Pest and on into Transylvania, Bucharest, Iaşi and eventually Ukraine, Kiev, Odessa and Constantinople. His very last professional recital was in Elisavetgrad in central Ukraine in September 1847.[4] But some time before that he had made up his mind to accept the offer of the post of Kapellmeister to the Grand Duke of Weimar. In Kiev he had met and fallen in love with a certain Princess Carolyne von Sayn-Wittgenstein, the estranged Polish-born wife of a Russian officer in the service of Tsar Nicholas I. After his final concert he spent three months with her on her estate in southern Ukraine. Then in February 1848 he proceeded to Weimar, where the princess soon joined him.

Meanwhile in Paris, five hundred miles away, a crowd gathered outside the Ministry of Foreign Affairs in protest at the banning of the banquets that were cover for political meetings. Someone in the front was pushed forward by the mass of people behind, a soldier lost his nerve and fired into the crowd, and before anyone could take cover more than fifty people lay dead.

In Dresden, Wagner was quietly putting the finishing touches to his *Lohengrin*, in which Henry the Fowler, tenth-century king of the East Franks, comes to Brabant to recruit soldiers for his army against the invading Magyars on his eastern border. But Wagner had one eye on the politics of his own day as well. In May 1848, with *Lohengrin* out of the way and a mere four days after submitting his plan for a German National Theatre, he wrote to the Saxon deputy to the National Assembly in Frankfurt with a four-point programme of political reform. The following month he addressed the Dresden political grouping known as the Vaterlandsverein with further proposals, including universal suffrage, the abolition of the aristocracy, and what he called 'the emancipation of the monarchy', placing the king at the head of the newly constituted republic. Between then and the following spring he published a series of increasingly inflammatory articles in the radical *Volksblätter* (edited by his assistant conductor, Auguste Röckel), ending in April 1849 with a grandiloquent piece of prose poetry unashamedly titled 'The Revolution'. 'The old world is crumbling,' it proclaimed; 'a new will rise therefrom.'[5] To us today the oddest thing about all this rhetoric – apart from the fact that it could be published at all – is the image, as Newman puts it, of 'princes, Parliament and public all being told what they ought to do on pain of incurring the disapproval of the second Kapellmeister of the Dresden Opera'.[6]

Lohengrin, however, for all its politico/historical context, is not a political opera. Like *Tannhäuser*, it descends from grand opera by way of German mythology and medieval romance. Lohengrin himself (as Loherangrin), in Wolfram von Eschenbach, is the son of the Grail king, Parzival, summoned to Brabant to protect the young heiress to the vacant throne, and agreeing to marry her on condition that she never ask his name or origin. In Wagner's version, the princess, now called Elsa, has been accused by the knight Friedrich von Telramund of the murder of her brother in order to gain the throne for herself, but Lohengrin arrives as her champion in a boat drawn by a swan, and defeats Telramund in single combat. As in Wolfram, he will marry Elsa on condition that she never ask the forbidden question, but Ortrud, the sinister pagan wife of Telramund, undermines Elsa's trust and goads her into asking it, at which point Lohengrin reveals his identity and leaves, having first changed the swan back into Elsa's lost brother, who had been transformed by the evil Ortrud.

Like much of *Tannhäuser*, *Lohengrin* is built around large ensemble scenes in which the chorus mainly functions as what Wagner would call 'scenery that has learnt to march and sing'. The entire first act is a spectacular crowd scene in which an intimate drama – Telramund's accusation of Elsa, her account of her dream of a knight in shining armour, his arrival in the swan-boat, her promise to him, etc. – is acted out in the presence of the people. Likewise the second half of Act 2, the bridal procession at the start of Act 3, and the whole of the long final scene, including Lohengrin's monologue about the Grail, his reproaches to Elsa, the transformation of the swan, Lohengrin's departure and Elsa's collapse: all is, so to speak, public. The most original music, though, is largely elsewhere. Above all, the Prelude to the whole opera is a masterpiece of spiritual scene-setting, a radiant description of the Grail itself, marvellously sustained through slow-moving diatonic harmony, transparently scored. Wagner had composed on a large scale before this, but he had written nothing of comparably long breath.

Also very fine, and in some ways new, is the scene between Telramund and Ortrud that opens the second act together with Ortrud's scene with Elsa that follows. Telramund, an honourable man led astray like Macbeth by a conniving wife, blames her for his downfall, as only the weak and well-meaning can do, while Ortrud displays the qualities that have brought him down, the scorn and vicious goading, the dark, self-confident power, then turns a quite different power on Elsa, appealing to her pity and warning her, with a malice she struggles to conceal, against her trust in Lohengrin. Wagner's technique here derives essentially from the Weber of *Euryanthe* and Marschner's *Hans Heiling*, but with a psychological edge they lacked. These are three-dimensional characters with ambivalent, fluctuating motifs, not the usual pasteboard creatures of Romantic opera. Their music works always in close conjunction with Wagner's text, is harmonically and rhythmically mobile, grippingly precise in expression, the perfect foil to the pure, otherworldly Grail music, like the darker world they inhabit.

In the conditions under which it was completed, there was little question of *Lohengrin* being staged in Dresden. Wagner was himself already engaging in activities that would have militated against it even if the circumstances had otherwise been favourable. That autumn he compiled a draft scenario which he called *The Nibelung Myth as Sketch for a Drama*; but by the spring of 1849 he was as much involved in revolution as in music. Some time in March, Röckel introduced him to Bakunin, and one shudders to think what he and the great anarchist, friend of Marx and Engels, may have said to each other at that first meeting. On Palm Sunday, Wagner conducted a performance of Beethoven's 'Choral' Symphony, and at the general rehearsal Bakunin walked up to the orchestra and called out that 'if all music were to be lost in the expected world conflagration, we should be willing to risk our lives to commit to the preservation of this symphony'.[7]

A month later the conflagration ignited in Dresden, and Wagner was prominent among the incendiaries. From the start he was active on the streets; he was seen with a gun and may also have carried grenades. He climbed the tower of the Kreuzkirche to report on the Prussian troops who had arrived in the city in support of the local Saxon force. He distributed placards urging the Saxon soldiers to defect, and he guided a posse of armed students across the barricades. When it was all over and the uprising had collapsed, he was lucky to escape arrest in Chemnitz, where the main ringleaders were apprehended at an inn in the centre of the town. Wagner had gone instead to his brother-in-law Heinrich Wolfram's house on the outskirts, from where Wolfram whisked him away in his private coach to Weimar, eighty miles to the west. The captured revolutionaries, including Bakunin and Röckel, were taken back to Dresden, tried and sentenced to death, sentences that were subsequently commuted to life imprisonment. Wagner, had he been caught, would certainly have suffered the same fate.

In Weimar now was Liszt, whom he had first met in 1840 in Paris, but whom he still barely knew. Liszt had no recollection of their Paris meeting, but had seen and admired *Rienzi* in Dresden in 1844, and had conducted *Tannhäuser* in Weimar earlier in 1849. He received its composer with warmth; but with a price on his head, Wagner would have to leave German territory without delay, and this he did, with travel money provided by Liszt. He went first to Zurich, proceeded to Paris, then, disappointed once again in Parisian taste and artistic judgement, returned to Zurich at the end of June, and settled down to plan his next revolution.

This was to be a two-pronged assault on the subject with which he was most qualified to engage: opera, the musical drama, its practice, its aesthetics and its purpose. His grand plan was to compose a drama of a nature and on a scale that would make all previous operatic work look frivolous and ephemeral. He had already sketched out a scenario for such a work, but it was still inchoate, a mere story and, as time would show, incomplete in a number of ways. At the moment its eventual character was tangled up with all kinds of general ideas about the theatre and its history, about music as a vehicle for serious drama, about philosophy, about Teutonic and Nordic mythology as a paradigm of world history, and other such trivial matters, which he needed to think out and write up in a series of extended essays. For four years after his arrival in Zurich he composed no music. Instead he wrote words, words and more words, the most extensive set of theoretical writings ever produced by a musician about his own work, writings of a deeply thoughtful kind, at times intensely practical, at times discursive and philosophical, largely expressed in a clotted and impenetrable prose that sends one back to his by no means always entirely transparent music with a sigh of relief.

The general drift of these extended essays was to spell out the idea of a new kind of music drama as something that emerges from the history of theatre and the history of the relation between theatre, poetry, music and the general culture of the people. Wagner's idea of revolution had always been, at bottom, an idea of revolution in art. Radical change in the arts would only happen through a complete reordering of society. In the first of the three main books, *Art and Revolution*, he argues that genuine art barely exists in modern society, having been commodified and debased into a pure diversion for the moneyed bourgeoisie. He compares the modern theatre with the theatre of the Greeks, which was a quasi-religious ceremony that united the entire population, and also unified the various art forms. Today, he says, the arts have gone their separate ways, been individualised, privatised. In Athens, art was fundamentally conservative, in that it expressed in integrated form the deep-rooted culture of society; true art now can only be revolutionary, 'because it exists only in opposition to the public as it stands'.[8] And that revolution will bring the arts back together, in something that he already calls a *Gesamtkunstwerk* – a total work of art.

The second book, *The Artwork of the Future*, extends this idea of a reunified art in the light of Feuerbach's theory of humanity alienated from nature by its gradual invention of spurious needs (Wagner's title plays on Feuerbach's *Principles of the Philosophy of the Future*). Art has suffered this same fate. It has become disconnected from its natural origins in music, poetry and especially dance, the most real art because the most directly connected to the human body. In music, Wagner sees counterpoint as the chief enemy, being a purely intellectual, non-sensory process, whereas the operatic aria is a direct emanation of the person by way of the voice (its place in his good books will, however, be short-lived). But dance he finds in its most elevated form in the classical symphony, and especially Beethoven, whose Seventh Symphony he famously calls 'the apotheosis of the dance', while the Ninth, the key work of all, recombines all this with poetry. Thus he lays out the elements of the *Gesamtkunstwerk*: dance, poetry, music, plus architecture (in theatre design, itself a social question to do with seating plans), sculpture and (especially landscape) painting. And this will be the communal work of everyone involved, including, as in old Athens, the people, or in Herderian terms *Das Volk*.

Finally *Opera and Drama*, the longest of the three books (1850–1), goes into more detail on the specifics of the new music drama. Wagner rails against the opera of his day, in which, he says, 'a means of expression (the music) was made the purpose, while the purpose of the expression (the drama) was made the means'.[9] He surveys operatic history, dismissing eighteenth-century opera, with its 'pointless' successions of arias and recitatives, tracing the partial reforms of Gluck on through French opera, exonerating Mozart in part, and attacking Rossini ('ear-tickling melody') and Meyerbeer ('effects without causes'). Meanwhile the straight theatre is nothing but novels transferred to the stage, and the novel, he claims, is bourgeois art writ large, its subject matter con-temporary bourgeois life in all its prosaic squalor. The only fitting sub-ject for the stage is myth, which is timeless and universal, conveys an enriched sense of reality, and goes with the desire to destroy the old society and remake it anew.

Wagner discusses the musical aspects of these ideas in detail. Words and music are to be organically connected, the one growing out of the other, the whole bound together by the orchestra, acting like a Greek chorus. The flow of the music, its rhythms and to some extent its con-tours, will be governed by the words, which must always be audible, and the main motifs (he doesn't use the term leitmotifs) will emerge from what he calls the poetic line. These motifs will then be taken up by the orchestra and serve both as glorified reminiscence motifs and as symphonic material. There will be no choruses and few vocal ensem-bles. What Wagner is envisaging here is a continuous, harmonically enriched orchestral stream, on which the voices travel, so to speak, conversationally, with none of the stops and starts of conventional opera. This is the ultimate world of the music drama, a world in which the characters live musically in the same way that we, in the material world, live verbally. The whole artifice of opera as previously under-stood is to be waved away, in favour of a kind of virtual realism, the ultimate Romantic concept of an alternative, parallel world into which, for a certain time, we sink our consciousness altogether.

Wagner was so convinced of the revolutionary character of this project that he decided it would need a specially built theatre for its realisation. In *The Artwork of the Future* he had already raised the issue of theatre design as a reflection of class structure. Now he is consid-ering the needs of his own work. This is first mentioned in another book-length essay of 1851, *A Communication to My Friends*, as well as in a letter of a year earlier, in which he reveals that, if he had the money, he would get built 'right here, where I am, out of boards, a theatre to my own design'.[10] Had he built his theatre then and there, he would have had nothing to put into it. That would be his next task.

In fact a draft scenario for his next work had existed since before his flight from Dresden. *The Nibelung Myth as Sketch for a Drama* is a prose story about Brünnhilde and the death of Siegfried, with a few preliminary details, based mainly on the thirteenth-century Middle High German epic *Nibelungenlied*. But when Wagner started working this up into a libretto called *Siegfrieds Tod* (*Siegfried's Death*) it became clear that the back story would need relating in a prefatory drama, which he called *Der junge Siegfried* (*The Young Siegfried*), and then that this in turn needed placing in context. Thus *Der Ring des Nibelungen* gradually became a tetralogy: a work in four parts, lasting in all some fifteen hours. He eventually got round to the actual music for the first part, *Das Rheingold*, towards the end of 1853, and in the next four years he composed that and *Die Walküre* and the first two acts of the third part, now called, simply, *Siegfried*, before setting the whole project aside in order to compose *Tristan und Isolde*, a work he hoped would have a better prospect of performance.

The one-act *Das Rheingold* is thus the work he composed soonest after writing *Opera and Drama*, and it's the one that reflects his theories most closely. Yet it is also, curiously, the most play-like, the least epic in flavour. Set by Marschner or Peter Lindpaintner as a Romantic opera about immortals it would hardly have raised an eyebrow. Set by Wagner as a music drama, with all that that implies and knowing what it led to, it is a culmination and a turning point. To some extent the mythical element is a mere distraction; this is a crisply plotted, swift-moving drama about sharply drawn characters with ordinary human motivations, albeit functioning in a world where magic sometimes intervenes and physical limitations don't always apply. The dwarf Alberich steals the river-gold underwater from the Rhinemaidens, renouncing love in order to do so, and forces his brother Mime to fashion a ring that theoretically gives him world power (though it will fail him when most needed). Wotan, the chief god, has just had Valhalla built by a pair of giants, Fafner and Fasolt, and now has to pay the bill. He hears from his messenger Loge about the stolen gold, himself steals it from Alberich with Loge's help, but is then forced to give it all up, including the ring, to pay the giants. Alberich lays a curse on the ring, the giants fight, Fafner kills Fasolt, and meanwhile the gods take up residence in Valhalla.

Wagner's new technique of short associative, mainly orchestral motifs accompanying a kind of long-limbed, word-sensitive vocal arioso is highly effective in animating this cosmic family saga. Above all it brings out a sheer harmonic range, from the almost totally static E flat major of the prelude to the flickering chromatics of the vivid scene changes, that was only intermittent in his earlier operas. It now provides a complete vocabulary, managed with consummate skill, pacing the narrative, helping establish character and, in collaboration with the leitmotifs, motivation. The motifs themselves, here some thirty in number, refer to all sorts of things: objects (the ring, the magic Tarnhelm), people, actions (renunciation, the curse), even abstract concepts such as servitude or – memories of Bakunin – *Vernichtungsarbeit*, the work of annihilation. In many cases they are versions of one another, a device that helps make dramatic or psychological points. You have to have studied the *Ring* to identify them (not to mention name them, which Wagner never did),[11] but they perhaps work subconsciously, intuitively, like symphonic themes.

Whether or not *Das Rheingold* fits Wagner's notion of *Gesamtkunstwerk*, one can say with confidence that the rest of the tetralogy does not. In the autumn of 1854, while working on *Die Walküre*, he read Schopenhauer's thirty-five-year-old treatise, *The World as Will and Representation*, and it transformed his conception of his own work. Where the *Opera and Drama* idea had been for a stage action of words heightened but by no means overridden by music,

Schopenhauer developed Kant's distinction between the phenomenal world (the one we experience with our senses) and the noumenal world, the deeper hidden reality beyond, and argued that only through music could we have any intuition of the noumenon. And where *Das Rheingold* had been the start of a drama about the decline of an old and weary political order and its replacement by a vibrant, youthful new order, Schopenhauer insisted that this phenomenal world was for ever hateful and evil, that it could never be anything else, and the only possible attitude towards it was to reject it wholesale, to will its annihilation and one's own. The curious thing is that Wagner's libretto, which existed complete, turned out to be already somewhat Schopenhauerian. Its central character, Wotan, wills his own destruction by the grandson he has deviously created as a way of retrieving the ring without his, Wotan's, complicity. Alberich renounces the life force, love. At the very end, Brünnhilde rides on to the funeral pyre, proclaiming the end of the gods, the end of everything except love. The implication here was meant to be the dawn of a new order; but nothing in the text contradicts the new idea that the world itself is coming to an end, and though Wagner added some new text to make this explicit, he never set it.

Something similar applies to the music. By the time he read Schopenhauer, Wagner had composed the first act of *Die Walküre*, the music of which is already more assertive, more in charge, the action less prosaic, more poetic, more lyrically paced. Siegmund, wounded from a fight, seeks shelter in the house of Hunding and is looked after by Hunding's wife, Sieglinde, who turns out to be his twin sister. He retrieves a sword left buried in an ash tree by their father (who the music tells us was Wotan), and the twins fall into a passionate embrace. Wotan intends to protect Siegmund in the coming fight with Hunding, but Fricka, his wife, outraged by his condoning of adulterous incest, makes him promise to let the fight take its course and to order his Valkyrie daughter, Brünnhilde, to do the same. But Brünnhilde disobeys him and in a fury Wotan smashes Siegmund's sword, enabling

Hunding to kill him, then strikes Hunding dead and sets off in pursuit of Brünnhilde and Sieglinde. Brünnhilde begs her sister Valkyries to protect them, but they recoil in fear of the All-Father. Sieglinde, pregnant with Siegfried, escapes into the forest, then Brünnhilde faces and gradually softens Wotan's rage. She must, he says, be put to sleep on the mountain-top, to be the wife of the first man to find her, but he rings her with fire to ensure that that man will be a hero (rather, presumably, than some passing mountaineer).

Siegfried, which Wagner began composing in September 1856, opens with our new teenage hero living in a cave with the dwarf Mime, who is trying to mend the sword that will kill Fafner, now a dragon guarding the ring in the deep forest. But Siegfried himself forges the sword, kills the dragon (and Mime) in Act 2, and sets off up the mountain with the ring (of whose power he is unaware), looking for the girl that a woodbird has told him is sleeping on the mountain. Wotan has figured in both acts as the Wanderer, observing but not influencing the events he has set in motion, but at the start of Act 3 he will confront Siegfried, who will shatter the spear of his authority with the sword that he made and proceed up through the flames to Brünnhilde. But Wagner broke off in July 1857 after finishing Act 2 and composed no more music for *Siegfried* or the final *Ring* drama, *Götterdämmerung* (*The Twilight of the Gods*), for nearly twelve years. Instead he almost immediately composed *Tristan und Isolde*, completing this long and complicated score in less than two years. Perhaps, as Newman suggests, he had begun to weary of his gods and dwarfs and to hanker after something more human and more melancholy.[12] He undoubtedly hoped that 'a simple work such as *Tristan*', as he described it to Liszt, would be easier to sell to publishers and theatres than a vast unfinished tetralogy.[13] On the other hand it is surely significant that he turned to a tale of passionate, all-consuming love at the precise moment when that very topic was pending in *Siegfried*. In any case, the striking thing about the new opera is that it took to an extreme the change from the *Gesamtkunstwerk* to 'deeds of music made visible', an expression he himself invented, slightly tongue-in-cheek, to describe music dramas like *Tristan*, 'where there is so little to look at'.[14]

Before the sidelining of *Siegfried*, he and Minna had moved into a house placed at their disposal by a Zurich patron, a silk importer by the name of Otto Wesendonck, and there he composed the first act of *Tristan*. Alas, the later acts had to be written elsewhere (Venice and Lucerne, respectively) because of a passionate and increasingly open relationship that developed between Wagner and Otto's wife, Mathilde, who seems to have served as Wagner's muse, if nothing more specific, in relation to the new work. On one never to be forgotten occasion, the composer read his *Tristan* libretto to a small party consisting of his own wife, Otto and Mathilde, and the pianist-conductor Hans von Bülow and his wife, Liszt's daughter Cosima: wife, mistress and future wife in one room. Perhaps not surprisingly, Mathilde 'had to be consoled'.[15] Minna and Cosima's reactions are not recorded.

Die Walküre and the first two acts of *Siegfried* already display an enriched version of the methods outlined in such detail in *Opera and Drama*. There are new leitmotifs to add to the *Rheingold* list, and they contribute to an increasingly sophisticated and eloquent musical texture. Perhaps in Wotan's torrid interview with Fricka in the second act of *Die Walküre* and here and there among the comings and goings of Act 2 of *Siegfried* it's conceivable still to think in terms of words and music on an equal footing; but in the outer acts of *Die Walküre* the music is now unquestionably the main engine of the drama. Act 3 is decisive in this respect. After 'The Ride of the Valkyries' the music gradually winds down, via Brünnhilde's frantic pleas to her sisters for protection, the brief exaltation of her scene with Sieglinde, and the Valkyries' terror at Wotan's approach, to his angry exchanges with Brünnhilde and their long final scene, calming into her attempts to reason with him, his initial refusal to compromise, but then his yielding to the emotion of their parting. Psychologically this is one of the most movingly beautiful sequences in all opera, and it is controlled entirely by the music, by a symphonic technique learnt, apparently through osmosis, from Beethoven, combined with a mastery of the art of transition that Wagner had learnt from conducting opera after opera that lacked it.

Nothing in *Tristan und Isolde* can quite compare with *Die Walküre* in psychological terms, but musically it surpasses it. Admittedly the scenario lends itself to a purely musical design, largely uncluttered by dramatic interventions. We are on a ship sailing from Ireland to Cornwall. Tristan, a Breton knight, is taking the Irish princess Isolde to Cornwall to marry his uncle, King Mark, but she claims a grudge against him over a previous encounter, and she demands that Tristan share a drink of atonement with her before they land. She intends this as poison, but her maid Brangäne substitutes a love potion, after drinking which and until the very end of the opera the two of them show no further interest in the material world and live only in and through their passion. In the second act they meet at night in an extended love duet, interrupted by occasional warnings from Brangäne, on watch in a nearby tower, and finally, at dawn, by King Mark himself and the treacherous knight Melot, who has deliberately arranged for the lovers to be caught *in flagrante delicto* and now attacks and wounds Tristan. In the final act Tristan lies dying in his native Brittany. His squire, Kurwenal, has sent for Isolde, but she arrives too late to save him, and he dies in her arms. King Mark arrives to forgive, having learnt the circumstances, but too late. Isolde sings the *Liebestod*, the love-death, and falls dead on Tristan's body.

This is not an eventful drama and it leaves a great deal to be assumed. Isolde and Tristan, one supposes, are really in love already but unable, for different reasons, to admit it. The potion releases their inhibitions because they believe it to be poison. Alternatively, Isolde's revenge may be genuine and the potion truly magical, in the best tradition of German Romantic opera. This hardly matters either way, since the sole point of the drama, as Wagner confessed to Liszt, is to 'erect a monument to the most beautiful of all my dreams, in which, from beginning to end . . . love shall be thoroughly satiated',[16] which he could do whatever the history of the passion. The connection of this idea to Schopenhauer, the concept of the renunciation of will and the attainment of the noumenon through love, is too obvious to need elaborating, especially by a non-philosopher, but it does suggest that the reading of *The World as Will and Representation* was the essential underlying cause of Wagner's temporary disillusion with the *Ring*.

The musical impulse for *Tristan*, in any case, had evidently been nagging him for some time before he yielded to it. As early as December 1856 he had written to Carolyne von Sayn-Wittgenstein's daughter, Marie, that 'Tristan has come between [me and Siegfried] in the shape of a melodic thread which, though I fain would have quitted it, kept on spinning itself, so that I could have spent the whole day developing it'.[17] This melodic thread is the key to the whole musical style of a work that has often been cited as one of the main sources for the harmonic adventures of twentieth-century music. The famous 'Tristan chord' (the first actual chord in the work) is merely an icon, as well as a motif, in itself a perfectly orthodox dissonance. More to the point is what happens to its component notes. If you have two or more musical lines playing together, they will either be consonant or dissonant, and in tonal music the rule is that if they are dissonant, they must at some point resolve into a consonance. In general, phrase endings will be consonant, so if resolving dissonance is delayed the effect is to spin out the phrase lengths; and since dissonance also creates tension, the spinning-out will increase that tension. The tension itself can denote different things, depending on the music's gestural language. In *Tristan*, the long, slow, melodic lines, rising in sequence, stand for the unsatisfied yearnings of the two lovers, though in the love scene of the second act those yearnings are temporarily satisfied and the harmony takes on a super-saturated quality, as if the tension were drawing us in, rather than along. Also important here are the gentle, offbeat syncopations, which tend to cancel out the strict bar-by-bar metre. Wagner's skill in managing this complex design is astonishing, and fascinated later composers like Debussy and Stravinsky who had little sympathy with the extended Wagnerian discourse. The precision of his ear in balancing the multiple instrumental lines into which the music divides, with Brangäne's haunting interjections drifting in from the real world, is something that even that curious breed of anti-Wagnerians (who ever heard of an anti-Bachian or an anti-Mozartian?) can surely unreservedly admire.

Tristan und Isolde was a superbly achieved masterpiece, but it was not without forerunners, as Wagner himself knew very well. In 1856 Liszt, now based in Weimar, published a group of orchestral works that he called *Symphonische Dichtungen*, symphonic poems, single-movement works of a programmatic character based mainly on subjects from literature and art: *Tasso* on Byron's poem about the sixteenth-century Italian poet; *Prometheus* on Herder's dramatic poem *Der entfesselte Prometheus* (*Prometheus Unbound*); *Orpheus* on an image on an Etruscan vase in the Louvre; and so forth. The generic title seems to have been Liszt's invention, though there was nothing particularly new in the idea of a descriptive, symphonic orchestral piece in one movement. It was Liszt's approach that was novel. Instead of adapting the idea behind the work to some standard classical form, he wanted the idea to generate a form out of its own particular nature, as a musical response to the feeling it inspired. In order to bind together a form of this kind, he used a technique that came to be known as the transformation of motifs, whereby a single theme would serve in various altered forms for the whole work. During his first ten years at Weimar, Liszt composed a dozen symphonic poems along these lines, as well as two large-scale programme symphonies, the *Faust Symphony* (1854–7) and the *Dante Symphony* (1855–6).

During that time, the whole concept of programme music had become an issue, in Germany at least. In 1852, the critic Franz Brendel, Schumann's successor as editor of the *Neue Zeitschrift für Musik*, published a *History of Music in Italy, Germany and France*, which already pinpointed Liszt, Berlioz and, to a lesser extent, Wagner as key figures in the new music of the time, a position which set him at odds with Schumann himself and his followers. Brendel was an enthusiastic advocate of programme music, and for a time even saw the Liszt of the symphonic poems as the most important living composer. Berlioz he also came to admire, after initial doubts about what he felt to be the music's too close adherence to the poetic (that is, verbal) idea. It was precisely the virtue of Liszt, Brendel argued, that his programme music avoided this fault. Brendel it was who invented the concept of the New German School, a strange, imaginary, not very German cabal of Liszt, Wagner and Berlioz, with various hangers-on, whose music responded to the 'poetic idea' with an approach to form, harmony and orchestral colour that broke away from classical models.

In 1854 there came a counterblast in the form of a book called *Vom Musikalisch-Schönen* (*On the Beautiful in Music*) by a young Viennese music critic called Eduard Hanslick. Hanslick had no time for the idea that music could express this or that emotion, describe this or that scene. 'Of music,' he insisted, 'it is impossible to form any but a musical conception, and it can be comprehended and enjoyed only in and for itself'.[18] Music might arouse emotion in the listener, but that had nothing to do with the composer. Hanslick located himself firmly on the side of the classical masters, and eventually in direct opposition to the New German School and Wagner's Music of the Future.

As it happened, the book came out almost simultaneously with the arrival on the scene of a young pianist-composer from Hamburg called Johannes Brahms, who would in due course be adopted as the mascot of the anti-New German School tendency headed by Schumann's widow, Clara. In April of the year before the book's appearance, Brahms had left Hamburg on an extended concert tour with a Hungarian violinist called Ede Reményi. In Hanover he had made the acquaintance of Joseph Joachim, an old friend of Reményi's and already, at twenty-one, one of the great violinists of the day. A few weeks later they were in Weimar, where they called on Liszt, who, with characteristic generosity, invited them to stay in his house, the Altenburg.[19] Pressed to play his music, Brahms shyly declined, whereupon Liszt sat down and sight-read his visitor's Scherzo in E flat minor and part of his C major Piano Sonata from barely legible manuscript copies. He then played his own enormous single-movement Sonata in B minor, a recently completed work that shared procedures with the symphonic poems. Alas for Hamburg manners, Brahms was seen to close his eyes in slumber. When the sonata finished Liszt left the room without a word.[20]

At the end of September that same year, 1853, Brahms called on the Schumanns in Düsseldorf and this time he played the C major Sonata himself. Schumann did not fall asleep. He noted in his diary 'a visit from Brahms (a genius)', and then he did something he had not done for ten years: he wrote an article for the *Neue Zeitschrift*, under the title 'Neue Bahnen' ('New Paths') hailing the arrival of the young master.[21] Brahms was to prove a ready-made figurehead for the conservative tendency to set up in opposition to the progressives of the New German School. His 1850s music consists mainly of works in classical instrumental genres: three piano sonatas, a pair of orchestral serenades, a piano trio, a string sextet, a piano concerto, some variation sets plus a few songs and choruses. But the music itself is not so easily pigeonholed. The descent from Beethoven is obvious enough, especially in the sonatas and variations. But there is always an element of repressed violence or passion remote from the Olympian muscularity of Beethoven. The openings of the B major Piano Trio and the B flat major Sextet may for instance suggest the 'Archduke' Trio in general character, but there is a kind of tremulous *Innigkeit* about this music that is far from any classical model. The sonatas, on the other hand, seem to explode out of the forms they pretend to inhabit, and the great D minor Piano Concerto was hissed at its first performance in Hanover in 1859 apparently because it did violence to the standard relationship between soloist and orchestra. Oddly enough, folk song is a major ingredient in Brahms's music of this time. He made lovely arrangements of children's songs, used folk tunes or poetry as the basis for the slow movements in his C major and F sharp minor Sonatas, and wrote a set of piano *Ballades* (op. 10) inspired by Herder's *Stimmen der Völker in Liedern*. Many of his original melodies have a folkish tinge, but always with something not quite innocent, some postlapsarian quality that (since we are all lapsed) enhances their beauty.

Brahms might not have seen himself as a traditionalist. He may have slept through Liszt's piano sonata, but he borrowed some of his motivic devices, and in the end became a master of thematic transformation. He got on well with Wagner and helped copy the orchestral parts for *Tannhäuser* and *Meistersinger* excerpts for their composer's 1863 Vienna concerts. But he opposed the New German School and its programme music and, with Joachim, composed a rather tame manifesto that was somehow leaked to the press before it had gathered signatures and was parodied in the *Neue Zeitschrift für Musik*. He was not by nature a controversialist, nor was he inclined to accept packaged opinion. It was his misfortune that after Schumann's death he attached himself closely to Clara, was for a time in love with her, and became the sounding-board for her entrenched hostility to everything to do with the Music of the Future.

Meanwhile in April 1857 the *Neue Zeitschrift für Musik* published an open letter from Richard Wagner to Marie von Sayn-Wittgenstein about Liszt's recently published first batch of symphonic poems, which Wagner, still in exile in Zurich, had presumably examined in score. He noted especially the difference between Liszt's approach to programme music and Berlioz's – a difference already discussed by Brendel in his history. When listening to Berlioz's *Roméo et Juliette*, a work 'so entrancing in its principal motifs', Wagner had suddenly lost the musical thread and found that the only way to go on following the music was to recall the equivalent events in the play. 'The musician', he pointed out, 'looks quite away from the incidents of ordinary life, entirely ignores its details and its accidentals, and sublimates whatever lies within it to its quintessence of emotional content, to which alone music and only music can give voice.' This was Liszt's achievement. 'With Liszt,' Wagner went on, 'this masterly grip in the musical conception speaks out with such power at the very outset of the piece, that after the first sixteen bars I often could not restrain the astonished cry: "Enough, I have it all!"' And with half an eye on his own next project, he adds the qualification that 'the difficulties that stand in the way of dramatic compositions, due to the far greater complexity of their media of expression, are smaller in the case of more purely orchestral works'.[22]

The comparison, nevertheless, is significant. Not only is *Tristan* a work that lives pre-eminently through its music, but it might even tempt one to echo Wagner's cry, 'Enough, I have it all!' if not after sixteen bars, at least by the end of the prelude, except that music is not information in that crude sense; what it's about is not all of what it is. But *Tristan* owed a debt to Liszt in other ways as well. From quite early in his compositional life, Liszt had been a harmonic and melodic adventurer, partly through improvising at the piano. Wagner, no great pianist, operated quite differently. The harmonies in *Tristan*, however tense and unresolved, nevertheless follow voice-leading rules, only stretching them to their logical limits. Liszt is sometimes careless about such matters. In *Prometheus*, for instance, the horror of the hero's situation, chained to a rock while an eagle pecks at his liver, suggests dissonant harmonies that strictly go nowhere, tortured melodies that cry out inarticulately. Here the dreaded Tristan chord pops up several times, alongside the more conventional diminished seventh, almost as isolated incidents. In this sense, Liszt's harmonies are like objects or images, Wagner's are part of a process. It was a distinction that would assume increasing importance as the century advanced towards its close.

The Nation Speaks

While Wagner languished in Zurich, writing, composing, conducting, philandering, but with his work largely unperformed, operatic life carried on elsewhere in blissful ignorance of the artistic minefield he was laying. When Liszt conducted *Lohengrin* in Weimar in August 1850, with its exiled composer tracking its course on a clock in a Zurich inn, it was the last Wagner premiere until he himself conducted the prelude to *Tristan* in a Paris concert in January 1860. One could read his books, if one had the stomach and the necessary German. But with none of the relevant music available, or even in existence, they would probably confuse more than they would elucidate. Imagine having struggled through *Opera and Drama*, then being confronted with the *Tristan* prelude and desperately trying to relate this strange, intense, wordless complexity to what you've been reading. Better to have read nothing. After attending Wagner's Paris concerts, the poet Charles Baudelaire wrote him a letter of rapturous appreciation that responded entirely to the atmosphere of the music and ignored any theoretical underpinning. The audience reaction to *Tannhäuser* at the Opéra the following year was admittedly somewhat less than rapturous, and certainly not because those responsible for the racket that accompanied all three performances had been reading about Wagner's theories. The background was almost certainly political: anti-Austrian in the person of the ambassador's unpopular wife, Princess Pauline Metternich, who had sponsored the production, and perhaps anti-German as well. The reason often given – that Wagner had failed to include a ballet in the traditional spot in Act 2 but had instead hugely expanded the Venusberg music that follows the overture – makes little sense. Successful recent operas had got by without significant ballets, or (like Rossini's *William Tell* or Meyerbeer's *Le Prophète*) with ballets in other acts.

The contrast between Wagner and Verdi in the 1850s could hardly be starker. By 1850 Verdi had established himself beyond question as the leading composer in Italy; but it was a status that demanded a continuous presence in the public eye. In Italy, at least, the idea of an operatic repertoire was still in its infancy, and it was almost impossible for a composer to retain his position without a flow of new work. Verdi no longer needed to churn out an opera or two every year, as he had been doing since 1839. Nevertheless between 1851 and 1853 he composed three works that have since become models of Italian opera: everyone's idea of what Italian opera is, even though, as it happens, they are already moving away from the standard model. Then over the following eight years he added another four operas, sharply differentiated from one another, driven, however, not by theory, but by the response of a vigorous, restless-minded genius to the varying circumstances that arose from his fame.

Between them the three great works of the early fifties – *Rigoletto*, *Il trovatore* (*The Troubadour*) and *La traviata* – are an object lesson in how to take a conventional genre by the scruff of the neck and force it to yield hitherto unsuspected secrets. Perhaps the most remarkable of all is *Il trovatore*, not because it's the greatest, which it perhaps is not, but because of the seemingly inexhaustible brilliance of Verdi's response to a plot and dramatis personae of the purest imaginable fatuity. There is a lurid and far-fetched back story set in fifteenth-century Spain which, rather as in the *Ring*, the various characters from time to time relate to one another; but what we see on the stage is an Italian tenor (Manrico) in love with an Italian soprano (Leonora), who is also loved by a morose Italian baritone (Count di Luna), who captures and kills Manrico then discovers he was his brother. The one interesting character in the whole piece is the contralto gypsy Azucena, whose mother was burnt at the stake as a witch, and who in revenge incinerated what she thought was the old Count's baby son but turned out to have been her own.

One way of looking at *Il trovatore* is that its plot is simply a vehicle, Wagner's 'deeds of music made visible'. Gabriele Baldini called it 'the perfect musical libretto, a text which allowed for the musical life of its characters, and for that alone'.[1] Baldini saw this as a revolutionary property, but it is perhaps better described as the apotheosis of a long tradition of Italian opera in which nobody bothered too much about the plot, and what mattered was strong situations as a platform for great singing. *Il trovatore* is at times almost a parody of that genre: unforgettable aria after unforgettable aria, chorus after chorus, in Verdi's most virile melodic and rhythmic vein, the harmony supplied mostly by elementary chord repetitions, performed by larger-than-life marionettes. Its timeless popularity proves the power of theatre as a state of being, in which a singer or actor steps forward and delivers something marvellous in some contrived situation or other, regardless of the before or after.

Yet Verdi aspired to a quite different kind of opera, one 'in which there were neither cavatinas, nor duets, nor trios, nor choruses . . . and the whole opera was one single piece'.[2] This was not quite the Wagner of *Opera and Drama*, though probably a response to some of the same influences. Even in Italian opera there was nothing particularly new about the idea; already in *Il trovatore* the design is in scenes rather than numbers, creating a generally more fluid narrative. But Verdi seems also to have had in mind a more probing, psychological kind of organism, in which set pieces still existed, but within a quasi-realistic conversational texture. Both *Rigoletto* and *La traviata* depend to some extent on this kind of discourse, and in that sense they are less purely operatic, more play-like, than *Il trovatore*.

Both works were in fact based on recent French plays, *Rigoletto* on Victor Hugo's *Le Roi s'amuse* (1832), *La traviata* on Alexandre Dumas's *La Dame aux camélias*, originally a novel, but staged as a play in February 1852, barely a year before the Venice premiere of Verdi's opera. *Rigoletto* is remarkable for the precise role played by set-piece numbers in defining the three central characters: the Duke of Mantua, an unscrupulous womaniser, stylish, elegant, emotionally superficial; the jester Rigoletto, a role-player whose own feelings lie hidden beneath professional ribaldry; and his daughter, Gilda, overprotected, lovelorn and naive. The Duke's arias, including two of the most famous in all opera ('Questa o quella' and 'La donna è mobile'), are masculine boasting, solo because he is the duke and an oversexed male. Gilda, virtually a prisoner in her father's house, can only soliloquise, in 'Caro nome' and (telling her story) 'Tutte le feste'. But the set-piece aria is otherwise largely subsumed into the conversational flow. Rigoletto's natural genre is backchat, but his true feelings come out in his one genuine human relationship, with his daughter. With her he shares aria-like duets, but Verdi allows him only one solo number, his magnificent outburst against the 'Cortigiani, vil razza dannata', the vile, damned breed of courtiers, and even this concludes in a kind of monologue as he pleads with these same courtiers to tell him where they have hidden Gilda. In these ways Verdi uses the set-piece convention flexibly to serve a variety of situations, culminating famously in the *coup de théâtre* when Rigoletto, believing he has the duke's corpse in the sack, hears him singing 'La donna è mobile' from the inn. We already know whose corpse is in the sack, and she was the one woman in the piece who was emphatically not 'mobile', which is why she ended up in the sack.

La traviata develops this technique into a genuine psychological study of the 'fallen woman' of the title, who to be exact starts out 'fallen' but picks herself up in the course of the opera, in an act of genuine self-sacrifice that makes Gilda's look merely hysterical. Here too the conflict is between sex and true love, but this time in the one person. Violetta Valéry, the opera's equivalent of the novel's Marguerite Gautier and her real-life model Marie Duplessis, is mortally ill with tuberculosis, and when Alfredo Germont declares passionate love for her, she is momentarily torn between the pull of a real emotion and the freedom of her courtesan life. She decides for Alfredo, moves to the country with him, and there she is visited by his father, who demands that she give Alfredo up for the sake of his sister, whose provincial betrothal is threatened by his association with a courtesan. The opera's second act, in which this confrontation takes place, is one of the great acts in opera. From the start it moves swiftly, through Alfredo's musing on his happiness, then his shame on learning that Violetta, who has been keeping them on her own savings, is selling her belongings. Off he goes to Paris, without her knowledge, to raise the money himself, and meanwhile his father enters, at first brusquely (after all, Violetta is a whore and no doubt a kept woman), then more respectfully when he observes her dignified deportment and learns who has been paying the bills. Still, she must give Alfredo up. For a time? No, for good. I would rather die, she says; in fact, I *am* dying. Remorselessly, he points out that her liaison with Alfredo is unblest; and she, a penitent, admits it. But now, he suggests, is her chance to make her peace with heaven by being 'a consoling angel'. So, she reflects bitterly, God is merciful but man is implacable; all right, tell your sweet daughter about the victim of misfortune who gave up her one ray of sunshine, and died. They part in tears, she for her old life in Paris, he to await Alfredo and urge him to come home to Provence.

This is a psychologically complex scene by operatic standards, but Verdi is equal to all its nuances. The pacing is masterly, the interleaving of aria and arioso, in a continuous discourse that nevertheless acknowledges those moments in any conversation where dialogue gives way to explanation, and that above all catches the changes of mood, the responses to things said, the contrasts of character: Alfredo, impulsive, volatile, unreflecting; his father, dull, upright, narrow-minded; Violetta, frail-bodied but strong-willed, a woman who knows her worth and her unworth, a beautiful, tragic soul. There are no 'great arias' here; they would be out of place; nor is it musically advanced in any particular way. It simply adapts with consummate skill what is to hand. The score is immaculate, perhaps inferior to *Il trovatore* in terms of highlights, far superior to it as stage drama. The ensuing scene, a party in the mansion of the *demi-mondaine* Flora Bervoix, builds a thrilling ensemble out of Alfredo's crazed abuse of poor Violetta, who cannot defend herself, knowing that he would return to her if he discovered the truth. Only at the very end of the opera, as she lies dying, do these reconciliations take place, and here too Verdi handles a scene that could easily descend into mawkishness with perfect tact. Perhaps a soprano dying of a chest complaint will always tempt satire, but Verdi disarms any such response by his control of the emotional temperature: nostalgia ('Addio, del passato'), rage against the dying of the light (in the great duet 'Gran Dio! morir si giovine'), and then the extraordinary moment – not, I'm told, altogether implausible clinically – when Violetta suddenly rises from her pillow, declares herself cured, then falls back stone dead.

The Venice premiere of *La traviata* was, according to Verdi himself, a fiasco. The performance was poor, and the whole concept of the work, a domestic tragedy set in Paris drawing rooms, was alien to audiences who expected opera to be about larger-than-life characters in olden times (though in fact the Fenice had lost its nerve about the contemporary setting and switched it to the time of Louis XIV). Worst of all, they laughed at a tubby Violetta dying of consumption, as have audiences sometimes since. In our own day, when new operas and productions of old ones are routinely presented in modern street dress as if this somehow guaranteed them 'relevance', it's worth recalling how bizarre it was thought in Verdi's day to see contemporaries treading the boards and singing as they went. It was not a mistake he, for one, ever made again.

He was to come closest with his next opera but two, *Un ballo in maschera* (*A Masked Ball*), which culminates in the assassination of the Swedish king, Gustavus III, at a ball at the Stockholm Opera House in 1792. But this subject ran into trouble for other, perhaps predictable, reasons. Regicide was not a happy topic for 1850s censors, even when (as here in Scribe's libretto, previously set by Auber) the motive is sexual rather than political. Various censors proposed various relocations: seventeenth-century Pomerania, fourteenth-century Florence, and – the solution adopted for the 1859 Rome premiere – pre-Independence Boston, with the king replaced by the English Governor, mysteriously renamed Riccardo. In fact the setting is not all that important. The assassin, Anckarström/Renato, is taking revenge for Gustavus/Riccardo's presumed infidelity with his wife, Amelia, and Riccardo himself, when not philandering, is mainly having fun, visiting the fortune-teller, Ulrica, with his entire court, and planning the guest-list for the masked ball. Politics barely figure. The score, one of Verdi's most sparkling, reflects these emphases. In the music for the page, Oscar, there are echoes of Parisian *opéra comique*, and Riccardo's own music often suggests his easy-going, unreflecting nature. Even the darker music for the crystal ball-gazing Ulrica has a tinge of pantomime. The whole opera, including the tense meeting of the lovers at the gallows at midnight, their discovery by Renato and his consequent mockery at the hands of a whole Gilbertian bunch of conspirators, not to mention the ball scene itself, breathes a spirit of sheer enjoyment, the pure pleasure of invention.

Any Parisian influence was straight from the horse's mouth. Verdi had been commissioned by the Opéra to compose a grand opera for performance during the Exposition Universelle of 1855, and he accordingly spent the whole of 1854 and 1855 until the premiere that June in the French capital, composing and overseeing the production. The subject was the Sicilian Vespers, an episode during the French rule in Sicily in 1282, complicated by the French viceroy's discovery that one of the chief Sicilian conspirators is his own illegitimate son, and ending with a historical massacre of the French triggered by the vespers bells of Palermo's churches. This might seem a suitable topic for a supporter of the Risorgimento. But from the start Verdi found Scribe's libretto absurdly ramshackle and implausible, and he took exception to its tendency, as he thought, to show the Sicilians in a poor light. He nevertheless did his best. There is magnificent music, some telling characterisation, and enterprising orchestration for the big Opéra orchestra; yet the piece as a whole hangs fire, and the ending, surprisingly, is tame.

Back in Italy, Verdi turned to another political subject with complications of paternity, and again it created problems. This was *Simon Boccanegra*, another epic tale of politics and passion, set this time in fourteenth-century Genoa. Verdi was to have more success with this work when he revised it with additional music in 1880–1, and the original version now seems a somewhat half-hearted attempt at what came to be known as *opéra dialogué*, opera in which the lyrical element is played down in favour of a kind of declamatory arioso. What is interesting about all three of these post-*Traviata* works is the way Verdi is suddenly drawn to subjects that suggest a conflict between political and personal loyalties, something he had first attempted in *Nabucco* but had generally avoided since.

What operas did Verdi hear in Paris? The possibilities are not inspiring. We know that he attended the first performance of Meyerbeer's *L'Étoile du nord*. He might have caught a new piece by a still comparatively unknown composer called Charles Gounod, *La Nonne sanglante* (*The Bleeding Nun*), a grand opera somewhat in the genre of *Robert le diable*, in which the hero marries the ghost of a nun by mistake and can only be released by killing her murderer, who turns out to be his own father. This reads like, but is not, a joke. The libretto (by Scribe and Germain Delavigne) had already been offered to Verdi in the late forties, and before that to Berlioz, who composed most of the first two acts before abandoning it. Had Verdi ventured to the Bouffes-Parisiens in July 1855, three weeks after his own first night, he might have witnessed a derisory little farce called *Les Deux Aveugles* by a certain Jacques Offenbach, a young German-born cellist and composer who had been conducting at the Opéra-Comique but had made barely any mark with his own work. His first – and greatest – success would come three years later with *Orphée aux enfers* (*Orpheus in the Underworld*), a brilliant spoof on the legend, featuring an Orpheus who is fed up with his wife Eurydice's complaints about

his violin-playing, delighted when she is bitten by a snake, but furious
at nevertheless being required by Public Opinion to retrieve her from
Hades. Not only were Offenbach's melody and general tone of musical
voice a good deal livelier than anything in *opéra comique* since Auber's
Fra Diavolo, but his sending-up of such earnest schoolroom material
as the activities of the Parnassian gods was guaranteed to set the educated Parisian middle classes rocking in the aisles. It was a recipe that
could stand repeating, and Offenbach duly repeated it, with no less
success, with *La Belle Hélène* (1864), a sparkling satire on the presumed
events leading up to the Trojan War.

Gounod took a somewhat different route in the treatment of
learned subject matter by turning Goethe's *Faust* into an opera,
apparently the first composer to risk such an impertinence.[3] Gounod
had spent time as a young man in Germany, was on friendly terms
with the Mendelssohns, and had discovered Goethe through Fanny
Mendelssohn as a Prix de Rome pensioner in Rome in the 1840s. His
Faust (1859: originally with dialogue, later turned into recitative) is a
curious yet effective blend of typically French, *boulevardier* elements
and the caustic diabolism and lurking tragedy of the play, with barely
a hint, however, of the lofty redemptive outcomes of Goethe's Part 2.
The work has aroused mixed responses, and its popularity has faded in
recent years; in Gounod's manner there is a blandness that sometimes
undermines the earnest intent, for all his smooth elegance of melody
and transparent orchestration. He wrote several more operas, including
an atmospheric dramatisation of Mistral's Provençal poem *Mireille*,
and an underrated *Roméo et Juliette*, and there is also some fine sacred
music, in much the same style (Gounod had for a time considered holy
orders). But outside France he has remained stubbornly a one-work
composer, which has at least kept him ahead of his slightly older contemporary, Ambroise Thomas, whose *Mignon* and *Hamlet* (1866 and
1868 respectively) have survived only in hard-working festival revivals.

Berlioz, meanwhile, had been composing a pair of sacred works so
violently contrasted in scale and character as to suggest some kind

of experimental approach to the genre. After all, Berlioz had 'long since fallen out' with the Catholic Church.[4] The hour-long Te Deum, with its vast choral and orchestral forces, had been composed in 1849, apparently for no better, if no worse, reason than the desire to recreate the complete image of a spectacular religious ceremony in the grandest church imaginable, and these were more or less the circumstances when the work was eventually performed in the church of Saint-Eustache in April 1855, by way of prelude to the Exposition Universelle, which opened in May.

The tone of the oratorio *L'Enfance du Christ* (*The Childhood of Christ*), which Berlioz conducted in the Salle Herz in December 1854, could hardly be more different. In a sense the account of King Herod's dream with its grim consequences, the Flight into Egypt, and the Holy Family's reception at Sais on the Nile delta, is as theatrical in its way as the Te Deum. Berlioz is no less painstaking with his instructions about the platform layout, and the score is graphic in the way that, for instance, the *St Matthew Passion* is graphic, with role-play for the chorus (soothsayers and angels in Part 1, shepherds in Part 2, a hostile *turba* in Part 3), and vivid writing for a theatre-size orchestra. But though not without its violent episodes, this is in the main a gentle score dominated by pastoral sounds, a Herod who is by no means brutal until his soothsayers force his hand, and a sad refugee family turned away from Egyptian doors but at last welcomed by Ishmaelites. The attitude to religion revealed by these two minor masterpieces is, at bottom, Romantic. The outsider looks in on ceremonies and legends he can no longer embrace, but yearns for the emotion he once felt kneeling to pray or, like the child Berlioz, going to the altar to receive communion while 'a chorus of fresh young voices [breaks] into the eucharistic hymn'.[5] Alas for the shades of Palestrina and Bach, the tune he heard was a sentimental ballad from Dalayrac's opera *Nina*, 'furnished with a text suitable for the occasion'.

For some time before composing *L'Enfance du Christ* Berlioz had been pondering a bigger project than anything even he had previously undertaken, an opera about the Trojan War and its aftermath, based on one of his greatest literary obsessions, Virgil's *Aeneid*. 'I am resisting the temptation to carry out this project,' he wrote in 1854, 'and shall, I trust, resist to the end. To me the subject seems magnificent and deeply moving – sure proof that Parisians would think it flat and tedious.'[6] He did write it, nevertheless, completing it in April 1858; and his prognosis of the Parisian response proved all too accurate. *Les Troyens* (*The Trojans*) is a grand opera fully in the tradition of Auber and Meyerbeer, on a comparable scale, in five acts, with spectacular scenic effects and the necessary conflict between the public and private spheres. Its main problem for the Opéra, the natural home for such a work, was Berlioz himself, a dangerous original who had moreover frequently attacked the Opéra in print. In due course, the work was taken on by the smaller, less well-equipped Théâtre Lyrique, who persuaded the composer to divide it into two evenings, *The Capture of Troy* and *The Trojans at Carthage*, then finally ditched the first part altogether and gave the second, heavily cut, a run of performances from November 1863. Nothing more was heard of the work in Berlioz's lifetime.

In this last respect its fate was not very different from that of every other French grand opera, with the possible exception of *William Tell*. There is even something Meyerbeerian, especially about the first two acts, set in Troy and dominated by the Trojan horse, the choral ceremonies and hubbub surrounding it, Cassandra's passionate warnings, Aeneas' vision of the ghost of Hector, and the mass suicide of the Trojan women. The Carthaginian acts are more spacious and lyrical. Aeneas and his Trojan survivors arrive in Carthage just as the city and its queen, Dido, are threatened with attack by the neighbouring Numidians; they offer their help and the Numidians are defeated. Dido and Aeneas fall in love, but Aeneas is summoned by Mercury to continue his journey to Italy to found the city of Rome, and in despair Dido orders a funeral pyre for herself, climbs on to it and stabs herself with Aeneas's sword.

The real inspiration here was Gluck; Gluckian turns of melodic and harmonic phrase crop up all the time in Berlioz's writing. Otherwise the old Berlioz qualities are fully on show: the fluid melodic lines of the *Roméo* love music and *Faust*, the mercurial rhythms of *Benvenuto Cellini*, the brilliantly coloured orchestral scoring. In all respects *The Trojans* is the climax of the French operatic tradition. Musically it shows hardly any Germanic influence, possibly excepting Weber in the Royal Hunt and Storm, where Dido and Aeneas consummate their love to the accompaniment of satyrs, wood nymphs and distant hunting horns. And it far outstrips its French models. Nothing in Meyerbeer or Halévy matches Berlioz's portrait of Cassandra, torn between her love for Coroebus and her vision of the certain destruction of Troy; or the Shakespearean love duet for Dido and Aeneas (inspired by the scene of Lorenzo and Jessica in Act 5 of *The Merchant of Venice*: Berlioz loved combining his obsessions); or the big choral and orchestral set pieces, always thrillingly bold and individual.

Then, having touched on Shakespeare in *The Trojans*, Berlioz turned to him once more for his last opera, *Béatrice et Bénédict* (1862), based on the main plot line of *Much Ado about Nothing*, the 'merry war' between the eponymous characters and their eventual marriage, but leaving out Don John's conspiracy against Claudio and Hero. This is a very different affair from any of Berlioz's previous dramatic works, lighter in touch and better formed than his only remotely comparable score, *Roméo et Juliette*, but to some extent compromised by the insertion of spoken dialogue, taken more or less straight from the play. The device creates casting problems: Shakespeare spoken by singers is rarely a pleasure, and in any case tends to interfere with the musical pacing. The music is some of Berlioz's most beautiful, but the opera never quite comes off in the theatre as well as the music deserves.

It's plausible to see the 1850s as some kind of culmination of early romanticism. In its various guises, romanticism had come into being as an assertion of the individual against the universals of the

Enlightenment. Three revolutions had fought this cause, with mixed success politically. Yet a lot had happened in the day-to-day world that looked like the product of an increasingly open, liberal environment, things that made life easier, and conducive to a longer and better one. Rail travel was not just four times quicker than the horse-drawn coach, it was more agreeable, and trains carried mail, which thus also became four times quicker, until the electric telegraph of the 1850s made it nearly instantaneous. Roads were improving and there were more and faster ways of getting about, including primitive bicycles, known as velocipedes ('fast walkers'). People were living longer, thanks to advances in medicine, especially in the treatment of diseases such as smallpox, puerperal fever and cholera. More was known about the world. In 1851 Léon Foucault hung a pendulum from the dome of the Pantheon in Paris, and proved (in case proof were still needed) that the earth rotated on its axis. Four years later David Livingstone crossed Central Africa and was the first European to see the Victoria Falls. Four years after that, in 1859, Charles Darwin published *On the Origin of Species*.

Darwin's theory somehow encapsulated the gradual demythologising of the material world. If evolution seemed to invalidate mankind's special status in the world, science in general was invading his perception of its mysteries. People were discovering not just new waterfalls, but new planets. Nicéphore Niépce and Louis Daguerre were taking photographs that would transform people's awareness of each other and the world they lived in. Perhaps worst of all, philosophers from Hegel onwards were expounding a view of history that implicitly denied human beings any control of their own destiny. The most terrifying example of this tendency, Karl Marx's *Das Kapital*, would not appear until 1867, but already in 1859 he had brought out a pre-echo of that book in what he called *A Contribution to the Critique of Political Economy*, whose preface announced, among other things, that 'it is not the consciousness of men that determines their existence, but their social existence that determines their consciousness'.[7] It was bad enough for any artist to be told that his inner world was nothing but a consequence of the people he knew; for the Romantic artist it was annihilation.

One response to this materialist threat might be a retreat into the self: into solitude, or remote places, into the distant past, into dreams, the irrational, into myth, magic and, if all else failed, chaos and insanity. One particular escape route was the one outlined almost a century before by Herder, and also incidentally, in a somewhat different context, by Voltaire: to cultivate your own garden. Musicians had been slow to follow this advice. Chopin and Liszt had both sampled their native earth, but from a safe distance. Isolated works by Moniuszko and Erkel had hinted at what might be possible on home ground. There was a kind of latent nationalism in Verdi and Wagner, but it was mainly a question of subject matter rather than musical material. Verdi's chorus could sing about its native land, but it did so in the same style as it sang about everything else. Wagner, and Weber before him, could plunge into the dark German forest, but their music descended, as before, from Beethoven and Schubert.

Around 1860 this situation was changing. In June 1859 the Austrian army was defeated in two key battles against the combined French and Sardinian armies, at Magenta and Solferino, with the result that Austria had to cede a part of its Italian territories and was weakened in its internal relations with its ethnic peoples. The most dramatic effect was in Prague and the Czech-speaking lands. Suddenly it was possible to perform plays and operas in Czech. Plans were laid for the building of a National Theatre in Prague, and meanwhile in November 1862 the so-called Provisional Theatre opened with a piece by the Czech playwright Vítězslav Hálek. Operas in Czech were still practically nonexistent, but this too would soon change, chiefly through the agency of a German-speaking pianist, conductor and composer who had been working mainly in Sweden for the past five years but hurried back to Prague early in 1861 full of patriotic intentions inspired, especially, by the announcement of a competition for Czech operas in Czech.

Bedřich Smetana was thirty-six years old and already the composer of a considerable body of piano music and several orchestral works, including a pair of Lisztian symphonic poems, *Richard III* (after Shakespeare) and *Wallensteins Lager* (*Wallenstein's Camp*) (after Schiller). He had written nothing for the theatre, but now produced for the competition a three-act opera, *Braniboři v Čechách* (*The Brandenburgers in Bohemia*), set in thirteenth-century Prague and the surrounding countryside at a time when Bohemia was being laid waste by German troops. The work won the competition but was not staged until January 1866, by which time Smetana had composed most of a second opera, this time a bitter sweet comedy, *Prodaná nevěsta* (*The Bartered Bride*), set in a Bohemian village.

The Bartered Bride has come down in the repertory as the archetypal national opera, though in fact preceded, as we saw, by Moniuszko and Erkel. But quality aside, Smetana's comedy is a subtly different affair from their work. In the original 1868 version, which had spoken dialogue and lacked the well-known dances, its Czechness was mainly confined to the subject matter, and a few polka rhythms here and there. The 1869 revision, with recitative and dances, has a more consistently 'local' feel, but this still has as much as anything to do with the plot, which partly hangs on specifically Slav social conventions. Mařenka and Jeník are in love, but Mařenka is being forced by her father to marry the son of a wealthy local landowner, by way of the characteristic Slav institution of the marriage-broker. This son, Vašek, turns out to be a half-wit with a stammer, and meanwhile Jeník is paid off by the broker to give Mařenka up, an act that nearly leads to an embittered ending until Jeník reveals that he is himself also the landowner's son, by his first wife, with an elder claim on Mařenka's hand.

To modern audiences, the work's musical idiom seems essentially Czech, but that may be partly because it was this opera, together with one or two later works by Smetana, that established the image of a Czech style. Smetana seldom quotes or mimics folk music directly, though the dances and simple song forms and the occasional melodic twist may remind us that we are in rural Bohemia; and his setting of Czech, not his mother tongue, is said to be unidiomatic. He wanted above all to celebrate the culture and history of the Czech lands and to be remembered as their chronicler. *Dalibor* (1868) reimagines the trial and death of a fifteenth-century Hussite knight who was executed for his part in a rising against the Catholic king of Hungary; *Libuše* (1872) makes a pageant out of the legend of the wise Czech queen who married a ploughman and foretold the founding of Prague. Above all, the cycle of six symphonic poems under the title *Má vlast* (*My Fatherland*, 1874–9) amounts to a complete manifesto of Czech identity, from the legendary heroines and heroes – the ferocious Šárka, who fought Libuše's ploughman widower in the so-called Maiden's War, and the Hussite warriors of *Tábor* and *Blaník* – to the landscape that echoes these tales, the great fortress of Vyšehrad in Prague, the Vltava river, and the beauties of the countryside itself in *Z českých luhů a hájů* (*From Bohemia's Fields and Forests*). Notwithstanding their Czech imagery, these are programme works in the Liszt tradition, complete with transformation of motifs, and forms that grow out of the subject matter. The results, it must be said, are uneven, with a tendency to dwell on not very interesting material. Only *Vltava* and *From Bohemia's Fields and Forests* are heard with any frequency outside Prague, but the complete cycle is still played every year in the Prague Spring Festival on the anniversary of Smetana's death.

One day in June 1866 a young Russian composer by the name of Mily Balakirev had arrived in Prague to organise a production of Mikhail Glinka's *A Life for the Tsar*. His timing could hardly have been worse. Two days after his arrival, the Austro-Prussian War broke out, and with the Prussians advancing on Prague poor Balakirev had to scuttle home to St Petersburg. But he was back in Prague in December, by which time the Glinka opera was in production, conducted by Smetana. Balakirev hated what he saw and heard, and he blamed Smetana, who 'deliberately gave them the wrong tempi in the performance in order to put them off'. He also suspected Smetana of pinching the score of Glinka's *Ruslan and Lyudmila* just before he, Balakirev, was due to conduct it, a scheme that failed, as he knew the work by heart. Behind all this there was probably a degree of pan-Slav jealousy between two domineering personalities. 'Smetana and I', Balakirev wrote to Glinka's sister, Lyudmila Shestakova, 'are no longer on speaking terms. We only bow to one another.'[8] But *Ruslan* nevertheless went off well and Balakirev returned to Russia full of warm thoughts about all but one of his fellow Slavs.

For ten years there had been a comparable movement in Russia towards a music that would be definably Russian, and Balakirev had been one of its prime movers. He had arrived in St Petersburg aged eighteen in 1855 from his native Nizhny Novgorod, and had met Glinka through the rich landowner who had been paying for his piano lessons. At Glinka's he had met Vladimir Stasov, a musically literate art historian with a passion for Russian history and a deep knowledge of its sources. Between them, these two would effectively create the agenda for a music that would be truly Russian and independent of western models.

This was a more difficult project than for the Czechs. They at least had a respectable, even distinguished tradition of composition, playing and instruction reaching back to Dussek, Hummel and Tomášek. In Russia the case was very different. Since Peter the Great had transferred his court to the newly built city of St Petersburg in the early 1700s, Russian music had been dominated by foreigners, brought in as part of a general policy of westernising Russian culture, society and economy. The focus of music was the Italian opera, though the court itself was dominated by Germans, and indeed the greatest of the tsars after Peter himself, Catherine the Great, was herself purely German.[9] There had been little opportunity for Russian composers to achieve serious prominence. Operas had been composed but were limited in scope, either vaudevilles with dialogue or provincial versions of western genres. Concert life was limited to the court and various private orchestras. Until the late 1850s there were no regular public concerts, no established orchestras except in the opera houses, no professional chamber groups, and above all no music conservatory until 1862, when the St Petersburg Conservatoire opened its doors. The most successful Russian composers before Glinka were songwriters like Alexander Alyabyev and Alexander Gurilyov, who wrote in a distantly folk-derived style that Richard Taruskin has dubbed the 'urban *style russe*',[10] and the church composer Dmitry Bortnyansky, who in the time of the Empress Catherine composed a large number of sacred concertos and choral music for the Orthodox liturgy, all for unaccompanied voices, and then used his position as director of the Imperial Court Chapel to standardise church music throughout the Orthodox communion. Glinka himself, the musically gifted descendant of Smolensk landowners, was a prime victim of this system, but was suddenly infected, while on an extended trip to Italy in the early thirties, with an urgent desire to hurry home and compose, as he recalled, 'like a Russian'. The result, *Zhizn' za tsarya* (*A Life for the Tsar*: St Petersburg, 1836), was literally the first grand opera by a Russian composer: a completely new kind of work, a hybrid of western, especially Italian, operatic idioms and Russianisms of various kinds, all attached to a scenario of so strongly emblematic a character, about the rescue of the first Romanov Tsar from invading Poles, that it rapidly became an officially approved nationalist icon, and even survived into Soviet times with, admittedly, an altered libretto and a new (though in fact Glinka's original) title, *Ivan Susanin*.

The work is, among other things, an unashamed pro-Russian tract in which Polish invaders, in search of the new Tsar Mikhail Romanov, are led astray into deep forest by the brave Russian villager Ivan Susanin, who knows they will kill him when they realise what he has done to them. For Glinka, as for most Russians of his day, the Poles were an evil bunch of Catholic heretics, and he ridicules them by having them do next to nothing but dance; even the cavalry detachment that arrives at Susanin's house demanding to know Romanov's whereabouts is accompanied by a sprightly polacca. Meanwhile the Russians are sympathetically if stereotypically portrayed through a potent mixture of folk song, Orthodox hymnody, and large set pieces including a final triumphal chorus in a ceremonial seventeenth-century Russian style known as *kant*.

Glinka's second opera, *Ruslan and Lyudmila* (1842), is a very different affair. Glinka had hoped to work out a scenario with the author of the original poem, Alexander Pushkin, but Pushkin had been killed in a duel in 1837, so Glinka got on with writing the music in the absence of any ground plan, not to mention any libretto, and this was eventually provided in bits and pieces by various writers, often having to be fitted to music that already existed. Not surprisingly, the work is dramaturgically a shambles, involving an abducted princess, a king who offers half his kingdom to her rescuer, an evil dwarf, Chernomor, with a long beard that houses his magic, rival suitors, rival magicians, and a huge severed head that gives Ruslan a sword with which to defeat Chernomor. Out of this farrago, however, Glinka invented an idiom that would serve his Russian successors for a whole series of magical fairy-tale operas and ballets over the next seventy years. He introduced strange, disorientating harmonic effects, notably the whole-tone scale for Lyudmila's abduction and Chernomor's enchanted garden; and he orchestrated with a glittering brilliance and freedom for which there was virtually no precedent in any western music of the day, especially for high woodwind and the brighter percussion instruments. Some of his string colourings too, especially in the magic dances, are sensational. Oddly enough, Russian folk song, a prominent feature of *A Life for the Tsar*, plays no part in *Ruslan*, though there is a Finnish tune sung at inordinate length by a sorcerer called Finn, and a Persian tune for the houris of the enchantress Naina. So the two operas approached Russianism from opposite angles, and between them initiated a double tradition. Only in a short orchestral piece called *Kamarinskaya* (1848) did Glinka return to his native folk song, working two tunes into a lively, crisply scored miniature based on multiple repetitions with varied orchestration: the 'changing background' method.

In the west, a Glinka would have been regarded as an irredeemable if gifted eccentric, and would probably have attracted only a fringe following. In Russia, in the total absence of good native models, he was treated as a father figure. Balakirev and Stasov, though they disagreed about his operas, agreed on his importance, and were soon acting as his prophets. They quickly assembled fellow travellers. Alexander Dargomïzhsky (1813–69) was older than either of them, had known Glinka since the thirties, and had himself had two operas staged, of which the more recent, *Rusalka* (1856, from an unfinished play by Pushkin), already embodied certain Glinkaesque tendencies, including the use of folk song, though on a more homely level. It also touched on a technique that Dargomïzhsky would develop fully in his last opera, *Kamennïy gost'* (*The Stone Guest*), where he studiously sets Pushkin's Don Juan play word for word in a quasi-speech style.

Rusalka was a modest work and a modest success, but its composer was nevertheless being regarded as a leading progressive on the strength of it. His own musical *soirées* testified to the fact. Balakirev began to attend them, and there he met a young cadet of the Preobrazhensky Guards who could play the piano and sing in an exceedingly unguards-like fashion. This was Modest Musorgsky, barely eighteen and a some-what affected creature who pomaded his hair and manicured his hands, and expressed himself with foppish gestures of the arms, but was clearly a talented musician. Another musical military man at Dargomïzhsky's was César Cui, an army engineer with an expertise in fortifications and high explosives. Cui was also writing a Pushkin opera, *Kavkazskiy plennik* (*A Prisoner of the Caucasus*). Musorgsky had already made the acquaintance of a slightly older graduate of the Medical-Surgical Academy called Alexander Borodin. Borodin, though a competent pianist and cellist, was not to be seen at Dargomïzhsky's. He was busy writing a dissertation about poisons and performing his duties as an assistant professor at the academy, but had still managed to compose at least parts of several chamber works and songs, of a charming, if not unduly original character.

Evenings of the Dargomïzhsky kind were typical of a society that, like any other, bred talented artists and thinkers but that afforded them little or no opportunity to develop their abilities in the public sphere. Russia was languishing under a repressive and inefficient centralised autocracy which stamped on free expression and which, outside the state civil service, offered no career possibilities to the minor, often landless aristocracy (what Nikolai Gogol called 'gentlemen of the intermediate category') that was Russia's nearest equivalent to the burgeoning western middle class. The economy was crippled by a serf system that trapped 40 per cent of the population on poorly managed land. Corruption was rife, and impossible to root out because of the sheer size of the country and its hopelessly inadequate communications. The system – to call it that – had been beautifully satirised by Gogol in his play *The Government Inspector* (1836) and his novel *Dead Souls* (1842).

The question, to quote the title of a novel by the socialist writer Nikolai Chernïshevsky, was: *What Is to Be Done?* Should Russia modernise, westernise; or should she cleave to her Russianness, her Orthodoxy, her (partly imaginary) ancient structures of land tenure and communal local decision-making, the policy of a group of Romantic religious thinkers known as Slavophiles? Stasov was no Slavophile, but he was attracted by their way of thinking about old Russia as a basis for an art, a music, that would be authentically Russian. In practice this might take a variety of forms. Folk music would be one obvious source. Balakirev himself made several trips into the Russian hinterland in the early sixties, listening to the peasants singing, and sometimes writing their songs down, as various more systematic collectors had done before him. Some of these tunes would turn up in works such as his *Second Overture on Russian Themes* (1863–4: the First Overture had pre-dated his collecting trips). The trouble with such works was that they were not much more than attractive medleys, brightly orchestrated. Folk tales, myth and ancient religious practice were another matter. That was a rich treasury of material for operas and orchestral programme music, and it was a treasury with which Stasov was familiar and which he liked to push in the direction of his composer colleagues, often bullying them until they finally did what they were told. The same was true of Russian history, about which more and more was becoming known. They were reading Sergey Solovyov's *History of Russia from the Most Ancient Times*, and much of this would resurface in ideas for musical works that Stasov would dream up and tout around among his composer friends.

For the next few years Stasov and Balakirev were the focus of a group that met regularly, in one or other apartment, just as they had met at Glinka's and Dargomïzhsky's. In due course they acquired a name. This was the *Moguchaya Kuchka*, the Mighty Handful, a name invented by Stasov in 1867 in a review of a concert of some of their works. But they were meeting long before that. At their core were the four young composers we have already met: Balakirev, Cui, Musorgsky, Borodin. Late in 1861, a seventeen-year-old naval cadet called Nikolai Rimsky-Korsakov appeared at Balakirev's and produced some piano pieces and parts of a symphony he had been writing. Balakirev's eyes must have lit up. Here was another talented youngster he could take in hand and mould in his own, somewhat haphazard fashion. Unfortunately for such plans, within a year Rimsky-Korsakov would be off on a three-year world cruise, part of his qualification as a naval officer, with only slow and unreliable correspondence to help him complete his symphony.

The *Kuchka* evenings were a celebration of collaborative dilet-tantism. Of the five composers who made up the core of the group (including Rimsky-Korsakov after his return in 1865), only Balakirev had ever had serious music lessons from anyone but Balakirev. They were all gifted musicians, but what they knew, technically, was a matter of chance. What was more, they affected to despise systematic study as tending to suppress the imagination. When Anton Rubinstein, having started Russia's first ever series of public concerts in 1859, opened her first Conservatoire in 1862, Stasov attacked the project as the work of 'a foreigner with no understanding either of the demands of our national character or of the historical course of our art'.[11] Rubinstein, one of the great pianists of the day, was by no means a foreigner. He was a Russian-speaking Jew from Transdniestria (modern Moldova) in the southern part of the Tsarist empire; but Stasov was making a common anti-Semitic point that Jews can never have a more than superficial grasp of European languages or cultures. His chief gripe was that Rubinstein was importing into Russia the dreaded rule-bound academic formulae of dull German professors. His own music had few if any identifiably Russian features. Its models were Mendelssohn and Schumann. It was fluent, technically competent, empty.

The *Kuchka* were not fluent. They suffered the usual impediment of the untaught in the difficulty of extending promising starts. Balakirev put Musorgsky through his paces, but was not good at imposing technical disciplines about which he was himself somewhat vague and to which he was in any case hostile. Musorgsky worked for a time on schoolroom projects, but gradually discovered two crucial things about himself: that he had a gift for setting words to music, and an intuitive feeling for dramatic situations. For three years in the mid-sixties he worked spasmodically on an opera based on Flaubert's *Salammbô*, not exactly a Russian topic, but an enticingly exotic one. Unfortunately Musorgsky, a landless younger son, had to take a job in the Ministry of Communications, *Salammbô* languished, and instead he toyed with an orchestral piece about witches that eventually emerged in 1867 as a symphonic poem called *Ivanova noch' na Lïsoy gore* (*St John's Night on Bald Mountain*). Musorgsky had recently heard Liszt's *Totentanz*; but where Liszt's variations have a well-behaved formality bracing their wild gestures, Musorgsky's witches' sabbath is an unkempt string of images, striking from minute to minute, not quite satisfying as a whole. It was never performed and he later twice revised it, after which Rimsky-Korsakov made yet another, better behaved version. The work generally known as Musorgsky's *Night on the Bare Mountain* is Rimsky-Korsakov's version.

Meanwhile Dargomïzhsky had been exciting his colleagues with his word-for-word setting of Pushkin's *Stone Guest*. This was a new kind of Russianness, a music that sprang directly from the language itself. Reality, Chernïshevsky had asserted, was superior to art. But what if art could approach reality? Realism was in the air. A group of young painters had recently left the Academy of Arts and formed an independent artel (later the *Peredvizhniki*, or Wanderers), opposed to the classical preoccupations of the Academy, and arguing instead for the representation of Russian life as it really was, in all its colour and squalor. Of course, Dargomïzhsky's realism was linguistic, not depictive, and his libretto was in verse. But it gave Musorgsky the idea of a specifically Russian, artel kind of realism, drawn from peasant life, and based on a prose play. In the summer of 1868 he began a word-for-word setting of Gogol's comedy *Zhenit'ba* (*The Marriage*), soon got bored with it, and turned instead to a much bigger project. Suddenly the twenty-nine-year-old dilettante who had barely managed to finish anything more than five minutes long was writing a three-hour opera that would, in the opinion of many good judges, rank among the dozen or so greatest of the century.

Pushkin's *Boris Godunov* is a very different matter from his *Stone Guest*: a grand historical tragedy on a Shakespearean scale, mixing public and private, prose and verse, and offering a broad panorama of Russian life at one of its most politically turbulent moments, the Time of Troubles in the early seventeenth century. Boris Godunov reluctantly accepts the crown under pressure from the crowd who are being whipped up into shouting for him. But he is wracked with guilt over the murder, ordered by him, of the young Tsarevich Dmitry, the heir apparent, and his torment doubles when a pretender, a runaway monk called Grishka Otrepiev, appears at the head of Polish troops. When the old monk Pimen tells the story of a miracle performed at the grave of the dead Tsarevich, it is finally too much for Boris, who collapses and dies.

It was probably the Russian premiere of *Lohengrin* in October

1868 that prompted Musorgsky to drop *The Marriage* and compose *Boris Godunov*. Not that he fell in love with Wagner, who, as a loud-mouthed German, was a *bête noir* to the *Kuchka*, though they hardly knew his music apart from excerpts he had himself conducted in St Petersburg in 1863. But *Lohengrin* showed what could be done with crowd scenes as backdrop to personal tragedy. Like Wagner, Musorgsky opens with the crowd, but his technique could hardly be more different. His orchestra never leads, only supports, while the people converse and chatter, quarrel and laugh, using an adaptation of the dialogue method from *The Marriage*. The musical style is folkish, demotic, and occasionally breaks into hymnody, but is never symphonic; rather, it's a kind of musical cinema before the fact (*Boris Godunov* has been filmed superbly). Later, in one of the most powerful scenes in all opera, the crowd outside St Basil's Cathedral begs Boris for bread, and the so-called Simpleton (the Russian holy fool, or *yurodivy*) confronts him and accuses him of the murder of the Tsarevich. Meanwhile there have been conversational scenes involving Pimen and Grishka, the escaping Grishka himself with a pair of drunken mendicants and the police, and, most masterful of all, a long scene in the Kremlin which shows Boris, first, as a loving, domesticated family man, then as a volatile, tortured ruler goaded almost to madness by the crafty, malignant boyar Prince Shuisky.

This first version of the opera, completed in 1869, revealed a hitherto unsuspected dramatic genius, a flair for portraiture and scenic timing, and a huge skill at matching music to words. Musorgsky had already composed songs that were like sharply observed vignettes, not essentially lyrical, but moments in time, pages from a story. But to make this work over a whole evening, in long self-contained tableaux that formed a loose, if not entirely sequential, narrative, was an astonishing, quite unpredictable achievement. Alas, the Imperial censors were unimpressed and, for reasons not wholly understood, rejected it. So Musorgsky went back to the drawing-board, revised or rewrote every scene (except St Basil's, which he removed), and inserted a whole new act, set in Poland, and a final 'revolutionary' scene with the unruly mob gathering round Grishka in Kromy Forest near Moscow. This revised *Boris Godunov*, performed in 1874 and today more or less the standard version, is a somewhat different kind of work from the original, less austere, more operatic, with more or expanded female roles, and more set pieces – songs and choruses. It shares much of the splendour of the original, but is in some ways less new, less startling. It retreats tactically from a theoretical position, and ends up as something not far off grand opera.

By the time *Boris Godunov* reached the stage, Musorgsky was working on another opera about Russian history, this time on a subject dreamt up by Stasov, about the disturbances surrounding the accession of Peter the Great in the 1690s. Unfortunately *Khovanshchina* (*The Khovansky Affair*) absorbed him so much that he spent more time researching it than composing the music; and meanwhile he started another, quite different opera on Gogol's Ukrainian folk tale *Sorochinskaya yarmarka* (*The Fair at Sorochintsi*). The result was that both works were left unfinished when he died of a surfeit of brandy in 1881. He did, however, complete a large number of songs, including three highly original cycles, together with a piano cycle, *Kartinki s vïstavki* (*Pictures from an Exhibition*), which in a way shows his genius for the evocation of images almost as well. It's in the songs, nevertheless, that the music is at its most fascinatingly radical. In *Detskaya* (*The Nursery*) the relation between words and music is often such as to override the normal procedures of harmony and metre, and these seven songs about childhood are like revue sketches, as vivid and fresh in their way as anything in the operas.

Nothing in the work of the other kuchkists compares with Musorgsky's sheer magisterial disdain for convention. The saddest case was Borodin, perhaps the most naturally gifted of the circle, but also the one with the busiest professional life and, incidentally, the most troublesome domestic circumstances (his wife was an insomniac who insisted that he kept her company as long as she stayed awake). He nevertheless completed two forceful and beautiful symphonies, leaving a third incomplete, as well as a pair of fine string quartets and some memorable songs. His masterpiece, though, would have been his opera *Knyaz' Igor'* (*Prince Igor*), on which he worked, in a depressingly disorganised way, for most of eighteen years, and which he left in chaos when he died suddenly in 1887. In the completed parts of this marvellous conception there are passages of a lyrical beauty that decisively bear out his remark (thinking of Dargomïzhsky and Musorgsky) that 'I lean towards song and cantilena rather than recitative'.[12] They also, of course, include the 'Polovtsian Dances', perhaps the most spectacular heir to the pseudo-orientalism of *Ruslan and Lyudmila*, which Stasov regarded as an authentic expression of Russianness quite apart from folklore or history, because 'the East' (which in kuchkist eyes included regions to the south such as the Caucasus and the Arab lands) is adjacent to Russia and not to the rest of Europe.

Balakirev was a different kind of victim of the circle's dilettantism. For as long as he presided over their activities, he himself composed very little. In 1859 he wrote a polka for piano and two or three songs; in 1860 he managed a couple of songs and a short unaccompanied chorus. In 1864 he started a symphony but failed to finish it until 1897. And so it went on. He planned a symphonic poem inspired by Lermontov's poem *Tamara*, about the beautiful Caucasian princess who lures travellers into her tower and, after a night of love, has them murdered and thrown into the river; and he would often play this piece at circle evenings, but seems not to have written it down. Only in 1882, after years of depression during which he virtually cut off communication with his fellow kuchkists, did he finish the work and have it published as the masterpiece we know, a key work in the stylistic development of the group, as becomes apparent if one listens to it alongside Rimsky-Korsakov's later and much better-known *Sheherazade*. The one work that Balakirev composed, wrote down, and that truly represents his best work during the *Kuchka* years is the oriental fantasy *Islamey* of 1869, a piano piece of such surpassing difficulty that only Balakirev was ever able to play it until it was taken up as a repertory piece by a second generation of Russian virtuosi.

The one kuchkist who recognised the value of discipline and regular work was the youngest, midshipman Rimsky-Korsakov. After returning, symphony in hand, from his world cruise, he joined the circle and fell briefly under Balakirev's, and perhaps even more Stasov's influence. The idea for his first reasonably mature work, a tone poem called *Sadko* (1867), based on the legend of the *gusli*-playing merchant who sinks to the bottom of the sea and plays for the wedding of the Sea King's daughter, was one that Stasov had been plugging for some time. And his next work (1868), a four-movement symphonic poem on the quasi-Byronic tale of Antar, the Arab chieftain who, tired of life, wanders in the desert and rescues a gazelle who turns out to be the beautiful peri Gul-Nazar, was suggested by Balakirev. Both are admirable, technically expert achievements for so inexperienced a composer, though Rimsky-Korsakov, who had a perfectionist streak, revised them both several times.

They already combine traditions and musical detail that bring them closer to the mainstream than almost any other music by the *Kuchka*. *Antar*, with its disaffected hero and its use of a motto theme to represent him, has obvious roots in Berlioz's *Harold en Italie*, while *Sadko* owes something to the Liszt of the symphonic poems, and makes use of Liszt's octatonic scale (alternating tones and semitones) to depict Sadko's descent to the seabed. Yet the Russian influence is just as strong. Glinka's orchestral brilliance finds a new home in Rimsky-Korsakov, and the subject matter chimes with Stasov's ideas about programme music, Russian myth and orientalism.

In the same year that he composed *Antar*, Rimsky-Korsakov began work on an opera about Ivan the Terrible, *Pskovityanka* (*The Maid of Pskov*). This time the subject, based on a play by Lev Mey, was pure Stasov, pure *Kuchka*. Tsar Ivan, having directed a massacre of the citizens of Novgorod as a reprisal for their supposed machinations with Poland, arrives in Pskov perhaps with the same intention, only to find there a grown-up daughter, Olga, from a long-ago affair in the city. Pskov, he announces, is protected. Alas, a band of guerrillas headed by Olga's lover attacks Ivan's men, the lover is killed and Olga is shot dead in the crossfire.[13] This whole subject created huge excitement in the circle; the libretto was endlessly discussed, and Rimsky-Korsakov would play over bits of music as it was composed. There was plenty of *Kuchka* input. Musorgsky supplied some chorus texts, and Stasov regaled them all about the *veche*, the public assembly which meets in the main square to decide how to respond to Ivan's approach. The fact that this and other details were historically inaccurate probably didn't bother him. The concept was purely Russian, the *veche* had once existed, and there was nothing like it in the west.

Like his orchestral works, Rimsky-Korsakov's music for *Pskovityanka* is mainstream in a way that *Boris Godunov* is not, but also, like them, incorporates Russian elements that distinguish it from possible western models such as *Faust* or *Lohengrin*. The absorption of folk song into, for instance, the first scene, where the two nurses gossip about the cruel Tsar Ivan while the young girls pick raspberries, is enchanting but hardly groundbreaking. The love music for Olga and her guerrilla lover Mikhail Tucha is on a high level of invention but not novel in its discourse. Even the *veche* scene, very effective in its way, is less adventurous than *Boris Godunov* in its treatment of the chorus. This is really to say no more than that Rimsky-Korsakov's leanings were always towards traditional musical design. And perhaps it was some recognition of this un-*Kuchka*-like tendency that led to his being offered a professorship at the Conservatoire in 1871, when he was a mere twenty-seven years old.

It was more or less the end of him as a kuchkist. Soon he was composing fugues and studying harmony and counterpoint, to keep ahead of his own students. No longer would he be one of Balakirev's men. He would become, instead, an organised and productive composer and teacher. 'Thirty years have passed by now', he would write in 1897, 'since the days when Stasov would write that in eighteen-sixty-so-and-so the Russian School displayed a lively activity: Lodïzhensky wrote one romance, Borodin got an idea for something, Balakirev is planning to rework something, and so on. It is time to forget all that and *travel a normal artistic path*.'[14]

His model for such a path in the late sixties and early seventies might have been one of the first Conservatory graduates in 1865, the son of a provincial mining engineer by the name of Pyotr Il'yich Tchaikovsky. Tchaikovsky had arrived in St Petersburg in 1850, aged ten, from the remote mining town of Alapayevsk. He enrolled in the School of Jurisprudence, but after graduating in 1859 and brief employment in the Ministry of Justice, he entered the Conservatory in the first cohort of students, studied there with Anton Rubinstein and the theorist Nikolay Zaremba, and emerged three years later a properly taught musician of exactly the kind most despised by Stasov and co. Nevertheless he soon befriended Balakirev in Moscow, where he had been given a post in the Conservatory that opened there in 1866, and Balakirev started treating him the way he treated his *Kuchka* colleagues, offering detailed criticism of his music, putting forward ideas for new works, and even outlining the form and character he thought they should take. The first product was Tchaikovsky's fantasy-overture *Romeo and Juliet*, suggested by Balakirev on a walk in Moscow in 1868, and overseen by him in correspondence to an almost comical degree.

On such occasions Tchaikovsky, who was pathologically lacking in self-confidence, would defer to his Petersburg colleague, who was not. But he quickly understood that the *Kuchka* way of doing things would never be his. He was always on good terms with them and would visit them when he was in the capital. But privately he was dismissive of their dilettantism. One has only to look at his work-list alongside theirs to see the difference. Not only are his works plentiful and, with one or two exceptions, finished, but they fall almost entirely into standard categories: they look like the *oeuvre* of any nineteenth-century western composer. There are seven symphonies, eight symphonic poems (variously classified), four or five concertos, three string quartets, nine or ten operas, three ballets, a large number of songs, and a good deal else besides. Tchaikovsky was interested in Russian folk music and often made use of it in his own work. But it was never an issue with him, and certainly never formative in point of style. His songs nearly all have Russian texts, and most of his operas (though none of his ballets) are on Russian subjects. But his technique, well taught by Rubinstein, owed at least as much to Mendelssohn, Schumann and Liszt as it did to Glinka. Even his mastery of the orchestra, which certainly did owe a lot to Glinka, was tempered by an admiration for Berlioz.

All the same, Tchaikovsky has often been criticised for his supposedly poor command of western forms and procedures; he criticised himself in this respect. And it is true that, when he tried too hard to write in a well-behaved symphonic way the result could be laboured, with repetition and sequence too obviously used to fill out the preconceived form. His great strength lay in the creation of vivid musical images, something that was naturally helped by the melodic genius that even his detractors have never denied him. *Romeo and Juliet*, in its final revised form of 1880, is a fine example, but there are many others: the symphonic fantasia *Francesca da Rimini*, *Hamlet*, the Fifth and Sixth Symphonies, the D major and E flat minor String Quartets, and of course the three great ballets. *Romeo and Juliet*, though a beautifully constructed sonata form, is equally a musical drama fashioned from the essential elements of the play. Even those works that gave him a reputation for coarseness or vulgarity, such as the *1812* overture, the Violin Concerto or the B flat minor Piano Concerto, are inventive scores that perhaps lack great subtlety and were certainly for a long time overplayed. On the other hand his songs, much less performed in the west than they deserve, are in many cases models of lyrical refinement and a sense of the voice and its needs.

The operas, too, have been neglected, apart from *Yevgeny Onegin* (1877–8) and, more recently, *Pikovaya dama* (*The Queen of Spades*, 1890), both based on Pushkin. At the time of writing *Yevgeny Onegin*, in which the young heroine, Tatyana, sends an unsolicited love letter to Onegin, a local landowner, and receives a patronising rejection in response, the homosexual Tchaikovsky had himself just received a declaration of love from a female former student, had become caught up in the parallel situation in the story, and contracted a disastrous marriage as a result. But even without the personal identification, *Onegin* is a work of instinctive theatre. Its two great solo scenes, Tatyana's Letter Scene and the poet Lensky's long aria before his fatal duel with Onegin, are telling portraits of sensitive, vulnerable characters at the end of their tether, while the genre scenes, and especially the ball in the final act, with Onegin having to endure the 'tedious' dances and Prince Gremin's stolid aria while seething with his newfound passion for Tatyana, are beautifully handled in a manner largely based on conventional French models. Of the other operas, the two versions of Gogol's *Christmas Eve* – *Vakula the Smith* and *Cherevichki* (*The Little Slippers*) – and *Mazepa* – also after Pushkin – should be heard more often than they are. *Mazepa*, especially, contains some of Tchaikovsky's best vocal writing set into a tragic drama about the conflicts between love, family and war.

The Road to Rome, and to Munich

Franz Liszt's years in Weimar were in many ways the most productive of his life. Not only did he compose a dozen symphonic poems and two large-scale symphonies, but he also wrote or completed several of his most powerful piano works, including the B minor Sonata, and the definitive set of *Harmonies poétiques et religieuses*, including the greatest of his consciously Hungarian pieces, *Funérailles*, and the biggest, if not the best, of his meditations, *Bénédiction de Dieu dans la solitude*. The *Harmonies poétiques et religieuses* are recognisably a culmination of the 1830s, the poet seeking oblivion, or the divine, in the remote regions of the mind. 'There are meditative souls', Lamartine had written in his preface (and Liszt had placed at the head of his score), 'whom solitude and contemplation raise irresistibly towards ideas of the infinite, that is towards religion'. Three of Liszt's *Harmonies* are transcriptions of choral pieces from the mid-forties, two of them settings of sacred texts ('Ave Maria' and 'Pater noster') which Liszt retains in the piano score. His pious leanings were by no means new, but they intensified in the late 1850s, no doubt to some extent because of difficulties, partly professional, partly personal, in his life.

Ever since arriving in Weimar, Princess Carolyne had been seeking an annulment of her Russian marriage, but it had been consistently obstructed or agreed only under ruinous conditions. In 1860, after more than a decade of dispute, she decided to take her case in person to Rome. Meanwhile Liszt's own position in Weimar was increasingly uneasy, mainly because of clashes with the intendant of the Hoftheater. The last straw snapped in December 1859, when Peter Cornelius's comic opera, *The Barber of Baghdad*, conducted by Liszt, was the target of a violent audience demonstration apparently organised by the intendant, Franz von Dingelstedt, and plainly aimed, not at Cornelius's opera, but at Liszt himself. In a fury, Liszt resigned as Kapellmeister, and eighteen months later followed Carolyne to Rome, where the Vatican had found in her favour over the annulment, and their wedding had been fixed for the day of his fiftieth birthday in October 1861.

The reasons why the wedding failed to take place are too elaborate to relate here. Enough to say that Vatican connections of Carolyne's daughter's husband secured a last-minute reversal of the annulment, and there they both were, stranded in Rome, their domestic situation unaltered, and their Weimar bridges burnt. But Rome turned out to be the perfect environment for the completion of two vast choral works that Liszt had had on the stocks since the mid-fifties. The first of these, *Die Legende von der heiligen Elisabeth* (*The Legend of St Elisabeth*), was in fact substantially composed before he arrived in Rome, and the plainchants that form its main melodic material were gathered for him in Pest National Library by the Hungarian composer Mihály Mosonyi. The second work, *Christus* – a three-and-a-quarter hour oratorio on the life of Jesus – was largely composed in Rome, in the Convent of the Madonna del Rosario, where Liszt was preparing for his admission as an abbé of the Catholic Church in 1865. The image of the great virtuoso and womaniser humbly ensconced in a monastic cell composing his spiritually grandest work as he awaited admission to the minor orders has been too much for many critics, who have doubted his sincerity as both Christian and artist. But Liszt was certainly troubled by the emptiness of his early life, and seems genuinely to have desired some kind of absolution. As for artistic sincerity, art is either good or bad (as Rossini once said), take it or leave it. The artist's motives may interest us, but they have, or should have, no bearing on our judgement of the art.

Of the two works, *Christus* is the more interesting and varied. Leaving aside its somewhat sprawling totality, it amounts to an anthology of biblical or quasi-liturgical tableaux nearly all of which lend themselves to excerpting in one way or another: the 'Stabat mater speciosa' in the Nativity, unaccompanied or softly accompanied throughout; the enchanting tableau of the shepherds piping at the manger, sweetly scored for alternate winds and strings; or, in the Passion, the long, very fine setting of the 'Stabat mater dolorosa' and the Agony in the Garden, which Wagner surely had at the back of his mind when composing the final act of *Parsifal. St Elisabeth* also has its longueurs and its beauties, but suffers from the basic problem, not shared by *Christus*, that as a narrative, rather than a series of tableaux, it lacks characterisation and even, for longish stretches, a real sense of drama. The tender plainsong opening is beautiful, but the piety soon wears thin, and the incessantly repeated 'Willkommen die Braut' of the first chorus is a little too redolent of those weddings we have all attended at which the bride does indeed arrive half an hour late.

Liszt had been to Rome before, but on this visit it affected him in new ways, some of which can be traced in his music. The pure chordal harmonies and multiple verses of the 'Stabat mater speciosa' might be a direct response to the music in the Sistine Chapel, where he went every Sunday 'to bathe and reinvigorate my spirit in the sonorous waves of Palestrina's *Jordan*'.[1] Palestrina had long been a symbolic figure in the slow revival of sacred music in the first half of the century. His music stood for a remote age in which piety and simplicity of spirit had irradiated the whole of life. Now, in the new age of the bourgeoisie, these things were more a kind of enclave, a small locked room in one wing of the house, to be opened only on special occasions and celebrated with one's hands together and eyes closed. Such occasions required a particular kind of music adapted to bourgeois taste, something not too elevated, not too complicated, not too difficult to perform or understand. It's a curious fact that, among the vast quantity of music composed for the practical liturgy, Catholic or Protestant, in the nineteenth century, there is hardly a single work of the front rank. Palestrina's music, by contrast, was seen as the essence of that purity of the religious spirit that had been lost at some time in the eighteenth century. It was perhaps fortunate for this attitude that the actual music was not well known, and was hard to come by in print. Even Hoffmann could describe it as music in which 'chord follows upon chord; most of them are perfect consonances, whose boldness and strength stir and elevate our spirits with inexpressible power'.[2] The description suggests the methodology of a badly taught music student struggling with a Palestrina harmony exercise. The idea that these chords were the by-product of an intricate polyphony of independent voices seems very far away.

In 1862 this situation was about to be remedied with the inauguration of the first modern edition of the great polyphonist's music, edited by F. X. Haberl in Leipzig. In Rome, Liszt met Franz Xaver Witt, a young Catholic priest and a composer of polyphonic church music that sought to reproduce the pure style of the sixteenth century. Witt was involved in the Cecilian Movement, a tendency, rather than an organisation, that had the long-standing objective of the reform of the music of the Roman Catholic liturgy, though it should be said that the idea of reform in the Cecilian sense seems to have been more an idea of revival. If only we all wrote like Palestrina or Lassus, it said, everything would be all right. But Witt's music, and that of other would-be neo-polyphonists, proves on the contrary that the spirit of one age cannot be co-opted as the spirit of another.

The Cecilian Movement was essentially a retreat from the bitter realities of industrialisation, and in that sense it had something in common with the Romantic response to both industrialisation and religion. Where they differed was in their attitude to the individual. For the Cecilians, the individual musician was to be subsumed into the liturgy, a willing self-sacrifice to the needs of simplicity and clarity. The Romantic composer would obviously have none of that. For him, the individual was, precisely, a kind of religion, and insofar as the individuality of the artist was a complex affair, its expression would be that as well. The first casualty of this particular form of hubris was in most cases religious belief itself. Few of the great religious works of the nineteenth century were composed by believers. Few were even formally liturgical, and those that were were mostly composed in such an elaborate way and for such extravagant forces as to put liturgical use out of the question. Beethoven's *Missa solemnis* and Berlioz's Requiem are extreme cases, but the Masses of Schubert, Cherubini and Liszt himself, who certainly was a believer of sorts, are also essentially concert works in sacred form, disguised choral symphonies. Brahms's *German Requiem*, composed between 1865 and 1868 after the death of his mother, avoids the liturgy altogether but assembles texts about death and grief from the Old and New Testaments. The nearest approach to a genuinely liturgical Mass by a composer of the front rank was written by the organist of Linz Cathedral, Anton Bruckner, in 1866. His Mass in E minor, for double choir accompanied only by wind instruments, has intonations for the Gloria and Credo as in an actual celebration, and many echoes of polyphonic and baroque music.

In all these settings, even Bruckner's, there is a tendency towards the theatrical, inspired of course by the drama that lies behind the sacrifice of the Mass, and by the grandeur of the architecture that surrounds it. For the Romantic artist, the divine mystery was an aspect of the Sublime, that which inspired awe and a fear of the unknown, and of which we had only a faint, tremulous intuition. It stood out against the normal, the quotidian, the rational. It was an object of helpless longing, a refuge from the disasters of the sublunary world, but an unattainable one, falsely represented by the religious impedimenta that are all around us, the churches and the cloisters, the monks and the priests, with their empty promise of redemption from the torments of desire, ambition and guilt. All these conflicting attributes had one thing in common: they were not the drab, material world. They were the nighttime of Wagner's Tristan, who, when caught at dawn *in flagrante delicto* with Isolde, exclaims 'the desolate day for the last time!'

Redemption, Christian or otherwise, is a serious matter in nearly all Wagner's mature operas. But in Romantic opera at large religion is more often a device than a theme. In Verdi's *La forza del destino* (*The Force of Destiny*), the heroine, Leonora, having been cursed by her father as he dies from a shot fired accidentally by her lover, becomes an anchoress at a monastery, to which in due course her lover, Don Alvaro, also coincidentally repairs. But the sanctuary is false. Leonora's brother, Carlo, turns up, bent on revenge. He and Alvaro fight, Carlo is mortally wounded but, dying, stabs Leonora as she bends over him. Verdi composed *The Force of Destiny* to a commission from the Bolshoi Theatre in St Petersburg, where it was premiered in November 1862, and was very probably seen by Vladimir Stasov and his friends. They may well have been struck by one aspect of the opera: its extensive crowd and battle scenes; perhaps also the curious way in which its principal characters vanish from the action for long periods while choruses of muleteers, peasants, soldiers, friars, drummers, pilgrims and what-not mill around the stage in an exciting, colourful, but essentially irrelevant cavalcade, spinning out the drama while contributing not a great deal to the plot. Perhaps Musorgsky took a hint from all this when starting *Boris Godunov* six years later, but if so it served only the stage picture. There is no detectable Verdi in Musorgsky's music.

By this time Verdi was so famous that he could afford to work only to commissions that appealed to him. Between 1859 and 1881, when the revised *Simon Boccanegra* had its premiere at La Scala, he wrote nothing for the Italian stage. His main contribution to the Italy of the 1861 reunification was to stand as a deputy in the new parliament, which he did reluctantly under pressure from Cavour and undid four years later. More importantly, in 1874 he composed his Requiem in memory of Alessandro Manzoni, the champion of the Risorgimento and himself a senator in the Italian parliament until his death in 1873. Verdi's Requiem is one of the great classics of religious romanticism, liturgical in form, liturgically impossible in practice, operatic in style and gesture. Yet while there are episodes in his operas that might conceivably have found a place in the Requiem, and equally episodes in the Requiem that suggest moments in this or that opera, the totality of the work is unique. Here for once Verdi is able to develop his choral thinking, evolved initially for the stage and there to some extent limited by the demands of the theatre. This is already the case in the opening Requiem Aeternam and Kyrie Eleison, a ten-minute piece of intense choral polyphony of the kind that would stop an opera in its tracks but provides a superbly taut, concentrated opening to this big concert work. In a different sense the Dies Irae applies operatic method on a grand but abstracted scale, chorus and solo alternating, but without the personal element that would dictate the progress of such music on the stage. The power here is architectural as much as dramatic; the drama is in the gesture and the discourse, but the ultimate power is in the marshalling of those elements into an impersonal design untainted by individual tragedy.

There is an intriguing comparison to be made between this work and the two operas Verdi had meanwhile composed for foreign theatres: *Don Carlos*, written for Paris and performed there in March 1867, and *Aida*, commissioned in 1870 for the new Cairo opera house built to mark the opening of the Suez Canal the previous November. In its original French-language version, *Don Carlos* is as rangy and discursive as *The Force of Destiny*, but its prolixity serves the drama in a more specific way. At its core is the historical fact of the betrothal of Carlos, eldest son of the Spanish king Philip II, to the French princess Elisabeth of Valois, who instead, for reasons of state, married Philip himself. The opera, like Schiller's play, imagines Carlos and Elisabeth passionately in love, with all that entails in the rigid context of the Spanish court and the Inquisition. Carlos's friend the Marquis of Posa has the king's ear, which he uses to speak up for Carlos, but also to passionately advocate more liberal policies in the Spanish Netherlands. The political theme and the doomed love are thus intertwined, and become hopelessly entangled at the moment when, at an auto-da-fé for the burning of heretics at the stake, Carlos pleads to be sent to Flanders as governor, is refused, then draws his sword on the king only to be disarmed by Posa. In due course, Posa is murdered by an agent of the Inquisition and Carlos is imprisoned, then condemned to death; but at the last minute, as he fights with his guards, a mysterious cowled figure emerges from the tomb of Philip's father, Charles V, and drags him back into it.

There are other motifs, too numerous to detail, in this extraordinary masterpiece of grand opera, but they all, in one way or another, serve the linking of the Romantic, political and religious themes. The Princess Eboli, herself in love with Carlos, betrays him and Elisabeth to the king, just at the moment when the Grand Inquisitor, in one of the great scenes in opera, is demanding from Philip the death of Posa and 'permitting' that of Carlos ('after all, God sacrificed *His* son'). This built-in coherence is thanks to Schiller. But Verdi cements it with music of commanding psychological richness and power. When Posa, in the original second act, pleads with Carlos to intervene in Flanders, Carlos ripostes with his own emotional troubles, and by the end of the scene their vow of brotherhood seems to embrace both torments. The individual character portraits are no less assured. Elisabeth is not just a passionate woman behaving dutifully; she is weak enough to yield, strong enough to resist. Eboli, engaged in an affair with the king, regrets too late the damage her machinations have done, and utters her remorse in an emotionally disturbed monologue ('O don fatale') that is moving in spite of its horrible air of self-pity. Philip's stern autocracy at court cracks as he takes Posa's boldness over Flanders as an encouragement to a breathless confession of his suspicions about Carlos and his wife. All this is music that flows in the channel of feeling and thought, largely uninterrupted by arias, cabalettas, and the rest of the Italian paraphernalia.

Though the Requiem shares its idiom, and is palpably the work of the same composer, its structural rhythm is different, that of a sequence of emotions and musical contrasts, rather than an organic, ongoing narrative. Cut into the Requiem at any point and, apart from the Latin text, you might be in the middle of an opera; let it run, and you soon couldn't be. Take the transition from the final repeat of the Dies Irae text into the Lacrymosa, the final part, with the Pie Jesu, of the entire sequence. In a narrative context this would be hard to explain, but in the ritual context of the Mass it is deeply affecting, marking the change from the wrath of the Dies Irae to the hope of mercy and repose, through the shared phrase 'dies illa' – on that day. Yet as it happens the music of the Lacrymosa actually began life in Act 4 of *Don Carlos*, where it originally grew out of the tense exchange between Carlos and Philip after the murder of Posa. In both works the music expands into an ensemble with chorus. But in the Requiem the emotion and musical material are shared, while in the opera the ensemble reflected in different music the different feelings of the two main characters and the chorus of grandees that had entered Carlos's prison with the king.

Aida, though it has always been the more popular work, is in some ways the more conventional, as well as the better made. Certainly it never underwent the cuts and alterations to which *Don Carlos* was subjected even before its first performance. The Pharaonic subject of *Aida* was of course chosen to suit the commission, but it seems to have appealed to Verdi from the start, and it enabled him here and there to write music of a vaguely exotic character, as well as some spectacular ceremonial music that fed on the quasi-barbaric atmosphere at Memphis. That in turn meant more set pieces than in *Don Carlos*, more dances, more processions, more religious ceremony and incantation.

On the other hand, it allowed a clearer trajectory from the public to the private: from the point at which Radames is named as commander-in-chief of the Egyptian army against the Ethiopian invaders to the point at the end of Act 3 where he unwittingly betrays the army's intended route to the Ethiopian king Amonasro and is accordingly, in Act 4, condemned to be buried alive in the subterranean temple vault. *Don Carlos* had proposed an ambiguity between love, the law and the ideal. In *Aida* the choice is clear, yet no less impossible to make. One might suggest that if Radames can betray his country so readily for love, he is not much of a commander-in-chief, especially as he is already in love with the enemy princess when he accepts the command. But Verdi makes this inadequacy in an otherwise brilliant man the whole point of his tragedy. From the start he portrays a soldier in an emotional muddle. How can he seriously imagine, as he does in his opening aria 'Celeste Aida', that he will be able to defeat her compatriots, led by her father, in battle, then come back and tell her 'for you I fought and for you I conquered'? The aria is serene, but the tragedy is there already, and Verdi works it skilfully through a series of confrontations that gradually take over from the superb but empty chanting and marching, and culminate in the dramatic concentration of the scene by the Nile, Amonasro's bullying of Aida into betraying her love by tricking Radames into revealing the army's movements, and, in the final act, Amneris's torment as she overhears Radames's trial and condemnation. These are straightforward situations in which everyone is both right and wrong and there is no villain. Even poor Amneris, the Pharaoh's daughter, though she has teased Aida cruelly, has merely behaved as any woman might do who can scarcely believe that her hero would fall for a captive slave. Life, Verdi's music tells us, offers simple solutions only to automatons, such as high priests, pharaohs and opera choruses. Flesh and blood can only struggle on the horns of dilemmas.

By the 1860s Verdi had achieved a stature and musical range against which his Italian contemporaries appeared as mere dwarfs. Two young composers, both destined for fame as collaborators with Verdi, had operas performed at this time. Franco Faccio's *I profughi fiamminghi* was staged at La Scala without success in 1863, and his *Amleto* in Genoa, not much more successfully, two years later. Three years after that, Faccio's *Amleto* librettist, Arrigo Boito, conducted his own *Mefistofele* at La Scala, again without success. Both composers were members of a group of artists known as the Scapigliatura (The Bohemians), which proclaimed a young Italian version of 'the artwork of the future'. But as far as composition went, the future was too much for Faccio and Boito. Faccio gave up composing altogether, but became one of the great opera conductors of his day, and conducted many important premieres at La Scala, including that of Verdi's *Otello* in 1887. *Mefistofele* (in an 1875 revision) fared better and still survives on the fringes of the repertoire, giving a good image of what was regarded as modernistic in Italy in the 1870s, but only rising patchily to the demands of its Faustian subject. But whatever his talents as a composer, Boito proved an outstanding librettist, and his texts for Verdi's *Otello* and *Falstaff* are beyond question the finest Shakespearean librettos ever written.

He had worked previously on the revised version of Verdi's *Simon Boccanegra* (1881), a radically restructured score with a completely new setting of the prologue and one major new scene, set in the Genoese Council Chamber, into which the mob breaks as it had done into the prison in the penultimate act of *Don Carlos*. It was apparently Boito's skilful working of this new scene that persuaded Verdi to accept him as librettist for *Otello*. But Boito was already experienced in the genre. Most notably he had written the libretto for Amilcare Ponchielli's *La Gioconda*, an adaptation of Hugo's play *Angelo, tyran de Padoue*. *La Gioconda*, which Faccio conducted at La Scala in 1876, is mainly famous today for its third-act ballet, *Dance of the Hours*, but in its own day it was an important link between middle-period Verdi and the so-called *verismo* composers of the century's end. Ponchielli seems to have been the first significant composer to use Verdi's example as a launching pad for anything particularly new in the world of Italian opera, and one can easily hear in the broad, volatile lyricism of his vocal writing, the explosions of emotional violence, and his rich orchestration, the starting point for the Mascagnis and Leoncavallos, not to mention Puccini, whose first teacher Ponchielli was at the Milan Conservatory.

To what extent Ponchielli, or for that matter Verdi himself, was influenced by Wagner – as was frequently alleged – is hard to decide, bearing in mind that Wagner's operas after *Lohengrin* made slow progress in Italy, and Verdi was certainly resistant for a time after seeing *Lohengrin* itself in Bologna in 1871. In any case, Wagner's way of doing things was well known by repute long before his music got known, and his scores were published. There was bound to be leakage, but there is not much Italian music that echoes Wagner in its sound or deep technique until, perhaps, Catalani.

As for Wagner himself, a huge change had come over his life in the mid-sixties. In 1860 the king of Saxony had issued a partial amnesty (excluding Saxony itself), as a result of which he had been able to conduct concerts of his music in Karlsruhe, Breslau and Vienna, as well as Prague. But he still failed to earn enough money to finance his increasingly extravagant lifestyle, and in March 1864 he had to sneak out of Vienna to avoid being arrested for debt. Six weeks later he was in Stuttgart when a man he had been avoiding as another creditor managed to corner him and announce that the new eighteen-year-old king of Bavaria, Ludwig II, was a huge admirer of his music and wished him to come to Munich and work there under royal patronage. The first great favour Ludwig did the composer, after installing him initially in a villa on the Starnbergersee, then in a large house on Munich's Briennerstrasse, and financing his taste for expensive silks, perfumes and the other accessories of his artistic noumenon, was to arrange for the premiere of *Tristan und Isolde*, which duly took place in June 1865. Meanwhile Wagner was working on *Die Meistersinger von Nürnberg*, and this had its premiere exactly three years later. But in between, as well as after, these two notable events, what had started as a loving relationship with the unusual young monarch underwent certain vicissitudes, due partly to a different sort of loving relationship.

In his autobiography, Wagner describes a carriage-ride he took with Cosima von Bülow in Berlin in November 1863, while her husband was busy preparing for an evening concert. 'We fell silent', he records, 'and all joking ceased.'

We looked silently into each other's eyes, and an intense longing to confess the truth overwhelmed us, a confession, for which no words were necessary, of a boundless misfortune that weighed on us. With tears and sobs we sealed the vow to belong solely to one another.[3]

A few weeks after Wagner settled in the Starnberg villa, Cosima came to stay, along with her two daughters and a nurserymaid, the unfortunate Hans being once again stuck in Berlin, and their affair began in earnest. Meanwhile in Munich, Ludwig's obsession with his composer favourite soon started to cause trouble with his court officials and ministers, who not surprisingly disapproved of his lavish expenditure on a mere artistic enthusiasm. They did their best to poison him against Wagner, and they succeeded in having the composer banished from Munich in December 1865, at which point he rented a house called Tribschen on Lake Lucerne, and there, in due course, Cosima joined him, in a more or less open domestic 'arrangement'. By 1868 Ludwig's relations with Wagner had reached a very low ebb, not least because of rumours, and more than rumours, about the composer's liaison with a married woman. Yet his passion for the music survived. After the *Meistersinger* premiere of June 1868, he insisted, against Wagner's increasingly vigorous objections, on mounting the first production of *Das Rheingold* (September 1869), and nine months later that of *Die Walküre*, both of them conducted by the local opera director, Franz Wüllner. The composer attended neither.

Die Meistersinger von Nürnberg (*The Mastersingers of Nuremberg*) was an even older conception than the *Ring*. It dated back to 1845 and had originally been thought of as a comic companion piece to *Tannhäuser* – a song contest with a worldly ending after a song contest with a redemptive ending. But Wagner was incapable of the compression called for by genuine comedy, and instead got caught up in the philosophical aspects of the subject, what it said about the moral basis of art, its native purity, and the relation between art and sexual love. These are big topics, and *Meistersinger* ended up as Wagner's longest work since *Rienzi*. Yet the story is simple. Walther von Stolzing, an aristocratic landowner who has sold his estates, arrives in Nuremberg with an introduction to the goldsmith, Veit Pogner, and falls in love with his daughter, Eva. But Pogner, a prominent member of the local mastersingers' guild, is offering Eva's hand to the guild member who composes the best master song, and Walther, though he has aspirations as a poet/composer, knows nothing of the guild's rules, and fails the trial for membership with a wild dithyramb that excites general ridicule from all except the cobbler, Hans Sachs. Walther and Eva plan to elope but are blocked by Sachs, and meanwhile the town clerk, Beckmesser, who has acted as 'marker' for Walther's trial and has hopes of his own where Eva is concerned, arrives outside Pogner's house to serenade her (though it is her nurse, Magdalene, who appears on the balcony). Sachs, working on Eva's shoes outside his house, marks each of the many crude mistakes in Beckmesser's song with a thwack of his hammer; but then Sachs's apprentice David (Magdalene's sweetheart) arrives, finds Beckmesser serenading his beloved, and picks a fight that quickly turns into a riot. Sachs has whisked Walther into his house, and the next morning he coaches him in the composition of a proper master song which, when he performs it at the public contest on the banks of the River Pegnitz, wins everyone over.

Dramaturgically, this could hardly be more different from *Tristan*. Where *Tristan* was a slow-moving, at times almost abstract interior drama, *Meistersinger* is rich in incident and individual character, something like a comedy of manners but with a deep undercurrent of ideas, presented, most unusually, as a conversation of musical styles and forms. Where *Tristan* was a virtually seamless score with hardly any identifiable 'numbers', *Meistersinger* is shaped by them. The first act begins with a Lutheran chorale, then comes David's song in which he tries vainly to drum the Masters' rules into Walther's mind; then Walther, so to speak, fills in his application form (answering questions about who he is, who taught him, etc.), and finally there is the Trial Song itself. In Act 2 Sachs sings his cobbler's song, and Beckmesser his serenade, leading to the riot finale, a rich and complex piece of fugal polyphony. In Act 3, after Sachs's 'Wahn' monologue (about the crazy world we live in), David sings his naive little Journeyman Song, and the rest of the act consists mainly of the gradual composition of the Prize Song, Beckmesser's disastrous attempt to sing it (having stolen the manuscript), and finally Walther's winning performance, with a brief episode at the start of the final scene in which the people acclaim Sachs in a motet of his own.

At one point Sachs, who is also in love with Eva, compares his situation with King Mark's in *Tristan*, but is too wise, he says, to risk Mark's fate. Wagner quotes *Tristan* here, but elsewhere is also too wise to impose the earlier opera's style on its successor. The prelude opens with a bang in the most absolute of C majors, and though there are of course plenty of harmonically more intricate stretches, they usually avoid the inconclusiveness that is the touchstone of the harmony in *Tristan*. Where *Tristan* generally avoided cadencing, *Meistersinger* cadences often, and where the word-setting in *Tristan* had tended to blur the scansion of lines that were mainly blank verse, *Meistersinger*, with a mostly rhyming libretto, often maps its music neatly on to the rhymes. This creates a curious effect of antique poesy, which goes with the period aspect of the work, but also seems to reflect the intricate and inflexible guild rules. Wagner understandably makes fun of the mentality that believes art can be judged by a set of precepts. But he is too subtle to argue the precise opposite, that art is exempt from rules. Through Sachs, he assures us that rules have their place, in art as in life; but he also realises that they are made, not by teachers or legislators, but by artists of genius. So when Sachs comes to coach Walther, he guides him according to the Mastersingers' norms, but accepts freedoms that make sense, even where they break the rules. Walther is an awkward character, unused to being tamed. He does many things that would have Beckmesser scratching his marker's board. But when he eventually sings at the contest, and radically extends each line of the song, masters and people alike recognise that they are in the presence of genius and the rules are in need of an overhaul.

While this may seem an optimistic view of public taste in general, it works well as the dramatisation of an idea about expert opinion, popularity and posterity. But the real beauty of *Meistersinger*, beyond its rich felicities of music and portraiture, and beyond its gratuitous warning, in Sachs's final monologue, of the danger to German art of 'welschen Dunst' and 'welschem Tand' ('foreign frippery and trumpery'), is the way its story about art and life is told in a tapestry of music styles, all bound together by a flowing orchestral texture learnt from *Tristan* but in a more lucid, 'reasonable' manner. It's as if the Wagner of *Tristan* had been coached by Sachs into an idiom that takes more account of tradition and convention, that accepts their principles but rejects their right to legislate.

13

Bayreuth: Its Friends and Its Enemies

It was now well over a decade since Wagner had done any work on the *Ring*, apart from orchestrating what he had already composed. He had left Siegfried at the start of Act 3, about to ascend Brünnhilde's mountain under instruction from the Woodbird; and *Götterdämmerung* still remained. Now in March 1869 he returned to *Siegfried* and composed the third act, in which the young hero meets Wotan, his double grandfather, alias the Wanderer, on the mountainside, cuts his spear in two with his sword, and proceeds to the summit through the magic fire to find and waken Brünnhilde and fall passionately in love with her (unaware, of course, that she is his aunt). Wagner completed *Siegfried* in all essentials by the autumn of 1869, and at once embarked on *Götterdämmerung*, the work that had been the original project before it had seemed necessary to supply a back story.

In fact, this culminating piece is as comprehensible on its own as most nineteenth-century operas. Siegfried, after spending time with Brünnhilde, sets out on a quest for heroic adventure (leaving the ring with her), and arrives in the Rhineland kingdom of the Gibichungs. The king, Gunther, has a sister, Gutrune, and a half-brother, Hagen, who we learn is the illegitimate son of Gunther's mother by the dwarf Alberich, and whose main purpose in life is to retrieve the ring. Hagen tricks Siegfried into blood brotherhood and drinking to it, but spikes the drink with a forgetfulness potion, which ensures that when Gunther, seeking a bride, mentions Brünnhilde, Siegfried displays no memory of her and agrees to help him win her for himself. On the mountain, Brünnhilde receives a visit from her sister Waltraute, who tries in vain to persuade her to return the ring to the Rhinemaidens, thereby releasing Wotan from the curse. Soon Siegfried comes up through the flames, disguised by the magic Tarnhelm as Gunther, takes her by force and seizes the ring. Back at the Gibichung court, Hagen is visited in his sleep by Alberich, then Siegfried returns (as himself), ahead of Brünnhilde with the real Gunther, and Hagen summons the Gibichung vassals.

Brünnhilde is of course astonished to see Siegfried and to realise that he doesn't recognise her. He has omitted to hand Gunther the ring which he, Gunther, is supposed to have taken from her, and when she notices it on Siegfried's finger, she breaks out in a fury, raging at Gunther, who is entirely ignorant of the ring, and at Siegfried for having stolen it from him and for his infidelity to her. Siegfried continues to behave in an amnesiac way, and after he and the vassals have left to prepare for his wedding to Gutrune, Brünnhilde, Gunther and Hagen plot to murder him, in a revenge trio that is Wagner's most spectacular denial of his old theories about ensembles. The next day Siegfried joins the Gibichungs in a hunting expedition, and as they pause for refreshments, Hagen persuades Siegfried to tell his life story, meanwhile slipping him a memory-recovery potion. Siegfried now remembers his excursion up the mountain, and as he recalls his first embrace with Brünnhilde, Hagen cries 'Vengeance' and stabs him in the back with his spear. His body is carried back to the Hall, and here the final rites are enacted, a funeral pyre is built for Siegfried, Brünnhilde takes back the ring, then rides her horse on to the pyre, the ring returns to the Rhine, which overflows its banks while, in the distance, Valhalla is seen engulfed in flames.

These four final acts of the *Ring* are a curious mixture, dramatically speaking, of straight grand opera and a strong dose of Schopenhauer. Suddenly, having denounced such things, Wagner has grand choruses, a revenge trio and a cataclysmic finale worthy of *La Muette de Portici*. But of course the ending of *Götterdämmerung* has profounder significance than the mere eruption of a volcano. The gods, after all, have taken Schopenhauer's advice about willing their own destruction.

Originally Brünnhilde's funeral pyre heralded a new world order; now, in the wake of *The World as Will and Representation*, it announces the willed end of the world as we know it, with nothing evident to follow. At least this is the Wagnerian interpretation, though nothing in the score or Brünnhilde's long final monologue says anything of the sort. As far as she is concerned, she is dying in order to be with Siegfried 'in the most powerful love', while the Rhineland suffers a catastrophic flood and her old family home goes up in smoke.

It's easy to ridicule this kind of dramaturgy, but in performance the whole business is rescued by the music, arguably Wagner's most magisterial score, and certainly the one that makes the most comprehensive and effective use of leitmotifs. Now, with the accumulation of old and new motifs, there are more than sixty in play, and these work, over the opera's four-and-a-half-hour span, both as symphonic material and as a continuous narrative subtext, arm-jogging reminders of things or individuals in the past, things the characters onstage may have forgotten or may not wish remembered, things they are thinking but not saying, as well as what Debussy later half-contemptuously called their brochure ('prospectus'), which they metaphorically hand out on arrival. The technique reaches its climax in Act 2 when Brünnhilde spots the ring on Siegfried's finger, and there ensues a whole network of motifs echoing the thoughts in the principal characters' minds, and the hidden causes of the situation. Often they are themes one recognises, but above all they bind the score together musically and psychologically. Musically this works because the motifs are related thematically in groups; dramatically it works because the musical connections express underlying causal connections in the plot. At the same time the score shows Wagner on top form, manipulating chromatic and diatonic harmony, the long musical line, the overarching structure, with complete assurance. And his command of the orchestra – the largest he ever used, including the so-called Wagner tubas and the bass trumpet, all of which he invented – is supreme, arguably superior to the earlier *Ring* dramas, more resourceful, if not better, than in *Tristan* or *Meistersinger*.

With the *Ring* close to completion towards the end of 1874, Wagner had started looking for a theatre in which to stage it. He had originally speculated on the possibility of building, or at least designing, one himself, but this plan had faded, and he was now looking around for some suitable existing theatre. This might seem strange, considering that the original impulse had been to get away from the hierarchical structure of conventional theatres, and it is little short of amazing that, having for some reason lighted on Bayreuth as a possible locale, he and Cosima actually went there to see whether the town's Markgräfliches Opernhaus, built in 1748, would fit the bill. Naturally, this pretty little rococo theatre was useless for the purpose, but Bayreuth stuck, the local authorities were enthusiastic, a site was found, and money somehow raised, with Ludwig coming belatedly to the rescue when the project seemed about to collapse. Almost thirty years after the first drafts of the scenario, the *Ring* had its first performance from 13 to 17 August 1876, in the amphitheatre-like auditorium, with its uniform sight-lines, uniquely balanced acoustics and punitive seats, that still survives today, somewhat altered, on Bayreuth's Green Hill. Only the audience will have disappointed Wagner's original revolutionary, populist intentions. Then, as now, the ticket prices were mostly beyond all but the deepest pockets, and the philosopher Friedrich Nietzsche, who attended the first cycle, reported that 'the whole idle riff-raff of Europe had been brought together, and any prince who pleased could go in and out of Wagner's house as if it were a sporting event'.[1]

In 1876 Nietzsche was emerging from his slavish devotion to Wagner, which had had its origins in a meeting in Leipzig in the autumn of 1868. He had become a regular visitor at Tribschen, had been there when Cosima gave birth to her son Siegfried in June 1869 and again at Christmas 1870 when the *Siegfried Idyll* was played on the stairs as a birthday present for her. For eight years Nietzsche and Wagner had met and talked on the most intimate terms about the composer's works, about Greek drama, its Dionysian and Apollonian aspects, the philosophy of Schopenhauer, and many other related and unrelated topics. But by the mid-seventies Nietzsche was beginning to fidget in his relationship with the great composer. He was thirty years Wagner's junior, and the association inevitably had a master–pupil dimension, whatever the intellectual reality. The whole furore over Bayreuth and the first *Ring*, with its well-heeled, upper-class audience fawning over the composer and radiating what Bryan Magee calls 'chauvinist triumphalism after the victory over France in the war of 1870–1', was almost the last straw for this still-young philosopher who detested the German bourgeoisie and regarded the French as in every way more civilised.[2] The absolute final straw was Wagner's last opera, *Parsifal*, with its elevation of Christian–Buddhist piety and renunciation at a time when Nietzsche was in full cry against every aspect of Christian morality.

Wagner had first read Wolfram von Eschenbach's epic poem *Parzival* in 1845, at the time of the prose sketch of *Lohengrin* and the first outline of *Meistersinger*, but thereafter it came and went in his mind until, with the *Ring* out of the way, he was at last able to give it his full attention and compose the music in time for the second festival in 1882. It has remained his most controversial work, both on account of its sacred subject matter and appurtenances (for example, the onstage celebration of Mass at the end of Act 1), and because of its complex and to some extent obscure underlying symbolism. The bare bones of the plot are already intricate enough. In the kingdom of the Grail[3] the Grail king, Amfortas, is in constant agony from a wound that will not heal. He had gone with the sacred spear against the castle of the sorcerer Klingsor, a former Grail suppliant who, unable to suppress his sexual urges, had castrated himself and turned to evil magic against the Grail. There Amfortas had been seduced by the mysterious Kundry, Klingsor's agent but also, as we soon discover, a penitent in the land of the Grail, reincarnated many times and seeking atonement for having laughed at Jesus on the Cross. Amfortas's sinful wound will only heal through the actions of 'a pure fool, made wise by compassion'.

All this (except for the details of Kundry's past) we learn gradually in a long opening sequence dominated by the old knight Gurnemanz, at the end of which a young man is hauled in who has shot a swan, in a land where all animal life is sacred. This is Parsifal, though he doesn't know his own name, nor where he comes from. In due course Gurnemanz suspects that this might be the pure fool of the prophecy, but when he confronts Parsifal with the suffering Amfortas at Mass, the young man shows neither compassion nor much interest in what he has witnessed. He is, however, being led gradually to understanding. He arrives at Klingsor's castle, easily resists the seductive Flower Maidens, and when kissed, like Amfortas, by Kundry, at once feels the wound bleeding in himself. Kundry, amazed by his resistance, tries to break it down by an account of her past and the curse she bears, but he thrusts her away and, when Klingsor hurls the sacred spear at him, it hovers above him, he seizes it and, with a sign of the Cross, brings the castle crashing down. After long wanderings, he arrives back one Good Friday in the land of the Grail, where spring is in the air but desolation reigns, the still-suffering Amfortas having long refused to celebrate Mass. But now Gurnemanz recognises in Parsifal the long-awaited redeemer and conducts him to the Grail Hall, where Parsifal touches and heals Amfortas's wound with the spear and assumes his role as king of the Grail.

This is a richly allusive scenario, profoundly involved with sexuality as a paradigm of human guilt, and with atonement whose mechanism (the wound in Christ's side, the wound in Amfortas's groin) suggests a, shall we say, enhanced reading of Christ's own humanity and sacrifice. A lot has also been made, down the years, of various supposed political and social undertones, the Grail kingdom as a male-only enclave, sexually chaste, racially pure, even, in some readings, covertly militaristic: a proto-Nazi haven of eugenics and medical experiment. Most of this, needless to say, is absent from the libretto, all of it from the music, which for the most part deals in generalised images of sanctity and depravity, by means of a sharp contrast of style between the Grail acts on the one hand and the central Klingsor act on the other.

The Grail music, typified by the long, reflective prelude, presents a serene, meditative environment within which the human agonies play out. Klingsor's music, on the other hand, is malevolence personified, used not only against Parsifal, but against Kundry herself, eventually creating the context for her bloodcurdling scene with Parsifal, which contains some of the most chromatic, tonally elusive music Wagner ever penned. In the final act the dark, anxious prelude accompanies Parsifal in his tortuous wanderings in search of the Grail land, but then retrieves its serenity as Gurnemanz recognises him and anoints him, Parsifal baptises Kundry, and the beautiful Good Friday music wells up as a sign that man (at least Grail man) is again at one with God and Nature.

Parsifal is a unique score, with a transparent beauty and psychic ferocity unlike anything in Wagner's earlier works. By localising the different harmonic colourings, it lends them a perspective that is also reflected in the orchestration, itself essentially new in its precise placing of wind and strings in a texture that Debussy later described memorably as 'as if lit from behind'. The use of leitmotifs is also different from earlier Wagner, the *Ring* especially. Motifs like the Dresden Amen or the pure fool prophecy remain entities that take on the colouring of their surroundings but retain their integrity. This enables Wagner, for instance, to infiltrate Grail elements into Klingsor's magic garden in a way that speaks the underlying idea as clearly as if it were put into words, but without any flavour of the didactic. In general, though, *Parsifal* is a profound masterpiece that leaves much unsaid. Nietzsche, who claimed to detest it, in fact never heard it, except for the prelude, of which, after finally hearing it in 1887, he rhetorically enquired: 'Did Wagner ever compose anything better?'[4]

According to Frederic Spotts, in the early years of the Bayreuth Festival every composer and conductor of importance attended at least once, with two notable exceptions.[5] One of these was Verdi, who had as we saw come late to Wagner, but who eventually acknowledged his genius without, perhaps, warming to his music. The other absentee was Brahms, and with him the situation was more complicated. On the one hand he had railed against the New German School and the Music of the Future. On the other hand, he could never quite share the almost hysterical antipathy to Wagner felt by Clara Schumann and, more publicly, Eduard Hanslick. Brahms respected Wagner as a composer and studied his music. He never went to Bayreuth, but he attended the Viennese premiere of *Meistersinger* in 1870 and heard both *Das Rheingold* and *Die Walküre* in Munich in 1870. After the Vienna *Meistersinger* he wrote to Clara that 'I do not wax rhapsodic – neither about this work nor about Wagner in general. But I listen to it as attentively as possible, that is, as often as I can stand it.'[6] However at the end of his life, in 1897, he wrote less guardedly to the music critic Richard Specht:

> Do you take me to be so dull as to have been unable to be as enchanted as anyone by the gaiety and grandeur of the *Meistersinger*? Or so dishonest as to conceal the fact that I regard a few bars of this work as worth more than all the operas that have been composed since? I an anti-pope? It's too stupid![7]

Wagner was less respectful in return. After meeting Brahms in Vienna in 1864 and hearing him play his Handel variations, he remarked, a shade condescendingly: 'One sees here what can still be done in the old forms when someone comes along who understands how to treat them.'[8] But the nature of his comments about Brahms recorded by Cosima is entirely contemptuous. It's perhaps worth noting that on both sides the less agreeable tone is in things said to adoring women. Wagner certainly knew that Brahms was a better composer than he allowed Cosima to think he thought.

The clue lay in his remark about 'the old forms'. The implication is that form precedes content. But variation is not a form, it is a process. One might as well say the same of *Tristan*, thinking of opera as a form. But Wagner's preference for the term 'music drama' similarly implies not a form but a process. This is not a quibble about words. Brahms's Handel variations of 1861 may be superficially old-fashioned, in that, as with Bach's *Goldberg Variations*, Beethoven's op. 120, and countless other sets by composers great and small in the past, the individual variations are distinct movements. But a cumulative design overrides the surface divisions. From the start there is a constant process of onward reference, often involving an actual exchange of material between consecutive variations, often a similarity of motion or rhythm, so that the half-hour work is eventually experienced more architecturally than sequentially. There is no name for this large form, which is perhaps unique. But that it *is* a form, and not just a series of interesting variations, would be hard to deny.

The same kinds of consideration apply to most of Brahms's works (the majority) that bear conventional generic titles. Throughout his life he composed abstract, non-programmatic, instrumental music in a long-standing German tradition, as against the supposed French and Italian preference for vocal music, and in defiance of the New German School's insistence on programmes and Wagner's belief that after Beethoven instrumental music was a dead duck. In one respect, though, Brahms agreed with Wagner. Beethoven could not readily be followed in those genres that he had himself so spectacularly transformed: the symphony, the string quartet, perhaps also the piano trio. In 1853 Brahms had composed his B major Trio, partly modelled on Beethoven's 'Archduke'; but he was never happy with it and eventually, in 1889, extensively rewrote it. His other two piano trios are later, more compact works, composed in the 1880s. As a young man he otherwise turned to genres not particularly associated with Beethoven. There are three big piano quartets, a piano quintet, and two string sextets. He certainly began a pair of string quartets in the sixties but held off completing them until 1873, when he was forty. And something similar happened with his First Symphony, whose first movement already existed in some preliminary form in 1862, but which he couldn't bring himself to complete until 1876, when it had its first performance in Karlsruhe three months after the Bayreuth premiere of the *Ring*.

Brahms was obviously more comfortable, early on, writing for or at least with the piano, his own instrument. And just as his three early piano sonatas have an uninhibited muscularity about them, so he transferred something of this sinewy energy to the piano writing in his chamber works. The scale of these works is at least partly the consequence of this keyboard manner of his. It committed him to finding a way of solving the notorious problems of balance in combining the piano with two or three string instruments, and since his solution to this was to have the strings playing all or most of the time, it tended to create an intensity of sound and workmanship that needed to be justified in terms of the musical content. The solution he found, no doubt intuitively, was to saturate the texture, the fabric of the sound, with thematic material. This might seem obvious enough, but it was not at all the classical way of doing things, which was still, even in Schumann, broadly based on the idea of theme and accompaniment. Of course, there is theme and accompaniment in Brahms as well; his openings, for instance, are nearly always of that kind. But soon, in first movements especially, the music begins to break down into units of melody passed to and fro between the instruments. Take the start of the Piano Quartet in G minor, op. 25 (1861). The piano opens with a winding unison melody which is taken up after four bars by the string instruments in dialogue. There is then immediately a new theme, piano and strings in dialogue, which soon leads back to the opening melody, varied, still in dialogue. After half a dozen bars this throws up a new semiquaver figure in the piano which at first sounds like an accompaniment but turns out to be another theme, once again discussed by the four instruments in dialogue (it is actually a rhythmic relative of the second theme). So after forty or so bars we have heard three separate themes, all very compact, in discussion and with hardly any padding or redundancy; and this, in terms of sonata form, is just the first subject.

The parallel with Wagner's leitmotif technique is hard to resist. In both cases, the result is a saturated texture in which everything carries meaning. I used to challenge my students to count, by ear, how many times the second symphony's opening three-note figure comes in the course of the first subject section (I make it thirty, including upside-down forms). And Brahms could even manufacture beautiful themes out of two-note motifs. The opening theme of the Fourth Symphony, a lovely melody in E minor for the violins, consists entirely of a cycle of thirds (minor and major), first down, then up, with octave changes, and the same interval then dominates the whole movement, and starts off the following Andante moderato. This combination of the lyrical and the cerebral can be extremely powerful. In the first movement of the First Symphony the intense working of motifs is several times interrupted by unexpected bursts of song, the second and third movements are essentially lyrical, and the finale, after a tense beginning, breaks into a radiant horn theme that Brahms unashamedly marks 'passionato'. The famous C major melody that follows, supposedly modelled on the finale theme of Beethoven's 'Choral' Symphony, is in reality pure Brahms, a close relative, for instance, of the first movement theme of the B major Piano Trio. But the obvious resemblance to Beethoven, in shape rather than sentiment, reinforced the widely held view that Brahms was an epigone of his great predecessor. His First was really Beethoven's Tenth.

It's a view that dies with the first bar of the symphony. Beethoven's C minor (in the Fifth Symphony) is a direct hit, Brahms's is an agonised quest, a search that continues throughout the movement and is only resolved after more striving in the finale. Yet at bottom Brahms was a lyricist, and a lot of his style can be traced back to his nearly two hundred songs and his numerous folk-song arrangements. Many of the songs are themselves folk-song-like in melody and sentiment, even when enriched by effusive piano parts that one can imagine the composer of the piano chamber music enjoying playing. A high percentage of the early songs, especially, are strophic, like folk songs, and deal with the usual topics, love and nature, love lost and gained, rustic scenes of one kind and another. The ballads of his one early cycle, the *Romanzen aus Tieck's Magelone*, op. 33 (composed at various times in the 1860s), are only half successful as a set, though they contain a handful of great songs, notably the lullaby, 'Ruhe, Süssliebchen', an obvious descendant of Schubert's 'Baches Wiegenlied'. Later a more reflective, quasi-philosophical, at times enigmatic note in the poetry finds an echo in the music. In one of Brahms's grandest and finest songs, 'Von ewiger Liebe', trouble is brewing in the opening, in a dark B minor, as a young man escorts his sweetheart home at night and talks to her about the shame of linking her name to his (we never find out why). But then comes an unexpected twist as the music switches to a warm B major, and the girl answers him: 'Our love shall not be severed: iron and steel are strong, but our love is stronger.' A more powerful answer to Romantic pathos would be hard to imagine. But there is a different answer in the ultra-concise 'Auf dem Kirchhofe'. The poet visits a graveyard in a storm and tries to read the gravestones. The names are illegible, but the words *gewesen* ('past and gone') and *genesen* ('recovered', but in this context perhaps 'released') speak from the stones. This might be pathos, but to Brahms it brings comfort, in a calm, almost radiant C major.

The ending of 'Auf dem Kirchhofe' expresses its sense of repose in what sounds like a phrase of Bach's Passion Chorale. There is a faint anticipation here of Brahms's final vocal work, the *Vier ernste Gesänge* (*Four Serious Songs*), composed in 1896 when Clara lay dying and the year before Brahms's own death. Settings of biblical texts about death, they apply a lieder technique to a style that frequently hints at the antique, but in an unspecific way, a modal touch here, a suggestion of plainsong there: a humanist Passion. Brahms was agnostic, but from early on he was an assiduous student of old music, not only Bach, but also the earlier baroque, especially Schütz, and Renaissance polyphony, and this inevitably drew him to religious music, whose flavour can often be detected in his own style. For a non-believer he composed a remarkable quantity of sacred music, though nothing liturgical. His *German Requiem* draws on biblical texts about death and the comforts of religion and is so devoid of false sentiment that it is hard to believe its composer did not intuitively feel the truth of the words he was setting, even while intellectually needing to distance himself from them. A feature of the work is the way it absorbs characteristics of old music into a perfectly modern, often complex style; for instance the second movement opens ('For all flesh is as grass', from the Epistle of St Peter) in a sombre unison B flat minor like some Lenten monastic processional, draws comfort from another epistle (St James's 'Be patient therefore, brethren') in a G flat major Chorale, then, after a reprise of the processional, ends with a big Handelian chorus from Isaiah ('The ransomed of the Lord shall return and come to Zion'), complete with canonic and imitative entries in the most learned baroque manner. Yet none of this sounds 'old' in the sense of pastiche. There is a certain parallel with Wagner's exactly contemporary *Meistersinger*, which apes antiquity for dramatic purposes and enters the same sort of timeless Lutheran world by a different door.

In December 1877, Brahms wrote to his Berlin publisher, Fritz Simrock, recommending a Czech composer in his thirties whose music had not yet penetrated beyond his homeland:

For several years I have enjoyed works sent in by Antonín Dvořák [for the Austrian State Stipendium]. This year he has sent works including a volume of ten duets for two sopranos and piano, which seem to me very pretty, and a practical proposition for publishing . . . He is a very talented man. Moreover, he is poor![9]

For three years Brahms had been on the panel for the Stipendium, and Dvořák had received an award each time. Yet he was thirty-six in 1877 and his music was still virtually unknown outside his native Bohemia. Brahms's recommendation created something like a chain reaction as a result of which Dvořák became one of the most successful and famous composers in Europe.

Unlike Smetana, whose father was a well-to-do German-speaking master brewer in eastern Bohemia, Dvořák was the son of a butcher and innkeeper in a village twenty miles north of Prague. The Dvořáks were Czech-speaking, and like most rural Czechs they were musical. Antonín studied violin and keyboard, and was a good enough organist to compete for serious church appointments in Prague, though in the end he settled down as principal viola in the orchestra of the new Provisional Theatre. Meanwhile he was composing and building up a local reputation. By 1877 he had written no fewer than nine string quartets, five symphonies, concertos for cello and piano, a string serenade, a set of symphonic variations for orchestra, four operas and a good deal else. Not a note had been heard outside Bohemia. Stylistically it had gone through various phases, influenced to some extent by Liszt and Wagner, a bit by Schumann and, eventually, Brahms; not much by Smetana. At a certain point in the early 1870s he had made a conscious decision to abandon these Germanic influences, partly by a study of Slavic folk sources, though his study does not seem to have been particularly penetrating. The *Moravian Duets* for two voices and piano that were among the pieces that won him the award and were the duets Brahms sent to Simrock, are charming settings of Moravian folk poems but musically hardly Moravian at all.[10] What happened in his music about this time was perhaps an attempt to individualise it for the benefit of those admiring Germans – and what better way than to assert his Czechness? Or perhaps the attempt was by Simrock, who promptly commissioned what became the first set of *Slavonic Dances*.

The dances, composed for piano duet then orchestrated, are Czech types: *furiant, sousedská, skočná,* and so forth, and they proclaim nationality, but without much in the way of melodic or harmonic oddity, a few modalisms apart. More interesting is the way that the same types start popping up in his chamber and (slightly later) symphonic works.

The D minor String Quartet (1877) has a polka for a scherzo, and the A major String Sextet (1878) a *dumka* slow movement and a *furiant* scherzo. A couple of years later, the scherzo of the Sixth Symphony is likewise a *furiant*. These are only superficially Czech features; after all, anyone can write a *furiant*, which is simply a quick triple-time dance with a hemiola cross-rhythm – three slow beats across two bars. The trickier question is, how specifically Czech is Dvořák's style at this point? The answer is probably not at all. According to Michael Beckerman, Dvořák is unlikely to have known very much about Bohemian or Moravian folk music; and certainly the kinds of exoticism that, for example, Bartók later discovered in the music of the Hungarian plain, is nowhere to be found in Dvořák. On the other hand, there is undoubtedly something fresh and faintly bucolic in his music of these years. The paired clarinets at the start of the Fifth Symphony, the drone-like pedal notes in the 'Alla Polka' of the D minor Quartet, the persistent enjoyment of slow harmonic effects such as the D major to B minor to F sharp minor progression in the slow movement of that same quartet, the point of which is that it studiously avoids the move to the dominant (A major) that would instantly align it with classical harmony. But there is nothing particularly Czech about this effect. One might see it as de-urbanising, but hardly more.

Dvořák probably turned to Smetana for some ingredients in this new style of his. The overture to his opera *Šelma sedlák* (*The Cunning Peasant*, 1877) is a patent chip off *Dalibor*. But in the end he was a more versatile, more profoundly gifted composer than Smetana, and he could turn out masterpieces in almost every genre, through a process of what Leon Botstein has called the civilising of 'folklike material', but might just as well be called the ruralising of the urban.[11] The Sixth Symphony is a beautiful example: the first and last movements, especially, sound like Brahms hung out on a breezy day. But it is a great mistake to regard Dvořák as a kind of rustic Brahms, a naturally gifted musical yokel, at his most effective when pulling melodies 'out of his sleeve', as Simrock once characterised his genius. On the contrary he was an expert, solidly trained composer whose best works lose little by comparison, technically, with Brahms. The D minor Symphony, No. 7 (1885), may have been prompted by hearing the Master's Third Symphony, but is itself not very Brahmsian except in the general sense of strongly worked material in a highly organised design. Most critics regard it as Dvořák's symphonic masterpiece. The Eighth (G major) and Ninth (E minor, 'From the New World') have always been more popular, because of their astonishing prodigality of melody and orchestral colour. But Brahms himself was severe on the Eighth: 'Too much that's fragmentary, incidental, loiters about in the piece. Everything fine, musically captivating and beautiful – but no main points!' About the Ninth he was more relaxed. 'Just as it stands,' he told the critic Max Kalbeck, 'it is so unspeakably gifted, so healthy, that one must rejoice in it.'[12]

The 'New World' symphony was one of several products of a three-year stay in New York (1892–5) as artistic director of the National Conservatory of Music in America, and it famously includes somewhat Czechified versions of negro spirituals and Amerindian melodies that he sought out with the aim of synthesising a national American style. The idea of a Czech nationalist inventing an American nationalism may seem quaint; but in fact Dvořák's music did have an influence on American composers, most obviously Charles Ives – though whether Ives can be regarded as a nationalist at all is an esoteric question that fortunately lies outside the remit of the present book.

Unsurprisingly, Dvořák was homesick in New York, and when the National Conservatory ran into financial difficulties, he took the opportunity to break his contract and return permanently to his native land. He brought back with him (apart from the symphony, the F major String Quartet, and the E flat major String Quintet) a Cello Concerto that, in both scale and feeling, stands apart from the other American works. In many respects it sums up the specifically Czech qualities in his earlier music, and at the same time raises once more the question whether these qualities are not simply a personal synthesis, based on a few superficially ethnic details, which has now lodged itself in all our brains as 'typically Czech': details like the modal touches in the main first movement theme, the Scotch snap and fourth intervals in the second movement theme, the polka rhythm of the finale. The personal character of the work is evident throughout, but becomes explicit in the second subject of the slow movement, which is a quotation from his German song 'Lasst mich allein' ('Leave me alone', op. 82/1), and in the coda which he added after returning from the States, where the same song is quoted by a solo violin. These quotes record his response to the illness and death of his sister-in-law, Josefina Kounicová, with whom he had been in love thirty years before, when she was a sixteen-year-old piano pupil of his. More importantly, the whole work is bound together by a constant engagement with the material, an obvious love of the cello, and a seamless integration of the solo and orchestral parts. Perhaps this Cello Concerto, actually Dvořák's second, is his finest and most beautiful work. It could certainly claim to be the most successful, even the greatest, of all cello concertos.

'Dvořák's music', the Viennese critic Robert Hirschfeld neverthe-less wrote in an obituary of the composer in 1904, 'has no profundity. He does not, like Bruckner, dig into the depths of his soul to bring forth an Adagio.'[13] Leaving aside the obvious fatuity of the criticism, the comparison itself is significant. For one thing Bruckner, who had died eight years before Dvořák, had often been reviled by the Viennese musical press, especially its mandarin-in-chief Eduard Hanslick (a supporter of Dvořák), his music treated as formless and incompre-hensible. But more specifically, it must have been obvious even to a Viennese music critic that the two composers had hardly anything in common musically and could not sensibly be used as sticks to beat each other. What they did have in common lay in their background. Bruckner, like Dvořák, was village-born, a church organist, and a late-comer as a successful composer. Dvořák had served as organist for three years at St Vojtěch's church in Prague. Bruckner was an organist from childhood, would occasionally play at Mass at his village church of Ansfelden, not far from Linz, was later assistant organist at the St Florian monastery, and ended his church career as cathedral organist in Linz itself. By the time he took up the Linz appointment in 1856 he was thirty-one and had composed practically nothing except church music, a number of motets and some Mass settings. Then for six years he studied counterpoint with the Viennese theorist Simon Sechter and composed, it seems, hardly anything. The earliest work by which he is now known, the D minor Mass, was completed in September 1864 when he was just forty. It was followed by two further Masses, the E minor with wind already mentioned, and a full orchestral setting in F minor. When he at last moved to Vienna to take up a chair at the Vienna Conservatory in September 1868, these sacred works, together with a single C minor Symphony, were his sole serious credentials as a composer. He never taught composition in Vienna, only harmony and counterpoint.

Misleading as it may be to think of Dvořák as a brilliantly gifted rustic, Bruckner did in some ways fit that description. A devout Catholic, he never completely shed his air of the village organ loft or his Upper Austrian way of speaking, continued to dress in an old-fashioned provincial manner, and was frequently the object of ridicule or satire for his gauche behaviour. Nor did he ever quite overcome his sense of awe towards those he regarded as far above him in genius or social status. In a sense, these qualities also colour his music. More than with any of his contemporaries, certainly more than with Brahms, his worship of Beethoven is audible in virtually every one of his, eventually, ten mature symphonies (including the so-called 'Nullte', No. o, composed after No. 1 but then withdrawn). Like Wagner, his other great idol, he seems to have been obsessed with the 'Choral' Symphony, especially its orchestral movements. All his symphonies except No. 1 begin with long pedal notes, high or low, usually tremolando, accompanying slow-moving, lapidary themes, exactly as at the start of Beethoven's Ninth (in No. 5 this happens after a slow introduction). The Adagio of Bruckner's Seventh is candidly modelled on Beethoven's: the second themes of the two movements are first cousins. As for Wagner, Bruckner's devotion was such that, after attending the premiere of *Tristan* and meeting the composer, he would thereafter boast of the acquaintance, not necessarily a credit point in Vienna. He probably went to all Wagner's subsequent premieres; his Third Symphony (1873) is dedicated to the Master, and his Seventh, completed early in 1883 when Wagner was at death's door, includes Wagner tubas for the first time (in the Adagio and Finale), and a long elegiac coda to the Adagio, tubas to the fore, added after Wagner's death in February. Yet Bruckner rightly denied that he was a Wagnerian symphonist. His music owes more to Schubert, but more still to his own background as an organist, the music he played and, no doubt, the way he played it.

His symphonies are grand, cyclopean structures, made out of large musical paragraphs that develop slowly through series of terraced climaxes, rather than by the classical method of organic interweaving of motifs. His shortest symphony, No. 1, lasts a good fifty minutes, while the longest, No. 8, lasts almost eighty. This was a scale unmatched even by the 'Choral' Symphony itself, or by Schubert's 'Great' C major, the two longest symphonies anyone knew about. But though Viennese audiences and critics complained that Bruckner's symphonies were too long, they are not. They are the length they need to be in view of their type of discourse, which simply cannot be curtailed. Listening to this music, one is irresistibly reminded of Bruckner the organist, not on his stool in Ansfelden, but in the great organ loft of St Florian. After years of study and experience he had become one of the finest improvisers of his day. When he auditioned for a teaching diploma in Vienna in 1861, the Hofkapellmeister, Johann Herbeck, said, 'He should have examined us.' At the organ he would set his stops, start perhaps with a long low pedal, introduce a theme on one manual, another theme on another manual, gradually build up the texture to a certain point, then press or kick a piston, changing to a new (pre-set) registration. Perhaps he would wait a second for the sound to die away in the echoing spaces, then set off again with some new idea treated in similar fashion. Each stage has its natural length, which sometimes has to be filled out by repetition; each stage has its 'registration'; each stage tends to build. Of course, in the nature of music the discourse is to some extent fluid. A symphony isn't, after all, a stone building but a narrative with a beginning, a middle and an end. So Bruckner does gradually develop his ideas, sometimes to a pitch of complexity, and he nods respectfully towards classical sonata form, without adhering to its orthodoxies.

The resulting works, all except the unfinished No. 9 in four movements with substantial slow movements and brusque, ternary-form scherzos, have a certain monumental splendour unlike anything else in late Romantic music. No music is more recognisable. But as with a long church service its enjoyment requires patience and a slow metabolism. Viennese audiences and musicians took time to develop these faculties. The Viennese premiere of the Third Symphony in 1877 was a notorious disaster; the orchestra took against the music, Bruckner conducted ineffectually, and most of the audience walked out during the finale. When the Vienna Philharmonic played through the Fourth Symphony in 1875 they found most of it 'idiotic' and turned it down for performance. Eventually Vienna came to terms with his music. The Seventh Symphony, having enjoyed a huge success in Leipzig under Arthur Nikisch in 1884, was almost as well received when Hans Richter conducted it in Vienna two years later. But still some in the city remained hostile. Hanslick continued either to abuse Bruckner's music or ignore it with acid politeness. Brahms, perhaps unsurprisingly, disliked 'these symphonic boa-constrictors, . . . a swindle which will soon be forgotten'. To be fair, Bruckner felt much the same about Brahms. 'He is Brahms,' he is said to have remarked, 'my profound respect. But I am Bruckner and I prefer my own stuff.'[14]

14

Ars Gallica, Ars Veritatis

The Franco-Prussian War of 1870–1, the Siege of Paris, and the Paris Commune that emerged briefly from them in March 1871, were arguably the most appalling sequence of events anywhere in nineteenth-century Europe. The military defeat, the capture of the Emperor Napoléon III, and the subsequent proclamation of the Prussian king as emperor of a united Germany in the Palace of Versailles: these were humiliations enough, one might think, to destroy a nation's self-confidence, even without the horrors of the siege and the vicious retributions of the Commune. Yet musical life, at least, seems to have proceeded with little more than a faint nod towards the chaos on the streets. Gounod vanished for a while to England; Georges Bizet, Camille Saint-Saëns, Vincent d'Indy and Jules Massenet all served in the National Guard. But life went on. On 25 February 1871, with peace negotiations still in progress at Versailles, two composers, Saint-Saëns and Marie-Alexis, Vicomte de Castillon de Saint-Victor, founded the Société Nationale de Musique in Paris, a patriotic gesture under the motto 'Ars Gallica' designed to initiate rehabilitation. On the 26th what was perhaps the most humiliating treaty even in France's somewhat chequered history was signed, and three days later thirty thousand German troops goose-stepped from Longchamp to the Place de la Concorde, braving the hostility of a population already infected with the republican fury that had set off three revolutions in the past century and was about to set off a fourth. But the mob were reserving their reprisals for each other. At the Concorde, Bismarck 'found himself surrounded by a glaring crowd . . . but with superb aplomb he took out a cigar and asked the most hostile-looking spectator for a light'.[1]

Not only was Paris shattered physically and morally by the siege and the Commune, but the whole of France laboured under a huge reparation bill. The atmosphere in the seventies was sombre where the sixties had been frivolous; the buoyant, corrupt but essentially stable Second Empire gave way to the dull, corrupt and at first unstable Third Republic, unsure of its direction, and lacking great figures able to dominate events. There were striking developments in the arts as well, but it would be hard to see them as reflecting the political and social changes in any straightforward way. The July Monarchy and the Second Empire had been a brilliant time for literature, but Stendhal and Balzac were long dead, Flaubert had done most of his best work, Victor Hugo had a single new novel up his sleeve. The realist flame of these writers was tended after 1870 most notably by Émile Zola, but the key to the future was in the hands of a group of anti-realist poets, followers of Baudelaire, Symbolists, who took their inspiration partly from music, especially Wagner. Meanwhile, the soon-to-be-labelled Impressionist painters had broken away from the Academy in 1863, held their own Salon des Refusés, and would soon, in 1874, form an independent co-operative. In their denial of photographic or descriptive realism, and their renewed appeal to inner experience, the individual eye, the immanent beauty and strangeness of being, seeing and feeling, the Symbolists and Impressionists not only, in their different ways, revived the spirit of the early Romantics, but also heralded a new, modern age in which art would no longer cater to the preferences and moral hypocrisies of a moneyed bourgeoisie, but would pride itself on its impenetrability, its perversity, even its perversion, its power to shock, to *épater le bourgeois*.

One will search almost in vain for anything of the kind in French music of the seventies and eighties. The various opera stages, though for a time inhibited by the straitened circumstances of the post-war years, continued to provide a bourgeois audience with the escapist fare it craved. Offenbach continued to churn out operettas, without ever achieving the success of his sixties works. His chief rival for frothiness,

Charles Lecocq, did somewhat better with *La Fille de Madame Angot* (1872) and *Giroflé-Girofla* (1874), both premiered in Brussels but brought quickly to Paris, but his was never the sort of work that would make an impact beyond the hallowed walls of the Folies-Dramatiques or the optimistically titled Théâtre de la Renaissance, not to mention the Brussels Théâtre des Fantaisies Parisiennes, where both pieces began their careers. Probably the most successful seventies work in anything like this vein was a ballet, *Coppélia*, by Léo Delibes, a composer in his thirties who had himself enjoyed some modest success with operettas and had worked as chorus master at the Opéra. In style, *Coppélia* (premiered in May 1870, just before the outbreak of war) hardly ventures beyond operetta, except that the absence of voices allows a certain Romantic sweep to the melody and orchestration that, on the operetta stage, might have dissolved into bubbles. As a story ballet with an intriguing plot (from Hoffmann's 'Der Sandmann') and real characterisation, it was destined to exert an influence well beyond its own superficially limited world. Tchaikovsky adored *Coppélia* when he saw it in St Petersburg in 1884; he adored Delibes's later ballet, *Sylvia*, even more, and both works lie behind his own two great ballets for the Imperial Theatre, *Spyashchaya krasavitsa* (*The Sleeping Beauty*) and *Shchelkunchik* (*The Nutcracker*).

The one French opera that made a lasting, indeed seismic, impact during these years was, perhaps precisely for that reason, a failure on its first performance at the Opéra-Comique in March 1875. Worse, its thirty-six-year-old composer fell ill with severe rheumatism soon after the premiere, then suffered two heart attacks and died three months later. Georges Bizet lived long enough to know that *Carmen* was not the failure it had seemed at first, but he never knew the astonishing extent of its eventual success. A Conservatoire pupil of Halévy and Gounod, Bizet had previously written seven operas, but hardly anything that gave warning of a musico-dramatic genius on the level of *Carmen*. After a trio of *buffo* comedies, one of which, the one-act *Le Docteur Miracle*, had been staged with success at the Bouffes-Parisiens in 1857, he had advanced to a five-act grand opera about Ivan the Terrible (*Ivan IV*) and his marriage to the Caucasian princess Maria Temryukovna. The scale and dramatic complexity of this Meyerbeerian subject were strictly beyond the twenty-four-year-old composer, though he managed several striking episodes and some memorable, if eclectic, individual numbers.

The two operas that followed, *Les Pêcheurs de Perles* (*The Pearl Fishers*, 1863) and *The Fair Maid of Perth* (*La Jolie Fille de Perth*, 1867, loosely based on the novel by Scott) were more consistently individual, without ever quite escaping from the orbit of Gounod and, in the case of *The Pearl Fishers*, Félicien David, whose *Lalla-Roukh* had had its premiere at the Opéra-Comique the year before. Both scores are marked by the growing assurance and precision of Bizet's orchestration, especially his feeling for the woodwind, which gives his textures a lightness and clarity that even Berlioz might have envied. Then, before *Carmen*, there was a lively, individual, one-acter, *Djamileh*, set in Cairo, with a strong central role for the slave-girl of the title, who, Sheherazade-like, tricks her owner into falling in love with her. But superior to any of these, and really the only work by Bizet that seriously anticipates his final masterpiece, is his incidental music to Alphonse Daudet's play *L'Arlésienne*, composed for its first production at the new Théâtre du Vaudeville in 1872. The play was an expansion of an exiguous short story in Daudet's *Lettres de mon moulin*, in which a Provençal farmer's son, engaged to a girl from the nearby city of Arles, learns that she has been unfaithful to him for the past two years, and throws himself out of a high barn window. Bizet, suddenly, seems inspired by the brutal, unembroidered tragedy of this rustic tale, in which the girl of the title, who never appears, takes on the character of a *femme fatale*, an image of the corruption of rural innocence by the lure of the urban or exotic.

In *Carmen*, the *femme fatale* appears, with results no less calamitous. Don José, a dragoon corporal in Seville, is betrothed to Micaëla, a simple girl from his native Navarre, but is seduced by the gypsy Carmen, then abandoned by her for the toreador, Escamillo. Trapped into deserting from the army, he becomes willy-nilly a member of a gang of smugglers to which Carmen belongs, and has to witness the start of her affair with Escamillo, who turns up in the smugglers' camp looking for her. At the bullfight in Seville José appears in a state of utter despair, pleads with Carmen to love him, and when she refuses stabs her, just as the shouts of triumph from the arena announce the death of the bull.

Freely based on a novella by Prosper Mérimée, *Carmen* is yet another tragedy that describes itself as an *opéra comique*, purely because of its spoken dialogue. It is not a particularly tidy piece. A lot of music was cut during rehearsal, and there are inconsistencies of style. There are conventional numbers, such as the Cigarette Girls' chorus in Act 1 (though the dramatic concept was shocking at the time), and Micaëla's aria in Act 3; and there are new ideas of real force and originality, starting with Carmen's *seguidilla* in the first act (the famous *haba-nera* was a crib of a song called 'El Arreglito' by the Basque composer Sebastián Iradier); then her *chanson bohème* in Act 2, each verse faster, and the fascinating little dance she performs with castanets for José, to the accompaniment of bugles sounding the retreat from his barracks. The third act, in the smugglers' camp, is mainly old-fashioned in its apparatus, including an outsize chorus of smugglers worthy of early Verdi, but the final act is beyond question one of the most powerful and inspired stretches of focused music drama in the entire repertory, the ultimate confrontation between injured domestic purity and the unfenced passion of the wild hills.

In the end, no doubt, *Carmen* is one of the half dozen or so most popular operas because of its vivid portraiture and narrative colouring and the sheer quality of its musical invention. Even in the action scenes – the opening with Micaëla and the sergeant, Moralès, or the scene between José and Escamillo in Act 3 – the melodies flow unabated, and there is hardly a weak number in the whole three-hour span. But beneath this surface prodigality there is something more profound, not a profundity of intellect, but a depth of dramatic and psychological realism. This is one of those rare operas (like *La traviata*) in which one follows the motivation with empathy: yes, that's how things happen, that's how people are. There is nothing artificial about José's entrapment. He loves Micaëla and resists Carmen for as long as he can; even when he has committed himself almost too far, he tries to evade her enticement, but circumstances outwit him, and his refusal to obey Zuniga's order to return to barracks is a natural impulse. Carmen is an instrument of Fate, as the work's most important theme tells us, but she is also a beautiful woman who knows she has men at her fingertips. The strong man knows this and rides it. As Escamillo, embarking on his affair with her, observes: 'Carmen's loves don't last six months.' But José is a weak, passionate man, in out of his depth.

Carmen shocked many in its first audiences by its apparent endorsement of lax morals and its horrible, graphic ending. Carmen was a free spirit, a Romantic icon, hence to be admired; but could one really respect such a person, a promiscuous, knife-wielding gypsy? The shock was made worse by the realism. These were flesh-and-blood creatures doing flesh-and-blood things to music that flowed through their veins. That was disconcerting to bourgeois Parisians, but it gained important professional admirers. Tchaikovsky, who loathed Wagner, adored *Carmen* when he saw it in Paris in 1876 and stole from it for his own operas, notably *The Queen of Spades*; Puccini and the young Italian school, the so-called *veristi*, copied its violent apparatus, without perhaps always penetrating to its deeper truths. Richard Strauss famously revered Bizet's orchestration. But *Carmen*'s most notorious admirer, or at least professed admirer, was not a well-known composer at all (though he did compose), but a philosopher, Friedrich Nietzsche. Looking, as he admitted in a letter to a friend, for 'an ironic antithesis to Wagner', he claimed in *Der Fall Wagner* to regard Bizet's masterpiece as the greatest opera of all. 'This music seems to me perfect,' he wrote. 'It emerges light, supple, courteous. It is amiable, it doesn't sweat . . .' Bizet's lightness was the opposite of Wagner. 'In the end, this music treats the listener as intelligent, as a musician himself – in this respect it is even the opposite of Wagner, who, whatever else, was in any case the most discourteous genius in the world.'² Nietzsche was being insincere, but his choice of insincerity was significant.

What Bizet might have achieved had he lived can only be guessed at, but in general French music of this period was patchy at best and, like French politics, lacked a commanding figure. Gounod lived on till 1893, composing operas that, after *Roméo et Juliette*, have been largely forgotten, and a good deal of sacred music, including several masses, of which probably the finest, the *Messe solennelle de Sainte-Cécile*, harks back to 1855. Gounod's near contemporary, César Franck (born in Liège, but Parisian by adoption) also composed a quantity of sacred music, likewise including large-scale oratorios, among them a *Redemption* and a *Béatitudes*, based on the Sermon on the Mount. But Franck was not a natural setter of words, and though these works, composed when he was already in his forties, show the beginnings of the style of his late instrumental scores, they nevertheless plod along in themselves, shackled by inept prosody and unhelpful vocal writing.

Franck, like Liszt, had been refused entry to the Paris Conservatoire as a foreigner. But unlike Liszt he took out naturalisation papers, entered the Conservatoire at the age of fifteen, and there studied piano and organ, among the usual other things. In 1851 he became organist at the church of Saint-Jean-Saint-François in the Marais, and then, seven years later, at Sainte-Clotilde, a newly built basilica close to the Invalides. Both churches had Cavaillé-Coll organs, and Franck was soon advising their famous builder, composing substantial works for them, and above all improvising on them, including large-scale closing voluntaries that began to attract audiences for their own sake. His superb *Six pièces*, including the *Grande pièce symphonique* and the *Prélude, fugue et variation*, are presumably more highly organised versions of these improvisations. They contain the seeds of Franck's late, highly chromatic style, with its intricate thematic connections, derived, ultimately, from Liszt's transformation technique. One of the useful skills of the church organist, who has constantly to improvise discreet background music while the priest performs silent parts of the liturgy, is to modulate, to move freely from one key to another, to drift around the musical landscape while avoiding intrusive musical gestures; and although it would be unfair to suggest that Franck's late music was no more than organised drifting, there is a certain obvious connection.

Nearly all Franck's well-known concert music was composed in the last ten years or so of his life; the exception is the symphonic poem *Les Éolides*, composed in 1876. Three more symphonic poems followed in the 1880s, together with the *Symphonic Variations* for piano and orchestra and the Symphony in D minor, and there were also three major chamber works, a piano quintet, a violin sonata, and a string quartet composed in 1889, the year before he died. These works embody Franck's peculiar harmonic language based on the free use of chromatic passing notes (notes not essential to the harmony) and frequent modulation, all of which generates a sense of continuous, often rather uneasy motion within a broadly conventional tonal language. Sometimes the chromaticism seems gratuitous, as if smeared over what would otherwise be fairly standard progressions. More often it creates genuine emotional tension which Franck controls by means of thematic connections within and between movements. The total effect is strenuous, with steep emotional gradients and grandiose climaxes. The critic Georges Jean-Aubry suggested the oxymoron 'serene anxiety' to describe this aspect of Franck's music, but the anxiety is often more apparent than the serenity. Debussy, who had studied improvisation with Franck and admired his music, referred to his 'wearying and persistent *grisaille*'.[3] Nevertheless these late concert works of Franck are among the finest by any French composer outside the opera house in the second half of the nineteenth century.

There were plenty of potential rivals. Partly no doubt because of the temporary shortage of funds for opera, partly because of outside influences, especially that of Liszt, French composers began turning to instrumental music much more after 1870. Franck himself was following a trend that already existed, especially in the work of a younger composer of positively Mendelssohnian talent whom we have already met, Camille Saint-Saëns. By the time he co-founded the Société Nationale in 1871, Saint-Saëns, a Conservatoire pupil of Halévy and already a brilliant pianist, had written three piano concertos, two violin concertos, two or three symphonies and a number of chamber works. He remained immensely prolific throughout a long life; he died aged eighty-six in 1921 and wrote three sonatas for wind instruments in that year. But as with many very fluent composers, his facility was often the enemy of substance. Profundity is a rare visitor to these acres of well-written, polished, invariably agreeable music, and when he seems consciously to have sought it, as for instance in the Third ('Organ') Symphony of 1886, the result is apt to be a spectacular mixture of the inspired and the sententious.

The beauty of Saint-Saëns's best music is its lucidity and poise, its uncluttered melodiousness, its clarity of form and texture. His melodic gift comes out in works of every type, from the sparkling and witty *Carnaval des animaux* (also 1886), to the more sustained, sensuous beauty of Dalila's arias 'Printemps qui commence' and 'Mon cœur s'ouvre à ta voix' in *Samson et Dalila* (1877), the only one of his dozen or so operas to have survived on the modern stage. In a way one might describe Saint-Saëns's best music as the quintessence of Romantic style stripped of its self-absorption. But this is not to call it inexpressive and certainly not cold. Quite apart from the controlled and objectified feeling that runs through *Samson*, there are tender episodes especially in the third and fourth piano concertos, at the start of the symphonic poem *La Jeunesse d'Hercule* (1877), and in the Allegretto of the A minor Cello Concerto (1872), and in many other places. But the feeling seldom bullies. There is a tact and delicacy that might be refreshing, or it might be a limitation. His chamber music, nearly all with piano (there are two late string quartets), often challenges the players, less often the listener. His piano trios (in F, 1864, and E minor, 1892) are typical in this respect, substantial works in point of length, attractive, athletic, but curiously inconsequential in effect.

Saint-Saëns's colleague in the Société Nationale, Alexis Castillon, promised as much or more but alas died of pneumonia when he was only thirty-four. He was also a late starter. An aristocrat from a military background, he studied for an army career but abandoned it in favour of music in his early twenties. A few years later he joined Franck's class, and it must have been from Franck's teaching and example that he developed a certain weight of musical thinking that distinguishes his few works from Saint-Saëns's many. They are mostly chamber music, notably a fine piano quartet, and a pair each of piano trios and string quartets. Another Franck pupil, Henri Duparc, also stopped composing in his mid-thirties, not because of actual illness but because of a condition called hyperaesthesia, in which all or some of the senses become hypersensitive, and the prescribed treatment includes not stimulating them. Unlike Castillon, Duparc composed songs, some fifteen of them, and little else. But these songs have a kind of perfection that makes them unique. Like Franck, Duparc was an indifferent setter of words, but his response to atmosphere and meaning was another matter. The richness of feeling in songs like 'L'Invitation au voyage' (poem by Baudelaire) and 'Phidylé' (Leconte de Lisle) is on a positively Schubertian level, with a marvellous range of harmonic colouring that may have come from study with Franck, but rarely echoes his extreme chromaticism.

With so much French music of this period there is some comparable feeling of limitation. With the late growth of an instrumental tradition, fine works were being composed, but few of outstanding quality. One composer who might detain us more than she has others is Cécile Chaminade, once described by Martin Cooper as a 'fashionable lady-composer', and less condescendingly by Ambroise Thomas as 'not a woman who composes but a composer who is a woman'.[4] Chaminade is a good illustration of the obstacles that confronted talented female composers throughout the nineteenth century and for most of the twentieth. Her father opposed her entering the Conservatoire, so she studied piano and theory privately, and when she came to compose, the market – for her work as for her playing – seems to have pushed her towards small-scale salon pieces, of which, like Fanny Mendelssohn before her, she wrote a large number. But she could, and occasionally did, do something more. A pair of piano trios (1881 and 1887), though not towering masterpieces, are elegantly written, with brilliant, filigree piano writing and a warm strain of melody, somewhat in the Saint-Saëns manner and losing little in the comparison. A *Concertstück* for piano and orchestra (1888) is weightier, messier, with shades of Wagner and Liszt and a certain intriguing grandeur. The later flute concertino (1902) is still in most flautists' repertoire. But the twentieth century otherwise took Cooper's view and consigned Chaminade to granny's piano stool, from which she was too polite to force her way out.

As for opera, here the French were on home territory, yet scarcely a single piece of lasting value, apart from *Carmen* and two or three operettas by Offenbach, reached the stage between *The Trojans* and 1881, when Offenbach's final, least characteristic, not quite complete but possibly best opera, *Les Contes d'Hoffmann* (*The Tales of Hoffmann*), had its posthumous premiere, four months after its composer's death in October 1880.

Offenbach had tried 'serious' opera before, but never with any success, and *The Tales of Hoffmann* is itself something of a halfway house. On the one hand it harks back to the Romantic fantasy opera of Hoffmann's own day, on the other hand it draws musically on what one might call the Romantic end of its composer's comic style. It would not have taken much to turn the piece into a satire on the Romantic lure of the unattainable: Hoffmann falling in love with a mechanical doll ('Der Sandmann'), with a singer forbidden to sing ('Rat Krespel'), and with a courtesan who steals his reflection (soul) then goes off with her servant ('Die Abenteuer der Silvester-Nacht'). But by linking these tales through the character of Hoffmann himself, Offenbach and his librettist, Jules Barbier, turned it into an allegory of artistic creation, a rather grand concept for an operetta specialist who had spent his career lampooning such things. Nevertheless the work, though too long, and textually corrupt because of changes and additions made after Offenbach's death, has held its place thanks to the quality of its music, its strong, faintly demonic atmosphere, and the opportunities it gives to star singers, especially the soprano who must turn her voice to three different styles and characters (often in practice given to three different singers), and the tenor lead, whose role is to sing passionately for three hours to a succession of doomed ideals.

This gallicisation by a German-born composer of a series of German Romantic tales is oddly symptomatic of French music in its entire development in the century after the 1789 Revolution, but especially after the Prussian defeat in 1870. At this traumatic moment, French music became not less but more Germanised, the main catalyst being, of course, Wagner. After all, opera was the special province of French music, and here was this German composer not merely theorising about it, but writing works on a magisterial scale that transformed the genre into something altogether more powerful and significant than anything previously known.

As we saw, the origins of this trend were initially literary. The sym-bolist poets, starting with Baudelaire, sought to emulate in verse the saturated emotional ambience and supra-rational discourse that they sensed in Wagner's music. The short-lived *Revue wagnérienne*, pub-lished in Paris between 1885 and 1888, had musicians among its founding members, but was pre-eminently literary in its focus, with contributions from the symbolist poets Stéphane Mallarmé and Paul Verlaine, from the novelist Joris-Karl Huysmans, and from the former Parnassian poet, now Wagner biographer, Catulle Mendès. These non-musicians were inspired partly by the Wagnerian atmosphere, partly by its subject matter, partly by its theories. Mendès urged French com-posers to cultivate their own myths and legends, as Wagner had done his, to integrate words and music as Wagner had advocated in *Opera and Drama*, and to 'reject recitatives, airs, strettos, even ensembles, unless these are demanded by the dramatic action, to which everything must be sacrificed'.[5] The fact that all this theory was thirty-five years old and had been to some extent overridden in practice by its author may or may not have escaped Mendès's notice. The ostensible point was that French opera needed to be shaken out of its routines; but Mendès, and the *Revue* in general, were really just as interested in the possibilities Wagner suggested for a new kind of literature and a new kind of theatre, a theatre of the mind and the senses, uncluttered by the day-to-day practicalities of logical storytelling and the theatre of four walls. What composers actually did was of secondary importance.

What they did was attend Bayreuth in considerable numbers, soak up the febrile, quasi-devotional atmosphere, and return home with somewhat vague ideas of its relevance to their own work. Saint-Saëns travelled to the first festival in 1876 with a young pupil of Franck called Vincent d'Indy. In 1879 (not a festival year), Duparc went with Emmanuel Chabrier and met Wagner himself, then the following year Chabrier heard *Tristan und Isolde* in Munich and sobbed his way through the prelude. Ten years later, a nineteen-year-old Belgian composition student, Guillaume Lekeu, heard *Tristan* in Bayreuth, fainted during the prelude and had to be carried out. In between, most of the leading French composers heard Wagner, either at Bayreuth or Munich or Cologne. It was a kind of *Hajj*, a career requirement, like the pilgrimage to Mecca. Only Franck seems never to have made it, but he too was deeply affected by the *Tristan* prelude when he heard it in Paris in 1874, and it could even be argued that the 'wearying and persistent *grisaille*' of his late works is the most strictly Wagnerian element, at least in harmony and texture, in any French music of the seventies and eighties.

For most the problem was to find a way of absorbing this overpowering influence without landing themselves with technical and aesthetic difficulties they were not equipped to solve. A few managed to avoid the problem altogether. Saint-Saëns admired Wagner but was not much affected by him in his own music, while his pupil Gabriel Fauré went on a fact-finding Wagner pilgrimage of his own without apparently feeling any need to tread musically in the Master's footsteps. With other composers, Wagnerism leaks into the music in various partial, sometimes interesting, sometimes uncomfortable ways. Édouard Lalo, a late-developing contemporary of Franck, had composed a series of lucid, melodious concertante works, including the *Symphonie espagnole* for violin and orchestra by which he is still chiefly known, before letting Wagner into his musical thinking in the shape of an opera based on the Breton legend of the sunken city of Ys (*Le Roi d'Ys*, 1875). Even here, though the texture and orchestration are sometimes heavy in the Wagnerian sense and there is some general flavour of the Germanic approach to myth, the music never really sounds anything but French, and becomes entirely so in the brilliantly catchy wedding music that opens the final act, a style Lalo exploited further in his ballet *Namouna* (1882), much admired by Debussy. A similar but even more interesting example is Chabrier, a younger composer whose musical instincts included hardly anything of the grandeur or self-importance of the worst kind of Wagnerian, but who could not resist introducing stray harmonic Wagnerisms into the wonderfully abstruse pages of his opera *Le Roi malgré lui*, a tangled comedy about the reluctance of Henri III of France to accept the Polish crown, and rather more than stray ones into *Gwendoline*, a tragedy about Saxons and Danes at the end of which the hero and heroine rise to Valhalla in a glow of redemptive light. But Chabrier, though he composed several other stage works, was at his most individual writing for the piano, an instrument he played with idiosyncratic virtuosity. His *Dix pièces pittoresques* (1881) are a curious mixture of pianistic inventiveness and style parody, influenced if anything by Schumann rather than Wagner, but with a kind of throwaway wit that looks forward to such quintessentially Gallic eccentrics as Erik Satie and Francis Poulenc. Chabrier is an intriguing case of Wagner's influence being more productive in its rejection than in its acceptance.

But there were counter-cases as well. The most extreme was Vincent d'Indy, another Franck pupil who, as we saw, attended the very first Bayreuth Festival and was overwhelmed by the experience of the *Ring*.

Of all the French Wagnerians, d'Indy is the one whose music reveals the influence most candidly. His cantata *Le Chant de la cloche* (1879–83, later turned into a stage work) is a fairly flagrant love child of *Meistersinger*, complete with guilds, leitmotifs and an artist hero, and the first and best known of his three large-scale music dramas, *Fervaal* (1889–93), is unashamedly Wagnerian in general style and subject matter, a mystical, mythological tale transferred from Montsalvat to the Ardèche, dense in texture, earnestly symbolic in tone. But d'Indy had lighter moods as well. His second opera, *L'Étranger* (1898–1901), is less heavy going musically, though still somewhat Wagnerian in its processes, and his best concert works, the *Symphony on a French mountain air* (1886) and *Istar* (1896) have a fresher, more open flavour. D'Indy shared with Wagner his right-wing politics and his anti-Semitism, which with d'Indy included support for the anti-Dreyfusards in the Dreyfus affair that erupted in 1894.

A more interesting counter-case is Massenet, who in his long career as a theatre composer (he wrote more than thirty operas, several ballets and a great deal of incidental music) managed to absorb what he needed from Wagner without ever making d'Indy's mistake of imitating his procedures. Massenet's work is the ultimate development of French grand and Romantic nineteenth-century opera. His subject matter is typically historical or literary, treated either on a broad canvas (*Hérodiade*, *Esclarmonde*) or as domestic or social tragedy (*Werther*, *Manon*), 'sensible' drama that has no truck with mythology or symbolism. His musical idiom is a kind of extended lyricism, drawing towards Wagner's *unendliche Melodie*, but never actually *unendliche* because Massenet generally sticks to the French preference for separate 'scenes', often ending them, rather arbitrarily, with loud chords that inform any inattentive audience member that something momentous has just taken place. This 'soliciting of the audience', as Martin Cooper memorably called it,[6] is something particularly French, a sort of emotional showmanship, a conscious theatricality that relates even lyric tragedy to the ethos of operetta and pantomime.

At his best Massenet composed some of the most beautiful stretches of lyrical music in any late Romantic opera. His melodic lines flow, expressively or sensuously, against rich harmonies that never venture too far from their tonal centres. His orchestration, usually for a large, expanded orchestra, is expert but discreet, the kind of scoring – the best kind, as Stravinsky remarked[7] – that one doesn't notice. His word-setting and vocal writing are immaculate, singable, fitting the lightly accented French language to perfection, and the portrayal of his characters is precise, especially those who are in love, like Werther, or Salome in *Hérodiade* (1881), who is a very different creature (based on Flaubert) from Strauss's Salome (based on Wilde). Massenet can sometimes note-spin when he feels, or at least appears, less involved with character or situation. One of his strengths was supposed to be the combining of sexual passion and religion, which d'Indy called his 'discreet, quasi-religious eroticism',[8] but at times he may seem to confuse the two. In the final act of *Hérodiade*, which consists largely of a love duet for Salome and a tenor John the Baptist, it is hard to remember that the original of this relationship is in the Gospels according to St Matthew and St Mark. The plot of *Thaïs* (1894) hinges on the same confusion, in which the monk Athanaël sets out to reform the courtesan Thaïs but, having succeeded, then lusts after her as she dies a saintly death. The famous Meditation describes Thaïs's change of heart by subtly hinting at both the before and the after, like an advertisement for anti-wrinkle cream.

The overwhelming impression of this quarter-century or so of French music is of a great deal of steady professional endeavour and a heap of worthwhile, likeable music, but hardly anything of world-shaking importance. With Italian music the situation could hardly be more different. Verdi's last two operas, *Otello* (1887, based on Shakespeare's play) and *Falstaff* (1893, based mainly on *The Merry Wives of Windsor*),

written in his seventies, are not only among his best works, they represent a new direction in Italian opera that affected a number of young
composers whose own work, though more variable in quality, achieved
a popularity that has mostly eluded French opera (and that incidentally
at first eluded these two Verdi masterpieces). Why this should be is not
easy to say. Opera was for long a traditionally Italian affair. Italy produced the best singers, Italian was and is the most singable language,
whereas French is a test that most foreign singers still fail. But there is
another, perhaps more important factor, which boils down to a certain
blatancy in the way Italians approach the stage. Even Verdi uses exag-
gerated gesture, a kind of emotional posturing, as a perfectly normal
and legitimate style device, a direct challenge to the audience's willingness to suspend disbelief in anything so improbable as, say, Azucena's
having thrown the wrong baby into the fire or Rigoletto's stupidity in
accepting a blindfold as a necessary part of the abduction of another
man's wife. Of course, in a sense all opera is absurd; but Italian opera
has always fed on this somewhat crude idea of dramaturgy, thrusting
everything in the audience's face then doing the same to their ears, and
overcoming their resistance by superb, unforgettable music, masterly
control of theatrical pacing, and, naturally, great singing.

All this is less absolutely true of *Otello* and *Falstaff*, but it is still
partly true. There is no equivalent in Shakespeare's *Othello* to Iago's
Credo ('I believe in a cruel God who created me in his image') in Act 2
of the opera, though in the play Iago soliloquises about his hatred of
Othello and on one occasion invokes Hell and all its devils. The actual
motive for his hatred, anger at having been passed over in promotion,
is thrown away in the opera in a brief recitative, as being unworthy of
a true operatic villain. On the other hand, the plying of Cassio with
drink naturally becomes the occasion for a grand *brindisi* (drinking
song) for the whole company led by Iago, one of Verdi's most thrilling
ensemble numbers. At the same time, the characters of both Otello
and Desdemona are appreciably simplified, Otello's disintegration is
swifter, more precipitate, her purity more one-dimensional, and even

their somewhat unorthodox relationship is never properly explained, as it is in Act 1 of the play, which Boito and Verdi left out.

Notwithstanding these purely 'operatic' features, *Otello* is in general a tighter, more dramatically concentrated score than its predecessors, a fact that was partly due to Boito's insistence, against Verdi's desire for a more spectacular, spacious treatment. Each of the four acts is made out of whole cloth, and the set pieces, such as they are, are set into an ongoing, often fast-moving music drama, not particularly of the Wagnerian type, rather a compression, or distillation, of Italian convention, with audience participation definitely excluded. Apart from Iago's 'Brindisi' and his somewhat overstated 'Credo', and Desdemona's exquisite 'Willow Song', the arias hardly stand out from the general discourse, but crystallise from it then blend back into it, often with conversational elements thrown in. In fact, conversation, over a fully developed orchestral accompaniment, is almost the default mode of the whole opera, and this was a technique that Verdi was then able to deploy, even more comprehensively, in *Falstaff*.

When it was premiered at La Scala in February 1893, *Falstaff* is said to have puzzled Verdi's Italian admirers with its mercurial pace and elliptical turn of phrase. Audiences were still inured to the idea of the set piece as a frozen moment, a point of reflection on the thoughts and feelings of the various characters. In *Falstaff* numbers of this kind hardly exist at all, at least until the final act in Windsor Forest, when Falstaff is tormented by a series of manifestations, preceded by Fenton's love-song to Nannetta and culminating in the great fugue, 'Tutto nel mondo è burla' ('All the world's a joke, and man is born joking'). Such arias as there are before this are themselves often like jests at the expense of the set piece. 'In the evening, when we go from pub to pub,' Falstaff sings to Bardolph in Act 1; 'that flaming nose of yours serves me as a lantern. But what I save on oil, you drink in wine.' The little song is gone in a flash. Later, when Falstaff delivers his cynical homily on the subject of honour, the middle section feels like the start of a lovely song in Verdi's best middle-period vein, but the words – 'even I must sometimes set aside the fear of God and, by necessity, deflect honour with stratagems and evasions' – soon puncture the lyricism and the tune vanishes. On the other hand melodic forms often sneak into the musical conversation, with a prodigality that even Shakespeare might well have appreciated. If music were as susceptible as words to quotation in ordinary social intercourse, *Falstaff* would be like *Hamlet* and *Macbeth*, nothing but quotes.

This is in effect a new form; or perhaps one should call it the ultimate state of a process that has gone on throughout the nineteenth century, a move towards natural, narrative or conversational forms that imagine a situation where singing, rather than speaking, is the normal mode of communication. The Wagnerian music drama was one route, towards a symphonic language dominated by the orchestra. Late Verdi, often thought of as influenced by Wagner, is strictly something different. Behind it still lies the kind of aria thinking that ruled Italian opera in the time of Rossini and Donizetti, and also the *scena* form of French and German Romantic opera. But *Falstaff* is neither arias nor scenas, but a kind of chain form whose links are fixed, in principle, by key moments or even key words, what Verdi called *parole sceniche*, in the swift passage of the drama. These are not scenes in the Shakespearean sense of new characters on the stage, nor in the sense of self-contained units of action, for which they are too short. They reflect changes in the balance of the dialogue, changes of tone and focus. Sometimes they are clear-cut musical units, sometimes not. The second scene of Act I is a good example of these changes, in the four ladies' discussion of the identical love letters Falstaff has sent to Alice Ford and Meg Page. In its first four or five minutes, the musical action passes through six or seven phases (links), each one musically distinct but individually too short to comprise a 'unit'. The opening scherzo, as the ladies greet each other and swap letters, quickly subsides into the reading of the letters, which has four phases matching their growing astonishment at the letters' identical content and culminating in Alice's aria-like 'Facciamo il paio' ('Let's make a pair'), which lasts all of forty seconds, then leads into the quartet that provides a link to the entry of the male characters and their quintet. Throughout this scene, melodies and fragments of melodies appear and disappear like subatomic particles, and as if to emphasise the evanescent character of the writing, Verdi has his four ladies all singing different texts simultaneously in their quartet, has his five men doing the same in their quintet, and finally combines the whole shebang into a nonet with nine different simultaneous texts.

At the age of seventy-nine, Verdi was working in an operatic environment peopled by much younger composers. The Scapigliatura had come and gone; a younger associate of theirs, Alfredo Catalani, had had success with two operas in particular, *Loreley* (Turin, 1890), and *La Wally* (Milan, 1892), but was dying of haemoptysis, brought on by tuberculosis; and a fellow Lucchese of Catalani's, Giacomo Puccini, had had an even greater success with his first opera, *Le villi* (Milan, 1884), and a painful failure with his second, *Edgar* (Milan, 1889). The year after *Edgar*, a competition for one-act operas run by the newspaper tycoon Edoardo Sonzogno was won by a young double bass player called Pietro Mascagni with his very first opera, *Cavalleria rusticana*, and almost exactly two years later Ruggero Leoncavallo's *Pagliacci* had its first performance in Milan. A third opera by Puccini, *Manon Lescaut*, was produced in Turin in February 1893, eight days before the Milan premiere of *Falstaff*.

These bald facts conceal some intriguing developments in Italian music in the eighties and early nineties. Both *Loreley* and *Le villi* were based on Germanic legends about unfortunate love affairs between mortals and denizens of the spirit world, and *La Wally* was also based on a German novel, by Wilhelmine von Hillern, about love in the Austrian Tyrol which ends in an avalanche that kills both lovers. This sudden interest in German Romantic tragedy goes back to the original Scapigliatura composers, who wanted to create a new kind of Italian opera, fed partly from foreign – especially German and French – sources. In the same way, both *Edgar* and *Manon Lescaut* were based on French originals, by Alfred de Musset and the Abbé

Prévost, respectively. Musically, as usual, the main issue here was the influence of Wagner, whose works were beginning to make belated headway in Italy. In Catalani, this comes out particularly in the orchestral writing, which is richer and above all more controlling than had normally been the case in Italian opera. To a lesser extent it also affects the continuities, though the number structure is still clear in an essentially un-Wagnerian way; and it also affects aspects of the harmony. Yet this remains Italian opera, with Italian voices and Italian melody, even when, with the horn solo that brings up the curtain in *Loreley*, one might half expect Siegfried to come sailing down the Rhine.

The Scapigliatura ideal of Italian opera enriched by foreign, and especially Wagnerian, influence reaches its true fulfilment in the work of the so-called *verismo* composers, and above all in the operas of Puccini. Nobody quite knows why, after *Pagliacci* and *Cavalleria rusticana* were first put together (that way round) as a double bill at the Metropolitan Opera in New York in December 1893, the pairing stuck, to the point where they are now treated as a kind of love duo under the affectionate title *Cav and Pag*, and rarely figure in other, adulterous partnerships. This is ironic, since both are about infidelity, which admittedly comes to a sticky end in both cases. Together, however, they make up a textbook example of *verismo*, that specifically Italian branch of realism that deals, not with your or my daily life, not with life in the village school or the suburban shopping centre, but with murder among the rural poor, in Sicily and Calabria, where, as recently as the composers' own time, and perhaps still to this day, such activities were governed by codes of honour that rendered them as necessary as they were unquestionably real. The idea that realism meant art about the poor had originated in Russia in the 1860s, where it arose as a reaction against the courtly academicism of contemporary portraiture and, in music, against Germanic formalism. Still in 1890 it seems that the well-to-do in Italy who bought theatre tickets or wrote about opera thought that squalor and violence were somehow more real than – well, buying theatre tickets or writing about opera. In the remote countryside they knew how to live, and how to die.

The musical idiom of, especially, *Cavalleria rusticana*, emphasises the coarseness of the emotional lives of these uneducated people. It draws on the crudity that had always existed as one ingredient in Italian opera, the often drastic contrast between ordinary life and the life of the passions, exemplified by Ponchielli's *La Gioconda*, but found here and there even in Verdi. The emotional gradients in *Cav* are steep, the orchestra often noisy. These Sicilians, evidently, are not nice people; their love is something desperate, not a normal affection, and it breeds hatred, betrayal and death. The title, in other words, is sarcastic; rustic chivalry means, treat each other as brutally as you like, but don't break the code. And meanwhile the church is there, physically and in the form of the brilliant Easter hymn, to reassure us that, if we repent in time, all will be well.

Mascagni found genuine inspiration in this depressing tale, and the one sad thing about his success is that he was never able to repeat it in more than a dozen attempts between then and his death in 1945. Curiously, much the same was true of Leoncavallo. He had composed a couple of operas but had had no performances and nothing published before writing *Pagliacci* (*The Players*) in 1892, in conscious imitation of *Cavalleria rusticana*. Its success and subsequent pairing with its model made its composer's name, but nothing he wrote thereafter, including a *La bohème* based, like Puccini's, on Murger's *Scènes de la vie de bohème*, made even modest headway. This may seem surprising, since *Pagliacci* is a well-made and effective piece with three or four strong individual numbers and a powerful and moving dramatic climax, in which Canio, the manager of the travelling theatre, turns the little *commedia* play into a real-life assault on his unfaithful wife, Nedda, and stabs her and her lover in full view of the stage audience. Musically, though, it is perhaps the less original of the two works. The influence of Wagner is audible, both in the general texture and the discreet use of motifs, and in one or two near quotations. Mascagni's score is less refined but bolder and more its own self, for better or worse, more *verismo*.

Like most such terms, this peculiarly Mediterranean form of realism quickly lost its original connotation and took on a quite different set of meanings. Of these, the most obvious was 'shocking'. Turiddu in *Cavalleria rusticana* is killed in a fight offstage, but Canio stabs Nedda on the open stage, something not new in itself (*Carmen* was the obvious precedent), but somehow more particularly horrible in *Pagliacci* because of the public setting of the act. What *verismo* rapidly ceased to mean was 'the depiction of the rural poor in our own time'. Umberto Giordano's *Andrea Chénier* (Milan, 1896) is about the revolutionary poet of the title and his aristocratic lover, both of whom end up on the guillotine. There are 'realistic', contemporary elements, revolutionary songs and eighteenth-century dances, but nothing of outstanding novelty in these respects. Giordano's next opera, *Fedora* (Milan, 1898), has a contemporary Russian setting and Russianisms in the music, but the main characters are again aristocrats. Francesco Cilea's *Adriana Lecouvreur* (Milan, 1902) is about an early-eighteenth-century French actress and her murder by a rival in love, the Princesse de Bouillon. Puccini's operas, too, are mostly set in exotic or remote places – Japan, gold-rush California, China – or remote times: eighteenth-century and revolutionary France. Even *La bohème*, the nearest to real life, is about starving artists, hardly the model of 'contemporary man and his problems', to quote one peculiarly obtuse definition of a *verismo* topic.

What most people think of when they hear or read the word *verismo* is music of a particular character, for which an equivalent English word might be 'excess'. Even in a relatively sedate example of the genre such as Puccini's *Manon Lescaut*, a work in which nobody is knifed, shot or poisoned and the only death is that of the heroine herself, exhausted and alone with her lover in the imaginary Louisiana desert, the slightest hint of passion is expressed through vocal and orchestral climaxes that would surely cause trouble with the neighbours. There is a parallel here with another phenomenon of late romanticism, expressionism, which similarly inflates the smallest tremor of mental distress into a violent trauma from which recovery seems doubtful. The important difference between these two versions of Romantic extremity is that, while expressionism brings a drastic extension of the musical language, *verismo* says much the same as before, only louder and amid cries of anguish.

Puccini is the test case for all this, because his works have nearly all survived in the repertory and in fact include three or four of the most popular operas ever written. He descended from a long line of professional musicians in the small Tuscan city of Lucca, pre-eminently church organists and composers, though his father composed two operas that seem to have been locally successful. At first young Giacomo followed this pattern. His earliest works are church music. But when he entered the Milan Conservatory in 1880 and began study with Ponchielli, his horizons broadened, he composed some orchestral music (including a *Capriccio sinfonico* that he later raided for *Edgar* and the opening of *La bohème*), and eventually his first opera, *Le villi*, which he entered unsuccessfully for the first Sonzogno competition in 1883.

Manon Lescaut is Puccini's first completely achieved, personal work. *Le villi*, on the same subject as Adam's *Giselle*, has two or three strong solo arias as well as, for the first and last time in Puccini, ballet music without voices. *Edgar* suffers from a libretto that is ludicrous even by the high standards of Italian opera, but still has many pages of unmistakable authorship and some music, in a subsequently discarded final act, that Puccini was able to transfer more or less intact to *Tosca*. In any case, he was a quick learner, and *Manon Lescaut*, though not without miscalculations, is an accomplished score and effective, if eventually somewhat morose theatre. The libretto, by a number of hands including Leoncavallo and Puccini himself, suffers from the steep contrast between the lively first two acts in Amiens and Paris and the almost unrelieved gloom of Manon's deportation and death in the last two; and Puccini only half solves this by thematic reminiscences that carry a heavy load of pathos along with their memories of times past.

But his idiom is now in place, with all its strengths and limitations:

that unique flair for melody that seems to grow out of the natural music of the Italian language and is able to turn even routine conversational exchanges into expressive phrases that linger in the mind; the acute sense of the voice; the usually dependable ear for orchestral colour and balance. The harmony, though in a sense adequate to Puccini's needs and always handled with skill, is somewhat over-dependent on a handful of devices, particular progressions and cadences, modalisms of one kind and another, and sequence – the repeating of a melody and its harmony in rising or falling series. On the other hand, his feeling for dramatic pace, still variable in *Manon Lescaut*, becomes totally assured in *La bohème* (1896), a work of utter mastery that never fails in performance, despite the mutterings of Californian professors about 'its somewhat chlorotic charm'.[9]

Like *Carmen*, *La bohème* is that precious creature, a supremely popular work admired also by professional musicians. No doubt its tale of a doomed love affair between an impecunious poet and a consumptive seamstress in a Parisian winter is marginally less seismic than the music's emotional contours might have us suppose. But after all its central characters are young men and their girlfriends, who inevitably believe themselves to be on the edge of life's precipice, and Puccini's music simply takes them at their word. In any case the narrative is not the main point of *La bohème*. Its four short acts are slices of life, in the spirit of Murger's own scenes of bohemian life. The story is featherlight, but the scenes are vivid, and as in *Falstaff* (surely an influence) they go past in a flash, with a quality of invention so dazzling that it has no need to protest. The psychology is fragile. The characters are defined behaviourally, hardly at all mentally.

None of this matters compared with the life they represent and that frames them. From the start Puccini paints a day in the life of four cold, hungry but happy young men, three artists and a philosopher, in a Paris garret of the 1830s. As in *Falstaff* the action is trivial but detailed. There is ragging and badinage, Rodolfo's play gets burnt for warmth, and as in *Falstaff* there is a landlord to pay and nothing to pay him with. All this speeds by, breathlessly, mainly in fast dance rhythms but with a lyrical undercurrent in the orchestra and here and there in the dialogue. The musician, Schaunard, appears with food and drink, having been paid by a rich Englishman to murder a neighbour's parrot with his violin-playing. Benoît comes for the rent and is shown the door. But strictly speaking nothing happens until three of the four go off to the Café Momus, Rodolfo stays behind to finish his article, and Mimì knocks on the door: her candle has gone out, and then she can't find her key. Their famous love scene ('Che gelida manina', and 'Mi chiamano Mimì') brings the drama into focus, but not for long. At Momus, in Act 2, even less happens in terms of the plot: the painter Marcello's ex-mistress, Musetta, appears with a sugar daddy, sings a seductive waltz, wins Marcello back, and the sugar daddy is left with the bill. But in musical incident, the twenty-minute act would be hard to beat. Puccini catches the atmosphere of nocturnal Paris *en fête*, the crowds, the colour, the excited children, the hawkers, pacing everything with diabolical precision, and again bringing the kaleidoscopic fragments into focus at just the exact moment in the shape of Musetta's waltz song, one of the great show-stopping numbers in late Romantic opera.

As in *Manon Lescaut*, gloom descends with the snow in the third act. But this time Puccini avoids wallowing in *morbidezza*. The colour is dark, certainly, but there is variety of tone and movement, helped by the vignettes of passers-by at the Barrière d'Enfer, the Orléans gate into Paris, and by a contrast in moods: Mimì ill and miserable, Rodolfo anxious and querulous, Marcello and Musetta quarrelling over her flirtatious behaviour with customers in the tavern where she is theoretically giving singing lessons. The music also has a delicacy of colour and texture that was lacking at the same point in *Manon Lescaut*, and it retains a discreet element of dance from the previous act, both in the reminiscences of Musetta's waltz, and, with surprisingly powerful effect, in Rodolfo's account of the terrible cough 'that shakes Mimì's frail chest', set by Puccini as a slow *valse triste*. Then finally Act 4, back in the garret, echoes the first act with some rather forced play acting, interrupted by an abrupt *coup de théâtre* as Musetta comes in with the dying Mimì, and the work ends in a mood of high tragedy with her death and Rodolfo's anguish.

It's hard to deny that this ending is laid on rather thick, in view of Mimì's sketchy characterisation, and the casual nature of her affair with Rodolfo. Here and elsewhere, Puccini expects us to weep on cue, as one might mourn a distant cousin. With him, pathos is never far away. In *Tosca*, his next opera (1900), *verismo* approaches Grand Guignol, with the scene of the (offstage but audible) torture of the painter Mario Cavaradossi, the onstage murder of the sinister police chief, Baron Scarpia, and the final suicide of Tosca herself, to music that again instructs us to weep. Cio-Cio-San's vigil waiting for the return of her faithless Yankee lover, Pinkerton, in *Madam Butterfly* (1904), is milked for all it's worth before her eventual suicide by *hara-kiri*, onstage but behind a screen. Even Puccini found it hard to complete his final opera, *Turandot* (1926, two years after his death), because the libretto expected it to end happily despite the messy onstage suicide of the work's most sympathetic character, the slave-girl Liù, in the last act.

By 1926 in any case pathos of this kind, and the music that went with it, were like voices from the past. Puccini was by no means ignorant of new trends in music before and after the First World War, and he often reflected them, in moderation, in his own work. *La bohème* certainly shows an awareness of recent French music, including Debussy, there are echoes of Debussy also in *Il tabarro* (*The Cloak*), the first of the three one-acters in *Il trittico* (New York, 1918), and *Turandot* is rich in discreet modernisms, including 'barbaric' rhythms in the manner of Stravinsky's *Rite of Spring*, a work he called 'sheer cacophony but strange and not without a certain talent'.[10] He heard Schoenberg's *Pierrot Lunaire* in Florence in 1923 and at least did not dismiss it out of hand, though it would perhaps be hard to find any specific echo of it in *Turandot*. Yet this opera, based on a *commedia dell'arte* play by

Carlo Gozzi, and set in remote, mythical China, has harmonic episodes that one feels could only be the result of an intensely musical ear confronted by alien sonorities that it could neither explain nor reject, so processed in its own way.

15

Clouds, Forests and More Clouds

Franz Liszt had always been an explorer and an innovator; it was the main thing that had set him apart from the run-of-the-mill virtuosos of the 1820s and 1830s. As the piano itself evolved, he had found ever newer ways of writing for it. Later, in Weimar, he had invented a new symphonic form, and finally, in Rome, he had taken holy orders and composed religious music on a grand scale. In his late fifties he might have been forgiven for vanishing into the monastery of Santa Francesca Romana, where he had had a first-floor apartment since 1866. But in 1869 he returned to Weimar at the invitation of Grand Duke Karl Alexander. Then the following year, distraught at the outbreak of war between France and Prussia, while Rome and the Papal States fell to the army of the unified Italian government, he fled to Hungary and remained there until the spring of 1871.

Thus began the so-called 'Vie trifurquée' – the three-way life – of his last fifteen years, much of which he would spend in railway trains or, less comfortably, in horse-drawn conveyances on the open road. He kept apartments in Weimar, Rome and Budapest, but also spent time in Vienna, Paris, and, near the end of his life, London. He was in Venice with Wagner, his son-in-law, at the end of 1882, but left a matter of weeks before Wagner died there in February 1883. He was in Bayreuth for the first festival in 1876, there again in 1884 for the first festival after the Master's death, a somewhat neglected guest of his daughter Cosima, and there he died at the end of July 1886, having returned at her request to provide moral support for the first Bayreuth performances of *Tristan und Isolde*, at a time when the future of the festival was shrouded in uncertainty. On these final visits he was not invited to stay at the Villa Wahnfried, nor is he buried there. His grave is nearby, in a small, specially built chapel, in the Bayreuth town cemetery.

Liszt was not one of the very greatest composers of the nineteenth century, but he was beyond question one of its greatest souls. While his sexual *mores* were perhaps not always what one might expect of the once and future Abbé, his generosity to other musicians was princely. He seems to have been immune to professional envy or any kind of artistic meanness. He may or may not have sired as many children as was claimed, but he certainly helped countless young musicians, both financially and in other ways, with advice and friendly support and mostly without partisanship. In Weimar in his final years he held regular masterclasses (a form of teaching he invented), had many individual pupils, though probably nothing like the number who called themselves his pupils, and seems never to have taken a penny in payment, though by this time far from wealthy, having given most of his money away.

Above all he continued to compose: a single symphonic poem, *Von der Wiege bis zum Grabe* (*From the Cradle to the Grave*), some short choral pieces, and a great deal of piano music. Some of these compositions are collected in what look like continuations of his earlier work. There is a third *Années de pèlerinage*, and a second, third and fourth *Mephisto Waltz*, though on closer inspection they turn out to be very different in character from their predecessors. The third *année*, for instance, is dominated by slow, elegiac and quasi-sacred pieces of one kind and another, and contains only a single virtuoso piece, *Les Jeux d'eaux à la Villa d'Este* (*The Fountains at the Villa d'Este*), that might conceivably have figured in one of the earlier books. Then there are the separate pieces, with morose titles and equally morose music: *Am Grabe Richard Wagners*, *La lugubre gondola*, *Nuages gris*, and perhaps darkest of all, *Unstern! Sinistre, disastro*. These pieces are remarkable for their experimental approach to harmony and texture. Sometimes the harmony verges on the atonal; in fact the very last piece is called *Bagatelle sans tonalité*. While the fountains of the Villa d'Este flash and glitter in the Tivoli sunshine, the next piece in the third *année*, *Sunt lacrymae rerum*, tunnels into the lower regions of the piano, to the point where, at one point, the harmony is completely lost in the darkness of the sound. In *Nuages gris* the material is reduced to a single two-bar melody, mysterious in tone, alternating with sequences of dissonant chords accompanied at first by dark left-hand tremolandi, then by a slow, rising chromatic scale in the right hand. The ingredients of *Unstern! Sinistre, disastro* are similar but fuller in texture, more dissonant, and more extended. *Nuages gris* ends in mid-air with two unresolved dissonant chords, *Unstern!* with an indecisive whole-tone melody deep in the bass: a strange, muted disaster.

The music may have been prophetic, but it had little influence on the developments it predicted. Several pieces were not published until years later, the *Bagatelle sans tonalité* not till 1956. Liszt's real influence continued to lie elsewhere. The symphonic poem had been to some extent a renaming of a genre that already existed in the concert overture, but it also embodied a whole set of new ideas that for a while provided a blueprint for much of the most brilliant orchestral music in the latter part of the century. Not surprisingly, the idea was seized on by nationalists as a way of distancing themselves from the Germanic mainstream, an ironic state of affairs since they were sailing in a vessel provided by the New German School. The Russian *Kuchka* had dabbled, if without complete conviction. Smetana had begun by basing symphonic poems, Liszt-fashion, on foreign literature, but later turned to his own country's landscape and history. Even Dvořák, after composing eight symphonies, rattled off a series of three 'concert overtures' in 1891 under the collective title *Nature, Life and Love*, with some shared material, then took the plunge and in the one year, 1896, composed four symphonic poems on the folk ballads of the Czech poet Karol Jaromír Erben: *The Water Goblin, The Noon Witch, The Golden Spinning Wheel* and *The Wild Dove*, charming, exquisitely orchestrated, if somewhat literal-minded pieces that broadly map their music on to the stories, while profiting formally from the repetitive nature of fairy tales.

This unexpected enthusiasm for subjects that might seem to belong to a time sixty or seventy years before, when fairies and witches were an antidote to the intellectual demons of the Enlightenment, in fact reflected a not dissimilar reaction to modern life in the 1890s. Dvořák had recently returned from New York, and this sudden embracing of Czech folklore was surely a sigh of relief at being home again. Nor did these four works completely satisfy the need. Four years later he composed his opera *Rusalka*, based on a Czech version of the *Undine* story, a subject much cultivated, as we saw, in the pre-1848 period but seemingly remote from the psychological concerns of the *fin de siècle*. In fact stage productions have shown that Dvořák's intensely beautiful music can accommodate all kinds of interpretation, from the socio-political – Rusalka as displaced migrant – to the psycho-sexual – Rusalka on the brink of sexual awakening. No fairies are required in either case.

For both Russians and Czechs the impulse behind these works may have been musically, if not politically, anti-German, but in Scandinavia purely local, in part linguistic, issues were involved. Edvard Grieg, though born and brought up in the Norwegian city of Bergen, like most middle-class Norwegians probably spoke what was essentially Danish with some Norwegian elements, the two languages being closely cognate. His first important musical contact was with the Norwegian violin virtuoso Ole Bull, and on Bull's advice he went to Leipzig, studied, without much enthusiasm, the usual Germanic things, then proceeded via Bergen to Copenhagen, the centre of Dano-Norwegian musical life, where he met Niels Gade, who sent him off to compose a symphony. Later, however, he made contact with a group of young musicians who were intent on creating a specifically Norwegian school, based on the peasant music of rural Norway. There was something dilettante about these would-be nationalists. They enthused about anything identifiably Norwegian, but appear not to have ventured far from Copenhagen in its pursuit. Grieg's closest friend in the group, a Dano-Norwegian composer by the name of Rikard Nordraak, was a big personality with a huge ego, but he died aged twenty-three in 1866 and left only a handful of songs and piano pieces, few of which show much trace of anything beyond the standard salon idiom of the period, with an occasional hint of folk modes and some rhythmic oddities.

Grieg said that Nordraak's influence on him was largely through his personality, and Grieg's music of these early years also consists mainly of miniatures with a handful of larger-scale instrumental sonatas (a couple for violin, one for piano) essentially in the Beethoven–Schumann tradition. In his whole life he composed few substantial concert works. The well-known Piano Concerto (1868), modelled on Schumann, is the obvious exception, along with the suites he drew from his incidental music to Ibsen's *Peer Gynt* (1874–5), and an ambitious but only partly successful string quartet (1877–8). These works often sound Nordic in some indefinable way, but as with Smetana it's hard to say how much of this is authentic folk style, how much simply Grieg's own individual voice. The voice is very clear in his various sets of lyric pieces and dances for piano, and in his songs. These are mostly salon miniatures with folkish titles and some off-the-peg ethnic touches: drone basses, dance rhythms, a modal flavour to the harmony, a few melodic embellishments. They rarely stray from a conventional kind of discourse, rarely suggest any new way of thinking musically. None of this is to belittle the composer's gifts in this field, or the wonderful service he performed for growing pianists of a later time in providing them with musical enchantment that they could get their fingers round. But Grieg was no Bartók, recasting the language by way of ethnic musics.

Though an admirer of Liszt, Grieg never composed any virtuoso solo piano music or anything approaching a symphonic poem, unless one includes the early concert overture, *I höst* (*In Autumn*), whose original orchestral version Grieg arranged for piano duet, destroyed, then redid in 1887. The case with two younger composers from the Baltic region, the Finn Jean Sibelius, and the Dane Carl Nielsen, was quite different. Sibelius composed upwards of a dozen symphonic poems, depending on how one defines the genre, since he used various names for it, most often tone poem, Hoffmann's term. Since he also composed seven symphonies, some of them in unorthodox forms, one can examine the difference between the two types of work, at least as he understood it. Nielsen wrote six symphonies, several solo concertos, and two or three short tone poems, initially in an individualised post-Brahmsian idiom, later in a powerful but idiosyncratic form of that same style, tonal but with harmonic twists that seem to express the bloody-minded northerner, unwilling to acquiesce in a received manner or anything approaching Romantic neurosis. The two finest symphonies, Nos. 4 and 5, composed respectively during and just after the First World War, express a kind of defiance, a blunt refusal to whimper about the state of the world or react against the past in any self-advertising way. The subtitle of the Fourth Symphony, 'The Inextinguishable', expresses very well the drift of Nielsen's music in general. Perhaps one or two of his late works, especially the Sixth Symphony ('Semplice') and the Clarinet Concerto, suggest some mild bewilderment about the direction modern music was taking in the late twenties. But of self-absorption there is no trace.

Sibelius, like the Slav composers by whom he was partly influenced, used the tone poem to tell musical stories about his homeland. But his relation to that homeland was, like Grieg's, ambiguous. Though Finnish-born, he came from a Swedish-speaking family and only began to learn Finnish at the age of ten. Finland had never had any existence as a nation state. Until 1809 it had been part of Sweden, but was then annexed by Tsarist Russia. The Finns, late converts to Christianity, had long remained unurbanised, a peasant culture ruled by a minority Swedish-speaking elite, with, latterly, a Russian governor and garrison in Helsinki. Their Uralic language was, and remains, baffling to outsiders who can muddle through with the Germanic Scandinavian tongues. Their cultural history had existed mainly as an oral tradition, with a certain amount of scattered publication, all of which had been decisively pulled together in the 1830s by Elias Lönnrot into a national epic called the *Kalevala*, a certain amount of which (as with *Des Knaben Wunderhorn* and Grimms' fairy tales) was probably the editor's own contribution. But as usual with such things, 100 per cent genuineness is less important than authenticity, and it was the mere possibility of such a work that excited Sibelius and his friends at the Helsinki Music Institute, where he enrolled as a student in 1885.

What Lönnrot and his colleagues heard on their collecting trips were songs: verses in trochaic tetrameters (ending with a spondee, two long syllables) sung to a certain number of formulaic melodies, and Sibelius himself went collecting in 1892 and no doubt heard these melodies from the horse's mouth. This was a new kind of musical folklorism. In Russia Balakirev had collected folk songs and Musorgsky had made a study of peasant speech, with a certain indirect impact on his own music. But Sibelius took the idea further; he began to draw on the *Kalevala* not only for his subject matter but for elements of his musical language. Because of the first-syllable accentuation of Finnish, the *Kalevala* tunes all start on downbeats, and because of the regular trochees of each line, the musical patterns are even, repetitive and monotonous. In 1892, Sibelius composed a tone poem called *En saga* which already derives its character from these features. Its themes start on downbeats and, without precisely fitting the tetrameter patterns, summon up the image of a pair of peasant singers, alternating verses, over and over, in the *Kalevala* manner. Sometimes these themes supply ostinato accompaniments; and in fact ostinatos – figures repeated over and over – are more or less ubiquitous, not all of them thematic. Sibelius proceeds by a kind of terracing, largely supported by fixed patterns, like the string arpeggios that accompany the main bassoon and horn theme at the start, or the pizzicato cello and long held bass E flat accompaniment to the second theme. There is something curiously static about these different episodes, despite their vigorous internal rhythms; the texture is lively, and harmony that changes very little on the terraces often goes through abrupt, even irrational change in between. It's a type of writing that exploits the ambiguity of musical time, the way music can seem to pass at speed yet stay in one place – something very different from the classical concept of ideas interacting and evolving

towards a resolution. In Vienna Sibelius had heard Bruckner's Third
Symphony, and there is something faintly Brucknerian about this
terraced design, though Sibelius's music, brusque and rough-hewn, is
about as un-Viennese as could reasonably be imagined.

En saga does not have a programme, but Sibelius was soon writing
tone poems in a similar style with stories taken from the *Kalevala*. In
the same year he composed a five-movement choral-orchestral symphonic poem about Kullervo, the most tragic character in the epic, a
Siegmund-like figure whose entire family is (he believes) wiped out,
but who seduces a girl who turns out to be his sister, after which both
she and, later, he commit suicide. Next (1895) the composer turned to
another *Kalevala* hero, Lemminkäinen, and wrote a suite of four tone
poems about incidents in the life of this tumultuous young man who,
among other adventures, descends to the land of the dead (Tuonela) in
order to kill the sacred swan only to be himself drowned, dismembered
and magically reassembled by his mother, then seduces almost the
entire female population of an island he visits, before being chased away
by their husbands, and finally rides home in well-deserved triumph.
In *Pohjola's Daughter* (*Pohjolan tytär*, 1906), the aged Väinämöinen
encounters the beautiful Daughter of the North weaving a cloth of
gold, offers to abduct her, but is set a series of impossible tasks, the last
of which (building a boat out of the girl's distaff) proves beyond him
and he is obliged to continue on his journey without her.

Sibelius diversified his style in these works, but the basic ingredients are similar. Lemminkäinen among the maidens of the isle obviously called for a more volatile music than the sombre tread of *En
saga*; the women seem alternately flirtatious and amorous, the scoring
for high woodwind suggestive of some Nordic *fête galante*. The Swan
of Tuonela, with her famous cor anglais solo, floats mysteriously on
the silent waters of the dark river. *Pohjola's Daughter* employs a proto-
cinematic device, cutting in montage fashion from the old hero riding
grandly along to the girl weaving away on her rainbow, then portrays
him struggling with the tasks and her laughing at his failures, before he

rides away, chastened but dignified in defeat. All this music is under-pinned and bound together by ostinatos, or by long-held pedal notes or slow-moving chords, while the melodies proclaim their ancestry in the rhythms and metrics of the *Kalevala*. The harmonic palette is often exceedingly simple, almost naive, but it can explode into violent dissonance, and Sibelius, having always treated textbook harmonic progressions as optional (his critics say because he never learnt them properly), is unafraid of drastic chordal gestures for drastic situations, usually emphasised by strident brass scoring. But this is only one end of his orchestral spectrum, which is often marked at the other end by extreme delicacy and a refined feeling for the character of individual instruments. In fact colour changes, like Bruckner's 'registrations', are frequently used as formal markers.

In 1899 Sibelius composed his First Symphony, and between then and 1924 he added a further six, after which his only large-scale work was the tone poem *Tapiola* of 1926. During his remaining three decades he composed nothing apart from a few miniatures and occasional pieces, and possibly an eighth symphony, about which rumours flew, but which, if it ever existed, he must have destroyed. The challenge of the symphony was quite different from that of the symphonic poem, which is one reason why this latter had come into being in the first place. The symphonic poem was a kind of musical short story, perhaps most akin to the fairy tale, in which things happen in a patterned, ritualised way. A symphony, at least in Sibelius's mind, was a tightly organised discussion of abstract ideas, a dialectic of tension and release, the musical imagination under the strict control of the intellect. When he met Mahler in Helsinki in October 1907, they discussed this question, and Sibelius remarked of the symphony that 'I admired its style and severity of form, and the profound logic that created an inner connection between all the motifs . . . Mahler's opinion was just the opposite. "No!" he said, "the symphony must be like the world. It must be all-embracing."'[1]

Sibelius's Third Symphony had had its first performance a month earlier, and it exemplifies his point of view. It had given him trouble. Its composition had got entangled with that of *Pohjola's Daughter*, a work in narrative form with contrasted episodes, whereas he evidently had a more lucid, integrated design in mind for the symphony. *Pohjola's Daughter* is a vivid, colourful, picture-book piece of writing. The Third Symphony is classical, in the sense of being concerned only with its musical material, presented and argued with disarming clarity and on the whole rather lightly scored. Its C majorishness is almost a statement in itself. The main first movement theme played by cellos and basses in unison and unaccompanied is pure C major and of a childlike rhythmic simplicity. After a time a vagrant F sharp appears, and helps swivel the music into B minor for the second subject, a very unclassical choice, but still handled directly and without ceremony. The second movement, usually taken too slowly (the marking is Andantino con moto, quasi allegretto, two threes against three twos, which suggests a minuet braced by a sarabande), has a curiously obsessive quality, enhanced by the extreme clarity of the ideas. The finale opens as if it intends to be a scherzo but soon generates a slow processional theme that gradually takes over and ends the symphony in the grand, glowing C major of *Meistersinger* or Brahms's First Symphony. Yet again the ideas are of surpassing simplicity. The opening figure of the finale might be a snatch of a nursery rhyme.

The acid test of this approach came with the Fourth Symphony, in A minor, first performed in 1911. These were the years when modernism was asserting itself not just as something impenetrable, but as actually uncomfortable, an expression of the agony of the modern world, epitomised by the paintings of Emil Nolde and the *Blaue Reiter*. Sibelius's Third Symphony seems blithely unaware of such terrors, but his Fourth confronts them head on, in music as dark and unforgiving as anything in Lemminkäinen's Tuonela, and a lot less garrulous. It's as if the composer, having found his style in the harsh, mysterious imagery of northern myth, washes out the imagery and is left holding nothing but the harshness and the mystery. The Romantic artist had sallied forth, alone with his dreams and his despair, luxuriating in the sweet anguish of rejection by a philistine world. But now, at journey's end, the dreams are dead and the despair is no longer anything but a husk of feeling. In the Expressionist music at the bitter end of German romanticism there is a rich, pulsating psychosis. In this symphony of Sibelius there is not even psychology. There are only the remnants of style and a kind of moral defiance, a refusal to yield but also a refusal of self-pity. So the familiar Sibelianisms – the simple melodic figures, the ostinati, the curious effects of rhythm created by offbeat entries and lines floated across barlines – are still there, somewhat curtailed, often reduced to the strange meanderings of small creatures in the nocturnal undergrowth, hardly ever with a strong sense of direction. The bold *fortissimo* attack on the very first note of the first movement subsides almost at once into an uncertain *pianissimo*. The A major finale opens in a brief, slightly etiolated mood of cheeriness. But it is wiped away, like an annoying butterfly, by the brusque A minor chords of the ending, a dismissive wave of the hand, the light of life simply switched off.

Any description of this work is apt to make it sound like a grim failure. But it is not. In its bleak, unloving, austerely beautiful way it is a masterpiece, perhaps its composer's finest work. Its main rival might be his Seventh Symphony (1924), or perhaps *Tapiola* (1926), single-movement scores that come from the opposite ends of his creative work-bench: the one a fusion of symphonic elements into a unified twenty-minute form *sui generis*, the other a rediscovery of the northern imagery but without the narrative, a fixed camera pointing towards the endless pine forests. It would be hard to imagine anything more remote from the literary models of Liszt's symphonic poems. But time had in any case run out for such things in the urbanised world of *neue Sachlichkeit*, and thereafter Sibelius retired to his wooden house near Järvenpää, north of Helsinki, and composed the occasional piece for violin or piano.

For the French, the image or the narrative had always been paramount. Opera and ballet they understood, the symphony and string quartet hardly at all. Bizet's symphony, like its model, Gounod's first (both composed in 1855), is a sparkling divertissement, and it made an excellent ballet score when George Balanchine choreographed it in 1947. Even Franck, a poor setter of words, wrote more vocal and choral than orchestral symphonic music, and only a single symphony. The one significant composer of chamber and orchestral music in the 1860s and 1870s had been Saint-Saëns; but then Saint-Saëns composed in every genre and in huge quantities without making huge waves. A very different case was his École Niedermeyer piano pupil, Gabriel Fauré, who composed many songs, two operas and a famous Requiem, but otherwise threw most of his creative energy into chamber music and music for solo piano. This body of work, often undervalued, was unique in French music of the nineteenth century, and had an appreciable, if discreet, influence on some important figures of the early twentieth.

Fauré came from the small cathedral city of Pamiers in the far southwest of France, but apart from a four-year stint as church organist in Rennes he spent his entire life from the age of nine in Paris. He never attended the Conservatoire, though he ended up as its director (from 1905 to 1920), and he was organist at the Madeleine from 1896. Yet according to his pupil Charles Koechlin, when the question came up of holding his burial service in that great church, one (unidentified) grandee is supposed to have enquired 'Fauré – who is he?'[2] Allowing for the habitual philistinism of the great and the good, the question was to some extent understandable. Fauré had neither sought nor composed for the limelight, and had written hardly any concert music of the kind that attracts headlines or big audiences. His work was neither comfortably popular nor sensationally modern. Even today it is possible to listen to Fauré and find him somewhat esoteric, often beautiful, but often inclined to wander in strange melodic and harmonic regions that leave the ear temporarily disorientated.

His hundred or so songs can give a route into this idiosyncratic style.

Leaving aside the way they were composed, one can think of them as melodic settings that sometimes deviate from the straight and narrow by flattening or sharpening this or that note. For instance, in 'Le Parfum impérissable' (1897) the melody starts with a simple up and down phrase in E major, but when it gets to G sharp the second time it decides to use this as a launch pad for a phrase in G sharp major, but still with the F sharp of the original E major – an effect that pulls the tune straight back to E. This is an elementary example of a device that Fauré often uses to wander into remote regions, but always return, sometimes (like the three kings) by a different route. Sometimes, as in this case, he doesn't go far but slips almost immediately back to his starting point, as if denying the intention to modulate. But Fauré's thinking is modal, treating all the notes as part of the 'field' of E major. This is thinking that can lead to considerable complications with the piano involved as well. Fauré, the church organist, likes to harmonise these deviant melodic notes with chords that fit the note but not the key and that, by pivoting on the note, lead off into new terrain apparently a long way from home. He had been an enthusiastic Wagnerite, and had travelled to Cologne and Munich in the late seventies and early eighties to hear the *Ring* operas, *Tristan* and *Meistersinger*, and had visited Bayreuth. Yet his own language owes hardly anything to Wagner in either style or method.

Perhaps it goes back instead to the École Niedermeyer, where Fauré had studied Gregorian chant and Renaissance polyphony, music of an essentially modal character that operates within fixed sets of notes and knows nothing of changing key. Modalism may be harmonically limited when it's at home, but when it is grafted on to the rich palette of advanced tonality it can produce some marvellously exotic results. It can justify the 'incorrect' treatment of dissonance; it can justify vagrant melody and harmony, provided only that the process is felt to be reasonable and comprehensible in its own terms. In the end it relies on the composer's ear, an educated organ, one hopes, that can persuade by virtue of something innate in the material and something consistent in the language. Whatever the discipline, rules are made, not by theorists, but, unintentionally, by creative geniuses. Fux discovered species counterpoint in Palestrina, but Palestrina did not know about species counterpoint.

Fauré's style evolves through harmony, but begins, like so much French music, with melody, under the influence of the lightly accented French language. In his early songs – 'Lydia', 'Après un rêve' or, somewhat later, 'Nell' – the expression is concentrated almost entirely in the melodic line. And line, in this context, is fundamentally something sensuous, not necessarily in any *risqué* sense of that word, but purely as feeling, the emotional content of the poetry translated into music. The intellectual or philosophical edge of the typical German lied is almost entirely absent, but so, on the other hand, is any trace of folkishness or the hearty outdoor life. These may not be subtle poems but they deal with sophisticated, adult emotions. When he came to set Verlaine, in 'Clair de lune', 'Spleen', and especially *La Bonne Chanson*, he responded more specifically to the verbal undercurrents, with the accompaniment more intricately engaged. In 'Clair de lune' the piano supplies the dance, a languorous minuet, while the voice elaborates Verlaine's fantastic, Watteauesque description of his lover's soul. And this sense of dialogue intensifies in *La Bonne Chanson*, a cycle of nine songs selected from Verlaine's ecstatic twenty-one poem offering to his fiancée Mathilde Mauté in 1869. Alas, by the time Fauré composed his cycle in the early 1890s, Verlaine had long since abandoned his wife, been imprisoned for homosexuality, shooting Rimbaud and trying to strangle his mother, and had sunk into an absinthe-soaked, diabetic, syphilitic squalor. But Fauré's songs beautifully recapture the radiant, richly ambiguous happiness of the *bonne chanson* time. The accompaniments now share the doubts and hopes of the vocal lines, seizing on the chromatics of, for instance, 'J'allais par des chemins perfides' to map a tortuous journey through the enharmonic byways out into the glowing F sharp major of the couple reunited by 'l'amour, délicieux vainqueur'. Perhaps only a French poet could imagine a 'delicious conqueror', but this is the key to the fundamentally sensuous nature of the quest, even at its most labyrinthine.

Fauré's piano music, though plentiful, is less played than it deserves, partly no doubt because it is mostly very hard. Liszt is said to have handed the *Ballade*, op. 19, back to him saying that it was 'too difficult', and most of the thirteen Nocturnes, thirteen Barcarolles and assorted impromptus and valses-caprices (there are no mature solo sonatas) make comparable technical demands. The chamber music, however, always with piano until his very last work, the string quartet, has established a firm place in the repertoire, a highly individual late flowering of a genre that was already beginning to lose its central place in the amateur market. Only the most talented amateurs will get far with these pairs of piano quartets, piano quintets, violin and cello sonatas, or even the single, and comparatively gentle piano trio that Fauré composed just before the string quartet. Yet they chart the evolution of his style as well as the songs, and with fewer lapses in quality.

In these instrumental works Fauré generally makes only a courteous nod towards classical forms, not least because his approach to harmony is not conducive to the normal play of tonalities that is the lifeblood of sonata-type forms. Here, too, the music's progress is essentially a matter of line, often lyrical, as in the first quintet and the trio, sometimes more muscular and energetic, as in the piano quartets. The late chamber works, especially the second quintet and the string quartet, embody Fauré's harmonic language at its most intricate, and the quartet is particularly intriguing in this way. If one were to grumble at anything in Fauré's music, it would be his sometimes excessive fondness for mechanical piano figuration, something that he himself, though no virtuoso, evidently found came readily under his hands. Lacking this recourse in the string quartet, he had to work every line for its proper value, and the result is an unusual and very intense musical conversation, if not one that yields its beauties to the casual ear. It's music, like some late Beethoven, that has to be listened 'into', and in this respect it is the real, if discreet, fulfilment of Fauré's entire life's work. Sadly, though he lived long enough to revise the finished score, he never heard it played.

By the 1920s there was nothing particularly modern about this late style of Fauré's. In no way was it in tune with the twenties spirit. It didn't set out to shock, made no statements about the necessity for this or that in art, had no agenda, rejected nothing. It was simply a natural growth from his own earlier music. Perhaps that is why, though it had an obvious effect on French composers, notably Ravel and Poulenc, and though it certainly was exploratory and new, it never found its way into histories of musical modernism. It's useful to compare Fauré's fate in this respect with that of a younger French composer who did take up a conscious stance in relation to the past and the way it was being imposed on him, and who went out of his way, like a petulant teenager, to avoid doing what the world expected of him.

Claude Debussy, unlike Fauré, did attend the Conservatoire and he did win the Prix de Rome, though having done so he groaned with disappointment at having to spend the next three years in Rome when in mid-affair with the wife of a Parisian architectural assessor. In general, he chafed against the conservatoire disciplines, the strict textbook rules of harmony and rhythm, the regular phrasings and barlines, the implication that the good professors knew what was what in the matter of music as an art form. Again unlike Fauré, he did not come from a musical family, and perhaps for that reason he seems never to have felt much obligation towards the conventions that had governed the teaching of music for the past two hundred years. His attitude was summed up in a response to his composition teacher, Ernest Guiraud, who had suggested that something could be beautiful but 'theoretically absurd', to which Debussy replied, 'There's no such thing as theory. You just have to listen. Pleasure is the rule.'[3]

Debussy had entered the Conservatoire at the age of ten as a pianist, and it was at the piano that he discovered the kind of music that he wanted to write, though he did not at first write it for the piano. The keyboard offered the hands a way of searching for the untheoretical pleasure he had talked about. Even dissonant chords could be beautiful, and strings of them, the same basic chord at different pitches, could be doubly, multiply beautiful, the hands moving without changing shape. The sustaining pedal allowed the blurring of such sounds, and there were degrees of blurring that created different textures, nearly all of them contrary to the normal rules of pedalling, which was supposed to respect the identity of the harmonies. Above all Debussy loved sound for its own sake, as a phenomenon and as a material. Like most French composers of his and the previous generation, he was fascinated by Wagner, learnt his operas at the piano, and went twice to Bayreuth, in 1888 and 1889. But he never cared for Wagner's discourse: the long, long musical paragraphs, the *unendliche Melodie*, the leitmotifs, and all the rest of the Teutonic paraphernalia. What he seems to have loved were the intense moments, the deep beauty of Wagner's orchestral fabric (he was less enthusiastic about the singing).

In his twenties he wrote songs that stole such moments: an early setting of Verlaine's 'En sourdine' which co-opts the sumptuous harmony of the Act 2 love duet in *Tristan und Isolde*; another Verlaine song, 'L'Ombre des arbres', which dwells on the first two or three bars of that opera; a Tristanesque setting of Baudelaire's 'Recueillement'. In 1889 he visited the Exposition Universelle on the Champs de Mars and was enthralled by the Javanese gamelan orchestra and the harsh music of the Annamite Theatre from modern Vietnam. Later he studied the Russian *Kuchka*, especially Musorgsky, with his unorthodox approach to harmony and metre. Anything to free him from the mediocrity, as he saw it, of recent French music. Like the early Romantics, he was distancing himself from the mentality of new money, and aligning himself, consciously or otherwise, with movements in other art forms away from the middle-class comfort zone: with the Impressionists, with their misty images that 'any fool could paint', the Symbolists, with their weird syntax and drug-induced nightmares, the collectors of Japanese prints, even the smoke-filled art cafés. Romanticism had come full circle, but was again branching out into unknown territory.

Debussy's style begins to emerge in the Verlaine songs, then evolves further in orchestral works of the 1890s, the *Prélude à l'après-midi d'un faune* and the *Nocturnes*, and in his only completed opera, *Pelléas et Mélisande*, which was largely finished by 1895. Between them, these works create a new kind of saturated beauty, in the process undermining the most basic assumptions of music as understood at the Conservatoire. By treating dissonance as something self-justifying and in no need of correct preparation and resolution, Debussy was ignoring what had been the most elementary rule of textbook harmony for five centuries. And because in tonal music rhythm, metre and phrase structure are inseparably linked to tonality, he was rethinking them as well. *Pelléas*, though indebted to Wagner in more ways, perhaps, than Debussy would have cared to admit, was in other respects consciously anti-music-drama. Like Maeterlinck's play, which it set more or less verbatim, it was in a large number of short scenes, it was unsingerly, with a prosodic kind of word-setting that allowed the French text to flow in its natural, unemphatic way, and the orchestral accompaniment was discreet, more Musorgsky than Wagner.

There are passion and deep sensuality in *Pelléas*, but they lie mostly beneath the surface conversation of these bewildered, fragile characters for whom life is a tortuous journey at night across a thickly sown emotional minefield. From the moment when Prince Golaud meets the mysterious Mélisande lost in the forest, takes her home and marries her, to her death in the final act giving birth to a child that may or may not be his, almost everything of importance is unknown. Even the love of Pelléas and Mélisande for each other seems to take them by surprise and is expressed obliquely, symbolically. With Pelléas in the castle park, Mélisande drops her wedding ring into a fountain, but when at Golaud's behest they go together looking for it, they search irrelevantly in a cave by the sea. Pelléas comes across her combing her long hair at a tower window and when it tumbles down he makes love to it and her white doves fly out of the tower. Yet when they finally declare and possibly consummate their love, spied on by Golaud who at once kills his half-brother, for them it's as if it were for the first time. Debussy's music catches these nuances by under-expressing them. Its default character is subdued, unemphatic. The vocal line is almost entirely syllabic, one note per syllable, with many note repetitions in low register and much use of what Debussy, in a letter to Ernest Chausson, called 'a device that appears to me rather rare, that's to say silence (don't laugh) as an expressive agent and perhaps the only way of bringing out the emotion of a phrase'.[4] When Pelléas declares his love, his voice at last rises with an urgency that is actually enhanced by the rattle of repeated notes: 'You don't know why I have to go away; you don't know that it's because . . . [silence] I love you.' And after another intense silence, Mélisande, a soprano, responds quietly ('in a low voice') on repeated middle Cs: 'Je t'aime aussi.'

The same kind of intensity pervades his prelude to Mallarmé's poem about the erotic fantasies of a faun on a hot Greek afternoon. In L'après-midi d'un faune, the emotion is an interior 'thickness' rather than anything gestural, starting with the flute solo that starts the piece off, floating chromatically between C sharp and G, tonally ambiguous, capable of various harmonisations or none. Scored for a moderate-sized orchestra without trumpets, trombones or percussion, apart from a pair of antique cymbals that chime softly at the end, the music seldom rises above mezzo forte, but instead vibrates internally, like the Act 2 love duet in Tristan, a tapestry of melodic threads woven into a pulsating stillness.

This quality of mobile immobility is the crucial factor in Debussy's revolutionary treatment of harmony. At its simplest, it involves prolonged or repeated consonant or dissonant chords that gradually lose their grammatical meaning and instead become sonorities, characters, in their own right. Nuages (Clouds), the first of the three orchestral Nocturnes, is an early example, and its subject matter is to the point. Clouds move all the time, yet the cloudscape stays much the same. When he started writing intensively for the piano in the early 1900s, these were the subjects he favoured: water and its reflections, rain, bells, foliage, moonlight, golden fish on a Japanese bowl, figures on a Greek vase, sails, wind, 'sounds and perfumes in the evening air' (Baudelaire), footsteps in the snow, and, perhaps most famously, a cathedral that rises out of the sea, its bells pealing, then sinks back to the ocean floor. These were the images of an eternal present that went with a harmony deprived of its natural tendencies. In *Cloches à travers les feuilles* (*Bells Through the Leaves*), the texture is intricate, like the synaesthetic title, but the harmony is almost static: whole tone for the first eight bars, then after a four-bar transition, a vibrating figure that starts to change, slowly, only after four more bars, beneath a melody of extreme stillness. With music of this kind, the composer has clearly taken trouble to lay the texture out accurately, like a painter blending his colours. He even writes it on three staves to make the layering clear. And he is no less careful with pieces that lack programmatic titles. In *Hommage à Rameau* everything hangs on the spacing of the subtly varied chords, and one can easily imagine Debussy sitting at the piano for hours on end testing, testing, listening into the resonance and exact design of each chord, many of them parallels that are not quite parallel. It was the same with orchestral music. He once told the wife he was trying to abandon that he had been unable to keep a rendezvous because he had spent the day orchestrating a single page of *La Mer*.[5] He may have been lying, but the lie must have been credible for him to have told it. *La Mer*, his greatest orchestral work, is indeed characterised by orchestration of needlepoint refinement, in which every note counts, long after the outlines have been settled.

Debussy stands on the cusp of a new musical century, without quite belonging to it. His insistence on beauty and gentleness of sound chimes oddly with modernism's early love of the tense and abrasive. On the other hand, his cultivation of dissonance as a kind of extract of tonality, and as an issue of sonority rather than grammar, was an idea that lent itself to a huge expansion of what was and was not acceptable in other hands; so when music historians identify him as the starting point of modern music, it may surprise those who find his music beautiful and modernism not, but it makes sense all the same. Curiously enough, the younger Maurice Ravel is less often saddled with that misdemeanour, though he initiated some important things that Debussy took up. Debussy's 'Soirée dans Grenade' is a candid theft from Ravel's *Habanera* and the starting point of various musical adventures in Spain, a country Debussy never visited apart from a day trip to San Sebastián. In a less obvious way Debussy's 'Pagodes' was probably inspired by Ravel's *Jeux d'eau*, and 'Pagodes' is the real start of his love affair with piano resonance. Both composers were influenced by Liszt in this respect, but in Debussy the influence seldom surfaces in keyboard technique, still less in musical style. Ravel is more Lisztian in both respects. The pianism of his most brilliant works, the *Miroirs*, *Gaspard de la nuit*, and *Jeux d'eau* itself, which Ravel said should be played 'like Liszt', clearly evokes the composer of *Mazeppa* and *Les Jeux d'eaux à la Villa d'Este*, and the musical discourse remains in the nineteenth-century tradition. The sounds in Ravel, the chord combinations, are superficially like Debussy, but when you look closely at what he does with them, they seem more decorative than formative.

16

The Shadow of Bayreuth

Perhaps the most striking thing about Wagner's immediate influence in the 1880s is that it came out so well in the work of a composer who was most at home on the small canvas of song. Up to the age of twenty-seven Hugo Wolf had looked like a normal, aspiring, not very successful young composer. Born at Windischgraz, in the Slovene part of Austria, he had persuaded his reluctant father to send him to the Vienna Conservatory in 1875, had been dismissed from that institution on disciplinary grounds in 1877, and had thereafter somehow kept body and soul together by teaching and, for three years from 1884, as a music critic for the *Wiener Salonblatt*. His main talent during these years seems to have been to make enemies. He had a touchy, volatile, somewhat quarrelsome temperament and a vitriolic pen, and it was unfortunate for him that, from early in his time at the Conservatory, he became an ardent Wagnerite, in a city whose most powerful musical voices were a chorus of anti-Wagnerism. He actually met Wagner, who advised him to compose on a bigger scale. Later he met Brahms, who said the same but also told him to take counterpoint lessons. Wolf seems to have reacted sharply against this latter advice, with the result that, when he took up music criticism, he used his pen to extol Wagner and excoriate Brahms. This was a dangerous tactic in Hanslick's Vienna, which duly took its revenge at Wolf's most vulnerable point, his own music. After meeting Liszt in 1883 and playing him some of his songs, he had composed a symphonic poem based on Kleist's play *Penthesilea*, and he had also been working on a string quartet. But his criticisms of the Vienna Philharmonic Orchestra came back to haunt him. When

Hans Richter conducted a run-through of *Penthesilea*, the orchestra performed chaotically, then at the end burst out laughing, and Wolf overheard Richter remark: 'Gentlemen! I should not have let the piece be played to the end, but I wanted to see for myself the man who dares to write in such a way about *Meister* Brahms.' And after he offered his quartet to the Rosé Quartet, whose members all played in the orchestra, he received a note: 'We have attentively played through your D minor Quartet and unanimously resolved to leave the work for you with the doorkeeper of the Court opera house.'[1]

No doubt revenge was only part of the reason for these responses. Vienna was a notoriously conservative city, and *Penthesilea* was a big, complex work in the tradition of Liszt, a composer poorly regarded in the Austrian capital. But Wolf had also been writing songs, settings of Goethe and Eichendorff, among others, including brilliant miniatures such as the Rückert setting 'Die Spinnerin', which had aroused Liszt's enthusiasm, and Mörike's 'Mausfallensprüchlein', a sadistic little tease urging the mice to come out and dance – with the cat. These were mostly occasional pieces, very patchy in word-setting and basic compositional technique. Like most young composers at that time, Wolf regarded the larger forms as the true goal, and even when, after abandoning music criticism in 1887, he suddenly started composing songs in quantity, he still regarded it all as preparation for larger-scale work. 'Today', he wrote to a friend early in 1888 in the first flush of songwriting, 'I have sketched out at the piano practically a whole comic opera. I believe I could write something really good of this kind. But I am afraid of the exertion. I am too cowardly for a proper composer.'[2] He would eventually produce a not very special comic opera called *Der Corregidor*. Meanwhile he was compiling an entire book of Mörike settings, moving on to Eichendorff and Goethe, nearly a hundred songs in 1888 alone, and more than fifty in 1889, including settings of Spanish poems in German translations by Emanuel Geibel and Paul Heyse. Towards the end of 1890 he embarked on a parallel book of Heyse translations from the Italian, then laid this aside in a state of depression, and was able to complete the Italian songbook only in 1896.

The problem was almost certainly a symptom of the tertiary stage of syphilis, which Wolf had contracted in his late teens as a result of one or more visits to a Viennese brothel. By 1897 he was beginning to show definite signs of insanity, and after a brief remission in 1898, in the latter stages of which he moved to the Salzkammergut, he tried to drown himself in the Traunsee, but came to his senses, swam to the shore, and was found wandering in nearby woods, cold and soaking wet. Like Schumann under similar circumstances, he was then admitted at his own request to a mental institution in Vienna, and there, after four years of virtual incoherence, he died in February 1903.

Thus, whatever might have been his potential for work on a larger scale (and *Penthesilea* suggests it was real), it is the songs of the years 1888–91 and 1896 by which he has been and will always be remembered. As a body of work, they can very well bear the weight. Wolf's contemporaries Gustav Mahler and Richard Strauss were also songwriters, but with them the lied was always subsidiary to grander projects, in Strauss's case the symphonic poem and opera, in Mahler's the symphony. Wolf's songs have no such feeling of subsidiarity. Even though many of them are short, they generally have an intensity, a kind of absolute insistence, that brusquely rejects any idea that more might be said if more time were given. Wolf composed lyrical songs in the Schubert manner: 'Verborgenheit' and 'Nimmersatte Liebe' in the Mörike book, for example, or 'Wenn du zu den Blumen gehst' in the Spanish book; and he composed long meditations like 'An eine Äolsharfe', also in the Mörike collection. There are erotic, tragic songs like the two 'Peregrina' settings in the Mörike book, and there are conciliatory love songs like 'Wir haben beide lange Zeit geschwiegen' in the Italian book. But for every song that delves into the fears and conflicts of love, there is one that makes fun of it or dismisses it out of hand. The Italian songbook is rich in such ironic vignettes. 'How I longed for a musician lover,' goes one, 'then God granted me one . . .

and here he comes . . . playing the violin,' and Wolf makes sure we get the point, with a 'violin' coda, 'feeble and hesitant' and ending on a ridiculously long trill. 'My beloved is so small', another reports, 'that without bending down he can sweep the floor with his hair.' And it ends: 'A curse on all flies, gnats and buzzing creatures, and people you have to bend down to kiss.' But Wolf can do genuine rapture with equal conviction. In 'Und willst du deinen Liebsten sterben sehen', also in the Italian book, the lover rhapsodises over the girl's hair, makes love to it almost, à la Pelléas, and the music winds itself sensually round the 'golden threads, silken threads, threads unnumbered'.

Apart from this immense variety of love songs, Wolf composed dramatic ballads, such as 'Der Feuerreiter' (Mörike), a kind of updated 'Erlkönig', and tragic monologues like Goethe's Mignon and Harper's songs, already famously set by Schubert and, less famously, Schumann. There are outdoor songs in the Schubert manner like 'Fussreise' and 'Auf einer Wanderung' in the Mörike book, and – perhaps surprisingly for a self-confessed agnostic – a whole section of religious songs in the Spanish songbook and several also in the Mörike volume, including 'Karwoche', whose text, like Parsifal, associates Holy Week with spring but, unlike Parsifal, regrets the connection and bids the birds be silent. Finally there are satires like 'Abschied', the final Mörike song, in which the author is visited by a critic, who surveys his nose, pronounces it too big, and is kicked downstairs for his pains, to the accompaniment of a merry Straussian waltz. The irony here is double, of course, in view of Wolf's own alternative trade, by this time, admittedly, in the past.

Wolf's real songwriting hero seems to have been Schumann. From Schumann he learnt the verbal precision and conciseness of the Mörike and Italian songs and the refined intricacy of his piano accompaniments. He set Schumann's poets, though mostly not the same poems, and in a few cases he openly modelled a song on one of Schumann's (for instance, 'Begegnung', in the Mörike book, an obvious derivative of Schumann's 'Lust der Sturmnacht'). There are, however, important differences. Wolf never composed a song cycle, despite his feeling that song composition was a preparation for opera; and his judgement of the quality of poetry, as opposed to its meaning and prosody, was superior to Schumann's. His sense of humour, his willingness to mock Romantic sentimentality, was not something Schumann would have been comfortable with. Above all, there was the small matter of Wagner, whose musical influence on Wolf distances him crucially from all his lieder forebears.

More than any lieder composer before him, Wolf wrote his music close to the text, in both prosody and meaning. One can rarely say of Wolf, as one sometimes can of Schubert or Brahms, that he forces a text into a preconceived melody. Even when he exceptionally composed a strophic song, as with Goethe's 'Kennst du das Land', he would make changes to reflect the natural fall of the words or the evolving imagery or feeling. More usually he would make what one might call a prose setting, in which the voice would dialogue freely with the piano, and the word-setting would reflect the verbal accents rather than the poetic metre. A good example is the Mörike song 'Im Frühling', which feels like a piano piece to which a free-wheeling vocal line has been added. Schumann sometimes wrote what amount to piano pieces with the voice doubling the top line. But this is not Wolf's way. Here the voice part is genuinely separate, laid in an informal fashion across the accompaniment, occasionally sharing a phrase, usually not. The poet, intoxicated by the spring airs and sounds, is in love with something or someone he can't identify, and the music breathes a drowsy, hypnotic atmosphere especially in the piano part, with its obsessive motto figure like an inner voice. The actual voice never echoes this figure, yet the whole song has an intensely integrated, almost symphonic kind of unity, and it's this quality, frequent in Wolf, that provides the specific gravity, what I called the absolute insistence, that sets his songs apart from those of other composers.

Continuities of this kind, with a free vocal line laid over a symphonic orchestral accompaniment, are the stuff of music drama. As in Wagner, the voice part can be more or less pure recitative, with little or no melodic character at all. The Italian songbook is full of such songs, either with unifying figures in the piano ('Man sagt mir, deine Mutter woll' es nicht'), or with actual melody ('Du sagst mir, dass ich keine Fürstin sei'). And, again as in Wagner, this seems to lead naturally to ever more elaborate harmony. Even innocent beginnings, like that of 'Auf einer Wanderung', can spawn surprisingly wandering harmonies. But just as many songs are chromatic from the start. There are extreme examples. The 'Peregrina' songs of Mörike, born of his disturbed erotic relationship with a mentally unstable young girl called Maria Meyer, take on in Wolf's hands a nervy, obsessive linear chromaticism plainly indebted to *Tristan und Isolde*. In 'Die du Gott gebarst', the second song in the Spanish book, the pain is by contrast penitential. 'You who bore our Redeemer,' it beseeches Our Lady, 'release us from our fetters,' and the piano part pleads with the voice in a succession of rising and falling semitones, the musical equivalent of supplication. Another of the sacred songs that form the first part of the Spanish book, 'Herr, was trägt der Boden hier', expresses the agony of the crown of thorns in dissonant harmonies that recall Parsifal's torments in Act 2 of Wagner's opera.

The Spanish songs are generally more spacious than the Italian set, the sacred ones much more so. Where the Italian songs dwell on the ironies of love, the Spanish set have touches of local character, dance rhythms, guitar and castanet noises, and rather more singerly vocal parts, though even here Wolf usually seems more concerned to catch the tone of the verse than to write conventionally good tunes. The best-known song in the book, 'In dem Schatten meiner Locken', makes the point nicely. The essential musical idea is in the light, skipping piano part, while the vocal melody tracks the scene: he is passionate when it suits him, then sleeps soundly 'in the shadow of my tresses', set quite freely but culminating three times in the lovely phrase: 'Should I wake him now? Ah, no!' Time and again in these songs the voice part moves by step, often chromatically, but in verbal rather than melodic shapes. Wolf's vocal lines would mostly make little sense without the accompaniment, which tends to create the form. And they would equally make no sense without the words. Wolf was not a tuneful songwriter. He was a genius in the musicalisation of poetry, and in terms of the integration of these two alien species his songs are among the greatest ever written.

Just before Wolf was discovering himself in this way, a young German composer from Munich had been publishing songs of a very different cut, and to a different kind of verse. But then, Richard Strauss came from a quite different background. His father, Franz Strauss, was principal horn in the Munich Court Orchestra, and a brilliant musician (Bülow called him 'the Joachim of the horn'), though one of conservative taste who played Wagner superbly but detested both the music and its composer. His professionalism (and his wife's money, inherited from her family brewery) ensured that Richard received a hyper-solid instrumental and compositional training from an early age, so that by his mid-teens he was already hearing his music performed by first-rate musicians. When he was eleven, his father became director of a fine amateur orchestra called the Wilde Gungl, an outfit that still exists in Munich, and Richard was able to sit in on their rehearsals, attend their concerts, and eventually write music for them. By the time he was twenty, the young Strauss had composed two symphonies, concertos for violin and horn, a serenade and a suite for wind, and various shorter orchestral pieces, several of which had been played by professional orchestras in Munich, Vienna, even New York. He had outgrown his father's preoccupation with the Viennese classics, had discovered Brahms and, in spite of his father, Wagner. In 1883 he met Bülow in Berlin, and two years later Bülow invited him to become assistant conductor of his Meiningen Court Orchestra. And so it went on: third in charge at the Munich Hofoper (1886), Kapellmeister at Weimar (1889), first Munich Kapellmeister (1894), principal conductor at the Berlin Hofoper (1898). By the age of thirty he was the most sought-after young conductor, and his music was published and widely performed.

Where Wolf's sudden emergence as a major composer came after years of struggle and out of the blue, Strauss's was entirely in the order of things, as if pre-planned through some process of musical eugenics. Franz Strauss had instilled in his son a strong work ethic, an impulse to work regularly and systematically, regardless of inspiration or mood, and the result was a steady rate of production on a high technical level with ups and downs in artistic quality. This is already apparent in songs composed in the eighties and early nineties, and published promptly in sets of five, six, or in the case of the first set, eight songs, op. 10, to texts by the minor Austrian poet, Hermann von Gilm. The first song of op. 10, 'Zueignung', is a wonderful example of elevated but slightly vacuous sentiment, ennobled by a beautiful, highly singable vocal melody and a sumptuous piano part that enters like someone walking into the room in mid-conversation. 'Allerseelen', the last in the set, is hardly less worthy, slightly fatuous in its conceit of All Soul's Day, the day of the dead, as a reminder of May-time love, but memorably set in Strauss's most *gemütlich*, cosy-Romantic vein. Lovely as these framing songs are, the most interesting song in op. 10 is 'Geduld' ('Patience'), which builds a powerful emotional charge out of the idea that, where love is concerned, every spring seems like the last and to wait for the next one is to court annihilation. Gilm seems to have had a habit of keying each verse to a single phrase: 'habe Dank' in 'Zueignung', 'wie einst in Mai' in 'Allerseelen'. These are verse ends. In 'Geduld' the phrase 'Geduld, sagst du' begins each verse, and enables Strauss to use it as a motif, starting with the piano's slightly elaborated version, then weaving its way through the whole song. Suddenly there is an emotional energy that almost matches Wolf.

In general Strauss takes hints from his poems in this way, rather than mapping the music on to them. The 'Mach auf!' motif in 'Ständchen', the opening phrase of 'Wozu noch, Mädchen', are like triggers for music that then flows on in its own way. Not that Strauss ignores his texts, but with him one is chiefly conscious of the music, whereas with Wolf the feeling is rather of words and music forming an alloy whose elements can no longer be separated. Perhaps this went with Strauss's frequent preference for setting minor poetry, where Wolf nearly always set first-rate verse. But even in Strauss's settings of Goethe and Rückert, for instance, the same is broadly true. In the excellent Rückert song 'Anbetung', for instance, the phrase 'wie schön, o wie schön' again acts as a trigger for a setting that gives free rein to the voice sometimes at the expense of the words.

In the summer of 1886, before taking up his post at the Munich Hofoper, Strauss went on a tour of Italy, and even while he was there he was sketching ideas for a symphonic poem – or symphonic fantasy, as he called it. *Aus Italien* is a four-movement travelogue that records things seen, heard and felt in musical form. It tries, with only partial success, to adhere to Liszt's idea that 'new ideas need new forms'. But Strauss almost immediately followed it with a series of three symphonic poems that come closer to Liszt's concept of the single-movement character study in a form distilled out of the elements of that character. The first of them, *Macbeth* (1888), is the least successful, perhaps because Strauss could not quite decide whether he was following the events of the play or writing an orchestral work in sonata form. But the other two, *Don Juan* (1888) and *Tod und Verklärung* (*Death and Transfiguration*) (1889), are purely musical masterpieces inspired by human situations: the Romantic lover in search of the ideal woman, and the dying man fighting against death, visited by memories of the past, its joys and failures, but finally transfigured into eternity where earthly failures become glorious successes (Strauss was an atheist, and his image of the next world was merely a poetic convenience). His Don Juan, meanwhile, is not the sexual athlete of Mozart's opera, but the idealist of Nikolaus Lenau's poem of 1844. His loves are not conquests but visions, and his end is not hell but a willed, unprotesting death, without transfiguration, on the sword of the father of a man he had killed.

Strauss was twenty-five when he wrote *Don Juan* and, more than any other, it was the work that established the Strauss style which would expand and contract, rise and fall, but remain essentially unchanged for the next sixty years. From its first bar, one of the most difficult starts in the whole repertoire, it has a coruscating brilliance of orchestral colour, a vitality of texture and movement, and above all a richness of melodic invention that, it must be said, Liszt never achieved. The style is in the best sense synthetic. It seems to have absorbed bits of other composers, notably Brahms and Berlioz, yet to be completely integrated in itself. *Tod und Verklärung* raises more problems, because the transfigured ending called for a genuinely elevated, spiritual quality that one is conscious of Strauss having to work to achieve. Admittedly, this is a problem posed by the programme more than the music. The work's design, derived from Strauss's idea of the man's death throes with radiant ending, is a good example of Liszt's remark about new ideas. But, music being what it is, this particular form could be fitted out with a variety of different programmes involving disquiet, struggle, hope and fulfilment. The stirring, if slightly over-lofty conclusion could just as well suggest recovery as transfiguration, which would at least avoid the sententiousness of an empty eschatology.

There is in these two works a distinct sense of something new happening. A year or two later, Debussy would be quietly undermining tonal harmony and rhythm in his *Après-midi d'un faune* and *Pelléas*. But Strauss's way is different. *Don Juan*, for instance, is entirely tonal. Its logic is that of traditional harmony, in which the part-writing obeys rules of combination, exactly as with Beethoven. Where Debussy dissolves these rules, Strauss stretches them, not yet to breaking point but, one might say, heading that way. For instance, in the work's opening pages the harmony moves so fast, sidestepping rapidly from key to key, that one could very well lose one's bearings altogether if it weren't for the composer's kindly habit of clinching each brief episode with a firm and definite cadence, often with a flourish that suggests a conjuror pulling a rabbit out of a hat. It's a technique that enables him to visit virtually any key at the drop of that same hat, but he doesn't yet use it to dissolve the sense of key altogether. *Don Juan* begins and ends in E major and has subsidiary themes in B, G and C. *Tod und Verklärung* starts in C minor and ends in C major, like Beethoven's Fifth Symphony.

After a brief foray into opera with the quasi-Wagnerian *Guntram*, a modest success in Weimar in 1894, a resounding failure in Munich the following year, Strauss reverted to tone poems, starting with *Till Eulenspiegel* (1895), a subject he had considered for an opera, then continuing with *Also sprach Zarathustra* (1896), *Don Quixote* (1897) and *Ein Heldenleben* (1898). The striking thing about these works as a whole is their tendency to blur the difference between concert and stage. *Guntram* is weakened as an opera by, among other things, the excessive concentration, musically, on the title character, an exhausting, non-stop tenor role. On the other hand the tone poems are so graphic, and so character-based, as to tend towards theatre, and towards forms that make questionable sense without knowledge of the programme. *Till Eulenspiegel* is still on the scale of *Don Juan*, and comparable with it in its rondo-esque form and thematic energy. But in the music's breath-taking description of its anti-hero's wild escapades, upsetting market stalls, escaping dressed as a priest, making fun of learned professors, ending with his trial and execution, the unprepared listener is likely to wonder what is going on even while enjoying the dazzling melodic and harmonic inventiveness and the sheer orchestral bravura. With *Also sprach Zarathustra* we are definitely in the land of the explanatory programme note, since Strauss's choice of subtitles from Nietzsche's chapter headings seems more or less random, made, presumably, for their musical attributes: 'Grablied', 'Tanzlied', 'Nachtwandlerlied', or possibilities: 'Von der Wissenschaft' ('Of Science'), which Strauss uses as pretext for a solemn fugue on a theme that contains all the twelve notes of the octave, though Nietzsche's chapter has really nothing to do with science in this positivist sense. Yet without these hints, the work might well seem baffling as a whole: a sequence of powerful images, linked thematically, but with no obvious rationale.

Don Quixote, a marvellously entertaining set of 'Fantastic Variations on a theme of Knightly Character' freely based on Cervantes, is practically cinematic, with its piping shepherds and bleating sheep (brass flutter-tonguing), imaginary flight (wind machine and harp glissandi), foundering boat (dripping pizzicato strings), and so forth. All this is combined with elements of a concerto, principally cello, but with an important part also for solo viola. Finally, *Ein Heldenleben* amounts to a shamelessly grandiose, episodic portrait of the composer himself, unblushingly in Beethoven's *Eroica* key, E flat major, and including a, to say the least, ambiguous portrait of his wife (the singer Pauline de Ahna, a notoriously sharp-tongued, complex personality), a battle sequence against a posse of cavilling, twittering music critics, and an *apologia pro vita sua* in the form of a gallery of quotations from his own 'works of peace'. By any conventional standards *Ein Heldenleben* is an indiscreet mess, but it proceeds with such confident brilliance and explains itself programmatically with such naive, amusing self-importance that, in a good performance (by no means a certainty), it comes off.

With all their errors of taste and problems of scale, these works add up to a crucial statement of the modernising tendencies of the 1880s and 1890s from one particular point of view. Turning shortly to Mahler, we shall encounter a composer fully in the Romantic tradition, a tormented soul pursuing his vision in the teeth of worldly incomprehension or, worse, indifference. But there is nothing tormented about Strauss. Like the opera composer he will soon become, he is on the look-out for subjects that enable him to deploy his technique and imaginative flair to best advantage, and even when that subject is himself he stands back, surveys his own image and, on the whole, likes what he sees. The objective, technical nature of Strauss's writing is its most striking feature. In *Ein Heldenleben*, for instance, there are long stretches where the polyphony is so complicated and chromatic as to produce an effect of virtual atonality or at least bitonality, the simultaneous presence of two keys at once; but Strauss always has the situation in hand and will close out these passages with clear cadences leading, often, to contrasting music of a purely diatonic character. In a way, these moments anticipate his subsequent reluctance to abandon tonality altogether. The soup always stays in the bowl.

Self-importance had always been a factor in the Romantic vision, but it seems that in the dying years of the century the artist's battle to assert his unique identity against bourgeois conformity and the political machine led inevitably to more complex and esoteric, often more outsize works. Strauss writes for a huge orchestra and deals, he would like us to feel, with large matters. Mahler told Sibelius in 1907 that 'the symphony must be like the world. It must be all-embracing,' having just written his own massive Eighth.[3] It's no coincidence that both Strauss and Mahler had been influenced by Nietzsche, particularly *Also sprach Zarathustra* and its concept of the *Übermensch*, though Nietzsche himself wrote concisely, often epigrammatically, even in *Zarathustra*, which consists of a large number of very short chapters. But there is something in Mahler of the idea of the artist as a kind of guru, a thinker and feeler for humanity grovelling in the dust of materialism. Where Strauss was a master craftsman dressed up as a great soul, Mahler was a true product of an age of increasing insecurity and dislocation, post-Darwin, post-Nietzsche, pre-Freud, profound even when cultivating the vulgar or trivial.

Mahler famously described himself as 'thrice homeless, a Bohemian in Austria, an Austrian among Germans, and a Jew in all the world'. He was born in the Bohemian village of Kalischt (now Kaliště), but brought up in nearby Iglau (Jihlava) in Moravia, the son of a German-speaking Jewish innkeeper who, it was said, beat his wife but encouraged his son's music. Mahler's childhood seems to have been a pattern of colourful and traumatic events that later affected his music. They lived near a barracks, and military music was often part of the local soundscape, as was the singing of the Czech peasantry. He told Freud that once, during a violent row between his parents, he ran out of the house and a street organ was playing 'Ach, du lieber Augustin', after which he could never separate the tragic and the trivial in his own music.[4] Later,

354

when he was eleven and staying with a family in Prague, he surprised the teenage son of the house making love to one of the maidservants, whose vociferous reaction led him to suppose she was being attacked. Naturally she was not best pleased at his gallant attempt at rescue. The point about these incidents and situations, commonplace enough in themselves, is their effect on the hypersensitive retina of Mahler's memory. Strauss, one feels, would have noticed them, then passed on. Mahler forgot nothing.

Yet his professional career was by most standards a success. Like Strauss, he held important conducting posts from the age of twenty-three until his death at fifty. He was a junior conductor at the opera houses in Kassel, Prague and Leipzig, chief conductor in Budapest, Hamburg (where he also took over the symphony concerts when Bülow died in 1894), Vienna and New York. There were many difficulties, but they were often of his own making. He was a fierce perfectionist with a tyrannical streak, demanded heavy rehearsal schedules and seems rarely to have controlled his temper if singers or players failed to live up to his high standards. As a forceful young conductor praised by the critics and liked by the subscribers, he was the object of jealousy on the part of older rivals, who on a couple of occasions engineered his dismissal. In Vienna he greatly extended the operatic repertoire, including into regions – for instance, recent Italian opera – not calculated to endear him to Austro-German traditionalists; and he took over the stage direction, importing modernist designers like Alfred Roller, and treating the stage as rigorously as the music, a rigour tempered by a habit of re-orchestrating standard repertory works. In Vienna he was naturally the victim of anti-Semitism, even though he converted to Roman Catholicism at the start of his tenure, and it's significant that, during his three years as conductor of the city's subscription concerts, he seldom conducted his own music. His beautiful but relatively conventional Fourth Symphony was the only major work of his premiered in the Austrian capital.

Mahler had been a contemporary of Wolf at the Vienna

Conservatory, and many of his early works are songs. But they are essentially different from anything by Wolf. From early on Mahler was drawn to the *Knaben Wunderhorn* collection, from which he tended to select poems with a strongly visual or narrative element. Often they are dialogues: the girl calls her lover to her window, the soldier marches off to war abandoning her, birds are instructed to carry this or that message. Tragedy is never far away. In one of the greatest of the *Wunderhorn* songs, 'Wo die schönen Trompeten blasen', the soldier who comes to her window is already dead, and calling her to join him beneath the green turf. In another, 'Revelge', the enemy is routed by dead soldiers brought briefly back to life by the dying drummer-boy beating his drum. Much of the imagery recalls Mahler's childhood. Military fanfares and march rhythms echo through song after song. Cuckoos call, nightingales sing. And behind everything is a kind of idealised folk music, memories of peasant life in Moravia, but clouded by vagrant harmony, major thirds drooping to the minor, chromatic passing notes of a faintly schmaltzy kind, a deliberate intrusion of urban sophistication and corruption into the simple country life.

Mahler might have stopped there or gone on writing these extraordinary, heart-breaking songs, that capture the sorrow at the heart of every simple joy in a way no composer had done since Schubert. But their emotional context was heavy with intellectual meaning for him, and his nine symphonies clearly emerge from the world of *Des Knaben Wunderhorn*, sometimes incorporating its music. The scale of these works, the shortest of which lasts only a little less than an hour, suggests the influence of Bruckner, whose classes Mahler sometimes attended at the Conservatory, but the prevailing tone of loss and alienation is remote from Bruckner's placid grandeur. Mahler himself felt it to be a Jewish trait, a symptom of displacement and not-belonging. And it's from these feelings that his music derives its narrative structure, something quite different from the monumental, quasi-architectural designs of Bruckner.

The first four symphonies, composed between the mid-1880s and

1900, all incorporate *Knaben Wunderhorn* ideas in one way or another. The first, in D major, actually draws on the song cycle *Lieder eines fahrenden Gesellen* (*Songs of a Wayfaring Lad*), for which Mahler had written his own texts. But he clearly modelled his poems on the *Wunderhorn*, and his settings are close in style to his *Wunderhorn* songs. They thus transport the quasi-folk style into the symphony, especially the first movement, whose first subject is the theme of the second Wayfarer song, and the third movement, which uses the final song as alternate to a sardonic minor-key version of 'Frère Jacques' played by a muted solo double bass (at least Mahler surely intended it to sound sardonic, though modern bass-players play it so beautifully that the effect is usually lost). The whole symphony is highly original in style and conception, but not quite as unprecedented as it now seems, since it owes significant elements to a now practically forgotten symphony by Hans Rott, a fellow student at the Conservatory who died, like Wolf, in an asylum at the age of twenty-five. Rott's E major Symphony, composed in 1880, anticipates Mahler in a number of details. Its scherzo theme is so close to Mahler's as to make the Mahler sound like a conscious borrowing, and the wisps of folkish melody in the first part of Rott's finale are pure Mahler before the fact. But it was left to Mahler to develop these ideas.

The key works are the Second and Third Symphonies, which establish for the first time the type of the Mahler symphony: massive, concert-length scores of a hyper-discursive character for a huge orchestra, drawing in all sorts of diverse ingredients, vocal and choral as well as orchestral, and presenting the whole as a disguised narrative, a kind of sprawling autobiography of the soul. Mahler's narratives are not like Strauss's. They don't concern other characters or events observed with a shrewd painterly eye, or even himself in the sense of 'the story of my life'. They are about the composer himself, but regarded as a solipsistic microcosm of the universe. The powerful first movement of No. 2, originally composed as an isolated symphonic poem called *Todtenfeier* (*Funeral Rites*), concerned 'the hero of my D major Symphony whom

I bear to the grave there'.[5] He poses a series of questions. 'Why did you live? Why did you suffer? Is it all nothing but a huge, frightful joke?' These questions he then 'answers' in his forty-minute finale, the second half of which is a grandiose choral setting of Klopstock's 'Resurrection' ode, a poem that does indeed answer at least the composer's first two questions: 'You were not born in vain, have not lived or suffered in vain!' Exactly what the three intervening movements have to do with this narrative is harder to explain. The second movement is a *Ländler*, a slow rustic waltz, which Mahler describes as 'the image of a long dead hour of happiness' after 'you have followed a loved one to the grave'. The third is actually an expanded version of his *Knaben Wunderhorn* song 'Des Antonius von Padua Fischpredigt' ('St Anthony of Padua's Sermon to the Fishes'), a bustling scherzo telling how the fish, unlike the parishioners, turn up for the sermon but still go back to their wicked ways as soon as it's over. The symphonic version, enriched by a radiant central section and, near the end, what Mahler called 'a cry of disgust', now depicts the meaningless scurry of existence in general. He then links this to the finale by way of another *Wunderhorn* poem, 'Urlicht' ('Primal Light'), beautifully set for alto solo, singing about the broad path to heaven, illuminated by the light of God.

The Third Symphony, even longer than the Second, has – or had – what looks at first glance like a more coherent programme. Mahler outlined it in slightly varying ways in correspondence. There was an overarching title, taken from Nietzsche: *Die fröhliche Wissenschaft*, then separate but related titles for each of the six, originally seven, movements, starting with a thirty-five-minute Allegro, 'Pan awakes. Summer marches in', then proceeding through a series of shorter movements with titles like 'What the meadow flowers tell me', 'What the woodland creatures tell me', and ending with a wonderful half-hour Adagio, 'What love tells me'. Here too there are vocal movements, a setting of Nietzsche's 'O Mensch! Gib Acht' from *Also sprach Zarathustra*, and another *Wunderhorn* poem, 'Es sungen drei Engel', magically set for children's and women's voices. The seventh movement would have been another *Wunderhorn* song for solo soprano, but Mahler decided that enough was enough, and kept it back as finale, instead, for the Fourth Symphony. 'There now!' he told a friend, 'you have a sort of programme . . . Nature in its totality, which is, so to speak, awakened from fathomless silence that it may sing and resound.'[6]

It's hard to know what to say about these explanations, except perhaps to express relief that Mahler withdrew them. Clearly they helped stimulate his creative juices, and by the same token they give some indication of the way his musical mind worked. He wanted to feel a unifying force making sense of these vast structures, and to a certain extent he succeeded, though with some perilous moments along the way. The first movement of the Third Symphony is a good case study. It sets out with a swinging march for eight horns in unison, but after a dozen bars it grinds to a halt and for the next ten minutes or so toys at slow tempo with fragmentary material presumably meant to represent the awakening of the god Pan. Eventually the movement picks up again and the march of summer proceeds. There is a lengthy middle section partly based on fanfares and sentimental horn and trombone tunes, then the march resumes and leads to a much-modified recapitulation with the same general attributes as the exposition.

This is an impossibly sprawling design that no programme could hold together. What saves it is the sheer fascination of the material and Mahler's amazingly original way of presenting it. His sources are obvious enough: the military marches of his childhood and the band concerts, the peasant songs and dance tunes, the music of itinerant Bohemian fiddlers. The material is often not much better than pretty trash, but through an alchemy of his own Mahler makes it movingly expressive. One could draw up a catalogue of his devices: the naive melodies twisted into strange shapes, the sinister drum rolls, the steep dynamic gradients, the chamber-music scoring for large orchestra, the use of 'wrong' instruments: trombones for sentimental tunes, strings for drum effects, the animal noises and subterranean grindings and rumblings, the constant tendency to disrupt whatever process is underway.

In general these ways of writing perpetuate Mahler's archetypal experience with the street organ: commonplace tunes and rhythms taking on painful associations. Mostly, Mahler's programme notwithstanding, they convey a sense of damage and loss.

In some ways early modernism relives the aims and attitudes of the early Romantics. In Mahler we still see the artist as an exceptional individual, in retreat from the material world and in quest of higher things. He searches in Nature, which he regards as an image of the divine. But the image is an illusion and the journey is fraught with torments, even at moments of greatest radiance. Everything is tinged with pain, even the child's dream of heaven in the Fourth Symphony, a place of slaughter in which King Herod himself participates – and can we be sure that it is only the animals that he butchers? Mahler's later symphonies (apart from the vast choral Eighth and the beautiful, valedictory *Das Lied von der Erde* (*The Song of the Earth*), intended as a ninth symphony until Mahler, who had been diagnosed with heart disease, lost his nerve about the historical significance of that number) abandon texts altogether, but develop the characteristics of his instrumental style towards, but never quite as far as, atonality. His melody becomes more sophisticated, less folkish; it never completely loses touch with the singable tonal line, but the stabs of pain get sharper, the textures denser and the harmonies more tangled.

The Fifth Symphony (1901–2), for instance, still preserves a certain quality of vocal melody in a design that to some extent reflects, orchestrally, the emotional journey of the Second Symphony, from funeral march to triumphant affirmation. The opening has an obvious affinity with the tragic militarism of the *Knaben Wunderhorn* songs, especially 'Der Tamboursg'sell' and the 'Lied des Verfolgten im Turm', while the well-known Adagietto (which Visconti used in his film of Thomas Mann's *Death in Venice*) is close in tone and style to the exactly contemporary Rückert song, 'Ich bin der Welt abhanden gekommen' ('I have become lost to the world'). But these quasi-vocal elements are a lot less prominent in the violent but superficially orthodox Sixth (1903–4),

Mahler's closest approach to the four-movement classical model, but a work utterly unclassical in expression and discourse, almost as if the composer had specifically set out to imprison his *Weltschmerz*, his world-weariness, in a form that would eventually explode under the pressure.

For many Mahlerians, the Sixth Symphony is his greatest work, perhaps because of its classicising tendencies. For others, Mahler's genius is better accommodated by the diffuse and episodic forms – those of the Third Symphony and the admittedly uneven Seventh – which come closer to his idea of the symphony being like the world, all-embracing. The Sixth and Seventh both in their different ways take Mahler's language into new territory. The start of the Seventh (1904–5), with its tenor horn theme in fourths, seems a conscious experiment in a new kind of harmony, based on fourths rather than the traditional thirds, an idea that Schoenberg pursued in his First Chamber Symphony of 1906. But in *Das Lied* there is a renewed simplicity of melody and harmony, apparently influenced by the beautiful, elegiac Chinese poems, but no doubt also by the return of the solo voice as a controlling factor; and this style still resonates at the start of the purely orchestral Ninth Symphony, before coming rapidly under scrutiny.

The first, D major theme, with its short, gasping phrases, expresses all the agony of life on the edge of the bearable, except that with each variant, each added appoggiatura, each chromatic twist, the agony increases. Although at first completely diatonic (entirely D major), the theme studiously avoids the keynote D, as does the second theme (in D minor). The note D is a point of rest; but this music cannot rest, or when it eventually does so (bar 25) the cadence rings false, as if to say, 'Oh well! nothing to be done,' and by the time the movement has run its lengthy course, the D of the theme has been subjected to so many added notes and appoggiaturas, chromatic as well as diatonic, that any serenity that might have survived the unsettled phrase structure has long since blown away. The *Ländler* that follows is a curiously gnarled, almost parodied version of its rustic original, while the

Rondo-Burleske third movement takes these distortions to the brink of atonality, still without ever quite tumbling over the edge. Then in the long slow finale, a semitone down in D flat, Mahler seems to seek repose but, in the vanishing music of the final page, achieves only annihilation.

Mahler's troubled soul was in some measure independent of the world around him. It was due, Freud told him when they met in August 1910, to an unresolved mother fixation; but in any case it was internal, an aspect of his character. One can hardly reduce phases in cultural history to such terms, and to the extent that the tensions in Mahler's work corresponded to the tensions in contemporary art, it may be because he took hold of the language as he found it and moulded it in his own image. The same could hardly be said of Strauss, whose soul never showed much sign of being troubled, but who certainly took hold of the language, and moulded it in ways that were implicit in its own nature and in keeping with certain tendencies in other art forms of the day, especially literature, painting and graphic design.

These tendencies seem to have started as an aesthetic and psychological reaction against gradual changes in society, social conditions and attitudes during the second half of the nineteenth century. In every sphere scientific discoveries and technological advances were doing away with the mysteries of life. Imagination was being outwitted by research. There was nothing for it but to come up with images from a world that, whatever the claims of the new psychoanalysis, was strictly beyond the reach of a Viennese couch or a Paris laboratory, images from deep in the psyche, from dreams and especially nightmares, from sexual obsession and exotic fantasies of one kind and another. The 1890s and 1900s were a time of artistic 'movements': symbolism, art nouveau, *Jugendstil*, *Sezession*, *Mir iskusstva* (The World of Art), expressionism, post-impressionism, cubism, abstraction. But whatever their technical differences, they were all trying to move art away from the certainties of modern technology and the clammy taste of the 'I know what I like' bourgeoisie; they were involved, to some extent like the early Romantics, in the project of making art strange again, at a time when the new money was on making it accessible. Here at least music could make common cause with its fellow art forms.

Strauss, as we saw, had been writing about characters on the fringes of respectable society but had barely strayed beyond the bounds of what a reasonably sophisticated Wagnerian might regard as mildly 'difficult' in point of style. Then suddenly in 1905 and 1909 he produced two big one-act operas that did that in no uncertain terms. Both *Salome* and *Elektra* were more or less straight settings of contemporary plays about women in the grip of pathological obsessions. Oscar Wilde's Salome is a beautiful, spoilt sixteen-year-old who conceives a sexual obsession with Jokanaan (John the Baptist), who has been incarcerated in an underground cistern by her stepfather, King Herod Antipas, for his denunciation of Herod's marriage to his widowed sister-in-law, Herodias. Hugo von Hofmannsthal's Elektra (in his adaptation of Sophocles) is completely taken up, to the edge of insanity, by her hatred of her mother, Clytemnestra, who, with her lover Aegisthus, murdered her husband Agamemnon on his return from the Trojan War. Herod's court in *Salome* is a nightmare of psychopathic inhumanity illuminated by a strange, symbolic moon, 'like a woman stepping from the grave', sings Herodias's page, 'like a crazed woman searching everywhere for a lover', sings Herod, anticipating precisely the theme of Schoenberg's monodrama, *Erwartung*, of four years later. Salome, having failed to seduce Jokanaan, agrees to dance for Herod in return for the Baptist's head on a silver charger, and when she gets it she makes such revolting love to it that Herod orders her to be killed. Elektra's frenzied longing for the return of her brother, Orestes, so that he can kill their mother with the axe that killed Agamemnon, is finally gratified after a long and beautiful recognition scene. But in between, Clytemnestra herself appears, a degenerate figure, pale and bloated, barely able to stand, decked out with jewels and amulets, each one a talisman against this or that demon, the image of moral and physical decay.

With these two subjects, Strauss approaches the world of expressionism, though the treatment is somewhat calculated, as if observing these horrible events from a safe distance. Reviewing the 1910 London premiere of *Elektra*, Ernest Newman complained that 'to make a play a study of human madness, and then to lay such excessive stress on the merely physical concomitants of madness, is to ask us to tune our notions of dramatic terror and horror down to too low a pitch', and that 'Strauss, of course, revels in this physical, and therefore more superficial, side of the madness'.[7] The result, all the same, is undeniably powerful, perhaps especially so in the scene with Clytemnestra, where Strauss paints an astonishingly vivid musical portrait of the psychotic, guilt-wracked queen as she describes the nameless, weightless something that crawls over her at night when she lies awake, and the dreams that freeze the marrow of her bones when she falls asleep. The dislocated orchestral textures, the breathless, fragmented vocal lines, the subterranean growlings of the contrabass trombone and tuba, the swirling chromatic string and woodwind figures, all this is the nearest Strauss came to the nightmare atonality of *Erwartung*. *Elektra* is never atonal in quite Schoenberg's sense: its harmonic extremities are reserved for moments of terror or violence, of which, admittedly, there are a good many. But where in *Erwartung* one feels that the subject has been chosen to fit the style, in *Elektra* the style varies with the incident, which was precisely the basis of Newman's criticism.

With *Elektra*, Strauss was generally considered to have established himself as a leading light of the modernist avant-garde. But it was clearly not a reputation he relished or wanted to cultivate. Soon after the first performance in Dresden in January 1909, he started a new opera with an original libretto by Hofmannsthal, set in 'the old Vienna under the Empress Maria Theresa'. *Der Rosenkavalier* (*The Knight of the Rose*) was emphatically not a scenario that called for music of any Expressionist cast. Essentially it is a piece of cultural nostalgia, with shades of Mozart, the Viennese Strausses, and a partial reversion to Richard Strauss's own pre-*Salome* idiom. Its most modern feature is its perfection of the conversational vocal style developed in *Salome* and *Elektra*. In other ways it is a masterpiece of sophisticated reaction, richly melodious, stuffed with 'Viennese' waltzes, superbly orchestrated, profoundly – perhaps excessively – sentimental. On behalf of both the composer and the librettist, it tells modernism: enough is enough, there is still plenty to be said in the old styles of music and drama, not to mention plenty of people willing to pay to hear and see it said. It was a philosophy Strauss and, until his death in 1929, Hofmannsthal stuck to, with mixed, occasionally memorable results.

If Strauss's modernism was usually a response to particular dramatic situations or psychological conditions, there were other composers who saw it as an essential, even inevitable, fulfilment of the implications of Romantic music itself. German and Austrian composers, especially, were inclined to respect procedures that had, after all, evolved largely in the work of their compatriots. And the outcome was a gradual divergence between composers who were content to go on writing in styles more or less directly indebted to Wagner, and composers who wanted to take forward what they saw as the implications of Wagner's own style and technique.

This was no mere temporary disagreement. Engelbert Humperdinck, who in *Hänsel und Gretel* (1893) had produced a delicious distillation of simplified Wagner and Brahms with folk song attachments, was still writing in essentially the same manner in *Dornröschen* (*Sleeping Beauty*, 1902) and *Königskinder* (1910). Hans Pfitzner's first opera, *Der arme Heinrich* (*Poor Heinrich*, 1895), is more ambitious, with dense, near-atonal harmony for an arcane redemption drama about an ailing knight who can only be saved by the sacrifice of a young virgin, a solution even Wagner had not thought of. But Pfitzner backed away from the full-blown atonality that might have seemed the logical continuation of these beginnings, and his best-known opera, *Palestrina* (1915), is something of a hybrid, mixing late Romantic tonal harmony with elements as diverse as Debussy and fanciful pastiche of Palestrina himself. However, the most interesting of these gradualists, apart from

Strauss, is Franz Schreker, an Austrian who found an eclectic route to a kind of modernism that combined the historical strain of German textbook-derived harmony with colouristic elements that owed something to French and even Italian music. Schreker's best works, the operas *Der ferne Klang* (*The Distant Sound*, 1903–10), *Der Schatzgräber* (*The Treasure-hunter*, 1915–18) and *Irrelohe* (1919–22), reveal a genuine lyrical gift combined with a fine ear for the orchestra which lends his more complex harmonic effects a clarity they often lack in the music of this period.

Something of a middle case is Max Reger, an instrumental composer *par excellence*, who like Bruckner began life as a church organist, and who, though a Catholic from Bavaria, was profoundly influenced by the Lutheran tradition of Bach and Brahms. Somehow the combination led to a heavy, essentially contrapuntal style, often extremely chromatic, to the point almost of atonality in a work like the *Symphonischer Prolog zu einer Tragödie* of 1908, an orchestral piece in a single movement lasting thirty-five minutes. Reger's best works, out of an enormous *oeuvre* for a composer who died at forty-three, are mostly chamber music, including half a dozen string quartets, a clarinet quintet and various works with piano, music that seems consciously to adhere to a more classical manner, for all its harmonic adventures. After the *Symphonischer Prolog* and the F minor Piano Concerto of 1910, atonality might have been a logical outcome. But Reger, too, stepped back, and his late orchestral works – the *Romantic Suite, Ballet Suite* and *Variations and Fugue on a theme of Mozart* – adopt an essentially 'reasonable' version of late Romantic tonality.

One can see in a lot of this music more or less unsuccessful attempts to find a way out of what the French theologian Jacques Maritain would later call 'the immense intellectual disarray inherited from the nineteenth century'.[8] It's as if Germanic composers especially felt bound to pick up the threads of Wagner, Liszt and to some extent Brahms, but then found them leading into a labyrinth they were wary of entering. Arnold Schoenberg summed the problem up in a different metaphor that includes his own reason for persevering. 'Personally,' he remarked,

> I had the feeling as if I had fallen into an ocean of boiling waters, and not knowing how to swim or to get out in another manner, I tried with my legs and arms as best I could . . . I never gave up.[9]

Schoenberg took the logical view that chromatic harmony led in one particular direction, and when he reached what he decided was the point of no return, he simply kept going. The connection is easy to hear, especially in his chamber music from the early string sextet, *Verklärte Nacht* (*Transfigured Night*, 1899): a beautiful, richly textured, entirely tonal work in D minor, through the First String Quartet (1905 also in D minor but more vagrant) and First Chamber Symphony (1906, E major), to the Second Quartet (1908, initially F sharp minor), whose last two movements include a soprano solo to texts by the Expressionist poet Stefan George. At a certain point in the Second Quartet, Schoenberg seems to have sensed that any feeling of key had dissolved in the polyphonic texture, so he simply dropped the key signature and carried on without one, trusting his immense skill as a contrapuntist to keep the music on track. 'I feel the breath of another planet,' as the second poem, 'Entrückung' ('Rapture'), begins. It may be a planet without gravity. But that's another story.

17

A Russian Autocrat and an English Misfit

Rimsky-Korsakov's problem, after accepting the Conservatoire professorship in 1871, was to transform himself into a properly equipped musical pedagogue, having spent the last ten years in an intellectual sphere that regarded pedagogy with contempt. Much of his time in the 1870s was spent remedying this situation, and undertaking work that arose from his newfound institutional respectability. In 1873 he was appointed Inspector of Naval Bands, a post that called for a knowledge of brass instruments he did not possess, but acquired by the simple process of learning to play them. He began to study orchestration as a technical discipline rather than a mere adjunct to composing. He also undertook editorial work. He set about revising earlier works of his own, and was soon working on other people's, editing Glinka in collaboration with Balakirev, tidying up *Prince Igor* in the hope of persuading Borodin to finish it, and most famously, after Musorgsky's death in 1881, doing the same for *Khovanshchina* and *Night on the Bare Mountain*, while at the same time producing his own, 'tidied up' edition of *Boris Godunov*.

His own composing inevitably suffered. In the wake of his theoretical studies he wrote some rather dry chamber music, and his inspectorial work gave birth to scores for military band, including a trombone concerto. The eighties were more productive. There was a somewhat Lisztian piano concerto and, later in the decade, the three orchestral works that, more or less alone, carried his name outside Russia: the *Spanish Caprice*, *Sheherazade* and the *Russian Easter Festival* overture. Then suddenly, in the 1890s, he embarked on the final series of operas that, in their professionalism and their sheer range of subject matter and methodology, finally distanced him from the *Kuchka*. Marina Frolova-Walker puts it neatly and with only the faintest hint of a tease. Rimsky-Korsakov died in 1908 'leaving no unfinished works behind'.[1]

A test case might be his second opera, *Mayskaya Noch'* (*May Night*), premiered at the Maryinsky Theatre in 1880, a well-made, charming, even somewhat old-fashioned genre comedy with fairy attachments, based on a short story by Gogol, in which the village mayor's son is helped by *rusalki* from a nearby lake to marry the girl his father is trying to steal. Rimsky-Korsakov's music descends from Glinka and Dargomïzhsky, but differs from them in its rich incorporation of actual Ukrainian folk songs, chosen for their aptness to the time and place of the action. For instance, there are Whitsun songs and a song about planting millet, such as one might have expected to hear sung in a Ukrainian village in the month of May in the 1830s. Everything about the work suggests careful thought and focused professionalism, something far removed from the wild, rambling historical research that had enriched *Khovanshchina* but stopped Musorgsky finishing it.

Rimsky-Korsakov's next opera, *Snegurochka* (*The Snow Maiden*, 1882), brings a new and decisive twist to the idea of folk tales and the intervention of the supernatural. Here the story of the *rusalka* who desires to be human but is unable to survive the condition is transformed into a seasonal (hence fertility) myth, in which Snegurochka, the love child of Winter and Spring, tries to learn human love, but when she at last does so she is melted by the first rays of the spring sunshine. This rather studious approach to ethnographic symbolism now looks like a pre-echo of the Russian Silver Age, whose climax in music would be Stravinsky's *Rite of Spring*. Rimsky-Korsakov again used a large number of folk tunes, in whole or part, and was again very conscious, as we know from his autobiography, of the sources and significance of these tunes. For example, there are songs to do with *Maslenitsa* (butter week, the week before Orthodox Lent), a time that proclaimed the coming end of winter.[2] As drama, this can all seem rather heavy-handed. But *Snegurochka* is a rich and colourful score, full of harmonic devices that bring out the distinctions between mystic nature (artificial, non-diatonic harmony, whole-tone and octatonic scales) and the human world of diatonic or modal (folk song) harmony, and withal vividly orchestrated.

Many of the elements of *Snegurochka* reappear in one form or another in Rimsky-Korsakov's numerous later operas: in *Sadko* (1898), in which he revisited the story, and some of the music, of his old symphonic poem; in *Skazaniye o nevidimom grade Kitezhe* (*Legend of the Invisible City of Kitezh*, 1904), the culmination of Rimsky-Korsakov's immersion in folk legend, with a strong admixture of pantheism and Christian mysticism, and a distinct flavour of Wagner in his Forest Murmurs garb; and in his final opera, *Zolotoy petushok* (*The Golden Cockerel*), a purely Russian – that is, fantastic, obscure, musically colourful – lampoon against political incompetence in the wake of Russia's humiliating loss of the war against Japan in 1904–5. Even at the very end of his life, Rimsky-Korsakov's style feels more than anything like an advanced and better organised version of Glinka, full of strange, magical harmonies governed by a hidden arithmetic, coloured by folk song and folk mythology, interesting and delightful, yet curiously inconsequential in relation to musical goings-on elsewhere.

Nevertheless Rimsky-Korsakov's influence in St Petersburg grew in these final years. The production of *Sadko* was paid for by a railway tycoon by the name of Savva Mamontov and presented in his private theatre in the capital. But many years before that Rimsky-Korsakov had already had an encounter with the new rich merchant class in the person of Mitrofan Belyayev, the music-loving heir to a timber fortune, who had been so impressed by a symphony by Rimsky-Korsakov's seventeen-year-old pupil Alexander Glazunov that he was now offering to sponsor its publication. Soon he set up an actual publishing company, dedicated solely to Russian music; and he started a concert series, the Russian Symphony Concerts, likewise devoted to Russian works that he would also proceed to publish. In all these ventures he came to rely on Rimsky-Korsakov's advice, and when, as a term in his will, the Glinka Prize was established in 1903, Rimsky-Korsakov was in charge of that as well.

The effect of all this on Rimsky-Korsakov's standing in St Petersburg music may well be imagined. As a senior composition professor at the Conservatory and the effective arbiter of what did and did not go in the new Russian music, he had become the biggest fish in a rather small pool. The results were not altogether wholesome. Orchestral works became the order of the day, and their character increasingly regressed to a bland average that picked up, one way or another, on the Glazunov style, usually without his brilliant, sub-Rimskian fluency. It's tempting to suggest, confronted by this parade of self-congratulatory mediocrity, that St Petersburg music in the 1900s was a good preparation for Soviet music in the late twenties and thirties. Yet, by a strange twist of fate, it also threw up one composer who would consign all the others to historical oblivion. Igor Stravinsky was the son of the leading bass at the Maryinsky opera, but he was not himself destined for a musical career, and ended up as a private pupil of Rimsky-Korsakov on condition that he also continued his law studies. He never attended the Conservatoire, was amiably looked down on by his fellow Rimskyites, and probably only emerged at all because Serge Diaghilev, desperate for a musical equivalent to the astonishing dancers, choreographers and designers he had presented in Paris in 1909, took a chance with this young man by whom he had heard a couple of lively orchestral pieces and commissioned him to compose *The Firebird* for his 1910 season. The result was an extraordinarily accomplished, derivative piece of superior kuchkism; but it was decidedly the last thing Stravinsky wrote of which that could be said. His next ballets, *Petrushka* and *The Rite of Spring*, dragged Rimskyism screaming into the new century, before their successors *Svadebka* (*Les Noces; The Wedding*) and *Renard* abandoned it altogether.

The one composer who could still move in St Petersburg musical circles in the late eighties and early nineties without depending on the Rimsky–Belyayev axis was Tchaikovsky. He conducted the first performance of his Fifth Symphony in a Philharmonic Society concert in November 1888 and almost exactly five years later his Sixth Symphony, the 'Pathétique', in the hall of the Assembly of the Nobles. In between there was a succession of major theatrical works for the Maryinsky: *The Sleeping Beauty* in January 1890, *The Queen of Spades* the following December, and finally the one-act opera *Iolanta* in a double bill with *The Nutcracker* in December 1892. He died in St Petersburg in October 1893, only a few days after the 'Pathétique' premiere, in circumstances that remain controversial.[3]

It probably helped Tchaikovsky that he did not live in St Petersburg but in the small town of Klin, sixty miles from Moscow, and was always only a visitor to the capital, on good terms with the musicians there, but by no means under their musical sway or involved in their politics. The personality differences are certainly marked in their works around 1890. Tchaikovsky had treated some of the same dramatic subjects as Rimsky-Korsakov. He had composed incidental music to Ostrovsky's *Snow Maiden* and an opera (in two versions) on Gogol's *Christmas Eve*. He had sometimes incorporated folk tunes in symphonic works, but these things had never seemed central to his musical thinking, which remained in essence a Russified version of western conventions. It's true that in the Fifth and especially Sixth Symphonies those conventions are to some extent turned on their head. Tchaikovsky did not understand symphonic music in the organic, dialectical sense of Brahms, in whose music he found 'something dry and cold that alienates my heart'.[4] For him, thematic material had something like a flesh-and-blood existence, and his typical way of developing it was to treat it as a creature to whom things happened, rather than as a concept to be dismantled, investigated then reassembled. In the first movement of the Fifth Symphony, after the opening motto theme, the main Allegro sets out on a journey in the course of which there are various encounters and events but not much argument. The first movement of the

'Pathétique' is a kind of music theatre in a series of short scenes divided by metaphorical curtains. It is a dramatic, not strictly a symphonic, form; and throughout there is a strong feeling of personal experience, a post-Byronic, post-*Manfred* emotional history, ending in catastrophe in an astonishing Adagio finale. It was inevitable that, when the composer died a few days after conducting the first performance, the symphony would be seen as autobiography, even as a suicide note. But intending suicides do not as a rule produce finished work of this quality; depression saps the concentration. The 'Pathétique' is a tragic masterpiece in the spirit of *Hamlet*, on which Tchaikovsky had recently written a superb fantasy-overture tone poem.

While Tchaikovsky's symphonies have sometimes been dismissed by earnest critics as ballet music, his ballets were criticised in his own time as too symphonic. *Swan Lake* had already in 1877 introduced a degree of musical and dramatic intensity that seriously disconcerted Russian audiences used to regarding ballet as frothy entertainment, and not much had changed by 1890. Even the Imperial Ballet, under the French *maître de ballet*, Marius Petipa, had generally treated the music as of secondary importance. There was an official post of Ballet Composer, occupied most recently by Ludwig Minkus, whose job it was to provide danceable, not too intrusive music for the lavish dance spectacles that were the stock-in-trade of the Imperial Theatres. Into this carefree world, Tchaikovsky's *Sleeping Beauty* stepped in January 1890 like a philosopher into a game of charades, not only in the grandeur and dramatic weight of the music, but in its sheer quality, which compelled attention that had habitually been directed elsewhere. The audience at the first night seems to have responded coolly, and even the Tsar, a Tchaikovsky fan, could only muster a 'Very nice!' Then three years later, at Christmas 1892, *The Nutcracker*, a ballet about children if not a children's ballet, was greeted with enthusiasm by the audience but with a certain bafflement by the press. Perhaps unhelpfully, it was presented as a double bill with the composer's one-act opera *Iolanta*, a charming but dramatically slow-moving piece not calculated to appeal to ballet lovers.

The popularity of these two ballets, as of some other Tchaikovsky scores, has tended to work against their standing as great music, but really it speaks for it. More or less single-handed they transformed a musically trivial plastic art into a kind of *Gesamtkunstwerk*, a total work of art that would soon help inspire two of the most exciting proto-modernist movements, *Mir iskusstva* and the Ballets Russes. The artist and stage designer Alexander Benois, a founder of both movements, was a balletomane who was eventually responsible for introducing Diaghilev to ballet as a serious art form. But he was also an opera-lover, and as thrilled by *The Queen of Spades* as by *The Sleeping Beauty*. For some reason, though, *The Queen of Spades* has never enjoyed the popularity of its companion ballets, and it has often proved hard to stage successfully, perhaps because of its awkward mixture of realism and the fantastic.

Hermann, a German officer in the Russian guards at the time of Catherine the Great, is in love with a girl he has seen but not met, who turns out to be Lisa, the granddaughter of an old countess. Another guards officer, Count Tomsky, tells a story of the countess as a beautiful young woman in Paris who was addicted to gambling, lost all her money at faro, but was told a secret of three cards which, if she called them in the right order, would unfailingly win. She had told the secret to two lovers, but then learnt that a third man would come and extract the secret by force, and she would die. Hearing this tale, Hermann becomes obsessed with the secret of the cards, and cynically uses Lisa's passion for him, which he has himself aroused, to gain entry to the old woman's chambers. He tries unsuccessfully to force the secret out of her, but she dies without revealing it. Later, however, he is visited by her ghost, who now names the three cards and says they will win if he marries Lisa. The lovers meet by the canal, but Hermann can think only of the cards, and Lisa, in despair, throws herself into the canal. At the tables, Hermann calls the three cards, but the third, instead of an ace, is the queen of spades, and at this moment the ghost of the countess reappears laughing at him. Hermann stabs himself.

Despite some problems of dramaturgy, *The Queen of Spades* is one of Tchaikovsky's most imaginative scores, and arguably his most powerful opera, for all the beauties of *Yevgeny Onegin*. The composer's biographer David Brown is critical of its lack of sympathetic characters, instancing Tatyana in *Onegin* as a counter-example. But while Lisa is certainly no Tatyana, she is hardly unsympathetic: her song to the night in the second scene sets up her awakened passion, which is then clinched in the powerful canal scene by music out of Tchaikovsky's very top drawer. It might be suggested, in fact, that all the characters in *The Queen of Spades* are sympathetic up to a point, even though Tchaikovsky is not in love with any of them. There is a vividness and intensity about the emotional atmosphere, which even invades the ball scene, and which is Tchaikovsky's own contribution to Pushkin's rather ironic little tale, where Lisa's affections are treated with a certain disdain, and she ends up marrying 'a very nice young man with a decent job somewhere or other'. Hermann goes mad and ends up in the Obukhov Hospital (room 17) muttering 'Three, seven, ace! Three, seven, queen!' at top speed, whereas Tchaikovsky has him begging forgiveness and apostrophising Lisa as he dies.

Tchaikovsky himself died in St Petersburg, but he remained, in a sense, a Moscow composer and a Moscow teacher. His own most gifted first-generation pupil, Sergey Taneyev, a child prodigy as a pianist, developed into precisely the kind of composer Stasov most despised, an assiduous student of counterpoint whose music is immaculately, painstakingly crafted, with barely a trace of conscious Russianism. The most famous thing today about Taneyev is that he was a close friend of Tolstoy, and that Tolstoy's wife Sonya was, probably unrequitedly, in love with him. But he was evidently a fine teacher, and his composition pupils included two very different composers, like him superb pianists, whose music, unlike his, has lasted: Sergey Rachmaninov and Alexander Skryabin.

Rachmaninov's career as a composer got off to a quick start. His First Piano Concerto dates from his graduation year (1891), and soon afterwards he wrote a one-act opera, *Aleko*, as a graduation exercise in composition, staged with modest success at the Bolshoi in May 1893. His style at this time was very much under Tchaikovsky's influence but with added ingredients, of which the most important was Russian Orthodox chant. The First Symphony of 1895 is saturated with chant motifs, and melodic shapes of this kind remained typical of Rachmaninov, even in the soulful lyrical style for which he became most famous. The main first movement themes of both the Second and Third Piano Concertos, much of the beautiful if somewhat sprawling Second Symphony, and the symphonic poem *Ostrov myortvïkh* (*The Isle of the Dead*), all have Orthodox chant in their ancestry, and much later he would set the Liturgy of St John Chrysostom (the standard daily liturgy of the Orthodox Church, previously also set by Tchaikovsky), and the All-night Vigil, both for unaccompanied choir.

But for all its promising start, his career soon ran into the quicksand. The St Petersburg premiere of the First Symphony in 1897 was savaged by the critics, notably César Cui, who described it as 'a programme symphony on the Seven Plagues of Egypt'[5] (it seems to have been atrociously played under Glazunov, who was said to be drunk). Thereafter Rachmaninov, badly scarred, wrote nothing for three years, but then, after consultations with a psychiatrist, returned to composition and wrote his C minor Piano Concerto, a much more amenable work with a strong lyrical thread and a big finale tune, in the manner of Tchaikovsky's first concerto. From then on he settled into this highly personal, somewhat morose form of late romanticism until his life, like that of the Russian aristocracy as a whole, was shattered by the Bolshevik revolution. At the end of 1917 he left Russia with his family, and for almost a decade composed no music at all.

The creative silence after 1917 perhaps suggests the troubles of exile as much as any particular stylistic crisis. Like most refugees from the revolutions of that year, Rachmaninov had left with few belongings and very little money, and his first concern was how to earn his keep. The obvious recourse was to tour as a virtuoso pianist. In any case, he wrote nothing new until 1926, when he completed a fourth concerto and a set of three Russian choruses; and after the failure of the concerto he went silent again until 1931, when he produced a set of piano variations on Corelli's 'La Follia', followed by the *Rhapsody on a Theme of Paganini* in 1934 and two big orchestral works, the Third Symphony (1936) and the *Symphonic Dances* (1940). The rhapsody, actually a non-stop set of variations on Paganini's well-known Caprice No. 24, is a minor masterpiece whose only concession to modernity is a certain mechanical dryness in the pianism, and a touch of diabolism in the form of the Dies Irae chant, which runs through the work as a counter-thread, alleviated by brief passages of reflection and the restrained tenderness of the D flat major variation No. 18. Whether the arms-length emotion of this music reflects some awareness that the old passion would no longer wash, or simply the exile's reluctance to give too much of himself, the result is a refreshing illustration of the possibilities of renewal in even the most jaded musical language.

Rachmaninov's fellow Taneyev pupil was a pianist and composer of a very different cut but of equal calibre. Skryabin's mother had died when he was a year old, and the boy was brought up, and mollycoddled, by his two grandmothers and a doting but dominating maiden aunt. Whatever the effect of this rather peculiar childhood, Skryabin remained delicate, effete and profoundly self-centred for the rest of his life. At the Moscow Conservatoire his playing was noted for its refinement, and the music he wrote at the time confirms that quality, along with a certain needlepoint sensuality that also seems to have come out in his behaviour towards young girls (he lost his job at St Catherine's School in 1903 after seducing one of the pupils). It may also have helped create a susceptibility to the more extreme manifestations of Silver Age spirituality, particularly theosophy, which he encountered in Brussels in 1905 and which he reprocessed in his own way into an idea for what he called the *Mysterium*, a vast multimedia work designed to bring about the regeneration of the entire human race, and intended to be performed in a temple at Darjeeling against the backcloth of the Himalayas. Unfortunately for the human race, he died in 1915 of septicaemia from a boil on his upper lip, before this interesting project could be realised.

Nearly all Skryabin's music is for or with piano. Early on, the list looks, and to some extent the music sounds, Chopinesque with hints of Liszt: waltzes and mazurkas, impromptus, studies, preludes, music of exquisite delicacy, beautifully composed for the instrument, and of an increasingly distinctive melodic and harmonic character. Then soon after the turn of the century a note of experimentation comes in, particularly in the harmony, but also in the treatment of form, which becomes more and more concentrated, especially the sonatas, which from No. 5 onwards are single-movement works of increasing density. Skryabin begins to explore certain types of dissonant chords for their own sake, mostly textbook chords with altered notes, but treated as static 'fields' rather than components of normal harmonic progressions. (He once said: 'One must be able to walk all round a chord.'⁶) The idea is not unlike Debussy's way with chords taken out of context, but the results are very different and gradually lead Skryabin, in the last three or four of his ten sonatas, to something close to atonality. The process is buttressed by two orchestral works, the *Poème de l'extase* (1905–8) and *Prometheus* (1910), which has an important piano part, and also a part for colour keyboard, fulfilling another of Skryabin's part-mystical enthusiasms, the association between sounds and colours, seldom realised in performance.

Skryabin is an immeasurably better and more interesting composer than his survival on the fringes of the piano repertoire and his reputation as a mad mystic might suggest. But for the revolution, his music would surely have provided a bridge from romanticism to some kind of coherent modernism; there were signs of something of the kind in Soviet music of the early twenties, notably in the work of Nikolay Roslavets. But that was quickly snuffed out.

Wagner's final legacy to European music of the *fin de siècle* was to the poor benighted British, who still by the 1890s had produced no composer of even vaguely international standing since Sterndale Bennett. London concert life still drifted along in the long shadow of Mendelssohn. The most successful British composer of the seventies and eighties was Arthur Sullivan, but his success came mainly in the Savoy operettas with W. S. Gilbert, and not a note of his concert or operatic music survives in the modern repertoire otherwise. Recent revivals have shown that composers like Alexander Mackenzie could write with polish and a certain elegant charm; but this is not a big recommendation for the best music of an epoch. Something in the Victorian air smothered any kind of musical individuality, and certainly any striking innovation. Composers, like English gentlemen, were expected to conform to the standards of the drawing room and the dinner table, where the discussion of sex, religion, politics or almost anything of intellectual substance was outlawed. It was an attitude that tended to restrict the profession to competent dullards. And this background proved an inhibition also on intellectually better equipped composers such as Hubert Parry and Charles Villiers Stanford, who stand out above their eighties contemporaries like Glastonbury Tor above the Somerset Levels. Yet even their music has hardly survived outside the Anglican church, apart from a few part-songs and, in Parry's case, the deathless 'Jerusalem'.

Stanford, a Dublin-born Protestant who became Professor of Music at Cambridge University and a composition professor at the Royal College of Music, composed a large body of choral and orchestral music, including seven symphonies, well made but rather too indebted to Brahms, several concertos and a series of Irish Rhapsodies, as well as eight or nine operas which, curiously, had more success in Germany than at home. A lot of this has now been recorded but still seldom figures in concert programmes and never on opera schedules. By contrast, Stanford's church music remains a pillar of the Anglican liturgy, towering above the other nineteenth-century repertoire which cathedral organists tend to favour because it has loud accompaniments that are fun to play and conceal rough edges in the singing. Parry is in some ways a more interesting case, not least because he was an obsessive Wagnerian at a time when Wagner was only slowly becoming acceptable in London circles. The early cantata *Prometheus Unbound* (1880) shows a definite influence, and the later choral and orchestral music (including four symphonies and a number of sacred and secular cantatas) at least display an enriched harmonic palette, even if they hardly upset any musical apple-carts. Perhaps the best of both Stanford and Parry is in the modest field of the unaccompanied motet: Stanford's three Latin motets of 1905 ('Justorum animae', 'Coelos ascendit hodie' and 'Beati quorum'), and Parry's *Songs of Farewell* (1916–18), not groundbreaking masterpieces but perfect in their way.

In this flat, muddy landscape, there arrived in the 1890s a no longer particularly young composer from the Three Choirs city of Worcester who owed nothing to the London or Oxbridge musical establishments, had not been to a public school or a university, and as a cradle Catholic was strictly an outsider in anything to do with the established Anglican church. Edward Elgar's father was an Anglican-if-required piano tuner, violinist and keyboard player who happened to have taken a job as organist at St George's Catholic church in Worcester, as a result of which his more religious wife converted and brought up all her seven children as Catholics. Young Edward had never studied music formally, but picked it up in the organ loft and in the music shop that his father opened when he was six. He learnt the violin well enough to play in the Three Choirs orchestra whenever the festival was in Worcester, and he conducted locally; in fact his entire musical background was local, working with amateur enthusiasts, choirs and chamber musicians, and writing music for them to play and sing. Success in the wider world came slowly and late. His *Froissart* overture was played at the 1890 Three Choirs Festival but made little progress elsewhere, and it was only with a series of big choral cantatas in the nineties that he began to establish a reputation as a superior exponent of a genre still mainly associated with provincial English festivals. The last of these, *Caractacus* (Leeds Festival, 1898), is a curious hybrid, part reflective, part narrative, full of potentially dramatic situations that, almost without exception, Elgar botches. What he emphatically does not botch is the choruses, many and varied, choruses of Britons, Druids and Druidesses, Soldiers, Maidens, Roman Citizens, mostly indistinguishable in terms of drama or character, but wonderfully varied in movement and texture, consistently inventive, superbly written for the voices, and throughout brilliantly orchestrated. A composer who could write like this, even one already in his forties, would surely soon break out of the provincial festival circuit.

Within a year he had done so, with an orchestral work he called *Variations on an Original Theme*, but which the world has ever since known as the 'Enigma Variations', thanks to a single word Elgar jotted over the main theme and a remark he made to the programme annotator for the first performance: 'The principal theme never appears, even as in some [recent] dramas . . . the chief character is never on the stage.'[7] He had gone on learning by listening. He had heard Hans Richter conduct in London on several occasions, music by Schumann, Brahms, Berlioz, Bruckner, above all Wagner. He had bought and studied Berlioz's treatise on orchestration. But it was Wagner that had excited him most. After hearing the Liebestod at a Crystal Palace concert in 1883, he noted in his programme: 'This is the finest thing of W's that I have heard up to the present. I shall never forget this.'[8] In 1892 he had attended the Bayreuth Festival, and heard *Tristan*, *Meistersinger* and *Parsifal* (for which he prepared with a painstaking study of the published vocal score). Many of the lessons he learnt are already apparent in the nineties cantatas, but they were to come out in full force in the oratorio he composed immediately after the 'Enigma Variations', a setting of Newman's poem about the mystical passage of a Catholic believer from death to eternal life, *The Dream of Gerontius*.

Gerontius could hardly have turned out the way it did without the Wagner model. The rich, through-composed design, the integrated texture, the leitmotifs, and the dramatic handling of an essentially reflective discourse, all show the effect of a close study of *Parsifal* in particular. Yet the music never sounds very Wagnerian. Its musical elements still descend essentially from the earlier choral works, especially the oratorio *The Light of Life* and the chorus writing in *King Olaf* and *Caractacus*. Something square-cut in the response to Newman's metric patterns and rhyme schemes still faintly recalls the solid Englishness of the earlier works; but the score never lapses into the stuffed-shirt absurdity of those works in their now-for-some-recitative moments. Everything is thought out in detail, the text setting is hypersensitive, the whole architecture expertly managed, the invention on a consistently high level. *Gerontius* may not be a perfect masterpiece, and of course it was at first regarded with great suspicion by the Anglican hierarchy; one bishop is supposed to have fumed that he would not let it into his cathedral. But it is beyond question the greatest choral work by an English composer since Purcell, in a field strewn with lifeless corpses. It got off to an uncertain start at its British premiere at the 1900 Birmingham Festival, but a Düsseldorf performance under Richter two years later established Elgar's reputation in Germany and drew praise from Strauss, who labelled him 'the first English progressive'.

Elgar tried again with the genre, but neither *The Apostles* (1903) nor *The Kingdom* (1906) was as successful in escaping from the blessed aura of the English oratorio, despite superb passages in both cases. Instead he fulfilled the promise of the 'Enigma Variations' in a brilliant series of large-scale orchestral works, starting with the A flat Symphony, which Richter conducted in Manchester in 1908, and continuing with the Violin Concerto, written for Fritz Kreisler and premiered by him at London's Queen's Hall in 1910. Both these works went swiftly round the world. They were followed by the E flat Symphony in 1911 and the symphonic study *Falstaff* in 1913. To what extent these great works proclaim their composer a 'progressive' might be disputed, bearing in mind that the competition included Schoenberg's early atonal scores, the *Five Pieces for Orchestra*, *Erwartung* and *Pierrot Lunaire*, Strauss's

Salome and *Elektra*, Mahler's Ninth Symphony and Stravinsky's *Rite of Spring*. Elgar probably in any case felt less than wholly sympathetic to these adventures on the edge of tonality. At the end of the war he composed a series of chamber works – a violin sonata and a string quartet, both in E minor, and a piano quintet in A minor – as well as the Cello Concerto, likewise in E minor, and thereafter wrote only occasional pieces and trivia until sketching a third symphony at the very end of his life. His late works in no way shirk the implications of post-Wagnerian harmony; but their finest, most moving passages equally accept the undiminished power of tonal harmony, and would be unthinkable without it.

Quite why a composer of Elgar's stature should suddenly materialise out of the fog of nineteenth-century English music is a hard question to answer. His unconventional background was doubtless a factor, and his early passion for Wagner will have helped, not in making his music Wagnerian, but in leading him to a detailed study of the complex scores of a supreme musical technician. Something similar might apply to his slightly younger contemporary, Frederick Delius, who arrived at his own level of mastery by an even more idiosyncratic route, though he did at least study for a couple of years in his mid-twenties at Leipzig Conservatory. Wagner was important to Delius as well. But perhaps in his case the crucial factor was that, though born in Bradford, he was ethnically German, his wool-merchant father having emigrated from Bielefeld in the late 1840s and married a Bielefeld girl in Bradford in 1856. Young Frederick had barely any contact with British musical institutions, including the church (he was a confirmed atheist), and in Leipzig his best musical friends were the Norwegian composers Grieg and Christian Sinding. For the last forty-five years of his life he lived in France.

Even Delius's admirers tend to characterise his music through the qualities it lacks. The influence of Wagner on its harmonic colourings is obvious, but the influence is in the sound more than the structure. There is something of Debussy's harmonic sampling, but without his precision of effect. Delius's harmonies drift and his melodies simply ride on top, like leaves on the wind. His text setting ignores the individual properties of the words, and instead uses them to generate atmosphere, usually without creating clear-cut forms or, in his various operas, strong drama. Described like this, it all sounds hopeless. Yet Delius invented a highly personal and distinctive kind of beauty, perhaps limited in expressive range, but still something more than miniaturist. His style is admittedly best approached through his short orchestral pieces, works like *On Hearing the First Cuckoo in Spring* and *Summer Night on the River*, where the drifting chromatic and added-note harmonies still allow the melody to speak, and form is not a serious issue. But Delius could succeed on a larger scale in this style as well: for instance, in his beautiful choral setting of part of Whitman's *Sea Drift*, and in his best opera, *A Village Romeo and Juliet*, a kind of stage tone poem, more poetic than dramatic, but affecting in its way. Though in no sense a folk-song composer, he wrote memorable sets of variations on an English tune, *Brigg Fair*, and what he called an 'Old Slave Song' in the choral-orchestral *Appalachia*, without going in the slightest degree folksy in manner. The essence of all these works is a certain vision of lost landscape, a slightly dreamy once-upon-a-time nostalgia. Yet Delius was an admirer of Nietzsche, and his most ambitious concert work, *A Mass of Life*, is a setting in German of texts from *Also sprach Zarathustra* in which the dreamy unexpectedly leaps to its feet and proclaims 'O Du, meine Wille! Du Wende aller Not!' ('O Thou, my will! Thou dispeller of all need!') in loud, boisterous tones. How well Delius's style fits the role of *Jasager* on this scale is a matter of taste.

Certainly nothing could seem more remote from Delius in this or any other vein than the English Folk-Song Society, which opened its doors in 1898, and was the nearest musical parallel to the activities of the Arts and Crafts movement initiated in the 1850s by William Morris and Edward Burne-Jones. Morris, the single most important figure in the English movement, was a lifelong socialist whose passion for the revival of traditional crafts went hand in hand with an ideal of restoring the supposedly decent working conditions of old labour. Not all Morris's artistic associates shared his political views, but they were clearly reflected in the activities of such composers as Gustav Holst and Ralph Vaughan Williams, while Cecil Sharp, a founder member of the Folk-Song Society and the founder, with Maud Karpeles, of the English Folk Dance Society in 1911, had become a closet member of the left-wing Fabian Society after hearing Morris lecture in Cambridge in the early 1880s. Holst also became a Morrisite, at least in his commitment to the role of the amateur in music-making. He joined the socialist club based at Morris's Hammersmith home, Kelmscott House, and conducted the Hammersmith Socialist Choir. Vaughan Williams co-founded the Leith Hill Music Festival, a competitive event for amateur choirs, in 1905, and remained its chief conductor until 1953. In his mind (and in his book, *National Music*) there was an intimate connection between a people's folk music and its national soul, in the Herderian sense.

In Herder's day the idea of ethnic identity had been an individualising affair, a direct counter to the universalism of the Enlightenment, but by 1900 the idea had gone into reverse, and ethnicity, at least in the social activity of music-making, had become an expression of community, of shared experience, an Enlightenment for the common people. Holst and Vaughan Williams composed a body of work that satisfied this new ideal: good sturdy choral music based on, or at least suggesting an origin in, folk music. Vaughan Williams, like Sharp, collected on his own account, with a practical as much as scholarly intention. Unlike the Hungarian Bartók, who painstakingly documented and classified his folk songs and drew conclusions for his own work from their unusual scales and sometimes outlandish tunings, Vaughan Williams took a limited view of authenticity, retained the modes but corrected 'errors' of tuning and other oddities, on practical grounds. The *English Hymnal*, which he co-edited in 1906, and the *Oxford Book of Carols* of 1928 both include folk tunes arranged by him into singable form.

For Holst and Vaughan Williams, in their own more personal and larger-scale work, folk music and, more generally, the community ideal were passports to a music that would be modern without the esoterism of Strauss or Schoenberg, the stridency of Bartók or Stravinsky, or the refinement of Debussy. Vaughan Williams studied briefly in 1908 with Ravel (who was three years his junior), and the French influence is apparent in his music thereafter, in the song cycle *On Wenlock Edge*, in the *Pastoral Symphony*, and even as late as the Fifth Symphony of 1943. But there is a certain bluffness about much of this music, a kind of Henry V not-French Englishness, that never loses touch with the amateur world of Leith Hill and the *English Hymnal*. Holst, on the other hand, knew all about continental modernism. His most famous work, *The Planets*, as good as proves that he knew Debussy (*Nocturnes* and *La Mer*), Stravinsky (*The Rite of Spring*), Schoenberg (*Five Pieces for Orchestra*), Dukas (*L'Apprenti sorcier*), probably Skryabin (*Prometheus*) and Strauss (*Till Eulenspiegel* and *Don Quixote*), and his own style never entirely settled as a result, notwithstanding the individual splendour of his best music, *The Hymn of Jesus*, *Egdon Heath*, the *Choral Fantasia*, as well as *The Planets* itself.

The folk song revival, like cultural nationalism everywhere in the nineteenth century, was at heart a Romantic phenomenon. It came out of Herder's idea of cultural individualism, and it fed into the idealisation of the past; but it eventually helped turn that idealisation into a scientific project, at which point it arguably lost contact with romanticism and became an element of modernism. Works such as Stravinsky's *Rite of Spring* (1912), Vaughan Williams's *Pastoral Symphony* (1922) and Holst's *Egdon Heath* (1927) stand on the verge of this change, which only goes to show how hard it is to date cultural movements in general. By 1911 Bartók was already writing folk-song-based piano music in an uncompromising modern style, and even his *Fourteen Bagatelles* of 1908 prompted the modern-minded Busoni to remark: 'At last something really new.'

18

The Song Ends but the Melody Lingers On

The longer you look at a 'period' of anything, whether it's music, or revolutions, capitalism or empire (to borrow Eric Hobsbawm's three divisions of what he called the long nineteenth century), the harder it is to decide when it begins and ends. If romanticism is, in the broadest sense, a style, then it was still going strong in 1934, when Rachmaninov composed his *Paganini Rhapsody* and the Austrian Franz Schmidt's valedictory Fourth Symphony had its premiere in Vienna. And this is without considering film or pop music, a lot of which trades on what are still essentially nineteenth-century idioms and gestures.

The attempt to ditch romanticism in favour of one or another type of modernism in the years just before and after the First World War was a messy failure, in the sense that it tried to subvert history, which will always take its revenge. Schoenberg announcing in 1921 that in serialism he had made a discovery that would ensure the supremacy of German music for the next hundred years; Jean Cocteau demanding in 1918, 'Enough of clouds, waves, aquariums, ondines and perfumes of the night . . . we need a music with its feet on the ground, an everyday music');[1] Stravinsky insisting in 1924 that his Octet was 'a musical object' with a form 'influenced by the musical matter with which it is composed'.[2] These were remarks made from inside the whale, in Orwell's phrase, like Jonah cut off from the real world. Seventy years after his death, Schoenberg has yet to achieve repertory status with a single work later than his op. 4, *Verklärte Nacht*, composed in the nineteenth century and even that only marginally canonic. Stravinsky, it's true, has achieved popularity with a growing number of works which may plausibly be considered to express something, if only the real desire to be heard and liked.

The avant-garde was, it needs repeating, essentially a Romantic invention. There was the artist way out in front of his public, taking risks, braving the dangers of the unexpected on their behalf. Beethoven, Berlioz, Schumann, Liszt, Wagner, Musorgsky, Debussy: these were the avant-garde. Most other composers followed along at a safe distance, not deviating much from their predecessors, sometimes with notable results, more often not. Above all, the Romantic avant-gardist was an individual, his own man, possibly mad, almost certainly eccentric, and at least in part of his consciousness uninterested in what the world thought of him and his work. The avant-gardist of more recent times, by contrast, has been a kind of modernist clone, regurgitating and recycling the latest techniques of a select number of guru grandees, safe in the knowledge that, however good or bad their own music, they are in the swim and up to the minute. In the twenty-first century we have arrived at the curious situation where the best composers have had to look for worthwhile ways of composing in the spaces left between romanticism and modernism, a big enough space, in all conscience, but one full of uncertainty as to how it relates to its musical surroundings, its before and after, and its present audience.

Some such feeling was already in the air in 1918, and it may have been why certain major composers, and some minor, lost heart and more or less stopped writing. A particular case was the American composer Charles Ives, who according to his beautifully named wife Harmony, 'came downstairs one day with tears in his eyes and said he couldn't seem to compose any more – nothing went well – nothing sounded right'.[3] That was early in 1927 when he was fifty-two, and he lived another twenty-seven years, revising but hardly composing at all. Ives is an unusual case because his music was in no straightforward sense Romantic. He was a radical whose style was nevertheless based on nineteenth-century models. He is best described as an experimentalist. He loved the sheer experience of sound, whether

it was Beethoven symphonies or revivalist hymns, and he was fascinated by chance concatenations of sounds, and by chaotic soundscapes
that included simple or familiar musical elements. Yet behind it all
– behind the densely textured impressionism of *Three Places in New
England*, the complex near-atonal harmony of parts of the *Concord
Sonata*, and the glorious sonic maelstrom of the second movement of
the Fourth Symphony – there remained an essentially Romantic sensibility. Ives composed plenty of music, including more than a hundred
songs and a good deal of chamber and ensemble music, in which the
Romantic or sentimental dimension is clear, even when he smuggles
deviant elements, irrational harmonies or rhythms or even pitch structures into the underlying idiom. His music recalls Schlegel's remark,
quoted in Chapter 1, about Romantic poetry being 'the expression of a
secret longing for the chaos which is perpetually striving for new and
marvellous births'. Ives would probably have found that way of putting
it too highfalutin, but it describes well his sheer delight in grabbing
music by the roots and shaking it until all its possibilities tumble out.

One composer who found a completely individual path through
these dilemmas was one whose music was practically unknown in
the west until after the First World War, the Czech composer Leoš
Janáček. Janáček, a Moravian from Hukvaldy, near the Slovak border, was only thirteen years younger than Dvořák, whom he got to
know well in the 1880s, and whose music influenced his own early
work; but until he was fifty he remained a provincial figure, respected
in the Moravian capital, Brno, as a teacher, administrator and composer, especially of works for chorus, but little known elsewhere, even
in Prague. His breakthrough came with his third opera, *Jenůfa*, which
was successfully staged in Brno in 1904 but had been in hand, on and
off, for ten years before that. Its spread was slow. Prague saw it first in
1916, and then only in a partial adaptation by the conductor, Karel
Kovařovic. Nearly all Janáček's repertory works, including four or five
more operas, the dramatic song cycle *The Diary of One Who Vanished*,
the *Glagolitic Mass*, a pair of string quartets, and the Sinfonietta, were

written between then and his death aged seventy-four in 1928.

Everything about Janáček's music proclaims its Czechness, but it is a Czechness fed from fresh sources, especially Moravian folk music and also patterns of speech, which Janáček made a habit of recording in a notebook as occasion arose. *Jenůfa* is still essentially a folk opera in the tradition of Smetana and Dvořák, but with a certain roughness that lends it an authenticity which, perversely, it may partly have learnt from Italian *verismo*. The dramatic treatment, though, is devoid of crude melodrama. Instead it absorbs violent and even tragic incident into a psychologically truthful train of events ending with a moving reconciliation between Jenůfa herself and Laca (the half-brother of her wastrel former lover, Števa), whom she has previously rejected but who stands by her when she is deserted by the villagers after the murder of her baby son.

Musically, *Jenůfa* initiates a style that seems both new and individual, largely tonal but with modal touches and a highly personal kind of discourse, abrupt, laconic and fast-moving but with tender moments that take us beneath the often tortured surface of the relationships. Janáček's continuities are intriguingly unlike anything in German or Italian music, influenced perhaps, though certainly not audibly, by Debussy. Short, crisp, sometimes punchy figures will alternate, interrupting one another like men arguing in a pub, but then suddenly overlaid with broad, lyrical melody that seems to ignore or at least regret the scrum of musical activity below. In the later operas Janáček evolved a method that on paper sounds like Wagner's theory of orchestral motifs originating in the vocal line, but is not in the least Wagnerian in musical effect. The word-setting, especially from *Katya Kabanova* on, is derived from a kind of Moravian speech melody that the orchestra picks up and moulds into more complete phrases which constantly generate new versions of themselves to carry the action forward from scene to scene. The result is a wonderfully integrated discourse which can even tolerate the chattering exposition of legal niceties in the first act of *Věc Makropulos* (*The Makropulos Case*), and yet lends itself to the emotionally overwhelming climax of that same opera, where the 337-year-old heroine pours out the misery and emptiness of her long life, the result of swallowing an elixir in Prague at the court of the Emperor Rudolf II in about 1600.

By the end of the war romanticism was officially dead. Practically everything that the nineteenth century had stood for – the magic, the mystery, the madness, the dreams, the nightmares, the artist as god, the artist as outcast, nature, antiquity, folk tales, the chaos and the sublime: all this was out of the window. 'A dreamer', Cocteau announced, 'is invariably a bad poet.'[4] Music was now to be urban, practical, useful, dry, economical, with sharp corners, like a Le Corbusier house. Not that artists like Cocteau, or for that matter Le Corbusier, relinquished their right to tell everybody else what to do. But what they had to do now had a certain appearance of not being all that worth doing. What was the point of a music you could 'live in, as in a house', especially if the house was Le Corbusier's 'machine to live in' or one of the sixty-storey skyscrapers in which he proposed to incarcerate the citizens of his Ville Contemporaine? The truth is that these were merely slogans reflecting a horrified realisation that the world had been upended by the society that had also produced Strauss's *Elektra*, Nietzsche's *Zarathustra*, Huysmans' *À rebours*, and various other expressions of the will to power and the will to self-destruction. When Stravinsky wrote, about his Octet, 'I have excluded all sorts of nuances, which I have replaced by the play of [. . .] volumes,' he was striking a pose while misrepresenting the Octet, whose score contains as many nuances as any other work for several players performing from individual parts.[5]

The newest thing about such statements was that it was felt necessary to make them at all. Romantic music had evolved in new ways. Its cultivation of individual experience and feeling had brought about a previously unheard-of diversification of styles and methods, so that the average music-lover who finds it hard to distinguish Palestrina from Victoria, or Handel from Bach, can easily tell Berlioz from Schumann or Wagner from Verdi. But the modernism of 1920 was hard to understand as a continuation of any of these styles. On the contrary, it set out to be a denial of them all. And though some romanticism leaked into post-war music, the results tended to be sidelined, marginalised, not taken seriously. The idioms of romanticism flowed into various types of popular music, mingling with one another in a kind of technical mishmash on the part of talented and not so talented composers who have been mainly content to use up the stylistic residue, while the 'serious composers' of the age have pursued what had been the Romantic dream of perpetual renewal and constant originality, but through the medium of technique and method rather than style or quality of vision, until it suddenly dawned on many of them that nobody loved their music and that maybe the Romantics, with their swooning melodies and tonal harmony, had been right after all. The so-called neo-romanticism of the 1970s and 1980s was almost the most gruesome phase of modernism, in that it seemed to admit that the whole thing up to that time had been some kind of ghastly mistake, yet signally failed to produce anything either better or (not necessarily the same thing) more likeable.

What, in the end, does all this tell us about romanticism itself? Perhaps only that the term is protean; it has both specific and general meanings which in varying degrees interact. Romantic music both charms and dismays, often both in the same work. Classical music had its own version of this paradox, but tightly walled into a *lingua franca* that civilised such distinctions into a matter of nuances and tones of voice. In what we call Romantic music, the windows are flung open, and everything to do with style, form, even technique, is exposed to the emotional and intellectual weather, the impulses and preferences of the individual composer. Instead of channelling his feelings into the narrow mainstream of an agreed way of writing, he now allows – encourages – them to take control of the discourse, to manipulate it in their own way; and since it was a first principle of romanticism that the artist was the subject of his own work, it's hardly surprising that the work itself becomes all of a sudden wildly, unpredictably diverse, in range, manner, subject matter and, most problematically, technique.

Yet nineteenth-century music has furnished the twentieth and twenty-first century repertoire, with some help from earlier times, which says a lot for the ability of great artists to work within constraints that they themselves may officially deplore. In fact, some constraints are obviously necessary. The Romantic idea of style as an individual matter might have led to the wrong kind of chaos, might even have produced the kind of stylistic and technical anarchy that has reigned in twentieth-century music since the 1960s and that, on the one hand, has imposed on artists the need to reinvent their method every time they put pen to paper, and on the other has guaranteed that their audiences will often consist only of music critics, agents, publishers and the homeless. Romantic music cultivated individuality and originality, the first age to do so. But it never lost a sense of responsibility to its public and to its own traditions; and perhaps that helps explain why, although Romantic art originated in a desire on the part of writers, painters and composers to distance themselves from the facile, habit-formed appreciation of a new, moneyed bourgeoisie, it became, and has largely remained, the preferred art of that same bourgeoisie's grandchildren and great grandchildren.

Notes

Introduction A Difficult and Dangerous Undertaking

1 Quoted in David Charlton (ed.), *E. T. A. Hoffmann's Musical Writings* (Cambridge University Press, Cambridge, 1989), 236–8. All translations from this book are by Martyn Clarke, and are quoted by kind permission.

1 Longing for Chaos

1 Quoted in Anthony Thorlby (ed.), *The Romantic Movement*, trans. René Wellek (Longmans, London, 1966), 2.

2 Johann Gottfried Herder, 'Extract from a Correspondence on Ossian and the Songs of Ancient Peoples', trans. Joyce P. Crick, in H. B. Nisbet (ed.), *German Aesthetic and Literary Criticism* (Cambridge University Press, Cambridge, 1985), 161.

3 Jean-Jacques Rousseau, *Émile, ou de l'éducation* (Édition Garnier Frères, Paris, 1961), 358; my translation.

4 Quoted in Isaiah Berlin, *The Crooked Timber of Humanity* (Fontana Press, London, 1991), 229.

5 Quoted in Daniel Heartz, 'Empfindsamkeit', in *Grove Music Online* (Oxford University Press, 2001); my translation.

6 Charles Rosen, *The Classical Style* (Faber and Faber, London, 1972), 44.

7 C. P. E. Bach, *Essay on the True Art of Playing Keyboard Instruments*, trans. William J. Mitchell (Eulenburg, London, 1974), 152.

8 H. C. Robbins Landon, *Haydn: Chronicle and Works*, vol. 2: *Haydn at Eszterháza* (Thames and Hudson, London, 1978), 389.

9 Amanda Holden (ed.), *The Viking Opera Guide* (Viking, London, 1993), 695.

10 My translation.

2 A Young Rhinelander

1 William Wordsworth, 'The French Revolution as It Appeared to Enthusiasts at Its Commencement' (1804).

2 Letter of 1798 to Nikolaus Zmeskall von Domanovecz, in *The Letters of*

Beethoven, ed. and trans. Emily Anderson, vol. 1 (Macmillan, London, 1961), 32.

3 Modern performances and recordings have usually substituted the recitatives composed by Franz Lachner in the 1850s.

4 David Wyn Jones, *The Symphony in Beethoven's Vienna* (Cambridge University Press, Cambridge, 2006), 171–2.

5 Before the invention of valves in about 1815, horns had crooks of different lengths to enable them to play in different keys. But changing these crooks took time. With three horns at his disposal, Beethoven naturally uses them to make extra noise, most spectacularly in the trio section of the scherzo.

6 Berlin, *Crooked Timber of Humanity*, 226.

3 Pleasing the Crowd and Escaping It

1 E. T. A. Hoffmann, Review of Beethoven's Fifth Symphony (1810), in Charlton (ed.), *Hoffmann's Musical Writings*, 236–7.

2 William Wordsworth, *Lines Composed a Few Miles Above Tintern Abbey* (1798).

3 My translation.

4 Quoted in H. A. Korff, 'Kant Romanticized by Fichte', in Thorlby (ed.), *Romantic Movement*, 110–11.

5 Quoted in Charles Rosen, *The Romantic Generation* (HarperCollins, London, 1996), 50. Translation slightly adjusted.

6 My translations.

7 My translation.

8 Charlton (ed.), *Hoffmann's Musical Writings*, 82.

9 Charlton (ed.), *Hoffmann's Musical Writings*, 80.

4 Operas Grand and Grotesque

1 Charlton (ed.), *Hoffmann's Musical Writings*, 189, 190.

2 Oliver Strunk, *Source Readings in Music History*, vol. 5: *The Romantic Era* (Faber and Faber, London and Boston, 1981), 32–3.

3 Winton Dean, 'French Opera', in Gerald Abraham (ed.), *The New Oxford History of Music*, vol. 8: *The Age of Beethoven 1790–1830* (Oxford University Press, Oxford, 1982).

4 In its original form, *Faust* was a singspiel with dialogue. The version with recitatives that is now occasionally performed and recorded was made by Spohr in 1851.

5 Winton Dean, 'German Opera', in Abraham (ed.), *New Oxford History of Music*, vol. 8, 486.

NOTES TO PAGES 73–111

6 John Warrack, *German Opera, From the Beginnings to Wagner* (Cambridge University Press, Cambridge, 2001), 383.

7 Charlton (ed.), *Hoffmann's Musical Writings*, 259.

8 John Warrack, *Carl Maria von Weber* (Hamish Hamilton, London, 1968), 35.

9 Weber's biographer John Warrack exonerates him from deliberate fraud in this affair, but subsequent research, notably by Joachim Veit, has proved his guilt. See Michael C. Tusa, 'Weber, Carl Maria (Friedrich Ernst) von', in *Grove Music Online*.

10 Letter to Hans Georg Nägeli, quoted in *Carl Maria von Weber: Writings on Music*, ed. John Warrack, trans. Martin Cooper (Cambridge University Press, Cambridge, 1981), 15. Sadly, Weber's famous remark about the Seventh Symphony proving that Beethoven was 'ripe for the madhouse' was almost certainly an invention of Beethoven's first biographer, Anton Schindler.

11 Donald Francis Tovey, *Essays in Musical Analysis*, vol. 4: *Illustrative Music* (Oxford University Press, Oxford, 1937), 54.

12 Richard Wagner, *My Life*, trans. Andrew Gray (Cambridge University Press, Cambridge, 1983), 292.

5 Landscapes of the Heart and the Mind

1 Germaine de Staël, *De l'Allemagne*, vol. 1 (Garnier-Flammarion, Paris, 1968), 211–14; my translation.

2 E. Eugene Helm, rev. Günter Hartung, 'Reichardt, Johann Friedrich', in *Grove Music Online*.

3 G major to B major via the common note B, a so-called enharmonic change of a kind much favoured by Schubert.

4 See, for instance, Schiller's review-article on the poetry of Friedrich von Matthisson in the *Jenaer Allgemeine Literatur-Zeitung* (11–12 September 1794), quoted and discussed in Rosen, *The Romantic Generation*, 126–32.

5 Quoted in Dietrich Fischer-Dieskau, trans. Kenneth S. Whitton, *Schubert: A Biographical Study of His Songs* (Cassell, London, 1976), 258.

6 Geniuses, Young and not so Young

1 An untranslatable play on the word *marche*, which means 'walk' but also 'work', in the sense of function.

2 Richard Wagner, *Mein Leben* (Kindle edn), 63; my translation.

3 Carl Czerny, 'Recollections from My Life', trans. Ernest Sanders, *Musical Quarterly*, 42/3 (July 1956), 314–15.

4 Quoted by Berlioz in a letter of 18 February 1825 to his uncle. David Cairns, *Berlioz*, vol. 1: *The Making of an Artist, 1803–1832* (Allen Lane, London, 1999), 171.

5 *The Memoirs of Hector Berlioz*, ed. and trans. David Cairns (Gollancz, London, 1969), 104.

6 From *The Dramatic Works of Victor Hugo*, trans. George Burnham Ives (Little, Brown and Company, New York, 1909).

7 Berlioz, *Memoirs*, 131.

8 Alan Walker, *Franz Liszt*, vol. 1: *The Virtuoso Years, 1811–1847* (Faber and Faber, London, 1983), 154, note 26.

9 Alan Walker, *Fryderyk Chopin: A Life and Times* (Faber and Faber, London, 2018), 187.

10 *Florentinische Nächte*, in *The Works of Heinrich Heine*, vol. 1, trans. C. G. Leland (William Heinemann, London, 1906), 32.

11 Letter of 2 May 1832, in *Franz Liszt: Selected Letters*, ed. and trans. Adrian Williams (Clarendon Press, Oxford, 1998), 7.

12 Walker, *Franz Liszt*, vol. 1, 138. In general I am indebted to Walker's great three-volume biography for much of my information on Liszt's life.

13 Walker, *Franz Liszt*, vol. 1, 187.

7 Opera as Politics, Politics as Opera

1 Mary Ann Smart and Julian Budden, 'Donizetti, (Domenico) Gaetano' (Maria), in *Grove Music Online*.

2 Dean, 'German Opera', 113.

3 Ernest Newman, *The Life of Richard Wagner*, vol. 1: *1813–1848* (Alfred A. Knopf, New York, 1960), 259.

4 Matthias Brzoska, 'Meyerbeer [Beer], Giacomo [Jakob Liebmann Meyer]', in *Grove Music Online*.

5 This was pointed out by Laurent Pelly in a short film introducing the DVD of the Covent Garden production of Meyerbeer's opera that he directed in 2012.

6 Robert Schumann, *Gesammelte Schriften über Musik und Musiker*, vol. 1 (Georg Wigand's Verlag, Leipzig, 1871), 325; my translation.

7 Quoted in Andrew Porter, 'Les Huguenots', *Financial Times*, 9 January 1968.

8 Quoted in Cairns, *Berlioz*, vol. 2; *Servitude and Greatness, 1832–1869* (Allen Lane, London, 1999), 66.

9 Cairns, *Berlioz*, vol. 2, 49.

10 Letter to his father, quoted in Cairns, *Berlioz*, vol. 2, 132.

11 Franz Brendel, *Geschichte der Musik in Italien, Deutschland und Frankreich* (Adolph Schumann, Leipzig, 1903), 522; my translation.

12 English translation from *Hector Berlioz Werke, Serie 1, Band 3* (Breitkopf and Härtel, Leipzig, 1901), 165.

13 But not *Undine*, which was not performed after 1821 and remained unpublished until 1906.

14 Holden (ed.), *Viking Opera Guide*, 1178.

8 The Mendelssohn Set

1 Angela Mace Christian, 'Hensel [née Mendelssohn (-Bartholdy)], Fanny Cäcilie', in *Grove Music Online*.

2 See for instance Siegfried Kross, 'Brahms the symphonist', in *Brahms: Biographical, Documentary and Analytical Studies*, ed. Robert Pascal (Cambridge University Press, Cambridge, 1983), 130.

3 *Robert Schumann: Tagebücher*, vol. 1, ed. Georg Eismann (Stroemfeld/Roter Stern, Basel and Frankfurt am Main, 1971), 91, 94, 330.

4 Schumann certainly succeeded in veiling the *Abegg* variations in mystery. The editor of the *Tagebücher* gives biographical details of a certain Countess Meta Abegg, a pianist Schumann is supposed to have known in Heidelberg, and the editor of the complete edition of Schumann's piano works even gives her birthday. But Schumann's biographer John Worthen dismisses the whole dedication as a fantasy, and suggests that Meta is an anagram of Tema = Thema (= Thème varié – my contribution). See John Worthen, *Robert Schumann* (Yale University Press, New Haven and London, 2007), 43.

5 The most complete source of information on the influence of Jean Paul on *Papillons* and on Schumann in general is Eric Frederick Jensen, 'Explicating Jean Paul: Robert Schumann's Program for *Papillons*, Op.2', in *Nineteenth-Century Music*, 22/2 (Autumn 1998), 127–43.

6 Jean Paul, *Walt and Vult [Flegeljahre]*, trans. Eliza B. Lee, vol .2 (James Munroe, Boston, 1846), 294.

7 Schumann, *Tagebücher*, 339, 344; my translation.

8 Schumann, *Gesammelte Schriften*, vol. 1, 1.

9 Rosen, *The Romantic Generation*, 100.

10 Schumann, *Gesammelte Schriften*, vol. 1, 39; my translation.

11 Schumann, *Gesammelte Schriften*, vol. 2, 40–2; my translation.

9 The Nation Takes the Stand

1 The identification of Heinrich von Ofterdingen and Tannhäuser was not quite original. Wagner had found it in a paper by a Königsberg professor, C. T. L. Lucas: *Über den Krieg von Wartburg* (Gebrüdern Bornträger, Königsberg, 1838).

2 As it happens, the historical pope in question, Urban IV, was a Frenchman. But when in Rome . . .

3 Today *verbunkos* is regarded as an authentic Hungarian style that had been adapted by gypsy musicians, then readapted by composers of concert music. The word itself is a Magyarisation of the German *Werbung* (recruitment), the style having supposedly originated in music associated with the recruitment of Hungarians for the Austrian army.

4 Schumann, *Gesammelte Schriften*, vol. 2, 360–1; my translation.

5 Private memo, quoted in Daniel M. Grimley, 'Berwald, Franz', in *Grove Music Online*.

6 Quoted in Clive Brown, 'Robert Schumann', in Holden (ed.), *Viking Opera Guide*, 967.

7 Quoted in Alan Walker (ed.), *Robert Schumann: The Man and his Music* (Barrie and Jenkins, London, 1972), 279.

8 His sole contribution to the upheaval seems to have been the composition of a set of marches (op. 76), one of which was known locally as the 'Barricades March' (see Newman, *The Life of Richard Wagner*, vol. 2, 62).

9 Including by the present author in a regrettable early book on Schumann's songs (Cassell, London, 1971), and by Eric Sams in his *The Songs of Robert Schumann* (Methuen, London, 1969).

10 New Paths, Different Directions

1 Schumann, *Gesammelte Schriften*, vol. 2, 95; my translation.

2 Schumann, *Gesammelte Schriften*, vol. 2, 207; my translation.

3 Walker, *Franz Liszt*, vol. 1, 286–7.

4 Walker, 'Liszt, Franz', in *Grove Music Online*. Elisavetgrad is now Kropyvnytsky.

5 Albert Goldman and Evert Sprinchorn (eds), *Wagner on Music and Drama* (E. P. Dutton, New York, 1964), 69. The anthology uses the translations of W. Ashton Ellis.

6 Newman, *The Life of Richard Wagner*, vol. 2, 7.

7 Wagner, *Mein Leben*, 472; my translation.

8 Quoted in Jürgen Kühnel, 'The Prose Writings', in Ulrich Müller and Peter Wapnewski (eds), *The Wagner Handbook* (Harvard University Press, Cambridge, Mass, 1992), 583.

9 Kühnel, 'The Prose Writings', 590.

10 Letter of 14 September 1850 to Ernst Benedikt Kietz, *Richard Wagner: Sämmtliche Briefe*, vol. 3 (VEB Deutscher Verlag für Musik, Leipzig, 1983), 404–5; my translation.

11 They were named by Hans von Wolzogen in a guide published in 1876 for the first Bayreuth Festival. Wolzogen seems also to have invented the generic term.

12 Ernest Newman, *The Wagner Operas* (*Wagner Nights*) (Putnam, London, 1961), 192.

13 Letter of 16 December 1856, in *Correspondence of Wagner and Liszt*, vol. 2, ed. and trans. Francis Hueffer (Haskell House, New York, 1969), 174.

14 'On the Term "Music Drama"' (1872), quoted in Arthur Groos (ed.), *Richard Wagner: Tristan und Isolde* (Cambridge University Press, Cambridge, 2011), 69–70.

15 Barry Millington, *Wagner* (J. M. Dent, London, 1984), 64.

16 Letter of 16 December 1854, in Goldman and Sprinchorn, *Wagner on Music and Drama*, 272.

17 Quoted in Newman, *Wagner Operas*, 193. The translation is by W. Ashton Ellis.

18 Eduard Hanslick, *The Beautiful in Music*, trans. Gustav Cohen (Novello, Ewer and Co., London and New York, 1891), 70.

19 The Altenburg was not Liszt's official address, as certain elements of Weimar society would not have accepted his liaison with Carolyne, who did live there. He officially lived at the Erbprinz hotel. See Hugh Macdonald, *Music in 1853: The Biography of a Year* (Boydell, Woodbridge, 2012), for these and many other details of Brahms's tour.

20 Macdonald, *Music in 1853*, 39, wonders whether Brahms truly slept or was merely transported.

21 Strunk, *Source Readings*, vol. 5: *The Romantic Era*, 104–5.

22 Richard Wagner, 'Über Franz Liszt's symphonische Dichtungen', in *Richard Wagner's Prose Works*, vol. 3, ed. and trans. W. Ashton Ellis (Keegan Paul, London, 1894).

11 The Nation Speaks

1 Gabriele Baldini, *The Story of Giuseppe Verdi*, trans. Roger Parker (Cambridge University Press, Cambridge, 1980), 210.

2 Quoted in David Kimbell, 'Giuseppe Verdi', in Holden (ed.), *Viking Opera Guide*, 1142.

3 Spohr's *Faust*, as we saw, was not based on Goethe; the Berlioz and Schumann settings were not intended for the theatre.

4 Berlioz, *Memoirs*, 31.

5 Berlioz, *Memoirs*, 32.

6 Berlioz, *Memoirs*, 468.

7 Gareth Stedman Jones, *Karl Marx* (Penguin, London, 2017), 407.

8 Letter of 11/23 January 1867, in Edward Garden, *Balakirev: A Critical Study of His Life and Music* (Faber and Faber, London, 1967), 73.

9 Catherine succeeded her half-German husband, Peter III, in whose death in 1762 she was possibly implicated.

10 Richard Taruskin, *Defining Russia Musically* (Princeton and Oxford, Princeton University Press, 1997), 29.

11 Quoted in Stuart Campbell (ed. and trans.), *Russians on Russian Music, 1830–1880* (Cambridge University Press, Cambridge, 1994), 74.

12 Letter of 1 June 1876 to Lyubov Karmalina, quoted in Stephen Walsh, *Musorgsky and His Circle* (Faber and Faber, London, 2013), 343.

13 In the play she commits suicide.

14 Letter to Sergey Kruglikov, quoted in Richard Taruskin, *Stravinsky and the Russian Traditions* (Oxford University Press, Oxford, 1996), 33, author's emphases. Nikolai Lodïzhensky was a *Kuchka* hanger-on who composed a few songs before entering the diplomatic service.

12 The Road to Rome, and to Munich

1 Letter of 25 December 1861 to his daughter Blandine, in Liszt, *Selected Letters*, 567.

2 Charlton (ed.), *Hoffmann's Musical Writings*, 357.

3 Wagner, *Mein Leben*, 890; my translation. The misfortune in Wagner's case was the usual one of pennilessness; Cosima's was her marriage to the respected but unloved Bülow.

13 Bayreuth: Its Friends and Its Enemies

1 Friedrich Nietzsche, *Ecce Homo*, quoted in Bryan Magee, *Wagner and Philosophy* (Allen Lane, London, 2000), 310–11.

2 Quoted in Magee, *Wagner and Philosophy*, 310.

3 The Grail is the chalice in which Christ's blood was preserved from the wound dealt Him on the Cross by the Roman soldier Longinus' spear.

4 Quoted in Magee, *Wagner and Philosophy*, 325.

5 Frederic Spotts, *Bayreuth: A History of the Wagner Festival* (Yale University Press, New Haven and London, 1994) 130.

6 Letter of 28 March 1870, in Styra Avins (ed. and trans.), *Johannes Brahms: Life and Letters* (Oxford University Press, Oxford, 1997), 404.

7 Richard Specht, *Johannes Brahms: Leben und Werk eines deutschen Meisters* (Avalun-Verlag, Hellerau, 1928), 286; my translation.

8 Specht, *Johannes Brahms*, 165; my translation.

9 Klaus Döge, 'Dvořák, Antonín', in *Grove Music Online*.

10 See Michael Beckerman, 'The Master's Little Joke: Antonín Dvořák and the Mask of Nation', in Beckerman (ed.), *Dvořák and His World* (Princeton University Press, Princeton, 1993), 142–5, for an expert discussion of this matter. Dvořák published three sets of *Moravian Duets*, opp. 20, 28 and 39. Which ones Brahms saw is not entirely clear.

11 Leon Botstein, 'Reversing the Critical Tradition: Innovation, Modernity and Ideology in the Work and Career of Antonín Dvořák', in Beckerman (ed.) *Dvořák and His World*, 41.

12 Quoted by David Beveridge, in 'Dvořák and Brahms: A Chronicle, an Interpretation', in Beckerman (ed.) *Dvořák and His World*, 82.

13 Quoted by Botstein in 'Reversing the Critical Tradition', 14.

14 Erwin Doernberg, *The Life and Symphonies of Anton Bruckner* (Barrie and Rockliff, London, 1960), 88–9.

14 Ars Gallica, Ars Veritatis

1 Alistair Horne, *The Fall of Paris: The Siege and the Commune 1870–1871* (Penguin, London, 1981), 320.

2 Magee, *Wagner and Philosophy*, 327; Friedrich Nietzsche, *Der Fall Wagner* (C. G. Naumann, Leipzig, 1895), 13–14; my translation.

3 Claude Debussy, *Monsieur Croche et autres écrits*, ed. François Lesure (Gallimard, Paris, 1987), 225.

4 Martin Cooper, *French Music from the Death of Berlioz to the Death of Fauré* (Oxford University Press, London, 1951), 188.

5 Quoted in Cooper, *French Music*, 56.

6 Cooper, *French Music*, 42.

7 Igor Stravinsky and Robert Craft, *Conversations with Igor Stravinsky* (Faber and Faber, London, 1959), 28.

8 Cooper, *French Music*, 23.

9 Specifically Joseph Kerman in *Opera as Drama* (Vintage, New York, 1959), 258.

10 Quoted in Mosco Carner, *Puccini* (Gerald Duckworth, London, 1958), 160.

15 Clouds, Forests and More Clouds

1 Erik Tawaststjerna, *Sibelius*, vol. 2, trans. Robert Layton (Faber and Faber, London, 1986), 76–7.
2 Koechlin, *Gabriel Fauré*, trans. Leslie Orrey (Dennis Dobson, London, [1946]), 15.
3 Stephen Walsh, *Debussy: A Painter in Sound* (Faber and Faber, London, 2018), 76. An excessively free translation of the whole conversation is in Edward Lockspeiser, *Debussy: His Life and Mind*, vol. 1 (Cassell, London, 1962), 204–8.
4 Letter of 2 October 1893, in Debussy, *Correspondance*, ed. François Lesure (Gallimard, Paris, 2005), 161; my translation. See also *Debussy Letters: 1872–1918*, ed. François Lesure and Roger Nichols (Faber and Faber, London, 1987), 56, for another translation.
5 Letter of February [?] 1905, in Debussy, *Correspondance*, 887.

16 The Shadow of Bayreuth

1 Frank Walker, *Hugo Wolf* (J. M. Dent, London, 1968), 183, 176.
2 Walker, *Hugo Wolf*, 202.
3 Tawaststjerna, *Sibelius*, vol. 2, 76–7.
4 The tune is more or less that of the English song 'The more we are together'.
5 Letter to Max Marschalk, quoted in Deryck Cooke, *Gustav Mahler* (Faber Music, London, 1980), 53.
6 Letter to Richard Batka, quoted in Cooke, *Gustav Mahler*, 63.
7 *Testament of Music: Essays and Papers by Ernest Newman*, ed. Herbert van Thal (Putnam, London, 1962), 118.
8 Jacques Maritain, *Art et scolastique* (Librairie de l'Art Catholique, Paris, 1920), 3; my translation.
9 Quoted in Charles Rosen, *Schoenberg* (Fontana/Collins, Glasgow, 1976), 10.

17 A Russian Autocrat and an English Misfit

1 Marina Frolova-Walker, 'Rimsky-Korsakov family: Nikolay Andreyevich Rimsky-Korsakov', in *Grove Music Online*.
2 Bearing in mind that, because of the Old Style calendar, Easter and every date connected with it are usually later in Russia.
3 According to his brother Modest, he died of cholera after drinking unboiled water during an epidemic. A more recent theory is that he committed suicide by arsenic poisoning on instruction from the School of Jurisprudence, to avoid

a scandal arising out of his homosexual relationship with the nephew of a high-ranking aristocrat. There is no hard evidence for either theory.

4 David Brown, *Tchaikovsky: The Final Years* (W. W. Norton, New York and London, 1991), 177.

5 Geoffrey Norris, 'Rachmaninoff, Serge', in *Grove Music Online*.

6 Quoted in Simon Nicholls, 'Introduction', in Simon Nicholls and Michael Pushkin (eds and trans), *The Notebooks of Alexander Skryabin* (Oxford University Press, Oxford, 2018), 6.

7 Jerrold Northrop Moore, *Edward Elgar: A Creative Life* (Oxford University Press, Oxford, 1984), 270.

8 Moore, *Edward Elgar*, 99.

18 The Song Ends but the Melody Lingers On

1 Jean Cocteau, *Le Coq et l'arlequin* (Stock/Musique, Paris, 1979), 61; my translation.

2 'Some Ideas about my Octuor', reprinted in Eric Walter White, *Stravinsky: The Composer and His Works* (Faber and Faber, London, 1979), 574–7. Its original first publication was in English.

3 J. Peter Burkholder, James B. Sinclair and Gayle Sherwood Magee, 'Ives, Charles', in *Grove Music Online*.

4 Cocteau, *Le Coq et l'arlequin*, 52; my translation.

5 'Some Ideas about my Octuor', 574.

Illustrations

16 Richard Wagner (Sueddeutsche Zeitung Photo/Alamy Stock Photo)

17 Balakirev Circle, 1871 (© RIA Novosti/Lebrecht Music & Arts)

18 Mahler in Toblach, 1907 (Internationale Gustav Mahler Gesellschaft)

19 Hugo Wolf, *c.*1895 (Photo by ullstein bild/ullstein bild via Getty Images)

20 Sibelius, 1915 (Photo by DeAgostini/Getty Images)

21 Debussy, 1902 (Lebrecht Music Arts / Bridgeman Images)

Index

Titles of works are listed under the name of the composer. Initial articles (A, An, The, Der, Das, Le, Il, etc.) are ignored for the purpose of alphabetisation.

INDEX

Mascagni, Pietro (1863–1945): compositional characteristics 314; *Cavalleria rusticana* 312, 313, 314–15

Massenet, Jules (1842–1912) 293, 307–8

Mattei, Stanislao 131, 133

Mayr, Simon (1763–1845) 65, 130, 132

Méhul, Étienne (1763–1817): *Euphrosine* 62; *Héléna* 32; *Mélidore et Phrosine* 62

mélodrame (accompanied speech) 32

Mendelssohn, Abraham 153, 154

Mendelssohn, Fanny (1805–47): compositional characteristics 155–6; influences 156; life 154–5, 157, 203, 234; *Das Jahr* 155–6; other works 155

Mendelssohn, Felix (1809–47): character 155; compositional characteristics 157–9, 161, 163; contemporary responses to 163; influence on other composers 156, 256; influences 158, 159, 162–3; life 153, 154–5, 157, 158, 159, 161, 163, 172, 189, 190, 202–3; romanticism 158; WORKS: CHAMBER: piano trios 160; string octet 153, 157, 158; string quartets 157, 158, 160, 203; string quintet 157; CHORAL: *Elijah* 163, 192; *Die erste Walpurgisnacht* 162; *Lobgesang* 163; *O Haupt voll Blut und Wunden* 162; *St Paul* 162–3; CONCERTOS: E minor Violin Concerto 158; OPERA: *Die Hochzeit des Camacho* 157; ORCHESTRAL: concert overtures 157, 159, 160–1; early orchestral works 157; symphonies 158, 159, 160, 163; PIANO SOLO: *Lieder ohne Worte* 170; *Rondo capriccioso* 156; VOCAL: 'Frage' 158; OTHER WORKS 157

Mendès, Catulle 304–5

Mercadante, Saverio (1795–1870) 130, 185, 186

Meyerbeer, Giacomo (1791–1864): compositional characteristics 139–41; contemporary responses to 139, 140, 141; influence on other composers 138–9, 236; life 136, 137; supports Berlioz 142–3; supports Wagner 151; OPERA: *Il crociato in Egitto* 137; *L'Étoile du nord* 233; *Les Huguenots* 140–1; *Margherita d'Anjou* 137; *Le Prophète* 141; *Robert le diable* 69, 136, 137–9

Middle Ages, significance for Romantics 9–10, 53

Minkus, Ludwig (1826–1917) 373

Mir iskusstva movement 362, 374

modalism 286, 317, 333–4, 370, 390

modernism: advent of 340–1, 360, 364, 365–6, 374; and romanticism 365, 387, 388, 392

Moguchaya Kuchka group 247–8, 250, 253, 254, 255, 337 *see also* Balakirev; Borodin; Cui; Musorgsky; Rimsky-Korsakov

Moniuszko, Stanisław (1819–72), *Halka* 184–5

Montgeroult, Hélène de (1764–1836) 156

Moore, Thomas, *Paradise and the Peri* 195

Mörike, Eduard 343, 344, 345, 346, 347

Morris, William 384–5

Moscow Conservatoire 255, 377

Mosonyi, Mihály (1815–70) 259

motifs: leitmotif 62, 215, 218, 275, 279, 283, 382; transformation 221, 224, 241

Mozart, Wolfgang Amadeus (1756–91): compositional characteristics 17–19, 36, 89–90; contemporary responses to 2; influence on other composers 63–4, 158, 159; influences 18; life 25, 40, 42; romanticism 21–2; WORKS: LIEDER 90; OPERA: *The Abduction from the Seraglio* 18; *Così fan tutte* 19, 20–1, 22; *Don Giovanni* 19, 20, 21–2, 114; *Idomeneo* 18–19, 25; *The Magic Flute* 70, 159; *The Marriage of Figaro* 19–20, 22, 114; ORCHESTRAL: G minor Symphony, K. 183 17–18; other symphonies 18, 34; PIANO CONCERTOS: 18

Müller, Wilhelm: *Poems from the Posthumous Papers of a Travelling Horn-player* 99; *Winterreise* 100

Murger, Henri, *Scènes de la vie de bohème* 314

Music of the Future (Wagner) 222, 224, 280

music publishing, growth in 41, 48, 108

Musorgsky, Modest (1839–81): character 245; compositional characteristics 250, 251, 337; contemporary responses to 250; editing by Rimsky-Korsakov 368; influences 249–50, 263, 327; life 245, 247, 248, 251; WORKS: OPERA: *Boris Godunov* 250–1, 254, 263, 368; *Khovanshchina* (unfinished) 251, 368, 369; *The Marriage* (unfinished) 249, 250; *Salammbô* (unfinished) 248; *Sorochinskaya yarmarka* (unfinished) 251; ORCHESTRAL: *St John's Night on Bald Mountain* 248, 368; SOLO PIANO: *Pictures from an Exhibition* 251; SONG CYCLES 251

Napoleonic Wars 29, 40, 108

national culture and identity: Czech *see* Czech (Bohemian) culture; Finnish 326–7; German *see* German culture; Hungarian 183–4, 258; Norwegian 324; Polish 120, 121; and romanticism 9–11; Russian 242, 246–7, 252, 253, 256

415